Preparing FISH & WILD GAME

Creative Publishing
international

Minneapolis, Minnesota

Creative Publishing international

President/CEO: Ken Fund
VP/Sales & Marketing: Kevin Hamric

PREPARING FISH & WILD GAME

Executive Editor, Outdoor Products Group: Don Oster
Editorial Director: David R. Maas
Managing Editor: Jill Anderson
Editor: Steven J. Hauge
Editor and Project Leader: Teresa Marrone
Copy Editor: Lee Engfer
Creative Director: Bradley Springer
Senior Art Director: David W. Schelitzche
Art Director: Joe Fahey
Photo Researcher: Angela Hartwell
Photographer: Bill Lindner
Photo Assistant: Peter Cozad
Food Stylist: Susan Telleen
Hand Model: Kay Wethern
Director, Production Services: Kim Gerber
Production Manager: Sandy Carlin
Production Staff: Nicole Hepokoski, Laura Hokkanen, Helga Thielen
Contributing Photographers:
  Phil Aarrestad/Waconia, MN
  © Phil Aarrestad: pp. 6, 68, 248
  Denver Bryan/Bozeman, MT
  © DenverBryan.com: p. 198
  Donald M. Jones/Troy, MT
  © Donald M. Jones: pp. 216, 270
  Bill Kinney/Redding, IA
  © BillKinney.com: p. 112
  Thomas Kitchin/Tom Stack & Assoc./Key Largo, FL
  © Thomas Kitchin/Tom Stack & Assoc.: p. 166
  Bill Marchel/Fort Ripley, MN
  © BillMarchel.com: p. 182
  Norm & Sil Strung/Bozeman, MT
  © Norm & Sil Strung: p. 279 all
Contributing Manufacturers: King Kooker

Printed in China
 10 9 8

Library of Congress Cataloging-in-Publication Data

Preparing fish & wild game.
    p. cm.
  Includes index.
  ISBN 0-86573-125-X
  1. Cookery (Fish) 2. Cookery (Game) I. Title: Preparing
  fish and wild game. II. Creative Publishing International.
TX747 .P74 2000
641.6'91--dc21   00-063857

Table of Contents

❖ ❖ ❖

Introduction

❖ ❖ ❖

In the 19th century, wild foods made up a significant portion of the average person's diet—not by choice, but by necessity. As times changed and the world became smaller, railroad cars and, later, jetliners, made it easy to transport fresh meat and fish (as well as fruits, vegetables and other perishable goods) across the country; refrigeration and modern food preservation techniques made it possible to serve seasonal specialties all year round.

As modern times advanced, an increasingly urbanized society lost touch with many of the seasonal rhythms that drove our forebears. Yet each spring, anglers still take to the swollen streams and lakes in search of fish, and in the fall, hunters pursue a wide variety of wild game in places ranging from the local woodlot to the wilds of the Arctic.

Fishing and hunting provide more than food for the table; they also provide nourishment for the spirit, a release from the cares of the day and a connection to the traditions of the past. We have developed to a point where hunting and fishing are no longer a necessity; they are a choice, but one that satisfies both body and soul.

This book is designed to help you make the most of your wild harvest. All aspects of fish and game care and preparation are covered. It begins with a comprehensive section on basic cooking techniques—useful to novice and seasoned cooks alike—and then goes on to present a stunning collection of recipes for fish and game. Helpful tips and sidebars guide the cook through variations and other recipe ideas. The book concludes with the most comprehensive guide to fish and game field care, butchering and final processing ever published in a single volume.

We are confident that *Preparing Fish & Wild Game* will become the most useful outdoor-related cookbook on your shelf.

Cooking Techniques

for

Fish & Wild Game

This section of *Preparing Fish & Wild Game* provides all the information you'll need to cook your wild harvest with confidence. Whether you're frying up a mess of panfish, grilling elk steaks or cooking up a hearty fish or game gumbo, you'll find the basic cooking instructions here.

The chapter starts on the stove top, where you'll learn the proper techniques for panfrying, stir-frying, blackening, poaching and steaming. There are even recipes and techniques explaining how to get the most out of your fish or game by making savory stock from the bones and trimmings.

Tabletop appliances are covered next. You'll learn how to deep-fry fish and game in a deep fryer, mini-fryer or electric skillet. Batter recipes and cooking suggestions make it easy to get perfect results. The section finishes with step-by-step instructions for cooking small game in a pressure cooker and includes a useful chart of cooking times.

Oven-cooking techniques range from baking and roasting to oven-frying to broiling. Fish and game are discussed separately for each of these useful methods.

Many cooks think of the microwave only for defrosting, but it's an excellent choice for cooking fish to keep it moist and tasty. Charts and photos explain how to bake and poach fish in the microwave.

Grilling is a natural for wild game, but it's also a great way to cook fish. Techniques for fish and game are covered, including how to grill foil-wrapped foods and how to keep fish from falling apart on the grill.

Smoking adds a wonderful flavor to fish and game and can be used to make jerky and other semipreserved foods. This section of the book takes the mystery out of this ancient technique and explains how to use cold smoke to flavor foods as well as how to smoke-cook foods at higher temperatures.

Sausage making can seem daunting to the inexperienced cook, but the step-by-step instructions and photos in the next section of this chapter make it easy. Both synthetic and natural casings are covered, so you can tackle any sausage-making chores with confidence.

Finally, you'll learn how to preserve fish and game by canning them in a standard stove-top pressure cooker.

Panfrying
FISH & GAME

Panfrying works well for lean fish and many types of game. The high cooking temperature (up to 375°F) seals in the juices, producing moist and tender results. Cooking times are generally quick; fish cooks in 5 to 10 minutes, while cut-up game birds or small game may take up to 15 minutes.

Fish with a low to moderate oil content are a good choice for frying; oily fish are too rich. The exception is small stream trout, which have less fat than larger ones; these are excellent panfried. Small fish of all types can be cooked whole. Remove the head and tail before cooking, if desired; small trout are usually fried with the head and tail intact. Whole fish such as crappies, sunnies and perch must also be skinned or scaled before frying. Bullheads, small catfish and trout need only a good wipe with a paper towel before breading to remove any moisture, fish

slime or loose scales. Larger fish must be filleted before frying; fillets thicker than 1½ inches should be sliced into thinner pieces (right). Arrange fish in a skillet with the thickest portions to the center.

Tender cuts of boneless venison, as well as game birds and small game, are excellent when panfried. Boneless game bird pieces cook more evenly and quickly than bone-in pieces and are easier to eat; however, it's hard to beat the appeal of a plate of chicken-fried rabbit or pheasant prepared with cut-up bone-in pieces.

Dredge foods to be fried in flour, cornmeal, cracker crumbs, cornflake crumbs or a seasoned coating mix. With heavier coatings such as cracker crumbs, the fish or game should be dredged in flour and dipped in beaten eggs before being coated with crumbs. This double coating helps prevent the breading from falling off during frying.

Use a large, heavy skillet to distribute the heat evenly. With most skillets, $1/8$ to $1/4$ inch of oil is sufficient; nonstick skillets require even less. Arrange floured pieces in the skillet evenly, without overlapping. If you overload the skillet, the oil will cool off, resulting in soggy food. If you cook more than one batch of food, you may need to add additional oil between batches.

Panfry over medium heat, leaving the skillet uncovered. Drain the cooked pieces on paper towels. Serve immediately, or keep warm in a 175°F oven while frying additional pieces or making a pan sauce.

Coating with Crumbs

1 Dip chilled fish or game in cold milk, cold buttermilk or a mixture of 1 beaten egg and 1 to 2 tablespoons cold milk or water. Egg helps to make the coating stick.

2 Coat dipped fish or game with flour, pancake mix, Potato Buds®, biscuit mix, cornmeal or fine bread, cracker or cornflake crumbs (right).

How to Panfry

1 Coat the bottom of a heavy skillet with $1/8$ to $1/4$ inch of vegetable oil. Heat over medium heat until a single drop of water added to the skillet sizzles and evaporates. If the skillet starts smoking, reduce heat and allow to cool before adding food.

2 Arrange coated fish or game in the hot skillet in a single layer. Fry over medium heat, turning several times, until cooked through and golden. (Fish cooks more quickly than game and is usually turned only once.)

3 Drain the cooked fish or game on a paper towel–lined plate. Serve immediately, or keep warm in a 175°F oven while frying additional pieces or making a pan sauce.

4 Pour off excess oil before making a pan sauce or gravy. Add sauce or gravy liquid to degreased skillet and stir to loosen browned bits. Proceed as directed in individual recipe.

How to Tell If Fish Is Done

UNDERDONE fish is transparent and watery. The flesh does not flake easily with a fork.

JUST-RIGHT fish is opaque and moist. The layers flake easily when tested with a fork.

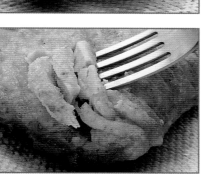

OVERDONE fish is dry and hard when tested with a fork. The flesh has little taste.

Panfrying Tips for Game

SPLIT small birds like quail or dove down the back, then open up and flatten before panfrying. This ensures even cooking.

POUND boneless venison steaks to an even thickness before panfrying. Pounding also helps tenderize the meat.

PRESSURE-COOK older squirrels, rabbits or raccoons before breading and panfrying. This tenderizes tough game.

Panfrying Chart for Fish

TYPE	SIZE	COOKING TIME 1ST SIDE	COOKING TIME 2ND SIDE
WHOLE	UP TO 1½ INCHES THICK	3 TO 5 MINUTES	2 TO 5 MINUTES
FILLETS	¼ INCH THICK	3 MINUTES	1 TO 2 MINUTES
	½ INCH THICK	3 MINUTES	1½ TO 3 MINUTES
	¾ INCH THICK	5 MINUTES	1½ TO 3½ MINUTES
	1 INCH THICK	5 MINUTES	2 TO 4 MINUTES

Stir-Frying
FISH & GAME

With this traditional Asian method, bite-sized pieces of fish or game are cooked over high heat in a wok or large skillet with a mixture of vegetables in a sauce. Hot vegetable or peanut oil is usually flavored with seasonings such as fresh gingerroot, garlic or chili peppers before the other ingredients are added.

Have all ingredients, including any sauce mixture, prepared and ready to cook

before heating the wok or skillet. Because the food is cooked over high heat, it must be stirred constantly to prevent burning. Stir-frying happens very quickly, and the finished dish should be served immediately. Rice or any other dishes to be served with the stir-fry should be prepared in advance and kept hot while the main dish is being stir-fried.

Always use firm-textured fish, so the stirring doesn't break up the pieces. Because it cooks so quickly, fish is often added after any vegetables have already been cooked. Stir as gently as possible to avoid breaking up the fish.

Boneless game works best for stir-frying. Cut the game into chunks or strips as directed in the specific recipe. Cubes are generally $1/2$ to $3/4$ inch in size, while strips are usually $1/8$ inch thick. These sizes promote rapid cooking. Because meat may take longer to cook than onions or other vegetables, it is usually cooked first; often, the cooked meat is transferred to a dish and kept warm while the vegetables are cooked in the wok. The meat is then returned to the wok for rewarming when the sauce is added.

1 Cut fish or game, as well as vegetables, into evenly sized pieces for stir-frying. Have all ingredients ready before starting to cook.

2 Heat wok or large, heavy skillet over medium-high heat until hot, then add a small amount of oil. Swirl the oil to distribute it in the wok.

3 Add seasonings, fish or game, and vegetables as directed in the your recipe. Stir constantly while adding food, and continue stirring until it is cooked.

Blackened
FISH & GAME

Blackened food is a hot item in more ways than one. Fish and game prepared in this spicy manner became popular in recent years as Cajun recipes spread northward from Louisiana and gained a following throughout the country.

Most restaurants use saltwater fish such as redfish, halibut, shark or swordfish. But you can also make blackened fish using firm-fleshed freshwater species, such as walleye, pike and perch. Venison, duck and other rich game are also well suited to blackening.

Always cook outdoors, because blackening creates billows of thick smoke that can fill a house.

Blackening isn't hard. Here's how you can make blackened specialties that are every bit as good as those served in the best restaurants.

HOMEMADE BLACKENING SPICES

- 4 TABLESPOONS PAPRIKA
- 3½ TEASPOONS CHILI POWDER
- 2 TEASPOONS ONION POWDER
- 1 TEASPOON DRIED THYME LEAVES
- 1 TEASPOON DRIED OREGANO LEAVES
- 1 TEASPOON GARLIC POWDER
- 1 TEASPOON WHITE PEPPER
- 1 TEASPOON SALT
- 1 TEASPOON PEPPER
- 1 TEASPOON CAYENNE

Mix the ingredients in a bowl. This recipe will make enough seasoning for four servings.

How to Cook Blackened Fish and Game

1. Heat a large cast-iron skillet over a charcoal fire for 20 minutes, so it is very hot. Rinse fish fillets and pat them dry; game usually doesn't need rinsing. Melt ½ cup (one stick) of butter in a saucepan.

2. Dip each piece in the melted butter, then coat the item evenly and generously with homemade blackening spices (see recipe, left).

3. Pour half the remaining butter from step 2 into the skillet. Drop the coated food into the pan. Drizzle the rest of the remaining butter over the pieces and flip them right away.

4. Turn the pieces every minute, cooking until they reach the desired doneness. Cooking time varies from two to six minutes, depending on the thickness of the pieces. Venison and duck are best when rare.

Poaching & Steaming

FISH & GAME

These cooking methods do not require the addition of fat, so they are among the healthiest ways to prepare fish. Poaching also works wonderfully for boneless pheasant breasts and other birds that can become dry during high-temperature cooking. Game birds cooked in this way are perfect for salads.

Poaching means cooking by immersing food in liquid heated to just below the boiling point. Poaching works especially well with oily fish because some of the fat leaches out into the cooking liquid.

Usually used with fish, steaming means cooking on a rack placed just above boiling liquid. With this technique, the fish are more likely to retain their natural flavor, shape and texture.

The liquid for poaching or steaming could be plain water, but wine, vinegar, lemon, apple or orange juice, or various vegetables, herbs and spices are normally added to enhance the flavor. If you plan to use the liquid to flavor a soup or sauce, use a bouquet garni, or seasoning bundle, (p. 18) so you won't have to strain out the herbs and spices. You can also poach or steam using court bouillon (p. 18) or milk. Poached foods are more likely to absorb flavor from the cooking liquid than are steamed foods.

When using an acidic liquid (such as vinegar or wine) for poaching or steaming, be sure to use cookware made of or lined with nonreactive material such as stainless steel, porcelain enamel, tin or glass. Don't use aluminum cookware unless it is coated or anodized.

HERBS AND SPICES for poaching and steaming include (1) fresh parsley, (2) coriander, (3) fresh marjoram, (4) peppercorns, (5) stick cinnamon, (6) fresh thyme, (7) whole allspice, (8) mustard seed, (9) fresh oregano, (10) whole cloves and (11) fresh rosemary.

FRESH VEGETABLES for poaching and steaming include (1) leeks, (2) carrots, (3) celery, (4) onions and (5) garlic. You can also add slices of fresh citrus fruit or citrus peel.

POACHING EQUIPMENT includes fish poachers, long roasting pans, deep skillets and saucepans. A rack with handles, cheesecloth or large spatulas are useful for removing the fish from the liquid.

STEAMING EQUIPMENT includes steamers, electric frying pans, woks, skillets and saucepans. A rack is necessary to keep the fish above the bubbling liquid. Cheesecloth can also be used to suspend the fish.

COURT BOUILLON

This classic "easy bouillon" can be used to poach fish or game birds, or as the stock in a variety of recipes.

 1   LEEK, CUT IN HALF LENGTHWISE AND RINSED
 4   SPRIGS FRESH PARSLEY
 3   TO 4 SPRIGS FRESH THYME
 1   LARGE BAY LEAF
 1   LARGE CLOVE GARLIC, CUT IN HALF
12   CUPS WATER
 2   MEDIUM CARROTS, THINLY SLICED
 2   RIBS CELERY, THINLY SLICED
 2   SLICES LEMON

Prepare the bouquet garni (seasoning bundle) as directed below. Set aside. Place water in a stockpot or fish poacher. Add the bouquet garni, carrots, celery and lemon. Cover. Bring to a boil over medium-high heat. Reduce heat to low. Simmer for 15 minutes.

If cooking fish or game birds in Court Bouillon, add to simmering stock. Cook, covered, for recommended time (see chart on page 20) or until fish is firm and opaque and just begins to flake; game birds should be just cooked through.

12 cups

Nutritional information not available.

How to Prepare a Bouquet Garni

1 Cut two 4-inch pieces from the outer layer of a halved and rinsed leek. Wrap and refrigerate remaining leek for future use. Place parsley, thyme, bay leaf and garlic on the concave side of one piece of leek.

2 Cover with remaining piece of leek. Tie in three places with string to secure seasoning bundle.

How to Poach Fish and Game Bird Fillets

1 Prepare ingredients for court bouillon as directed at left. Place poacher on stove, covering two burners, if necessary. Heat to boiling. Reduce heat; cover. Simmer 15 minutes.

2 Measure a whole fish at the thickest point to determine the cooking time. Estimate the total cooking time at 9 to 11 minutes per inch thickness. Wipe fish inside and out with paper towels.

3 Place fish on rack; lower into the simmering liquid. If cooking fish without a rack, wrap them in a long piece of cheesecloth. Use the ends as handles to lift the fish.

4 Add boiling water, if necessary, to cover the fish. Cover poacher and quickly return the liquid to boiling. Reduce heat. Simmer for the estimated time. Test for doneness by inserting a fork at the backbone. Twist tines. The fish is done when it flakes easily.

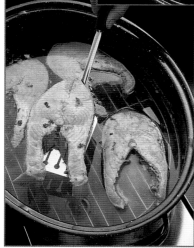

5 Fish steaks should be poached, using the same technique, until they flake easily. See chart for times. Remove with a large spatula.

6 Boneless game bird fillets are poached, using the same technique, until just cooked through. To check doneness, make a small cut at the thickest part; the meat should no longer be pink.

How to Steam Fish and Game Bird Fillets

1 Boil 1 inch of water or a combination of 10 parts water to 1 part white wine in the steamer. Grease rack with oil. Place in pan over the liquid.

2 Place whole fish, fillets or steaks, or game bird fillets on the rack. Leave enough space between the pieces for steam to circulate. Cover the pan.

3 Steam over the boiling liquid. See chart (below) for times. Cook until the fish flakes easily at the thickest part; game bird meat should no longer be pink.

Poaching & Steaming Fish & Game

TYPE	SIZE	COOKING TIME
WHOLE FISH	ANY SIZE	9 TO 11 MINUTES PER INCH
FISH FILLETS	1/2 INCH THICK	4 TO 6 MINUTES
	3/4 INCH THICK	6 TO 8 MINUTES
	1 INCH THICK	9 TO 11 MINUTES
FISH STEAKS	3/4 INCH THICK	6 TO 8 MINUTES
	1 INCH THICK	9 TO 11 MINUTES
PHEASANT OR GROUSE	BREAST HALVES (BONELESS)	20 TO 30 MINUTES
PHEASANT OR GROUSE	CUT UP (BONE IN)	35 TO 55 MINUTES
TURKEY	BREAST HALVES (BONELESS)	35 TO 45 MINUTES

FISH & GAME
GAME
Stock

Good stock is fundamental to good cooking. It's used as the base for sauces and as the cooking liquid in many recipes. Stock is made by boiling the bones of fish, big-game animals, birds or small game, usually with vegetables and seasonings. Homemade stock adds more flavor to recipes than commercial broth. For convenience, freeze stock in 1-cup batches (page 307). Or can it in the pressure cooker (page 65). Leave a 1/2-inch head space in pint jars; process at 10 pounds pressure for 20 minutes.

If you make a large batch of stock, you may want to try a technique used by professional chefs. Prepare the stock without adding salt, then strain it through a double thickness of cheesecloth. Allow the strained stock to cool completely, then skim off any fat. Boil the strained, skimmed stock until it is reduced by half to make a *demi-glace* (half glaze), which is the base for many classic French sauces. Reducing the *demi-glace* even further produces a hard, rubbery glaze that can be cut into small chunks and frozen. A small chunk of the glaze added to a sauce or braising liquid intensifies the flavor of the dish without adding liquid. If a recipe calls for a teaspoon of instant bouillon granules, you can substitute a small chunk of glaze and a bit of salt.

VENISON STOCK

Browning the bones in the oven makes the stock rich and dark. Venison stock requires long cooking to bring out all the flavor from the large bones.

ENOUGH DEER, ANTELOPE, ELK OR MOOSE BONES TO FIT STOCKPOT (5 TO 10 POUNDS)

4 TO 6 CARROTS, CUT INTO 2-INCH PIECES

3 OR 4 STALKS CELERY, CUT INTO 2-INCH PIECES

2 MEDIUM ONIONS, QUARTERED

2 BAY LEAVES

10 WHOLE BLACK PEPPERCORNS

4 OR 5 SPRIGS FRESH PARSLEY

1 SPRIG FRESH THYME, OR 1/2 TEASPOON DRIED THYME LEAVES

---

about 3 quarts

See photo instructions at right.

Nutritional information not available.

How to Prepare Venison Stock

1 Arrange bones in a roasting pan. Heat oven to 450°F. Roast until well browned, about 1 hour, turning bones once during roasting. Transfer bones to a stockpot.

2 Loosen browned bits from roaster by stirring, adding 1 cup water if necessary. Pour liquid into a large measuring cup. Skim fat; discard. Return liquid to stockpot.

3 Add remaining ingredients to stockpot. Cover with cold water. Heat to boiling over medium-high heat. Reduce heat. Skim foam from top of stock. Simmer for about 8 hours, skimming periodically, and adding water as necessary to keep the bones covered.

4 Strain stock through a double thickness of cheesecloth. Discard bones and vegetables. Pour stock back into cleaned stockpot. Heat to boiling over medium-high heat. Cook until reduced to about 3 quarts. Cool slightly. Refrigerate overnight. Skim any solidified fat from top.

GAME BIRD STOCK
(PHEASANT, PARTRIDGE, GROUSE, TURKEY, OR WATERFOWL)

Save the backbone and neck when portioning birds, and any bones left after boning, until you have enough to make stock. Game bird stock cooks more quickly than venison stock.

1½	TO 2 POUNDS UNCOOKED GAME BIRD BACKS AND BONES
1	SMALL ONION, QUARTERED
1	STALK CELERY, CUT INTO 1-INCH PIECES
1	CARROT, CUT INTO 1-INCH PIECES
¼	CUP SNIPPED FRESH PARSLEY
½	TEASPOON DRIED MARJORAM LEAVES
½	TEASPOON DRIED THYME LEAVES
6	WHOLE BLACK PEPPERCORNS
2	WHOLE CLOVES
1	BAY LEAF
1¼	TEASPOONS SALT, OPTIONAL
4	TO 6 CUPS COLD WATER

About 3 cups stock

In a large saucepan, combine all ingredients, adding enough water to completely cover the bones and vegetables. Heat to boiling over medium-high heat. Reduce heat. Skim foam from top of stock. Simmer for 1½ to 2 hours, skimming periodically. Strain through a double thickness of cheesecloth. Discard bones and vegetables. Cool stock slightly. Refrigerate overnight. Skim any solidified fat from top.

Nutritional information not available.

RABBIT STOCK

Follow the recipe above, substituting 1½ to 2 pounds rabbit backs, ribs and other bones for the game bird bones. Continue as directed, cooking for 2 to 2½ hours.

How to Make Fish Stock

1 Remove the guts, gills, fins and tail, after cutting out the cheeks (arrow). Use kitchen shears or a sharp knife. Scale the head, if necessary. Rinse the head under cold running water. Wipe off slime with paper towels. Cut the skeleton into small pieces that fit easily into a saucepan or stockpot, depending on quantity.

2 Cover the skeleton with water. Add a dash of salt and pepper. Heat to boiling; reduce heat. Simmer for 30 minutes. Remove head and bones.

3 Strip the cooked flesh from the bones and head; discard the bones. Freeze or refrigerate the flaked fish in plastic containers or freezer bags.

4 Strain the cooked fish stock through a double layer of cheesecloth to remove any remaining bones and scales. Return stock to the pan. Boil the stock over high heat to reduce it by half for storage; cool. Freeze or refrigerate in plastic containers. Label as fish stock.

Deep-Frying
FISH & GAME

The trick in deep-frying is to form a tasty golden crust to seal out fat. Deep-fried foods are best when served quickly. The crust may become soggy if serving is delayed.

One secret to successful deep-frying is proper oil temperature; 375°F is recommended. This is the point at which vegetable oil bubbles if a small amount of batter is dropped into it. A deep-frying or candy thermometer is helpful to monitor oil temperature.

Vegetable oils for deep-frying must have a high burning point. Corn, peanut, cottonseed or safflower are popular because they do not change the flavor of the fish.

You can use a variety of batters, but make sure the batter is cold; otherwise, it will soak up too much oil. Dry the fish or game with paper towels before dipping into the batter, to ensure that the batter sticks. A layer of newspapers or paper towels under the fryer and the batter bowl makes cleanup easier.

Lean fish deep-fry better than oily fish. Fillets, strips or chunks must be of a uniform size and shape to deep-fry evenly. Pieces no thicker than 1 1/2 inches are best for deep-frying. Panfish and other small fish can be deep-fried whole if they are less than 1 1/2 inches thick. Bullheads and catfish that are less than 8 inches long can be deep-fried whole; bigger fish should be filleted.

Boneless game makes an excellent appetizer when deep-fried. Before breading, cut venison steaks into fingers; the meat from game birds and small game can be cut into chunks or strips. This is a good way to stretch a single pheasant or other limited amount of game, enabling many guests to get a taste. Bone-in game birds or small game can also be cut up, then breaded and fried, similar to fried chicken.

DEEP-FRYING TECHNIQUES

There are two methods of deep-frying. The most common method requires 2 or more inches of oil in a traditional deep fryer or tall saucepan. This is the easiest way, because the deep container controls oil splatters. The other method uses a large skillet or electric frying pan. Use about 1 1/2 inches of oil, and turn the food during cooking.

Before deep-frying a batch of fish or game, test-fry one piece. If the batter falls off, it is too thin; add more flour to the mixture. If the batter is too thick, add a few drops of water. Dredging the pieces in cornstarch before dipping helps the batter adhere better and also makes the coating crisper.

When deep-frying several batches, allow the oil temperature to return to 375°F between batches before adding more fish or game. Add oil as needed between batches. If the batter and food to be fried are both cold and the oil is hot, the coating will seal immediately.

DEEP-FRYING EQUIPMENT includes a deep fryer, mini-fryer, electric frying pan or deep skillet. Other useful tools are a thermometer, wire basket, tongs and a slotted spoon.

How to Cook Fish and Game in a Deep Fryer

1 Chill fish or game pieces in the refrigerator before deep-frying. Pat dry with paper towels. Pour 2 to 3 inches of oil into the deep-fat fryer. Heat oil to 375°F.

2 Dip a piece in cold batter with fingers, fork or tongs. Use paper towels or newspapers under the bowl and fryer to catch any splatters.

3 Drop the pieces gently into the hot oil, one at a time. Do not crowd or the oil will cool. Fry until golden brown. Drain and keep warm while frying more.

How to Deep-Fry in a Skillet

2 Fry 2 to 3 minutes. Turn with spatula and fork to avoid splatters. Fry until golden brown and cooked through, turning again if needed.

1 Pour 1 to 1½ inches of oil into a deep skillet or electric frying pan. Heat oil to 375°. Gently add batter-covered fish or game, using tongs or your fingers.

COATINGS & BATTER FOR DEEP-FRYING

FLOUR COATING

1   EGG
1   TABLESPOON MILK OR WATER
1   CUP ALL-PURPOSE FLOUR
1   TEASPOON SALT
1/8   TEASPOON PEPPER

Blend egg and milk. Mix flour, salt and pepper. Dip fish in egg mixture, then in flour mixture. Deep-fry as directed.

PACKAGED COATINGS

Popular packaged coatings for deep-frying include corn flour, cracker meal, seasoned coating mix, tempura and other batter mixes. Prepare mixes as directed on package. For variety, substitute beer for the liquid in package directions.

BEER BATTER

1   CUP ALL-PURPOSE FLOUR
3   TABLESPOONS CORNSTARCH
1   TEASPOON SALT
1/2   TEASPOON PAPRIKA
     DASH NUTMEG, OPTIONAL
1   CUP BEER
1   TABLESPOON VEGETABLE OIL

1 1/2 cups batter

In a medium bowl, mix dry ingredients. Blend in beer and vegetable oil until smooth. Dip fish into batter. Deep-fry as directed.

Tips for Deep-Frying

TEST the oil to make sure it's hot enough by dropping in a small piece of bread or fish. It should brown in less than a minute. Don't test with water; it will pop and cause the hot oil to splatter.

KEEP deep-fried foods crispy by placing them on a wire rack over a paper towel–lined plate. Keep them in a warm oven while frying another batch. If you put them directly on paper towels, the coating may not stay as crisp.

STRAIN cooled oil through cheesecloth so you can use it several times. Place a potato slice in the hot oil to remove flavors before straining. Store oil in a sealed container in the refrigerator.

Pressure-Cooking
SMALL GAME

Although you can cook many types of game in a pressure cooker, these stove-top appliances are most commonly used by wild-game cooks to prepare small game. The process tenderizes game that might otherwise be tough, and it's also the most efficient way to produce cooked meat for use in casseroles, salads and other recipes.

Pressure cookers are also used in canning big game; see pages 66-67 for instructions.

How to Cook Small Game in a Pressure Cooker

1 Place cut-up game in the pressure cooker, on a trivet if desired. Do not exceed two-thirds of the cooker's capacity. Add 1 to 1½ inches of water, or the amount specified in the cooker manual. Seal the cooker, then set the control for 15 pounds of pressure.

2 Heat to full pressure as directed by the manual. Normally, the control starts to jiggle when full pressure is reached. Begin timing, then lower the heat so the control jiggles only one to four times per minute.

3 Cook as long as recommended by the chart (below), then remove the cooker from the heat. Do not remove the control or open the cooker until it cools completely. Escaping steam could cause serious burns.

4 Cool according to the pressure-cooker manual. Generally, the cooker is allowed to cool naturally for about 5 minutes, then is placed under cold running water until it's cool enough to touch. Remove meat with tongs.

Pressure Cooking Times for Small Game

TYPE OF GAME	COOKING TIME
SQUIRREL, YOUNG	15 MINUTES
SQUIRREL, OLD	20 MINUTES
COTTONTAIL RABBIT	20 MINUTES
SNOWSHOE HARE	25 MINUTES
RACCOON, YOUNG	20–25 MINUTES
RACCOON, OLD	30 MINUTES

Always follow the manufacturer's directions when using your pressure cooker. Consult the manual for specific recommendations. You may heat oil in your pressure cooker and brown the game before pressure-cooking, if desired. Add water carefully to the browned game, and seal the cooker immediately to prevent water loss.

TECHNIQUES FOR
Oven Cooking

The three basic methods of oven cooking are baking (also called roasting), broiling and oven frying. Any fish or game can be cooked in an oven, but some of these methods work better than others for a specific piece of fish or game.

BAKING OR ROASTING

Both of these terms refer to the same technique: cooking foods in the oven in a dish, which is often uncovered. "Baking" is generally used when discussing fish, while "roasting" typically refers to game birds, small game or a big-game roast. Baking can cause lean fish or meats to dry out. Marinating the food before cooking or basting with pan liquids during cooking can help keep fish and game moist.

In moist-heat roasting, foods are baked with at least a small amount of liquid in a covered pan. Pot roasting is included in this category and is often used to tenderize tougher big-game cuts. Similar results can be

obtained on the stove top by braising foods with liquid in a covered pan; however, oven braising is easier and more suited to large cuts such as roasts.

One more special roasting technique should be mentioned: roasting in an oven cooking bag. These special poly bags keep moisture in, yet allow the food to get deliciously browned. Oven cooking bags are most commonly used for big-game roasts and whole game birds, but also work well for cut-up game birds and small game.

BROILING

This high-heat cooking technique browns food more than baking does, adding extra flavor, texture and eye appeal. The fish or game to be broiled is placed on a special slotted or perforated broiling pan, which allows fat to drip through to a pan underneath. This technique is particularly good for fatty or oily fish such as salmon. It also works well for venison steaks and similar cuts, especially if they are cooked to no more than medium doneness. Well-done big-game steaks and chops can be dry and tough. Basting helps prevent leaner fish and game from excessive drying during broiling and can also add a nice crust to broiled ribs, chops and steaks.

OVEN FRYING

With this technique, you get the flavor and crispness of panfrying with less mess. Just as with panfrying, foods to be oven-fried are dipped in a milk or egg and milk wash, then into crumbs; the breaded pieces are placed into a preheated pan with a little oil in it. Fish and game cooked in this fashion are lower in fat than foods that are panfried or deep-fried.

Utensils for oven cooking include (1) broiling pan with rack; (2) baking pan or roaster with 2-inch sides for oven frying; (3) large spatula, for handling whole fish; (4) glass baking dishes; (5) deep-dish pie plate; (6) baster; (7) casserole; (8) porcelain enamel or (9) Teflon-coated baking pans and (10) heavy-duty foil.

BAKING FISH

Baking is ideal for stuffed whole fish and for thick cuts that might dry out under direct heat. Fillets and steaks can also be baked.

This technique is used most often for oily fish because they're not likely to dry out. But lean fish can also be baked if you marinate them first, coat them with crumbs or sauce or bake them in a small amount of liquid, which is then used for basting.

Other ways to conserve moisture are to bake the fish in a covered pan, or wrap it with aluminum foil, vegetable leaves or oiled baking paper. These techniques also help retain flavor.

Basting with pan juices helps prevent dryness. To brown a dish of baked fillets or steaks before serving, baste with pan juices and place them under a hot broiler for about a minute.

You can bake steaks, fillets or whole fish. The latter are often stuffed to add flavor and keep them moist. The baking temperature and time depend on the thickness of the fish pieces. Fish more than 3 inches thick are usually baked at 325° to 375°F; fish less than 1 inch thick, 400° to 450°F. As a rule, bake 10 minutes per inch of thickness.

Leave the head on a whole fish if there is room in the pan. Whole fish can be baked with a rice, vegetable or bread stuffing, which adds flavor and keeps them moist.

A large whole fish is difficult to remove from the pan. If desired, place the fish on greased aluminum foil before putting it in the pan. Pick up the foil to remove the fish. Large spatulas are also helpful.

Utensils for baking whole fish include long roasting pans or casseroles. Use a rack to keep oily fish out of the cooking juices. Bake fillets and steaks in a shallow 8 × 8- or 13 × 9-inch baking pan.

How to Bake Fish

1 Wipe fillets, steaks or a whole fish with paper towels. Heat oven to 375°F. Oil a baking pan or rack. Place the fish in the pan. Brush with a mixture of 1 tablespoon lemon juice and ½ cup melted butter, or as directed in the individual recipe.

2 Cover the baking pan with a lid or aluminum foil and place it in the hot oven. Bake, basting with the lemon-butter mixture two times during cooking. Fish is done when it flakes easily.

3 Remove the fish carefully from the pan. Place it on a heated serving platter. Save the pan juices for use in chowder or sauces.

ROASTING BIG GAME

There are two basic ways to roast big game: with dry heat and moist heat. Dry-heat roasting includes high- and low-temperature methods. The most common method of moist-heat roasting is braising, which includes pot roasting.

Only prime roasts are candidates for dry-heat, high-temperature cooking. These include the top round, sirloin tip, backstrap (page 286), and rump roasts. The tenderloin of a moose, elk or large deer may also be used. These prime cuts are naturally tender and do not need long, slow cooking for tenderizing.

For high-temperature cooking, select a roast between 2 and 5 inches thick, or a thinner piece you can roll and tie (page 289). First, brown the meat in hot fat, then roast it

in a hot (400° to 450°F) oven. With these high temperatures, roasts should be cooked only rare to medium. If cooked well done, they dry out and shrink.

Low-temperature roasting is another option for these same prime cuts. And it's necessary for such medium-tender cuts as the bottom round and eye of round, which need longer cooking to ensure tenderness. Cover

the meat with bacon or a sheet of beef or pork fat (available from your butcher), or baste it frequently. Cook it in a slow (300° to 325°F) oven. With low heat, roasts may be cooked rare, medium or well done.

When roasting with dry heat, use a meat thermometer to check for doneness. The chart below gives temperatures for various stages of doneness. Remove the meat from the oven when it reads 5° below the ideal temperature; it will continue to cook on the platter. It will slice better if you wait 10 to 15 minutes before carving.

Moist heat tenderizes shoulder roasts and other tough cuts, and also works well with the bottom round and eye of round. Brown the roast in hot fat, then add liquid and seasonings and cover the pan tightly. Cook the meat until tender, in a moderate (325° to 350°F) oven. When pot roasting, add vegetables during the last hour or so of cooking. Braised meat is always served well done.

Internal Temperature Doneness Chart

DONENESS	INTERNAL TEMPERATURE
RARE	130° TO 135°F
MEDIUM-RARE	135° TO 140°F
MEDIUM	140° TO 145°F
MEDIUM-WELL	150° TO 155°F
WELL DONE	155° TO 160°F

ROASTING GAME BIRDS & SMALL GAME

Birds with the skin on can be roasted in an open pan in a slow (325°F) oven. Frequent basting helps keep the meat moist and makes the skin crisp and brown. Some cooks prefer roasting in oven cooking bags; the birds baste themselves, the skin browns well and cleanup

is easy. See page 31 for information about using oven cooking bags.

Skinned birds and small game should be handled differently. Moist cooking methods such as braising or steaming work better than open-pan roasting. If you choose to roast small game or a skinned bird, cover the meat with strips of bacon or rub it with softened butter and baste it frequently. Small birds like doves, quail and woodcock can be wrapped in cabbage or grape leaves to retain moisture.

Only young birds and small game should be roasted. Older, tougher specimens should be cooked with moist heat.

Insert a standard meat thermometer into the thigh of a large bird before roasting, or check near the end of the roasting time with an instant-read meat thermometer. Upland birds are done when the thigh temperature reaches 185° F. Waterfowl may be cooked medium-rare (150° to 160° F) if desired.

If you are roasting smaller birds, test for doneness by wiggling the leg. When it moves freely, the bird is done. You can also prick the thigh; the juices should run clear. Judge the doneness of small game by checking for tenderness, not temperature.

How to Truss a Game Bird for Roasting

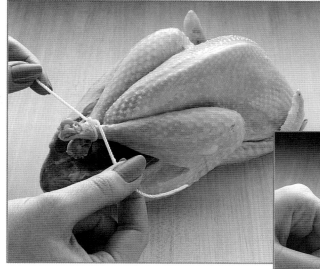

METHOD 1: Secure the legs together, using kitchen string.

METHOD 2: Cut a hole in the skin of the bird at the base of the tail, and tuck the ends of the legs into the hole.

BROILING FISH

Broiled fish has a pleasing flavor, but the high heat dries fish faster than other cooking methods. There are many ways to reduce this dryness.

Select naturally oily fish. Trout, salmon and lake trout are excellent, because they are basted by their own fat, which drips through the rack into the broiler pan during cooking. Baste lean fish often with butter, margarine or vegetable oil to prevent them from drying out. Watch them carefully so they do not overcook.

Lean fish fillets or steaks can be marinated for a few minutes before broiling in a mixture of 1/2 cup melted butter and 1 tablespoon lemon juice. Use the same mixture for basting. Oily fish can be basted to enhance flavor.

Professional chefs have a secret for serving moist broiled fish. They poach or steam the fish until it is almost cooked. Then they baste the fish with butter and brown it quickly under the broiler.

Another tip for adding moisture is to pour $1/4$ to $1/2$ inch of boiling liquid, such as a fish stock, wine, beer or vegetable juice, into the broiler pan. Place the fish on the oiled rack and cook as directed. The fish will be bathed with hot steam while it is browning.

When cooking fillets with skin, place the skin side up first. Small whole stream trout can be broiled with or without the head. Most fish are placed 4 inches from the heat. Thin fillets are set 5 inches from the heat to keep them from drying out. Slash whole fish on both sides before broiling. Cuts about $1/4$ to $1/2$ inch deep ensure that the fish will cook through evenly.

Many cooks line the broiler pan and rack with aluminum foil for easy cleanup. To avoid flare-ups, poke holes in the foil so the oil drains into the pan.

If using an electric range, broil with the door slightly ajar. This keeps the heat constant since the broiling unit is always on. Close the door if using a gas range.

How to Broil Whole Fish

1 Select a whole fish that is about 10 to 14 inches long. It should be no thicker than 2 inches. Pat the fish dry with paper towels. Arrange on oiled broiler pan. Set oven to broil and/or 550°F. Baste the fish with vegetable oil, melted margarine or butter. Adjust broiler pan so it is 4 inches from the heating element. Broil for 5 minutes on the first side; baste once during cooking.

2 Turn the fish carefully with a spatula or tongs. Try to avoid piercing the skin. Baste again. Broil for 4 to 8 minutes; baste once more during cooking.

3 Test for doneness by pulling the dorsal fin. If it is easily removed, the fish is cooked. The flesh next to the backbone should flake easily. Save the juice from the broiler pan to use in sauces or chowder.

Broiling Chart

TYPE/SIZE	COOKING TIME 1ST SIDE	COOKING TIME 2ND SIDE	DISTANCE FROM HEAT
WHOLE UP TO 2 INCHES THICK	5 MIN.	4 TO 8 MIN.	4 INCHES
STEAKS: 1 INCH	5 MIN.	2 TO 4 MIN.	4 INCHES
FILLETS: $1/4$ INCH	3 TO 4 MIN.	———	5 INCHES
$1/2$ INCH	3 MIN.	1 TO 3 MIN.	4 INCHES
$3/4$ INCH	3 MIN.	$2 1/2$ TO $3 1/4$ MIN.	4 INCHES

How to Broil Fish Steaks

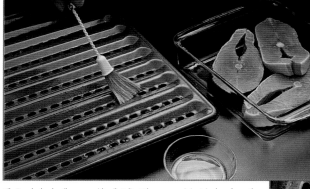

2 Turn the steaks over; broil on the second side for 2 to 4 minutes, depending on the thickness. Baste again. The steaks are done when the flesh flakes easily.

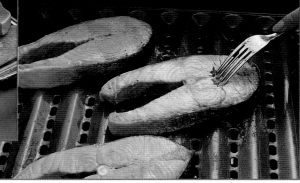

1 Brush the broiler pan with oil. Adjust the pan so it is 4 inches from the heat (5 inches for fillets less than ½ inch thick). Set oven to broil and/or 550°F. Place steaks on the pan; baste. Broil on the first side for 5 minutes.

How to Broil Fillets

2 Baste the fillets with oil, margarine or butter. If the fillets have skin, start them with the skin side up. Broil on the first side. See chart (page 39) for cooking times.

1 Cut the fillets into serving-size pieces. Brush the broiler pan with oil. Adjust the pan so it is 4 inches from the heat. Set oven to broil and/or 550°F. Place fillets on the pan.

3 Turn and broil on the second side, basting again. Test for doneness with a fork. The fish is done when the flesh flakes easily at the thickest part.

4 Thin fillets (¼ inch) are arranged on an oiled broiler pan 5 inches from the heat. Broil as directed for other fillets, but do not turn over. See chart for times.

BROILING BIG GAME & GAME BIRDS

Many types or cuts of wild game are not suitable for the high heat used in broiling. Small game, for example, is so lean that it dries out very quickly under the intense heat of the broiler. Large cuts of venison and other big game are too thick for broiling.

However, prime big-game chops and steaks are excellent when broiled. Boneless waterfowl breasts are similar to big-game steaks and also broil up nicely. For the best flavor and texture, broil big game and waterfowl just until medium doneness; medium-rare is even better (if you like medium-rare beef, you'll love medium-rare venison or duck). Note that wild pig and bear always must be cooked to

well done, whatever cooking method you use.

Small waterfowl and upland game birds other than turkey work well in the broiler if halved or quartered; the smallest birds can be split down the back and opened up flat for broiling (see page 11). For best results, leave the skin on game birds to be broiled; the skin helps ensure moist meat.

Marinating game prior to broiling provides additional moisture; save the marinade and brush it over the game during broiling. If you have not marinated the game, use a baste of fat and an acid ingredient, such as vinegar-oil dressing or lemon-butter sauce, to provide needed moisture.

How to Broil Big-Game Steaks or Chops

1 Choose tender big-game steaks or chops for broiling. If the cuts are thin, slash edges at half-inch intervals to prevent curling (inset). Season meat with salt and pepper. Place meat on oiled broiler pan; brush with oil or melted butter. Adjust broiler so the pan will be 4 inches from the heat. Broil until meat is nicely browned, 3 to 6 minutes.

2 Turn meat over and brush second side with oil or butter. Continue broiling until meat reaches the desired doneness. For best results, do not cook to well done.

How to Broil Game Birds

1 Split small birds like quail down the back and open up flat; if cooking larger birds, cut into serving pieces or use boneless breast and thigh meat.

2 Arrange birds skin side up on oiled broiler pan. Brush with melted butter; sprinkle with salt and pepper. Broil 4 inches from the heat for 5 to 6 minutes.

3 Turn birds and brush with butter. Broil second side for 5 to 6 minutes. Turn and brush birds again. Broil for 3 to 5 minutes longer, or until juices run clear.

Tips for Broiling Game

BROIL boneless duck breasts or big-game steaks on one side until they are almost the desired doneness, then turn and top with buttered bread crumbs. Continue broiling until the crumbs are browned and the meat is cooked.

GLAZE baked ribs or other barbecued big-game cuts by finishing under the broiler. Brush the cooked meat with barbecue sauce, then broil, 4 to 5 inches from the heating element, until the sauce is deliciously crusty.

OVEN-FRYING FISH & GAME

Oven-frying is very similar to panfrying, but instead of being cooked in a skillet on the stove top, the breaded food is placed in a baking dish that has been preheated with a small amount of oil. The heat of the oven accomplishes the same thing as the heat under the skillet, with less mess, fewer calories and reduced cooking odors.

As with panfrying, lean fish are a better choice for oven-frying than oily ones. Fillets work better for oven-frying than whole fish or steaks. Boneless game bird pieces and tender boneless venison are suitable for oven-frying; cut-up squirrel and boned rabbit back-straps also work well. Bone-in game bird pieces and cut-up bone-in rabbit take too long to cook with this method.

The techniques for oven-frying fish and game are the same, but cooking times will be longer for game than for fish.

How to Oven-Fry Fish & Boneless Game

1 Heat oven to 450°F. Place ⅛ inch of vegetable oil in a baking pan. Heat the pan in the oven for 5 minutes. Wipe fillets or game pieces with paper towels.

2 Beat 1 egg and 1 tablespoon milk in a shallow bowl. Spread ½ cup dry seasoned bread crumbs on a plate. Dip pieces in egg, then coat in crumbs.

3 Place the coated pieces in the hot pan, turning to coat both sides with oil. Oven-fry until cooked through; time will usually be from 9 to 15 minutes.

Microwaving FISH

Timing is critical when microwaving fish because they can easily be overcooked. Ideally, the fish should be removed from the oven just before it flakes. Watch carefully as it cooks.

Lean fish is usually microwaved at 100 percent power. Oily fish is microwaved at 50 percent power because the fatty flesh may "pop" at a higher setting.

When cooked and flaked fish is needed for a recipe, microwave the fish using the basic technique (right) or the steaming technique (page 20).

Unless a specific recipe gives instructions, avoid microwaving game. There are too many variables to provide general instructions for this technique, and results are often unsatisfactory.

How to Microwave Fish

1 Brush fish with melted butter or lemon juice. Roll in crumbs, if desired. Place on the roasting rack.

2 Cover with waxed paper (except crumb-coated fish, which gets soggy). Microwave half the time; see chart. Rearrange fish, placing less cooked parts to the outside. Microwave remaining time, until fish flakes.

Microwaving Chart

TYPE	THICKNESS	POWER LEVEL	BASIC MICRO-WAVING TIME	POACHING TIME	STEAMING TIME
SMALL WHOLE FISH	1 TO 1¾ INCH	50 %	8 TO 11 MIN./LB.	6½ TO 10 MIN./LB.	6½ TO 9½ MIN./LB.
LEAN FILLETS	½ TO 1 INCH	100%	2 TO 5 MIN./LB.	3½ TO 6½ MIN./LB.	2½ TO 4½ MIN./LB.
OILY FILLETS	½ TO 1 INCH	50%	5 TO 8 MIN./LB.	5½ TO 8½ MIN./LB.	5 TO 7 MIN./LB.
LEAN STEAKS	ABOUT 1 INCH	100%	5 TO 8 MIN./LB.	7 TO 9 MIN./LB.	4½ TO 7 MIN./LB.
OILY STEAKS	ABOUT 1 INCH	50%	8½ TO 11½ MIN./LB.	9½ TO 12 MIN./LB.	7½ TO 9½ MIN./LB.

POACHING INGREDIENTS

1/4	CUP WATER	3	SLICES LEMON
1	MEDIUM CARROT, CUT INTO 1/2-INCH PIECES	1/8	TEASPOON WHOLE PEPPERCORNS
1	STALK CELERY, CUT INTO 1-INCH PIECES	1	BAY LEAF
		1	TEASPOON DRIED PARSLEY FLAKES
1	SMALL ONION, SLICED	1/4	TEASPOON SALT

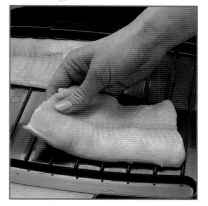

How to Steam Fish in the Microwave

1 Place fish on the microwave roasting rack. The thickest portions should be to the outside.

How to Poach Fish in the Microwave

1 Place poaching ingredients in a 12 x 8-inch glass baking dish. Cover with plastic wrap and microwave at 100 percent power until water is bubbling, 4 to 6 minutes.

2 Put fish in dish. Cover tightly with plastic wrap, turning one edge back to allow steam to escape. Microwave for half the time given on the chart (page 44).

3 Turn fish over. Arrange fillets so thick parts are to the outside and thin parts overlap. Cover with vented plastic wrap and microwave for the remaining time.

4 Remove fish from the oven. Test for doneness by probing the thickest part with a fork. Serve immediately.

2 Cover the baking dish tightly with plastic wrap. Turn back one edge to allow steam to escape.

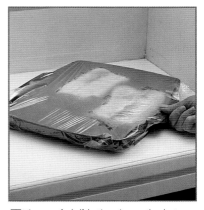

3 Microwave for half the time given on the chart (page 44). Rotate dish; microwave for the remaining time, or until fish flakes easily.

Grilling FISH & GAME

To many people, outdoor grilling is the perfect cooking method for big-game steaks, chops and ribs. The naturally smoky flavor seems totally suited to the meat. However, fewer people associate outdoor grilling with fish, small game and game birds. The fact is, these foods have the same delicious charred-wood flavor as grilled red meat.

Oily fish such as trout and salmon are best suited to grilling because they stay moist despite the high-heat cooking process. Lean fish such as walleye or largemouth bass tend to get dry unless you select thick cuts or grill them in foil (page 49).

You can grill fish steaks, fillets or whole fish. As with most other fish cookery, allow an average of 10 minutes cooking time per inch of fish thickness.

Waterfowl, with its rich, dark meat, is similar to venison and grills up just as nicely. Boneless breasts or cut-up birds work equally well. If you have a choice between skinless and skin-on waterfowl, choose skin-on. The fat under the skin bastes the meat naturally as it grills.

Upland birds need special care to remain moist during grilling. Marinating before grilling and basting during grilling add needed moisture. Birds with the skin on will be juicier when grilled than skinned birds. Indirect heat also prevents the flesh from drying out.

Grilling small game is similar to grilling upland game birds: cook "low and slow." Frequent basting provides needed moisture; a pan of water set between two banks of coals will also provide needed humidity, helping keep the meat moist and tender.

Types of Grills

CHARCOAL GRILLS are inexpensive, portable and impart a distinct charred-wood flavor. You can regulate the heat by adjusting the air vents. But they heat up more slowly than gas grills and require more cleanup time.

GAS GRILLS cook the food over a bed of hot lava rocks. They start easily and heat up quickly, and you can control the temperature by regulating the gas flow. But they're costlier and less portable than charcoal grills.

Equipment for Grilling

EQUIPMENT for grilling includes (1) grilling screen and (2) grilling basket, to prevent fish from sticking to the grate; (3) long-handled tongs, for moving coals and turning food over; (4) long-handled spatula, for turning and removing food from the grill; (5) nonstick vegetable cooking spray, for oiling the grate prior to cooking; (6) heavy-duty aluminum foil, for wrapping food and to prevent sticking; (7) long-handled basting brush, used to baste the food with marinades or sauces; (8) fine-mist spray bottle, for controlling flare-ups; (9) electric charcoal starter; (10) liquid charcoal starter and (11) charcoal.

Tips for Using a Gas Grill

PLACE a pan of soaked wood chips on the lava rocks in a gas grill to add flavor. If you sprinkle chips over the rocks, ash could clog the gas vents.

SET one burner of a double-burner gas grill at a lower temperature. This way, you can cook fish or game over high heat and vegetables over lower heat.

REMOVE hardened grease from your grate with a foaming-type oven cleaner. Keep the grate clean by washing it frequently in soapy water.

HOW TO GRILL FISH AND GAME

To start coals in a charcoal grill, pile briquets in a mound, douse with charcoal lighter fluid and ignite; or use an electric starter. When the coals turn white, use tongs to spread them in a layer an inch larger than the cooking area; or arrange coals in two banks for indirect cooking.

Spray the grate with nonstick cooking spray after cleaning it thoroughly with a stiff wire brush or oven cleaner. Place the grate over the coals. If cooking fish fillets, use foil or a grilling screen to keep the fish from falling apart.

Close the lid of the grill and adjust the vents (below) to regulate the heat. You can also increase heat by lowering the grate or bunch-

ing the coals more closely; reduce heat by raising the grate or spreading the coals. Turn foods at least once during cooking.

Grilling in a Foil Packet

1 Spread butter or oil over the center of the shiny side of a large piece of heavy-duty foil. Add fish or game. Season as desired, and top with additional butter or oil. You may also add sliced onions, carrots or other vegetables; do not overcrowd the packet or make it too thick.

2 Bring the long sides of the foil together over the food. Roll-fold until the foil is snug against the food, using at least three roll-folds. Roll the ends in tightly, using at least three roll-folds. Press the foil against the food to make a neat package.

3 Grill the packet over hot coals, turning at least once. Fish generally takes 15 to 20 minutes; game may take longer, depending on the thickness. To check for doneness, open one packet only. Rewrap and continue grilling if needed.

How to Keep Fish from Falling Apart

PLACE lightly oiled skinless fish steaks or fillets on foil, shaped to match the fish. The foil keeps the fish from sticking to the grate and falling apart.

USE a grilling screen or a special fish-grilling cage for fillets or steaks. Some grilling cages are shaped like whole fish and work well if your fish happens to be the same size.

Tips for Grilling Fish and Game

SKEWER small or medium-sized game birds on a rotisserie spit by running the rod through the body cavity; snug the birds together before securing with meat holders. If skewering three or four birds, you may skewer through the ribs, changing the direction of every other bird.

ARRANGE coals in two banks on the sides of the grill, leaving a space in the center, for indirect cooking. This method provides more gentle heat and helps prevent flare-ups. For additional humidity, place a disposable aluminum pan between the coals and fill it with water.

PLACE skin-on whole fish directly on the grate; oil the skin first to make turning easier. Turn fish over carefully with tongs or a large spatula, taking care not to break the skin. Whole fish usually cook in 10 to 20 minutes.

MONITOR grill temperature by clipping a deep-frying thermometer into a wooden clothespin; insert the tip into a vent in the lid. The clothespin keeps the thermometer from coming in contact with hot metal.

TOSS a handful of wood chunks on the hot coals for a slightly smoky flavor. Use hardwood or fruitwood chunks; sporting goods stores usually sell wood chunks for smoking. Do not use wood from conifers.

Smoking
FISH & GAME

Smoked fish and game are delicious and easy to prepare. Home-smoked fish makes a mouthwatering appetizer and adds a distinctive flavor to chowders, casseroles, salads and other dishes. Smoke and wild game seem to go together naturally; the tangy, sweet smoke flavor is reminiscent of a day in the woods or field.

There are two basic methods of smoking. Cold smoking is done at temperatures below 120°F, and works well for drying and flavoring jerky and cured sausages or for flavoring fresh sausages prior to cooking. It also is the method used by commercial processors to preserve fish so it can be kept as long as 3 months. Temperatures used for preserving fish never exceed 100°F during the commercial smoking process, which may take as long as a week. This method is not usually attempted by home cooks.

Hot smoking, also called smoke-cooking, is not a preservation technique, but simply a cooking method. Temperatures range from 150° to 250°F. Fish and game are fully cooked with this method and they pick up a delicious smoky flavor.

Many types of smokers are available, ranging from sheet-aluminum smokers with an electric hot plate to produce smoke and limited heat, to charcoal or electric-powered water smokers, to insulated variable-temperature smokers. You can also use a covered grill as a hot smoker, or turn an old refrigerator, range or even a garbage can into a smoker. Many smokers can be used for either hot or cold smoking, depending on the weather and the heat source.

Use (1) wood chips, tree trimmings or smoking saw-dust to provide smoke. Use a digital thermometer (2) to monitor the internal temperature of summer sausage or large cuts of meat without opening the smoker, which causes heat loss, and an instant-read thermometer (3) to monitor smoker temperature. Insert the thermometer into the smoker's vent hole or a hole designed for a thermometer.

Most smoking is done with dry heat, but water smokers are readily available and are the choice of many cooks. A pan of water placed above the heat source produces steam that helps keep foods moist during smoking.

All smokers require wood to produce smoke. Sports stores and specialty catalogs sell chips and sawdust of various woods used for smoking, including hickory, cherry, alder, apple and mesquite. Trimmings from your own hardwood or fruitwood trees also work well. Other smoke-producing materials include pecan shells, sassafras bark and cobs from dried corn.

Soak wood chunks in water for at least an hour before using them. They will produce more smoke and are less likely to burst into flames than dry chunks. Small chips or saw-dust used over small electric hot plates can be sprayed with a mister bottle to dampen them.

Temperature control is important when smoking, especially when making foods like salami that will receive no further cooking. An insulated electric smoker is perfect for this, because the temperature is easy to adjust and maintain. Monitor the smoker temperature constantly with an instant-read or oven thermometer. If your smoker doesn't have a built-in thermometer, add one by clipping a candy thermometer in a wooden clothespin and inserting the tip into a vent hole (see page 51). A digital thermometer is useful for monitoring the internal temperature of salami and large cuts of meat during smoking.

Weather greatly affects smoking time. In hot weather, even smokers with small hot plates may get too warm for cold smoking. Cold and windy weather lowers the temperature in any smoker. To increase the smoking temperature, move the smoker to a protected location. If your smoker is electric, you may be able to slip a large box over it for insulation. If it's charcoal-fueled, just add extra charcoal. Insulated variable-temperature electric smokers are easiest to control.

Judge the doneness of hot-smoked meat by checking its temperature with a thermometer. Smoke-cooked fish is just like fish cooked by any other method: when the flesh flakes easily near the backbone, it's done.

When using cold smoke to flavor meats or sausages prior to cooking, use the color of the meat as a guide. A golden color on a pheasant, for example, indicates light smoke flavor, while a deep golden brown indicates strong smoke. After cold smoking, roast the meat in the oven to the desired temperature.

Types of Commercially Available Smokers

Types of Homemade Smokers

WATER SMOKERS have a heat source, either gas or electric, at the bottom and an extra grate below the food for holding a pan of water. The steam keeps the food moist and, if you substitute wine or other flavored liquids for the water, imparts a unique flavor to smoked foods.

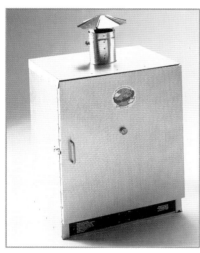

INSULATED VARIABLE-TEMPERATURE SMOKERS offer excellent temperature control and are a growing favorite among serious cooks. These tend to be the most expensive smokers available but are very easy to use.

KETTLE GRILLS double as hot smokers, although their capacity is limited. Simply put a small pile of charcoal briquets on the bottom and spread them when they're hot. Add a few hardwood sticks and place the food on the grate. Control the heat by adjusting the air vents.

STEEL GARBAGE CANS, preferably new ones, easily convert to smokers. Drill holes in the sides and insert metal rods to support grates. Set a burner on the bottom, cut a hole large enough for a frying pan and save the metal to make a closing flap. Cut vent holes in the lid.

OLD STOVES, especially gas models, make ideal smokers. They're insulated, have heat-resistant racks and usually require no extra venting. Just remove the broiler rack, put a pan of charcoal briquets or a large electric burner in the broiler compartment and add a few hardwood sticks or a pan of shavings. Drill a hole in the top for a thermometer.

ELECTRIC SMOKERS are the most popular type. A pan of hardwood chips rests on a burner at the bottom, and the food is placed on removable wire racks. These smokers are convenient and are available in several sizes, but they don't work well in cold weather.

OLD REFRIGERATORS can be converted into dry smokers. Remove the electric mechanism and drill ventilation holes in the top and bottom.

SMOKING FISH

Virtually any kind of fish can be smoked, but oily fish such as salmon and trout are best. They absorb the smoke better than lean fish and aren't as likely to dry out during the smoking process. Skin-on fillets and steaks no more than 1 inch thick are easiest to smoke, but thicker pieces or whole fish may also be used.

Either fresh or defrosted fish can be smoked. You can also smoke fish and then freeze it, but smoked fish tends to be watery when defrosted.

Before smoking, fish must be soaked in a salt solution, or brine. This helps kill any microorganisms and provides much of the distinctive flavor of smoked fish. Brining times vary from 6 to 24 hours, depending mainly on the size of the fish pieces. Some species absorb the salt more readily than others, and previously frozen fish take the brine more rapidly than fresh ones, so you may have to experiment to find the degree of saltiness that suits your taste.

Experiment also with the brine recipe at right. Many cooks try less salt, more sugar or a little red pepper or Tabasco sauce. The herbs can be changed, and maple syrup or molasses can be substituted for the sugar.

Dry smokers reduce the fish in size and take much longer than water smokers do. Dry-smoked fish has an intense flavor and is usually served as an appetizer or used in salads or chowders. It can be refrigerated up to 2 weeks. Fish cooked in a water smoker is usually served as a main course. The fish is lightly flavored and moist. It can be refrigerated for only a few days.

BRINE SOLUTION

1 CUP PICKLING SALT
10 CUPS WATER

OPTIONAL:

¼ CUP GRANULATED OR
PACKED BROWN SUGAR

BAY LEAF

CHILI POWDER

THYME

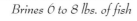

Brines 6 to 8 lbs. of fish

Mix brine solution in a nonaluminum container. You may heat the solution on the stove or in the microwave to help dissolve the salt; cool completely before using.

Brining Chart

TYPE/SIZE	BRINING TIME
WHOLE	
UP TO 4 LBS.	12 TO 18 HOURS
4 LBS. OR MORE	24 TO 48 HOURS
FILLETS, STEAKS AND CHUNKS	
½ TO 1 INCH	12 TO 18 HOURS

How to Smoke Fish

1 Soak the fish in a brine solution (above, or as noted in recipe). Cover bowl with plastic wrap and refrigerate at 40°F for the recommended time.

2 Air dry the fish on a wire rack after patting it dry with paper towels. A shiny film, called a pellicle, will form in about an hour; this helps seal in juices. You can use a fan to form the pellicle faster.

3 Preheat the smoker to 100°F, checking the temperature with an oven thermometer. In cold or windy weather, put an insulating cover over the smoker (following page) to maintain the desired temperature. Place fillets (skin side down) or steaks on greased racks. The racks may have to be rotated during the smoking process; fish on the bottom rack tend to cook more quickly. There is no need to turn the fish over on the racks.

4 Place a pan of hardwood chips on the burner, put the cover on the smoker and allow the fish to smoke. The air temperature inside the smoker should reach about 225°F. Add more chips as needed for desired flavor.

5 Test fish for doneness using an instant-read thermometer. When the internal temperature of the fish reaches 180°F, try to maintain that temperature for an additional 30 minutes before removing the fish from the smoker.

SMOKING WILD GAME

Wild game, unlike fish, is not always brined before smoking. Many people prefer to smoke it plain, or lightly seasoned. But brining before smoking does add a unique flavor and makes the meat firmer. It also helps retain moisture in game birds and small game.

Hot smoking is used to cook game; cold smoking is used to flavor game, especially sausages, before cooking.

Any type of game can be smoked, so you are limited only by your imagination and the contents of your freezer. Because game is typically low in fat, it is sometimes covered with bacon or with an oil-soaked cheesecloth before smoking.

Follow the same basic procedure shown on page 57 for smoking fish, eliminating the brine if you prefer. It's helpful to use a digital thermometer to monitor the temperature of larger cuts of meat during smoking.

Tips for Smoking Fish and Game

ADD wine or flavorings such as stick cinnamon or lemon slices to the water pan when wet smoking to flavor the fish or game.

MAKE a loose-fitting cover from ceiling tiles and 1 × 2-inch strips of wood to hold the heat in an electric smoker when smoking in cold weather.

SMOKE-COOK game of different sizes at the same time by placing large items on the bottom rack and small ones on top rack. Game on top is farther from the heat and easier to remove if it gets done sooner.

How to Make Jerky

1 Slice meat evenly, about ⅛ inch thick. Meat sliced with the grain produces chewy jerky; for more tender jerky, slice across the grain. Meat is easier to slice if it is partially frozen. Special slicing boards (pictured), available at sporting goods stores, help ensure even slices.

2 Combine marinade ingredients in a large nonmetallic mixing bowl. Stir to dissolve salt. Add meat strips. Cover with plastic wrap. Refrigerate 24 hours, stirring occasionally. In a large mixing bowl, cover wood chips with water. Soak for 1 hour. Place oven thermometer in the smoker and heat to 120°F.

3 Spray smoker racks with non-stick vegetable cooking spray. Set aside. Drain wood chips. Drain and discard marinade from the meat strips. Pat strips lightly with paper towels. Arrange strips at least ¼ inch apart on prepared racks. Place racks in smoker.

4 Open damper. Place a handful of wood chips in the smoker. Close damper, cracking slightly when wood chips begin to smoke. Smoke meat strips for 3 to 6 hours, or until dry but not brittle, adding wood chips as necessary. Cool completely. Store jerky, loosely wrapped, in refrigerator for no longer than 1 week, or wrap tightly and freeze up to 2 months.

Oven Method for Making Jerky

1 Add 2 teaspoons liquid smoke flavoring to any marinade. Continue with recipe as directed, except place oven thermometer in oven. Heat the oven to the lowest possible temperature setting, using a wooden spoon to prop open the oven door about 7 inches at the top to maintain 120°F.

2 Spray 4 14 × 10-inch cooling racks with nonstick vegetable cooking spray. Arrange meat strips on prepared racks, spacing as directed. Dry for 3 to 4 hours, or until dry but not brittle.

Game Sausages

There are few things more satisfying than making your own sausages, whether fresh or smoked, and doing the job well.

The art of sausage making is not as difficult as you may think. Special sausage-making equipment and ingredients are available to anyone through mail-order sources. All it takes is a little patience and practice to produce wholesome, delicious sausages you'll be proud to serve.

For big-game sausages, use trimmed meat from any part of the animal; the meat doesn't need to be tender. Game bird sausages work well with a combination of breast and thigh meat. Generally, fatty pork butt or plain pork fat is added to the lean meat. Be sure to specify hard pork *back fat* when you order the fat from your butcher; tell the butcher what you'll be using it for to be sure you get the right thing. Lard is too soft and will produce a greasy sausage. It should not be used.

Keep your meat grinder blades sharp when grinding meat for sausage. Dull blades squeeze juices from the meat, resulting in dry, less flavorful sausage.

If your grinder slows down during use or if the texture of the meat suddenly becomes fine and mushy, partially disassemble the grinder and check the blades and plate. Sinew and other tough material can get caught in the mechanism, causing poor performance. Clean the blade and plate, then continue. You may need some help when making sausages. One person can turn the crank while the other guides the casings off the horn and twists the links.

Temperature control when smoking is extremely important for proper drying of sausages and for quality control. Most fresh sausages are cooked by methods other than smoking. They may be smoked at a low temperature for flavoring, but are later grilled, broiled or panfried. Salami and other cured sausages, however, receive no further cooking.

Because low smokehouse temperatures and airtight casings create an ideal environment for bacteria growth, we recommend adding cure (page 62) to all sausage that is smoked. This prevents the growth of organisms that cause food poisoning. Cure can be found in stores that specialize in smoking and outdoor cooking equipment.

Equipment for Making Sausage

SAUSAGE-MAKING SUPPLIES & EQUIPMENT include (1) optional heavy-duty sausage stuffer, helpful for large quantities; (2) non-metallic mixing bowl or tub; (3) kitchen scale; (4) kitchen twine; (5) sausage casings; (6) meat grinder with two grinding plates and stuffing horns; and specialty ingredients and optional equipment for cured sausages, including (7) powdered dextrose, (8) soy protein concentrate, (9) premixed cure/seasoning blends, (10) curing powder, and (11) sausage pricker for eliminating air bubbles.

Tips and Techniques for Sausage Making

GRIND lean meat separately from fat for juicier fresh sausages. Cut fat into chunks, partially freeze it, then grind it finer than the meat. Mix ground meat and ground fat together. This way, the fat will be more evenly distributed and there won't be any large pieces in your sausage.

KEEP meat as cold as possible during sausage making. If meat is to be ground twice, chill it thoroughly and wash and refrigerate the grinder between grindings. When working with a large batch of meat, grind only a small portion at a time and leave the rest refrigerated.

USE a cure for all sausages that will be smoked, to prevent botulism, a type of food poisoning. For a fresh-sausage recipe that makes 5 pounds, *substitute* 8 level teaspoons Morton® TenderQuick® mix for 5½ level teaspoons canning/pickling salt; or, *add* 1 level teaspoon InstaCure No. 1 (formerly Prague Powder No. 1) to the salt already in the recipe.

SPRINKLE mixed dry seasonings over coarsely ground meat. Mix well and refrigerate overnight to blend the flavors. Mix with liquid called for in recipe, then grind through the finer plate and stuff immediately. If using already ground meat, mix dry seasonings with liquid before adding to meat.

CHOOSE (1) lamb casings for breakfast sausages; (2) collagen casings for snack sticks; (3) hog casings for polish-size sausages; or (4) synthetic-fibrous casings for salami. Fresh-sausage recipes need not be cased. Form into patties (5) and fry or broil.

USING SYNTHETIC & NATURAL CASINGS

Synthetic casings used in this book include 22 mm and 32 mm collagen casings, which are edible, and 3½-inch synthetic-fibrous casings, which are peeled and discarded before the sausage is eaten. Salami-size casings can also be made from clean muslin. Before stuffing, sew one end shut in a half circle and turn it right side out to prevent unraveling. Stuff tightly and tie off as directed below.

Natural sausage casings include lamb casings (22 to 24 mm), which are used for breakfast links, and hog casings (commonly 32 to 35 mm), which are used for Italian, Polish and country-style links. A butcher shop that specializes in sausages may sell you a *hank*, a bundle of casings packed in salt. You can also order casings from specialty sources.

The casing you select is based on the sausage you'll be making. Natural casings are usually used for fresh sausages, since they are tender and edible. Synthetic-fibrous casings are perfect for salami and are easier to find than natural alternatives. Collagen casings are available for both fresh and smoked sausages in sizes for small links or bratwurst. They are easier to use than natural casings, but they don't hold a twist well and may need to be hand tied at the ends.

Preparing & Stuffing Synthetic Casings

1 Soak synthetic-fibrous casings in a mixture of 3 tablespoons white vinegar to 2 quarts lukewarm water for 30 minutes, or as directed by manufacturer. The vinegar helps the casing to peel smoothly from the finished salami and helps prevent mold growth. Wet a homemade muslin casing before stuffing.

2 Wrap the middle of a 20-inch piece of kitchen string tightly around one end of the casing several times; then fan out the end like butterfly wings. Wrap one end of the string tightly around one wing several times. Repeat on the other side. Wrap both ends of string around main neck again. Tie securely.

3 Stuff with sausage mixture by hand or with a stuffing horn. Pack the casing tightly, squeezing to force out air pockets. Tie off with a butterfly knot; make a loop in the string for hanging the sausage. If there are small air bubbles trapped under the surface, pierce the casing with a sterilized needle or sausage pricker.

Preparing & Stuffing Natural Casings

1 Spread out a hank of salted casings carefully on a clean work surface. Find the beginning of the hank and gently pull one length out of the bundle until it is free, being careful not to twist the remainder of the lengths. Remove as many lengths as you need. Resalt and freeze the remainder for future use.

2 Open one end of the casing and slip the end over a faucet. Hold your hand over the casing to keep it from slipping off. Run a steady, medium stream of cold water through the casing until it is completely filled and the water runs through. Continue flushing for a few minutes. Rinse the outside of the casing.

3 Place the rinsed casing in a large measuring cup filled with cold water after draining out all water and air from the casing. Let one end of the casing hang over the edge of the cup. Rinse remaining casings, adding them to the measuring cup, until you've rinsed all the casings you will need.

4 Slip one end of a rinsed, wet casing over the sausage-stuffing horn; push until the end of the casing is at the back end of the horn. Continue pushing until the entire length is gathered onto the horn. Pull the casing forward until about 1 inch hangs over the open end of the horn.

5 Turn the crank of the sausage stuffer slowly until some of the sausage mixture comes out of the horn. Tie off the end of the casing with kitchen string, pinching off a small bit of meat. The pinching helps eliminate air at the end of the link. Continue cranking until sausage is desired length; have a helper guide the link away from the horn.

6 Twist the first link several times; then crank until a second link is formed. Support both links with one hand while using the other to keep the casing on the horn until it's firmly filled. Be sure to let casing slip off easily before it overfills and breaks. Continue twisting and filling until you come to the end of the casing; keep casings on horn wet so they slip off without sticking. Tie off the last sausage with string.

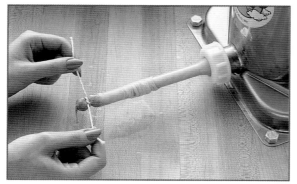

Canning
FISH & BIG GAME

Home canning preserves fish or game for up to 1 year. It is an excellent alternative to freezing, especially when freezer space is limited. It is very useful for preserving a large catch of oily fish such as salmon, which have a short freezer life. It's also perfect for canning boneless chunks of venison that you're left with after boning a deer.

Fresh fish fillets need not be totally boneless before canning. Pressure cooking softens the bones (much like commercially canned salmon) so they can be eaten. The skin can also be retained. Smoked fish is delicious when canned; the great flavor is retained.

Canned big-game chunks are a great pantry staple. For added flavor, smoke the meat lightly before canning.

Home canning is easy if a few rules are followed. Use a pressure cooker because it kills bacteria during the cooking process.

One-pint jars are best; processing times are very long for larger jars, and foods cook unevenly. A 1-pint jar holds about 1 pound.

Wash the jars and bands in hot, soapy water. After rinsing thoroughly, keep them in a sink filled with hot, clear water until you are ready to fill the jars.

Put the lids in a saucepan with hot water and place them over low heat on the stove. This will soften the rubber and the lids will seal better.

Add vinegar to fish before canning to raise the acidity level. It is an additional safeguard against bacteria growth. Include 1/2 teaspoon of salt for flavor, if desired, whether canning fish or game. To change the color of white fish to that of canned salmon, blend 2 teaspoons of ketchup with the oil and vinegar. Dribble the mixture evenly over each layer of fish after it is placed in the jar.

After processing and cooling, check the jar seals carefully before storing. Turn the jars upside down to see if they leak. Also, use thumb pressure on the center of the lid. If the lid pops or the jar leaks, it is not sealed properly. Refrigerate and use within 2 days.

When opening home-canned fish or game, listen for the vacuum release when the lid seal is broken. Discard, without tasting, any food from a jar that does not appear to be tightly sealed.

Canned fish is used as the basis of many fine dishes. Because it is already cooked, it is not as versatile as frozen fish. Canned fish can be used in fish cakes, loaf, quiche, patties, appetizers, sandwiches, salads or any recipe calling for cooked fish. Once opened, canned fish should be drained, refrigerated and used within 2 days. Canned big game makes excellent sloppy-joe type sandwiches and works well in a quick stew or stroganoff.

How to Can Big Game in a Pressure Cooker

2 Pack warm smoked chunks into jars, leaving 1 inch of space at the top. Unsmoked meat cubes can also be canned; cook to rare, and pack while hot. Add boiling broth, leaving 1 inch space at the top. Wipe rim with clean cloth.

1 Wash pint jars, bands and lids in hot, soapy water. Rinse well. Place jars and bands in sink filled with hot, clear water. Place lids in saucepan; cover with hot water. Heat to barely simmering over low heat.

3 Place warm lid and band on the jar. Tighten firmly but lightly. Place sealed jars on trivet in pressure cooker. Follow pressure-cooker manufacturer's directions for the number of jars and amount of water to add to cooker. Heat until 10 pounds pressure is reached, then begin timing. Process for 1¼ hours at 10 pounds pressure.

4 Allow pressure to drop naturally. When pressure has dropped completely, remove jars with tongs. Place in a draft-free place for 12 hours. Check seals according to lid manufacturer's directions. Refrigerate any jars that have not sealed properly; use within 3 days. Store jars in a dark, cool place; use within one year.

How to Can Fish

1 Slice the skinless fish fillets into two thin pieces if they are thicker than 1 inch. Then cut them into 1- to 1½-inch chunks.

2 Stuff the fish into clean jars, allowing a ½-inch air space. Add 1 tablespoon vinegar to each jar. With lean fish, add 1 teaspoon vegetable oil.

3 Wipe the jar rim thoroughly. Place the warm lid and band on the jar, and tighten them according to the lid manufacturer's directions.

4 Put the jars in the pressure cooker. Follow the instruction book for number of jars and amount of water. Process 90 minutes at 10 pounds pressure.

5 Remove the jars with tongs; place on a thick towel in a draft-free place for 12 hours. Take off bands and check seals according to lid box guidelines.

6 Label the jars. Write the fish species and canning date on freezer tape. Store the jars in a dark, cool place and use them within a year.

Recipes

for

Fish & Wild Game

Freshly caught fish, and wild game that you've harvested yourself, are truly satisfying to cook and serve. You know exactly how the food you are about to set on the table was handled before it reached your kitchen. You also know that it's free of hormones, antibiotics and other chemicals frequently given to domestic livestock.

Just as free-range chickens have a more robust flavor and better texture than coop-raised chickens, the meat from animals that roam the wild open spaces all their lives has more character than that from domestically raised animals confined to small pens. The same seems to hold true for fish. Connoisseurs believe that wild salmon, for example, is superior to farmed salmon, even of the same species.

Of course, you are free to use farm-raised fish and game in any of these recipes. Shooting preserves, game farms and areas where one can fish for farmed salmon and other fish are within the reach of many hunters and anglers; and game-farm meat is becoming easier to find at large supermarkets. Farm-raised game tends to have more fat than its wild counterpart, so information is included in this book to help you adapt to this. We also provide substitution information throughout the recipe section, enabling you to substitute a different type of game or fish for the type specified in a recipe.

Whether you harvest your fish and game in the wild, at a game farm or at the supermarket, you'll find inspiring new ways to prepare it in the chapters that follow.

RECIPES FOR
Cooking Fish

Cooking methods differ for oily and lean gamefish. Oily fish are best cooked with little or no added oil. They can be broiled, baked, poached, steamed, grilled or smoked. These cooking methods allow the oil to drain from the fish before serving. Small stream trout, however, are often panfried, because they have less fat content than large oily fish such as coho and chinook salmon.

Baste lean fish to keep them moist. They can be panfried, deep-fried, oven-fried, baked, broiled, steamed, poached, grilled or smoked.

A common rule of thumb is that white-fleshed fish is lean; dark or pink flesh is oily. Although fish usually have a delicate or mild flavor, oily fish sometimes are strong-tasting. To reduce the oily taste, choose a recipe using lemon or lime juice, wine or vinegar.

Lean fish have fewer calories than oily ones. However, vegetable oil, butter, margarine and sauces add extra calories. Poaching and steaming are the only cooking methods in which no calories are added. On the right is a guide to the average number of calories per 4-ounce serving of uncooked fish.

Calorie Chart

TYPE	SPECIES NAME	AVERAGE CALORIES (4-OUNCE SERVING)
OILY FISH	SALMON	223 TO 254
	TROUT (SMALL)	115
	TROUT (LARGE)	223
LEAN FISH	BLACK BASS	119
	MUSKELLUNGE	125
	NORTHERN PIKE	101
	STRIPED BASS	120
	WALLEYE	106
	PANFISH	104
	WHITE BASS	112
	CATFISH	118
	BULLHEAD	96

Cooking Methods Chart

■ EXCELLENT □ GOOD

	PANFRY	DEEP-FRY	BROIL	POACH	BAKE	OVEN-FRY	MICROWAVE	BARBECUE	SMOKE-COOK	OPEN FIRE	FISH BOIL
LARGE OILY:											
SALMON			■		■		■	■	■		■
TROUT									■		
SMALL OILY:											
SALMON		■			■				■		
TROUT											
LARGE LEAN:											
BLACK BASS			■		■						
MUSKELLUNGE					■						
NORTHERN PIKE			■								
STRIPED BASS					■				■		
WALLEYE					■						
SMALL LEAN:											
PANFISH	■										
BLACK BASS	■										
WHITE BASS			■								
CATFISH											
BULLHEAD											

FISH SUBSTITUTION GUIDE

All of the gamefish listed in this book's recipes can be replaced by other fish. But for best results, use a fish from the same grouping on the fish substitution chart (below).

For example, northern pike, walleye or muskellunge can be substituted in a recipe that calls for largemouth bass.

Fish Substitution Chart

TYPE	SPECIES NAME	OTHER COMMON NAMES
LARGE OILY (2 POUNDS OR LARGER)	SALMON:	
	CHINOOK	KING SALMON, TYEE
	COHO	SILVER SALMON
	SOCKEYE	RED SALMON
	PINK	HUMPBACK
	CHUM	DOG SALMON
	ATLANTIC	LANDLOCKED SALMON, SEBAGO SALMON
	TROUT:	
	BROOK	SQUARETAIL, SPECKLED TROUT
	BROWN	LOCH LEVEN TROUT, GERMAN BROWN
	RAINBOW	STEELHEAD, KAMLOOPS
	CUTTHROAT	YELLOWSTONE TROUT
	LAKE	GRAY TROUT, TOGUE, MACKINAW
SMALL OILY (UP TO 2 POUNDS)	SALMON:	
	KOKANEE	SOCKEYE, RED SALMON
	TROUT:	
	BROOK	SQUARETAIL, SPECKLED TROUT
	BROWN	LOCH LEVEN TROUT, GERMAN BROWN
	RAINBOW	STEELHEAD, KAMLOOPS
	CUTTHROAT	YELLOWSTONE TROUT
LARGE LEAN (2 POUNDS OR LARGER)	BLACK BASS:	
	LARGEMOUTH	BLACK BASS
	SMALLMOUTH	BRONZEBACK, BLACK BASS
	MUSKELLUNGE	MUSKIE
	NORTHERN PIKE	JACK, PICKEREL, SNAKE
	STRIPED BASS	ROCKFISH, STRIPER
	WALLEYE	WALLEYED PIKE, PICKEREL, DORÉ
	WHITE BASS	STRIPER, SILVER BASS
SMALL LEAN (UP TO 2 POUNDS)	PANFISH:	
	BLUEGILL	BREAM, SUNFISH
	YELLOW PERCH	RINGED PERCH, STRIPED PERCH
	CRAPPIE	PAPERMOUTH, SPECKLED PERCH
	PUMPKINSEED	BREAM, SUNFISH
	BLACK BASS:	
	LARGEMOUTH	BLACK BASS
	SMALLMOUTH	BRONZEBACK, BLACK BASS
	WHITE BASS	STRIPER, SILVER BASS
CATFISH AND BULLHEADS	CATFISH:	
	FLATHEAD	YELLOW CAT, MUD CAT
	CHANNEL	FIDDLER
	BLUE	WHITE CAT, SILVER CAT
	BULLHEAD	HORNED POUT

THAWING FISH

Thawing fish frozen in water is a simple process. Melt the block of ice under cold, running water. When the fish are free from the ice, place them on a plate lined with paper towels. Cover the fish with plastic wrap and thaw in the refrigerator.

Thaw ice-free fish by refrigerating them for 24 hours. To speed the process, place the fish in a heavy, waterproof plastic bag. Seal the bag, put it in a bowl of cold water and refrigerate until thawed.

Glazed fish and those frozen without ice can be thawed in the microwave. Separate frozen serving-sized pieces before thawing. If this cannot be done, break them apart as soon as possible. A block of ice must be removed as described above before microwave thawing, because fish can partially cook before the ice melts. Wipe ice off glazed fish as it thaws and remove water that accumulates in the roasting rack.

Place fish on a microwave roasting rack. Shield the thin ends with foil. Microwave for half the time listed on the chart below. Turn fish over. Rearrange the fillets so the thick parts are to the outside and the thin parts overlap. Remove shields and microwave for the remaining time, until pliable but still a bit icy in the thick parts. Let stand 5 minutes to complete thawing. Drain and cook immediately, or cover and refrigerate until mealtime.

Removing Bones from Cooked Fish

Loosen the skin with a knife. Using your fingers and a knife, carefully peel the skin, starting from behind the head and working across the body to the tail.

Insert a fork at the backbone. Lift the side carefully away from the spine. On a small fish, the entire side may come off in one piece.

Grasp the spine behind the head with your fingers. Use the fork to hold the fish on the plate. Remove the spine from the fish and discard.

Remove fins with the fork and discard. Check both sides of the fish for little rib bones. If any remain, remove them. The fish is now ready to eat.

Microwave Thawing Chart

TYPE	SIZE	POWER LEVEL	FROZEN WITHOUT ICE	GLAZED
SMALL WHOLE	1 TO 1¾ INCHES THICK	50 PERCENT	3½ TO 6½ MIN./LB.	4 TO 6½ MIN./LB.
FILLETS	¼ TO 1 INCH THICK	50 PERCENT	3 TO 5 MIN./LB.	3½ TO 5½ MIN./LB.
STEAKS	ABOUT 1 INCH THICK	50 PERCENT	3 TO 5½ MIN./LB.	3½ TO 6 MIN./LB.

Deep-fried Corona® Catfish

MUSTARD BATTER FISH

⅓	CUP PREPARED OR DIJON MUSTARD
¼	CUP PLUS 1 TABLESPOON WATER
1	TEASPOON FRESH LEMON JUICE
1	TEASPOON WORCESTERSHIRE SAUCE
⅛	TEASPOON CAYENNE
1½	CUPS SEASONED COATING MIX
2¼	LBS. ANY FRESHWATER FISH FILLETS (6 OZ. EACH), SKIN REMOVED, CUT INTO 1½-INCH PIECES
	VEGETABLE OIL

6 servings

In small mixing bowl, combine mustard, water, lemon juice, Worcestershire sauce and cayenne. Place coating mix in shallow dish. Dip fish first in mustard mixture and then dredge in coating mix to coat.

In 10-inch skillet, heat ½ inch oil over medium heat. Add fish. Fry for 3 to 4 minutes, or until golden brown, turning over once. Drain on paper towel–lined plate.

Per Serving: Calories: 504 • Protein: 37 g. • Carbohydrate: 21 g. • Fat: 30 g. • Cholesterol: 116 mg. • Sodium: 1556 mg. — Exchanges: 1½ starch, 4½ lean meat, 3¼ fat

DEEP-FRIED CORONA® CATFISH

This spicy batter makes a superb catfish feast. It also works well for deep-frying shrimp.

1	CUP ALL-PURPOSE FLOUR, SIFTED
1	CUP CORONA® BEER, DIVIDED
⅓	CUP FINELY CHOPPED ONION
1	TABLESPOON OLIVE OR VEGETABLE OIL
1½	TEASPOONS SALT-FREE HERB AND SPICE BLEND
1½	TEASPOONS CAJUN SEASONING
⅛	TEASPOON RED PEPPER SAUCE
	VEGETABLE OIL
2¼	LBS. CATFISH FILLETS (6 OZ. EACH), SKIN REMOVED, CUT IN HALF CROSSWISE

6 servings

In medium mixing bowl, combine flour, ¾ cup beer, the onion, olive oil, spice blend and Cajun seasonings. Stir in remaining ¼ cup beer and the pepper sauce. Cover with plastic wrap. Set aside at room temperature for 30 minutes.

In deep-fat fryer, heat 2 inches vegetable oil to 375°F. Dip fish in batter to coat. In hot oil, fry fish, a few pieces at a time, for 5 to 6 minutes, or until golden brown, turning over once. Drain on paper towel–lined plate.

Per Serving: Calories: 389 • Protein: 33 g. • Carbohydrate: 19 g. • Fat: 18 g. • Cholesterol: 99 mg. • Sodium: 324 mg. — Exchanges: 1¼ starch, 4¼ lean meat, 1 fat

GARLIC-FRIED TROUT

2¼ LBS. STREAM TROUT, WALLEYE, OR OTHER FRESHWATER
FISH, FILLETS (6 OZ. EACH), SKIN REMOVED
1 CUP MILK
1 CUP SEASONED DRY BREAD CRUMBS
10 TO 12 CLOVES GARLIC, PEELED
¼ CUP OLIVE OIL
¼ CUP VEGETABLE OIL

6 servings

Arrange fillets in single layer in 13 × 9-inch baking
dish. Pour milk over fillets, turning to coat. Cover
with plastic wrap. Refrigerate 12 hours or overnight.

Place bread crumbs in shallow dish. Drain and
discard milk from fillets. Dredge fillets in bread
crumbs to coat. Place coated fillets on wax paper–
lined baking sheet. Chill ½ hour.

In a 12-inch skillet, heat oils and 5 or 6 cloves
garlic over medium heat. Add fillets. Fry for 7 to 9
minutes, or until golden brown, turning once and
adding the remaining cloves of garlic after half the
cooking time.
Drain on paper
towel–lined plate.

Per Serving:
Calories: 426
• Protein: 38 g.
• Carbohydrate:
16 g. • Fat: 22 g.
• Cholesterol: 99 mg.
• Sodium: 582 mg.
— Exchanges:
1 starch, 4½ lean
meat, 2 fat

BUTTERMILK DELIGHT

Especially good with bass, walleye, perch and all panfish.

2½ CUPS BUTTERMILK
2¼ LBS. ANY FRESHWATER FISH FILLETS (6 OZ. EACH),
SKIN REMOVED, CUT IN HALF CROSSWISE
VEGETABLE OIL
¾ CUP SELF-RISING FLOUR*
¼ CUP YELLOW CORNMEAL
1½ TEASPOONS ONION SALT

6 servings

Place buttermilk in medium mixing bowl. Add
fish. Stir to coat. Cover with plastic wrap. Chill
45 minutes.

In deep-fat fryer, heat 2 inches oil to 375°F. In
shallow dish, combine flour, cornmeal and onion
salt. Drain and discard buttermilk from fish
pieces. Dredge fish in flour mixture to coat. In
hot oil, fry fish, a few pieces at a time, for 3 to 4
minutes, or until golden brown, turning over
once. Drain on paper towel–lined plate. Serve
with tartar sauce, cocktail sauce, sweet and sour
sauce or salsa, if
desired.

*You may substi-
tute all-purpose
flour for self-rising
flour by adding
1½ teaspoons
baking powder and
½ teaspoon salt.*

Per Serving:
Calories: 447
• Protein: 36 g.
• Carbohydrate:
27 g. • Fat: 21 g.
• Cholesterol: 117
mg. • Sodium: 758
mg. — Exchanges:
1¾ starch, 4½
lean meat, 1½ fat

Garlic-fried Trout

HEARTY FRIED FISH

2	CANS (12 OZ. EACH) BEER
2	EGGS, BEATEN
3	BAY LEAVES
1/2	TEASPOON DRIED THYME LEAVES
1/2	TEASPOON DRIED MARJORAM LEAVES
1/4	TEASPOON SALT
1/4	TEASPOON FRESHLY GROUND PEPPER
2 1/4	LBS. ANY FRESHWATER FISH FILLETS (6 OZ. EACH), SKIN REMOVED, CUT IN HALF CROSSWISE

SAUCE

1	CUP SPAGHETTI SAUCE
1	TABLESPOON FRESH LEMON JUICE
2	TEASPOONS PREPARED HORSERADISH
1/4	TEASPOON RED PEPPER SAUCE
	VEGETABLE OIL
1	CUP UNSEASONED DRY BREAD CRUMBS
	LEMON WEDGES

6 servings

Combine beer, eggs, bay leaves, thyme, marjoram, salt and pepper in large mixing bowl. Add fish. Cover with plastic wrap. Refrigerate overnight.

Combine sauce ingredients in small mixing bowl. Cover with plastic wrap. Chill at least 1 hour.

Heat 2 inches oil to 375°F in deep-fat fryer. Drain and discard beer mixture and bay leaves from fillets. Place crumbs in shallow dish. Dredge fillets in crumbs to coat.

Fry fish in hot oil, a few pieces at a time, for 3 to 4 minutes, or until golden brown, turning over once. Drain on paper towel–lined plate. Serve with sauce and lemon wedges.

Per Serving: Calories: 410 • Protein: 36 g. • Carbohydrate: 20 g. • Fat: 20 g. • Cholesterol: 134 mg. • Sodium: 593 mg. — Exchanges: 1 starch, 4 1/4 lean meat, 1 vegetable, 1 1/4 fat

PRETZEL FISH

This recipe is very simple and works well with any firm-fleshed fish.

4	CUPS PRETZEL TWISTS
2	EGGS, BEATEN
1	CAN (5 OZ.) EVAPORATED MILK
3	TABLESPOONS BEER OR CLUB SODA
2¼	LBS. WALLEYE, SUNFISH OR OTHER LEAN FISH FILLETS (3 TO 6 OZ. EACH), SKIN REMOVED
	VEGETABLE OIL
	LEMON WEDGES

6 servings

Place pretzels in food processor. Process until powdery. (Pretzels may also be placed in a large plastic food-storage bag and crushed with a rolling pin.) Place powdered pretzels in large plastic food-storage bag. In medium mixing bowl, combine eggs, milk and beer. Dip fillets in egg mixture, then shake in pretzel powder to coat.

In 12-inch skillet, heat ¹/₈ inch oil over medium heat. Add fillets. Fry for 3¹/₂ to 6 minutes, or until golden brown, turning over once. Drain on paper towel–lined plate. Serve with lemon wedges.

Per Serving: Calories: 523 • Protein: 41 g. • Carbohydrate: 32 g. • Fat: 25 g. • Cholesterol: 193 mg. • Sodium: 820 mg. — Exchanges: 2 starch, 4³/₄ lean meat, ¹/₄ skim milk, 2 fat

Five Variations on Pretzel Fish

Parmesan Fish—Substitute 1 cup buttery cracker crumbs mixed with ¹/₂ cup grated Parmesan cheese for the pretzel crumbs; use ¹/₂ cup regular milk and 1 egg in place of the egg/evaporated milk/beer mixture.

Italian-Flavored Bites—Cut fish into bite-sized chunks and soak for 30 minutes in milk to coat; drain and discard milk. Substitute 1 cup Italian-seasoned bread crumbs for the pretzel crumbs; use 1 egg beaten with 1 tablespoon water in place of the egg/evaporated milk/beer mixture.

Caraway Rye Fried Fish—Substitute ³/₄ cup dried crumbs from caraway rye bread (about 6 slices), mixed with 1¹/₂ tablespoons dried oregano leaves, for the pretzel crumbs; use 2 eggs beaten with salt and pepper to taste in place of the egg/evaporated milk/beer mixture. This is good served with sweet and sour tomato sauce.

Fritos® Fillets—Soak fillets in beer to cover, mixed with a little lemon juice, for 1 hour; drain and discard beer. Substitute 2 cups finely crushed Fritos® corn chips mixed with 2 tablespoons grated Parmesan cheese and 1 teaspoon cayenne for the pretzel crumbs; use 2 eggs beaten with 1 tablespoon olive oil and ³/₄ cup beer in place of the egg/evaporated milk/beer mixture.

Honey-Fried Fillets—Substitute 2 cups coarsely crushed soda crackers mixed with ²/₃ cup flour and salt and pepper to taste for the pretzel crumbs. Use 2 eggs, beaten with 2 tablespoons honey, in place of the egg/evaporated milk/beer mixture.

GINGER BEER-BATTERED BASS

	VEGETABLE OIL
1	CUP CORNSTARCH
2	EGGS, SEPARATED
3/4	CUP BEER
2	TABLESPOONS SOY SAUCE
1/2	TEASPOON GROUND GINGER
1/2	TEASPOON DRY MUSTARD
1/2	TEASPOON SALT, DIVIDED
1	CUP ALL-PURPOSE FLOUR
1/4	TEASPOON PEPPER
1 1/2	LBS. BASS OR OTHER LEAN FISH FILLETS (6 OZ. EACH), SKIN REMOVED, CUT INTO 1 1/2-INCH PIECES

4 servings

In deep-fat fryer, heat 2 inches oil to 375°F. In medium mixing bowl, combine cornstarch, egg yolks, beer, soy sauce, ginger, mustard and 1/4 teaspoon salt. Set aside.

In another medium mixing bowl, beat egg whites at high speed of electric mixer until stiff but not dry. Fold into beer batter.

In shallow dish, combine flour, remaining 1/4 teaspoon salt and the pepper. Dip fish first in batter and then dredge in flour mixture to coat. In hot oil, fry fish, a few pieces at a time, for 3 to 4 minutes, or until golden brown, turning over once. Drain on paper towel–lined plate.

Per Serving: Calories: 560 • Protein: 39 g. • Carbohydrate: 56 g. • Fat: 17 g. • Cholesterol: 222 mg. • Sodium: 944 mg. — Exchanges: 3 1/2 starch, 4 1/4 lean meat, 1 fat

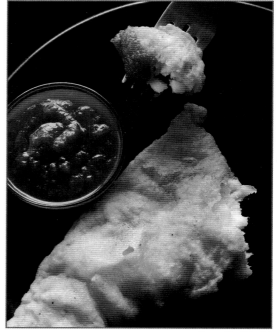

Lemon Fried Panfish

LEMON FRIED PANFISH

1	CUP ALL-PURPOSE FLOUR
2	TEASPOONS GRATED LEMON PEEL
1/2	TEASPOON SALT
1/4	TEASPOON PEPPER
1	CUP WATER
	VEGETABLE OIL
1 1/2	POUNDS PANFISH OR OTHER LEAN FISH FILLETS
	ALL-PURPOSE FLOUR

4 to 6 servings

In medium bowl, combine 1 cup flour, the lemon peel, salt and pepper. Blend in water; cover. Refrigerate at least 30 minutes.

In deep-fat fryer or deep skillet, heat oil (1 1/2 to 3 inches) to 375°F. Coat fish with flour, then dip in chilled batter. Fry a few pieces at a time, turning occasionally, until light golden brown, about 3 minutes. Drain on paper towels. Keep warm in 175°F oven. Repeat with remaining fish.

Per Serving: Calories: 220 • Protein: 24 g. • Carbohydrate: 14 g. • Fat: 7 g. • Cholesterol: 102 mg. • Sodium: 827 mg. — Exchanges: 1 starch, 3 very lean meat, 1 fat

CORNMEAL-COATED FRIED FISH

COATING

1/2	CUP YELLOW CORNMEAL
1/4	CUP MASA HARINA (CORN FLOUR)
1	TABLESPOON BAKING POWDER
1 1/2	TEASPOONS DRIED PARSLEY FLAKES, CRUSHED
1/2	TEASPOON GARLIC POWDER
1/2	TEASPOON ONION POWDER
1/2	TEASPOON PAPRIKA
1/2	TEASPOON CELERY SEED
1/4	TEASPOON PEPPER

2 1/4 LBS. ANY FRESHWATER FISH FILLETS (6 OZ. EACH), SKIN REMOVED
VEGETABLE OIL

6 servings

In shallow dish, combine coating ingredients. Dredge fillets in coating to coat. In 12-inch skillet, heat 1/8 inch oil over medium heat. Add fillets. Fry for 5 to 7 minutes, or until golden brown, turning over once. Drain on paper towel–lined plate. Top with salsa, if desired.

Per Serving: Calories: 419 • Protein: 34 g. • Carbohydrate: 13 g. • Fat: 25 g. • Cholesterol: 116 mg. • Sodium: 334 mg. — Exchanges: 1 starch, 4 1/2 lean meat, 2 1/4 fat

FISH CAKES

2	CUPS ANY FLAKED COOKED FRESHWATER FISH
1	CUP CORNFLAKE CRUMBS
1/2	CUP SLICED GREEN ONIONS
3	EGGS, DIVIDED
1	TABLESPOON SHERRY
1	TABLESPOON WORCESTERSHIRE SAUCE
1	TEASPOON SESAME OIL (OPTIONAL)
1/4	TEASPOON SALT
1/4	TEASPOON PEPPER
1/2	CUP SEASONED DRY BREAD CRUMBS
2	TABLESPOONS VEGETABLE OIL

3 servings

In medium mixing bowl, combine fish, cornflake crumbs, onions, 1 egg, the sherry, Worcestershire sauce, sesame oil, salt and pepper. Divide mixture into 6 equal portions. Shape each portion into a 1/2-inch-thick patty.

In small mixing bowl, lightly beat the remaining 2 eggs. Place bread crumbs in shallow dish. Dip patties first in eggs and then dredge in crumbs to coat.

In 10-inch skillet, heat vegetable oil over medium heat. Add patties. Fry for 2 to 4 minutes, or until golden brown, turning over once. Drain on paper towel–lined plate. Serve with lemon wedges, tartar sauce or cocktail sauce, if desired.

Per Serving: Calories: 543 • Protein: 40 g. • Carbohydrate: 50 g. • Fat: 19 g. • Cholesterol: 289 mg. • Sodium: 1333 mg. — Exchanges: 3 1/3 starch, 4 lean meat, 1 1/2 fat

Fish Cakes

WOK FISH SUN

1 1/2 LBS. SUNFISH OR OTHER LEAN FISH FILLETS
       (2 TO 3 OZ. EACH), SKIN REMOVED
1 1/2 TEASPOONS CORNSTARCH
1   TABLESPOON WATER
1   TEASPOON SESAME OIL
1/2   TEASPOON SALT
1/4   TEASPOON WHITE VINEGAR
1/8   TEASPOON FIVE-SPICE POWDER
2   TABLESPOONS VEGETABLE OIL
2   CLOVES GARLIC, MINCED
4   SLICES PEELED FRESH GINGERROOT
2   MEDIUM TOMATOES, EACH CUT INTO 8 WEDGES
1   PKG. (9 OZ.) FROZEN SUGAR SNAP PEAS, DEFROSTED
1   MEDIUM RED PEPPER, CUT INTO 1-INCH CHUNKS
1   MEDIUM GREEN PEPPER, CUT INTO 1-INCH CHUNKS
1/2   CUP THINLY SLICED GREEN ONIONS
2   TABLESPOONS SOY SAUCE

4 servings

Arrange fillets, slightly overlapping, in 13 ×
9-inch baking dish. In small bowl, combine cornstarch, water, sesame oil, salt, vinegar and
five-spice powder. Spread cornstarch mixture
evenly over fillets, turning to coat. Cover dish
with plastic wrap. Chill 1 hour.

In wok, heat vegetable oil over medium-high
heat. Add garlic and gingerroot. Stir-fry for 30
seconds, or until browned, stirring constantly.
Using slotted spoon, remove and discard garlic
and gingerroot from oil. Add fish. Stir-fry for 3
to 5 minutes, or until fish is firm and opaque and
just begins to flake. Remove fish from wok. Place
on serving platter. Cover to keep warm. Set aside.

Add remaining ingredients to wok. Stir-fry for 3 to
4 minutes, or until mixture is hot, stirring constantly. Stir in fish. Serve over hot cooked rice, if desired.

Per Serving: Calories: 303 • Protein: 37 g. • Carbohydrate:
17 g. • Fat: 9 g. • Cholesterol: 114 mg. • Sodium: 937
mg. — Exchanges: 4 lean meat, 3 vegetable

ALMOND FRIED TROUT

1/4 CUP ALL-PURPOSE FLOUR
1/8 TEASPOON PEPPER
1 EGG
3 TABLESPOONS MILK
1 CUP CRACKER CRUMBS
1/2 CUP SLICED ALMONDS, COARSELY CHOPPED
1 1/2 POUNDS TROUT FILLETS, ABOUT 1/2-INCH THICK
2 TABLESPOONS MARGARINE OR BUTTER
1/4 CUP PLUS 1 TABLESPOON VEGETABLE OIL

4 servings

Heat oven to 450°F. On plate or waxed paper, mix flour and pepper. In shallow dish or pie plate, blend egg and milk. On another plate or waxed paper, mix cracker crumbs and almonds. Cut fish into serving-size pieces. Coat fish with flour, dip in egg, then coat with almond mixture, pressing lightly.

In 13 × 9-inch baking pan, combine margarine and oil. Place pan in oven for 5 minutes to heat oil. Add fish, turning to coat with oil. Bake 5 minutes. Turn fish. Bake until fish is golden brown and flakes easily at thickest part, about 5 minutes. Drain on paper towels. Serve with lemon wedges, if desired.

Per Serving: Calories: 623 • Protein: 42 g. • Carbohydrate: 22 g. • Fat: 41 g. • Cholesterol: 153 mg. • Sodium: 406 mg. — Exchanges: 1 1/3 starch, 5 1/2 very lean meat, 7 1/4 fat

CHEESY BAKED CATFISH

1 CUP CRUSHED CHEESE-FLAVORED CRACKERS
1/4 CUP SESAME SEEDS
1 TABLESPOON SNIPPED FRESH PARSLEY
1/2 TEASPOON SALT
1/4 TEASPOON PEPPER
1/4 TEASPOON CAYENNE
1/2 CUP MARGARINE OR BUTTER
2 1/4 LBS. CATFISH FILLETS (6 OZ. EACH), SKIN REMOVED
2 TABLESPOONS SHREDDED FRESH PARMESAN CHEESE

6 servings

Heat oven to 400°F. In shallow dish, combine crackers, sesame seeds, parsley, salt, pepper and cayenne. Set aside.

In 1-quart saucepan, melt margarine over medium heat. Pour into another shallow dish. Dip each fillet first in margarine and then in crumb mixture, pressing lightly to coat. Arrange fillets in single layer in 13 × 9-inch baking dish. Bake for 20 to 25 minutes, or until fish is firm and opaque and just begins to flake. Sprinkle fillets evenly with Parmesan cheese.

Per Serving: Calories: 447 • Protein: 34 g. • Carbohydrate: 10 g. • Fat: 30 g. • Cholesterol: 100 mg. • Sodium: 707 mg. — Exchanges: 3/4 starch, 4 1/2 lean meat, 3 1/4 fat

Almond Fried Trout

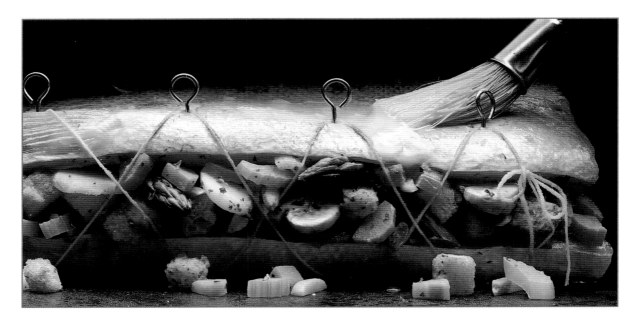

TROUT VALORA

1/3	CUP MARGARINE OR BUTTER
1	CUP CHOPPED ONIONS
1	CUP CHOPPED CELERY
1	CUP CHOPPED CARROTS
4	OZ. FRESH MUSHROOMS, SLICED (1 CUP)
1/2	CUP CHOPPED FRESH ASPARAGUS SPEARS
1	CAN (8 OZ.) SLICED WATER CHESTNUTS, RINSED AND DRAINED
2	CUPS UNSEASONED DRY BREAD CUBES
1/4	CUP PLUS 2 TABLESPOONS TOASTED SLIVERED ALMONDS
1/4	CUP HALF-AND-HALF
2	TABLESPOONS SNIPPED FRESH PARSLEY
1	TEASPOON BOUQUET GARNI SEASONING
1/2	TEASPOON SALT
1	WHOLE DRAWN LAKE TROUT OR SUBSTITUTE (6 1/2 TO 8 1/2 LBS.), HEAD AND TAIL REMOVED

BASTING SAUCE

1/3	CUP MARGARINE OR BUTTER, MELTED
1	TEASPOON GRATED LEMON PEEL
1/4	CUP PLUS 2 TABLESPOONS LEMON JUICE

8 to 10 servings

Heat oven to 375°F. In 12-inch skillet, melt 1/3 cup margarine over medium-low heat. Add onions, celery, carrots, mushrooms, asparagus and water chestnuts. Cook for 8 to 10 minutes, or until vegetables are tender, stirring frequently. Remove from heat.

In large mixing bowl, combine vegetable mixture, bread cubes, almonds, half-and-half, parsley, bouquet garni and salt. Spoon stuffing mixture into cavity of trout. Wrap any extra stuffing in foil packet. Set aside. Insert short metal skewers through underbelly of fish, and lace cavity shut by crisscrossing with string.

In 1-cup measure, combine basting sauce ingredients. Set aside. Spray 15 1/2 × 10 1/2 × 1-inch jelly roll pan with nonstick vegetable cooking spray. Place fish and stuffing packet on prepared pan. Bake for 1 hour to 1 hour 10 minutes, or until fish begins to flake when fork is inserted at backbone in thickest part of fish, basting frequently with sauce during baking.

Per Serving: Calories: 490 • Protein: 45 g. • Carbohydrate: 11 g. • Fat: 29 g. • Cholesterol: 119 mg. • Sodium: 408 mg. — Exchanges: 1/2 starch, 6 lean meat, 1 vegetable, 2 fat

LEMON-CUCUMBER STUFFED TROUT

½	CUP CHOPPED, SEEDED, PEELED CUCUMBER
½	CUP SHREDDED CARROT
2	TABLESPOONS CHOPPED ONION
½	TEASPOON LEMON PEPPER
¼	CUP MARGARINE OR BUTTER
½	CUP HOT WATER
1	TEASPOON INSTANT CHICKEN BOUILLON GRANULES
2	TABLESPOONS SNIPPED FRESH PARSLEY
3	CUPS DRY BREAD CUBES
4	SMALL DRAWN TROUT, ABOUT ½ POUND EACH

4 servings

Heat oven to 375°F. Grease 13 × 9-inch baking pan. In small skillet, cook and stir cucumber, carrot, onion and lemon pepper in margarine over medium heat until tender, about 6 minutes. Blend in water and bouillon granules. Heat to boiling. Add parsley. Remove from heat.

In medium bowl, stir bread cubes into vegetables until coated. Place fish in prepared pan. Stuff each trout with one-fourth of bread mixture. If desired, brush fish with 2 tablespoons melted margarine or butter before baking. Bake until fish flakes easily at backbone, about 20 minutes.

Per Serving: Calories: 353 • Protein: 30 g. • Carbohydrate: 18 g. • Fat: 17 g. • Cholesterol: 77 mg. • Sodium: 651 mg. — Exchanges: 1 starch, 3¾ very lean meat, ½ vegetable, 3 fat

Three Simple Flavored Butters That Are Good with Baked Fish

In small bowl, combine 6 tablespoons butter or margarine, softened, with one of the following:

Citrus Butter—¼ teaspoon grated orange, lemon or lime peel.

Lemon-Parsley Butter—1 tablespoon snipped fresh parsley, ¼ teaspoon fresh lemon juice.

Dill Butter—⅛ teaspoon dried dill weed.

WALLEYE WITH RICE STUFFING

1	PACKAGE (6 OZ.) WILD AND LONG GRAIN RICE MIX
1	TEASPOON INSTANT CHICKEN BOUILLON GRANULES
1½	CUPS SLICED FRESH MUSHROOMS
1½	CUP CHOPPED CELERY
2	TABLESPOONS MARGARINE OR BUTTER
1	JAR (2 OZ.) SLICED PIMIENTO, DRAINED
⅛	TEASPOON GROUND SAGE
2	TO 2½-LB DRAWN WALLEYE

4 to 6 servings

Prepare rice as directed on package, adding bouillon granules to water. Set aside. Heat oven to 375°F. Grease broiler pan or 13 × 9-inch baking pan.

In small skillet, cook and stir mushrooms and celery in margarine over medium heat until mushrooms are tender, about 5 minutes. Stir in pimiento and sage. Stir vegetables into rice.

Place walleye on broiler pan. Stuff with rice mixture, placing any extra stuffing around fish. Cover rice only with foil. Bake until fish flakes easily at backbone, 20 to 25 minutes. If desired, serve with one of the flavored butters above.

Per Serving: Calories: 221 • Protein: 17 g. • Carbohydrate: 23 g. • Fat: 7 g. • Cholesterol: 66 mg. • Sodium: 669 mg. — Exchanges: 1⅓ starch, 2 very lean meat, ⅓ vegetable, 1 fat

BAKED STUFFED BASS

1 PKG. (6 OZ.) WILD RICE AND MUSHROOM STUFFING MIX
1/4 CUP MARGARINE OR BUTTER
1/4 CUP ALL-PURPOSE FLOUR
1/2 TEASPOON SALT
1/8 TEASPOON WHITE PEPPER
2 CUPS MILK OR HALF-AND-HALF
1 1/2 LBS. BASS OR OTHER LEAN FISH FILLETS (6 OZ. EACH), SKIN REMOVED, CUT IN HALF CROSSWISE, 1/4 INCH THICK*
1 TABLESPOON LEMON JUICE
1/2 TEASPOON GRATED ORANGE PEEL
2 TABLESPOONS FINELY CHOPPED ALMONDS
2 TABLESPOONS GRATED PARMESAN CHEESE
1 TABLESPOON SNIPPED FRESH PARSLEY

6 servings

Heat oven to 350°F. Prepare stuffing as directed on package. Set aside to cool. In 1-quart saucepan, melt margarine over medium-low heat. Cook just until margarine begins to brown, stirring constantly. Remove from heat. Stir in flour, salt and pepper. Stir until mixture is smooth. Blend in milk. Return to heat. Bring mixture to boil over medium heat, stirring constantly. Reduce heat to low. Simmer for 3 to 4 minutes, or until mixture thickens and bubbles. Remove from heat. Set white sauce aside.

Spray 13 × 9-inch baking dish with nonstick vegetable cooking spray. Top each fillet with a thin layer of stuffing, then roll up jelly-roll style. Secure with wooden picks. Arrange in prepared dish. Sprinkle evenly with lemon juice and orange peel. Spoon white sauce evenly over fish. Sprinkle evenly with almonds, Parmesan cheese and parsley. Bake for 25 to 30 minutes, or until fish is firm and opaque and just begins to flake.

*Thick fillets may be cut in half horizontally to yield 1/4-inch-thick fillets.

Per Serving: Calories: 522 • Protein: 30 g. • Carbohydrate: 26 g. • Fat: 33 g. • Cholesterol: 90 mg. • Sodium: 867 mg. — Exchanges: 1 1/2 starch, 3 1/2 lean meat, 1/3 skim milk, 4 1/2 fat

SALMON LOAF WITH HORSERADISH SAUCE

2 CUPS FLAKED COOKED SALMON OR OTHER OILY FISH
2 EGGS, SLIGHTLY BEATEN
1 CUP MILK
1/2 CUP FINE DRY BREAD CRUMBS
1 TABLESPOON SNIPPED FRESH PARSLEY
1 TABLESPOON SLICED GREEN ONIONS
1/2 TEASPOON GRATED LIME PEEL
1/2 TEASPOON SALT
1/8 TEASPOON PEPPER
3 TABLESPOONS PREPARED HORSERADISH
1 TABLESPOON PLUS 1 TEASPOON SOY SAUCE

4 to 6 servings

Heat oven to 350°F. Generously grease 8 × 4-inch loaf pan. In medium bowl, combine all ingredients except horseradish and soy sauce. Spread in prepared pan. Bake until center is firm and loaf is golden brown, 55 to 60 minutes. Loosen edges with spatula and turn out of loaf pan; cut into slices.

In small dish, blend horseradish and soy sauce. Serve with salmon loaf.

Per Serving: Calories: 178 • Protein: 18 g. • Carbohydrate: 10 g. • Fat: 7 g. • Cholesterol: 100 mg. • Sodium: 575 mg. — Exchanges: 1/2 starch, 2 very lean meat, 1/8 whole milk, 1 fat

GRILLED CATFISH MEXICANA

½	CUP MILK
½	TEASPOON GROUND CUMIN
1½	LBS. CATFISH FILLETS (6 OZ. EACH), SKIN REMOVED
2	TABLESPOONS OLIVE OIL
1	MEDIUM ONION, FINELY CHOPPED (1 CUP)
½	CUP CHOPPED GREEN, RED OR YELLOW PEPPER
¼	CUP SNIPPED FRESH CILANTRO LEAVES
¼	TEASPOON SALT
¼	TEASPOON FRESHLY GROUND PEPPER
4	TEASPOONS TACO SAUCE OR SALSA (OPTIONAL)

4 servings

Combine milk and cumin in large, sealable plastic food-storage bag. Add fillets, turning to coat. Seal bag. Chill 1 hour.

In 8-inch skillet, heat oil over medium heat. Add onion. Cook for 2 to 3 minutes, or until onion is tender. Reduce heat to low. Stir in chopped pepper, cilantro, salt and pepper. Simmer, uncovered, for 1 to 2 minutes, or until chopped pepper is tender-crisp. Set aside.

Prepare grill for high direct heat. Drain and discard milk mixture from fish. Cut 4 14 × 12-inch sheets of heavy-duty foil. Place 1 fillet on each sheet of foil. Top each fillet with one-fourth of vegetable mixture and 1 teaspoon taco sauce. Fold long sides of foil together in locked folds. Fold and crimp short ends; seal tightly.

Place packets on cooking grate. Grill, covered, for 11 to 17 minutes, or until fish is firm and opaque and just begins to flake. Garnish with lemon and lime wedges, if desired.

Per Serving: Calories: 290 • Protein: 33 g. • Carbohydrate: 5 g. • Fat: 15 g. • Cholesterol: 101 mg. • Sodium: 259 mg. — Exchanges: 4 lean meat, 1 vegetable, ½ fat

PANFISH ASPARAGUS BISCUIT BAKE

  1   CUP DICED CARROT
  1   SMALL ONION, CHOPPED
  2   TABLESPOONS MARGARINE OR BUTTER
  2   CUPS FLAKED COOKED PANFISH OR OTHER LEAN FISH
  1   CAN (10¾ OZ.) CONDENSED CREAM OF
       MUSHROOM SOUP
  1   PACKAGE (10 OZ.) FROZEN ASPARAGUS CUTS, THAWED
  ¼   CUP MILK
  2   TEASPOONS FRESH LEMON JUICE
  ¼   TEASPOON SALT
  ⅛   TEASPOON PEPPER
  1   CUP BUTTERMILK BAKING MIX
  ⅓   CUP MILK
  1   TEASPOON DRIED PARSLEY FLAKES
       DASH PAPRIKA

4 to 6 servings

Heat oven to 375°F. In 9-inch skillet, cook and stir carrot and onion in margarine over medium heat until tender, about 11 minutes. Remove to 1½-quart casserole. Stir in fish, cream of mushroom soup, asparagus cuts, ¼ cup milk, lemon juice, salt and pepper. Set aside.

In small bowl, combine baking mix, ⅓ cup milk, parsley flakes and paprika. Mix with fork. Drop 8 mounds of dough on fish mixture in casserole.

Bake until biscuits are golden brown and casserole is bubbly, about 35 minutes. Brush biscuits with melted margarine before serving, if desired.

Per Serving: Calories: 270 • Protein: 17 g. • Carbohydrate: 24 g. • Fat: 12 g. • Cholesterol: 58 mg. • Sodium: 858 mg. — Exchanges: 1 starch, 1½ very lean meat, 1½ vegetable, 2¼ fat

FISH CHEESE PUFF

  2¼   LBS. NORTHERN PIKE OR OTHER LEAN FISH FILLETS
         (6 OZ. EACH), SKIN REMOVED
  ½   CUP SOUR CREAM
  ½   CUP SHREDDED CHEDDAR CHEESE
  2   EGGS, SEPARATED
  2   TABLESPOONS SLICED PIMIENTO-STUFFED GREEN OLIVES
  1   TABLESPOON FINELY CHOPPED ONION
  ¼   TEASPOON SALT

6 servings

Heat oven to 350°F. Spray 11 × 7-inch baking dish with nonstick vegetable cooking spray. Arrange fillets, slightly overlapping, in prepared dish. Set aside.

In large mixing bowl, combine sour cream, cheese, egg yolks, olives, onion and salt. Set aside.

In medium mixing bowl, beat egg whites at high speed of electric mixer until stiff but not dry. Gently fold egg whites into sour cream mixture. Spread mixture evenly over fillets. Bake for 25 to 30 minutes, or until fish is firm and opaque and just begins to flake, and puff is light golden brown.

Per Serving: Calories: 259 • Protein: 38 g. • Carbohydrate: 1 g. • Fat: 10 g. • Cholesterol: 156 mg. • Sodium: 314 mg. — Exchanges: 5 lean meat

Panfish Asparagus Biscuit Bake

SALMON WITH TARRAGON SAUCE

1   WHOLE DRAWN SALMON OR SUBSTITUTE
    (3 1/2 TO 4 1/2 LBS.), HEAD REMOVED

2   TABLESPOONS SNIPPED FRESH PARSLEY OR 1 TEASPOON
    DRIED PARSLEY FLAKES

1   TABLESPOON SNIPPED FRESH TARRAGON LEAVES OR 1/2
    TEASPOON DRIED TARRAGON LEAVES

1/4   TEASPOON SALT

1/4   TEASPOON PAPRIKA

1/8   TEASPOON PEPPER

1   TABLESPOON FRESH LEMON JUICE

SAUCE

1/4   CUP MARGARINE OR BUTTER

1/4   CUP ALL-PURPOSE FLOUR

1   TABLESPOON SNIPPED FRESH TARRAGON LEAVES OR
    1/2 TEASPOON DRIED TARRAGON LEAVES

1/2   TEASPOON CURRY POWDER

1/4   TEASPOON SALT

1/8   TEASPOON PEPPER

1   CUP CHICKEN BROTH

1   CUP MILK

2   TABLESPOONS DRY WHITE WINE

6 to 8 servings

Heat oven to 375°F. Cut a 28 × 18-inch sheet of heavy-duty foil. Place salmon on foil. Sprinkle cavity and outside of fish with parsley, 1 tablespoon tarragon, 1/4 teaspoon salt and paprika, 1/8 teaspoon pepper and the lemon juice. Fold long sides of foil together in locked folds. Fold and crimp short ends; seal tightly. Place on large baking sheet. Bake for 40 to 50 minutes, or until fish begins to flake when fork is inserted at backbone in thickest part of fish.

Meanwhile, prepare sauce. In 2-quart saucepan, melt margarine over medium heat. Stir in flour, tarragon, curry powder, salt and pepper. Blend in broth and milk. Cook over medium heat for 3 to 5 minutes, or until mixture thickens and bubbles, stirring constantly. Stir in wine. Serve salmon with sauce. Garnish with additional fresh tarragon sprigs, if desired.

Per Serving: Calories: 233 • Protein: 22 g. • Carbohydrate: 5 g. • Fat: 13 g. • Cholesterol: 59 mg. • Sodium: 385 mg. — Exchanges: 1/3 starch, 3 lean meat, 1 fat

WALLEYE ITALIANO

3 TABLESPOONS MARGARINE OR BUTTER

3/4 CUP CHOPPED ONION

3/4 CUP CHOPPED GREEN PEPPER

1 CUP TOMATO JUICE

1 TEASPOON CHILI POWDER

3/4 TEASPOON SALT, DIVIDED

1/4 TEASPOON GARLIC POWDER

1/4 TEASPOON DRIED THYME LEAVES

1/4 TEASPOON DRIED OREGANO LEAVES

1/4 TEASPOON PEPPER, DIVIDED

2 LBS. WALLEYE OR OTHER LEAN FISH FILLETS
(8 OZ. EACH), SKIN REMOVED

1 CUP WATER

1/2 CUP WHITE WINE

1 1/2 CUPS SHREDDED MOZZARELLA CHEESE

---

4 to 5 servings

Heat oven to 350°F. In 2-quart saucepan, melt margarine over medium-high heat. Add onion and green pepper. Cook for 4 to 5 minutes, or until vegetables are tender-crisp, stirring constantly. Stir in tomato juice, chili powder, 1/2 teaspoon salt, the garlic powder, thyme, oregano and 1/8 teaspoon pepper. Bring to a boil. Reduce heat to low. Simmer for 15 to 20 minutes, or until sauce thickens.

Meanwhile, place fillets in deep 10-inch skillet. Sprinkle with remaining 1/4 teaspoon salt and 1/8 teaspoon pepper. Pour water and wine over fish. Bring to a boil over medium-high heat. Reduce heat to low. Simmer, covered, for 8 to 10 minutes, or until fish is firm and opaque and just begins to flake.

Drain and discard poaching liquid. Place fillets in 11 × 7-inch baking dish. Spoon warm sauce over fish. Sprinkle evenly with the cheese. Bake, uncovered, for 5 to 8 minutes, or until cheese is melted.

Per Serving: Calories: 353 • Protein: 42 g.
• Carbohydrate: 6 g. • Fat: 17 g. • Cholesterol: 183 mg.
• Sodium: 759 mg. — Exchanges: 5 1/2 lean meat, 1 vegetable

Walleye Italiano

PERFECT SALMON

You may substitute Walla Walla or other sweet onions for the green onions.

1/2 CUP MAYONNAISE

1/2 CUP THINLY SLICED GREEN ONIONS

1 TEASPOON PREPARED MUSTARD

1 SALMON OR OTHER FRESHWATER FISH FILLET
(2 1/4 LBS.), SKIN ON

1/4 TEASPOON SALT

1/4 TEASPOON PEPPER

1/4 TEASPOON GARLIC POWDER

---

6 servings

Spray rack in broiler pan with nonstick vegetable cooking spray. Set aside. In small mixing bowl, combine mayonnaise, onions and mustard. Set aside.

Place fillet skin side down on prepared broiler pan. Place under broiler with surface of fish 7 inches from heat. Broil for 10 minutes. Spread mayonnaise mixture evenly on fillet. Sprinkle salt, pepper and garlic powder evenly over mayonnaise mixture. Broil for 10 to 15 minutes, or until fish is firm and opaque and just begins to flake, and mayonnaise mixture is golden brown.

Per Serving: Calories: 376 • Protein: 34 g.
• Carbohydrate: 1 g. • Fat: 25 g. • Cholesterol: 104 mg.
• Sodium: 280 mg. — Exchanges: 4 3/4 lean meat, 2 fat

MARINATED SALMON STEAKS

1/2	CUP VEGETABLE OIL
1/2	CUP WHITE WINE VINEGAR
1	TEASPOON SUGAR
1	TEASPOON DRIED PARSLEY FLAKES
1/2	TEASPOON DRIED ITALIAN HERB BLEND
1/4	TEASPOON GARLIC SALT
1/4	TEASPOON ONION POWDER
1/8	TEASPOON PAPRIKA
1/8	TEASPOON PEPPER
4	SALMON STEAKS, ABOUT 1 INCH THICK

4 servings

In shallow bowl, blend oil, vinegar, sugar, parsley flakes, Italian seasoning, garlic salt, onion powder, paprika and pepper. Place fish in plastic bag. Pour marinade over fish. Seal bag. Refrigerate 1 1/2 hours, turning bag over two or three times.

Set oven to broil and/or 550°F. Grease broiler pan. Remove fish from marinade. Reserve marinade. Arrange fish on broiler pan; baste with marinade. Broil 4 to 5 inches from heat for 5 minutes; turn. Baste with remaining marinade. Broil until fish flakes easily in center, about 5 minutes.

Per Serving: Calories: 463 • Protein: 30 g. • Carbohydrate: 2 g. • Fat: 36.5 g. • Cholesterol: 82 mg. • Sodium: 157 mg. — Exchanges: 4 1/4 lean meat, 5 fat

FAT CAT MULLIGAN

3 SLICES BACON, DICED

3 MEDIUM ONIONS, SLICED THIN

2 LBS. CATFISH FILLETS, CUT IN BITE-SIZED PIECES

2 LBS. POTATOES, DICED

1/2 TEASPOON CELERY SEED

2 LARGE CARROTS, DICED

1/4 CUP DICED GREEN PEPPER

1 TABLESPOON SALT

2 TEASPOONS FRESHLY GROUND BLACK PEPPER

3 CUPS BOILING WATER

31/2 CUPS CHOPPED CANNED TOMATOES

2 TABLESPOONS FRESH PARSLEY, CHOPPED FINE

8 servings

Sauté bacon in a deep kettle until lightly browned; remove bacon bits and set aside. Sauté onion slices in bacon grease until tender. Stir in fish, potatoes, celery seed, carrots, green pepper, salt, black pepper and water. Simmer, covered, until vegetables are tender, about 30 minutes. Add tomatoes and heat through. Garnish with chopped parsley and bacon bits.

Per Serving: Calories: 327 • Protein: 26 g.
• Carbohydrate: 34 g. • Fat: 10 g. • Cholesterol: 72 mg.
• Sodium: 1191 mg. — Exchanges: 11/4 starch, 21/4 lean meat, 3 vegetable, 1/2 fat

CRAYFISH CREOLE

1/3 CUP SHORTENING

1/4 CUP ALL-PURPOSE FLOUR

1 CAN (28 OZ.) WHOLE TOMATOES, UNDRAINED AND CUT UP

1 CUP CHOPPED ONION

1 CUP SLICED GREEN ONIONS

1 CUP WATER

1/2 CUP CHOPPED GREEN PEPPER

1/2 CUP CHOPPED CELERY

1 TABLESPOON WORCESTERSHIRE SAUCE

2 CLOVES GARLIC, MINCED

1 TEASPOON HOT PEPPER SAUCE

1/2 TEASPOON SALT

1/4 TEASPOON PEPPER

1/8 TEASPOON CAYENNE

11/2 TO 2 LBS. STEAMED PEELED CRAYFISH TAILS

4 to 6 servings

In 6-quart Dutch oven or stockpot, melt shortening over medium heat. Add flour. Cook for 5 to 8 minutes, stirring constantly, until dark golden brown. Remove from heat.

Add remaining ingredients, except crayfish. Bring to a boil. Reduce heat to low. Simmer, covered, for 30 minutes. Add crayfish. Cook for 4 to 6 minutes, or until mixture is hot. Serve over hot cooked rice, if desired.

Per Serving: Calories: 317 • Protein: 34 g.
• Carbohydrate: 14 g. • Fat: 14 g.
• Cholesterol: 236 mg. • Sodium: 548 mg.
— Exchanges: 1/4 starch, 4 lean meat, 2 vegetable, 1/2 fat

Fat Cat Mulligan

NORTHWOODS MINESTRONE

2 TABLESPOONS OLIVE OIL

1/2 CUP SLICED GREEN ONIONS

1/2 CUP CHOPPED RED OR GREEN PEPPER

2 CANS (28 OZ. EACH) WHOLE TOMATOES, UNDRAINED AND CUT UP

1/2 CUP WATER

2 TEASPOONS SUGAR

1 TEASPOON ITALIAN HERB BLEND

1/2 TEASPOON SALT

1/4 TEASPOON GARLIC POWDER

1/8 TO 1/4 TEASPOON CAYENNE

1 1/2 LBS. WALLEYE OR OTHER LEAN FISH FILLETS, SKIN REMOVED, CUT INTO 1 1/2-INCH PIECES

1 CAN (15 1/2 OZ.) DARK RED KIDNEY BEANS, RINSED AND DRAINED

1 PKG. (9 OZ.) FROZEN ITALIAN OR CUT GREEN BEANS

1 CUP UNCOOKED ROTINI

6 to 8 servings

In 6-quart Dutch oven or stockpot, heat oil over medium-high heat. Add onions and chopped pepper. Cook for 3 to 5 minutes, or until vegetables are tender, stirring constantly. Stir in tomatoes, water, sugar, Italian seasoning, salt, garlic powder and cayenne. Bring to a boil. Reduce heat to low. Simmer for 5 minutes.

Stir in remaining ingredients. Return mixture to a boil over medium-high heat. Reduce heat to low. Simmer for 15 to 20 minutes, or until fish is firm and opaque and just begins to flake, stirring occasionally.

Per Serving: Calories: 242 • Protein: 21 g. • Carbohydrate: 29 g. • Fat: 5 g. • Cholesterol: 61 mg. • Sodium: 569 mg. — Exchanges: 1 starch, 2 lean meat, 2 vegetable

SNAPPING TURTLE STEW

2 LBS. SNAPPING TURTLE MEAT, TRIMMED AND CUT INTO 1-INCH CUBES

4 CUPS SEEDED CHOPPED TOMATOES

4 1/4 CUPS WATER, DIVIDED

1 CUP CHOPPED ONIONS

1/2 TEASPOON SALT

1/2 TEASPOON DRIED THYME LEAVES

1/4 TEASPOON DRIED ROSEMARY LEAVES

1/4 TEASPOON PEPPER

1/4 TEASPOON GROUND NUTMEG

1/8 TEASPOON GROUND CLOVES

1 TABLESPOON LEMON JUICE

2 TABLESPOONS ALL-PURPOSE FLOUR

1/2 CUP SNIPPED FRESH PARSLEY

1/4 CUP DRY SHERRY

4 servings

In 6-quart Dutch oven or stockpot, combine turtle meat, tomatoes, 4 cups water, the onions, salt, thyme, rosemary, pepper, nutmeg, cloves and lemon juice. Bring to a boil over medium-high heat, stirring occasionally. Reduce heat to low. Simmer, uncovered, for 2 1/4 to 2 1/2 hours, or until meat is tender, stirring occasionally.

In small bowl, combine flour and remaining 1/4 cup water. Blend until smooth. Add to stew, stirring constantly, until mixture thickens and bubbles. Just before serving, stir in parsley and sherry.

Nutritional information not available.

Northwoods Minestrone

HOT & SOUR BASS SOUP

5 CUPS WATER

2 TABLESPOONS INSTANT CHICKEN BOUILLON GRANULES

1/4 CUP WHITE VINEGAR

1 MEDIUM ONION, CUT INTO THIN WEDGES

8 WHOLE PEPPERCORNS

3/4 POUND BASS OR OTHER LEAN FISH FILLETS, ABOUT 1/2 INCH THICK

1 CAN (4 OZ.) SLICED MUSHROOMS, DRAINED

1 TABLESPOON SOY SAUCE

1 CLOVE GARLIC, MINCED

1/4 TO 1/2 TEASPOON DRIED CRUSHED RED PEPPER

2 TABLESPOONS CORNSTARCH

2 TABLESPOONS COLD WATER

1 EGG, BEATEN

1 GREEN ONION, CHOPPED

4 to 6 servings

In Dutch oven, combine 5 cups water, the bouillon granules, vinegar, onion and peppercorns. Heat to boiling. Add fillets. Reduce heat. Cover and simmer until fish flakes easily, about 5 minutes. Remove fish. Cut into 1-inch pieces; set aside. Remove peppercorns. Stir mushrooms, soy sauce, garlic and red pepper into soup. Heat to boiling. Reduce heat. Cover and simmer for 15 minutes.

In small bowl, blend cornstarch into 2 tablespoons water. Stir into soup. Heat to boiling. Cook, stirring constantly, until soup is thickened, about 1 minute. Add fish. Reduce heat and simmer for 1 minute. Remove from heat. Pour beaten egg slowly in thin stream over soup; do not stir. Top with green onion.

Per Serving: Calories: 116 • Protein: 12 g. • Carbohydrate: 8 g. • Fat: 3 g. • Cholesterol: 74 mg. • Sodium: 1307 mg. — Exchanges: 1 3/4 very lean meat, 1 vegetable, 1/2 fat

Hot and Sour Bass Soup

HEARTY CATFISH STEW

2 CUPS PEELED RED POTATOES (3 MEDIUM), CUT INTO 1/2-INCH CUBES

2 CUPS SEEDED CHOPPED TOMATOES

1 CUP CHOPPED ONIONS

1 CUP CHOPPED GREEN PEPPER

1 CUP FROZEN CORN

1 CUP TOMATO JUICE

1 CUP WATER

2 TABLESPOONS MARGARINE OR BUTTER

2 CLOVES GARLIC, MINCED

1/2 TEASPOON SALT

1/2 TEASPOON DRIED THYME LEAVES (OPTIONAL)

1/4 TEASPOON PEPPER

1/8 TO 1/4 TEASPOON CAYENNE

4 CATFISH FILLETS (6 OZ. EACH), SKIN REMOVED, CUT INTO 1-INCH PIECES

4 servings

In 6-quart Dutch oven or stockpot, combine all ingredients except catfish pieces. Bring to a boil over medium-high heat. Reduce heat to low. Simmer, uncovered, for 10 to 12 minutes, or until potatoes are tender, stirring occasionally. Add catfish. Simmer for 10 to 15 minutes, or until fish is firm and opaque and just begins to flake, stirring occasionally.

Per Serving: Calories: 395 • Protein: 36 g. • Carbohydrate: 33 g. • Fat: 14 g. • Cholesterol: 99 mg. • Sodium: 684 mg. — Exchanges: 1 1/4 starch, 4 lean meat, 2 vegetable, 1/4 fat

SOUTH OF THE BORDER CHEESY FISH SOUP

¹/₂ CUP CHOPPED ONION

¹/₂ CUP CHOPPED CELERY

¹/₂ CUP CHOPPED RED PEPPER

¹/₂ CUP CHOPPED GREEN PEPPER

2 TABLESPOONS MARGARINE OR BUTTER

¹/₄ CUP ALL-PURPOSE FLOUR

¹/₂ TEASPOON SALT

¹/₈ TEASPOON PEPPER

2 CUPS MILK

8 OZ. MILD MEXICAN-FLAVORED PASTEURIZED PROCESS CHEESE LOAF, CUT INTO 1-INCH CUBES

1¹/₂ CUPS WATER

1 TEASPOON INSTANT CHICKEN BOUILLON GRANULES

1¹/₂ LBS. YELLOW PERCH OR OTHER LEAN FISH FILLETS, SKIN REMOVED, CUT INTO 1-INCH PIECES

SNIPPED FRESH CHIVES

4 servings

In 6-quart Dutch oven or stockpot, combine onion, celery, peppers and margarine. Cook over medium-high heat for 3 to 4 minutes, or until vegetables are tender, stirring constantly. Reduce heat to medium. Stir in flour, salt and pepper. Blend in milk. Cook over medium heat until mixture thickens and bubbles, stirring constantly. Add cheese. Stir until melted. Remove from heat.

In 2-quart saucepan, combine water and bouillon. Bring to a boil over medium-high heat. Add fish pieces. Return mixture to a boil. Reduce heat to low. Simmer for 8 to 10 minutes, or until fish is firm and opaque and just begins to flake. Add fish and bouillon mixture to cheese mixture. Mix well. Cook over medium heat for 2 to 5 minutes, or until hot, stirring frequently. Sprinkle each serving evenly with chives.

Per Serving: Calories: 486 • Protein: 49 g. • Carbohydrate: 21 g. • Fat: 24 g. • Cholesterol: 210 mg. • Sodium: 1641 mg. — Exchanges: ¹/₄ starch, 6 lean meat, 1 vegetable, ³/₄ skim milk, 1 fat

WALLEYE & CLAM CHOWDER

4	SLICES BACON, CUT INTO 1/2-INCH PIECES
1/2	CUP THINLY SLICED CELERY
1/4	CUP SLICED GREEN ONIONS
2	CUPS PEELED RED POTATOES (3 MEDIUM), CUT INTO 1/2-INCH CUBES
1	CAN (14 1/2 OZ.) CHICKEN BROTH
1/2	TEASPOON DRIED DILL WEED
1/2	TEASPOON CELERY SEED
1/4	TEASPOON SALT
1/8	TEASPOON PEPPER
3	TABLESPOONS ALL-PURPOSE FLOUR
3	CUPS MILK
1 1/2	LBS. WALLEYE OR OTHER LEAN FISH FILLETS, SKIN REMOVED, CUT INTO 1-INCH PIECES
1	CUP WHIPPING CREAM
1	CAN (6 1/2 OZ.) MINCED CLAMS, UNDRAINED
1	PKG. (10 OZ.) FROZEN CHOPPED SPINACH, DEFROSTED AND DRAINED

6 to 8 servings

In 6-quart Dutch oven or stockpot, cook bacon over medium heat until brown and crisp. Drain, reserving 2 tablespoons bacon drippings in the Dutch oven. Set bacon aside.

Add celery and onions to bacon drippings in Dutch oven. Cook over medium-high heat for 3 to 5 minutes, or until vegetables are tender-crisp, stirring constantly. Stir in potatoes, broth, dill weed, celery seed, salt and pepper. Bring to a boil over medium-high heat. Reduce heat to low. Simmer, uncovered, for 10 to 15 minutes, or until potatoes are tender.

In 4-cup measure, combine flour and milk. Blend until smooth. Stir into broth mixture. Bring to a boil over medium-high heat. Reduce heat to low. Add walleye pieces. Simmer for 3 minutes, or until fish is firm and opaque and just begins to flake, stirring occasionally. Stir in bacon, cream, clams and spinach. Cook over low heat (do not boil) for 5 minutes, or until chowder is hot, stirring occasionally.

Per Serving: Calories: 355 • Protein: 27 g. • Carbohydrate: 17 g. • Fat: 20 g. • Cholesterol: 140 mg. • Sodium: 507 mg. — Exchanges: 1/2 starch, 3 lean meat, 1/2 vegetable, 1/2 skim milk, 2 1/4 fat

CREAM OF SALMON SOUP

1   CUP SLICED FRESH MUSHROOMS

1/4 CUP FINELY CHOPPED ONION

1/4 CUP MARGARINE OR BUTTER

3   TABLESPOONS ALL-PURPOSE FLOUR

2   TABLESPOONS SNIPPED FRESH PARSLEY

1/2 TEASPOON SALT

1/8 TEASPOON WHITE PEPPER

1/8 TEASPOON DRIED ROSEMARY LEAVES

1 1/2 CUPS MILK

1 1/2 CUPS HALF-AND-HALF

1 1/2 TO 2 CUPS FLAKED COOKED SALMON

---

4 to 6 servings

In 2-quart saucepan, cook and stir mushrooms and onion in margarine over medium heat until just tender, about 5 minutes. Stir in flour, parsley, salt, pepper and rosemary. Remove from heat. Blend in milk and half-and-half. Cook over medium heat, stirring constantly, until thickened and bubbly, 7 to 10 minutes. Add fish. Cook and stir 1 minute.

Per Serving: Calories: 291 • Protein: 18 g. • Carbohydrate: 10 g. • Fat: 20 g. • Cholesterol: 54 mg. • Sodium: 366 mg. — Exchanges: 1/4 starch, 2 very lean meat, 1/4 vegetable, 3/8 whole milk, 3 fat

FISHERMAN'S BOUILLABAISSE

1   MEDIUM GREEN PEPPER, CHOPPED

1   MEDIUM ONION, CHOPPED

2   CLOVES GARLIC, MINCED

2   TABLESPOONS OLIVE OR VEGETABLE OIL

3   CUPS FISH STOCK (PAGE 23)*

1   CUP CLAM-TOMATO JUICE COCKTAIL

1   CAN (16 OZ.) WHOLE TOMATOES

1/2 TEASPOON SUGAR

1/2 TEASPOON SALT

1/4 TEASPOON DRIED THYME LEAVES

1/4 TEASPOON GROUND TURMERIC

1/8 TEASPOON PEPPER

1   BAY LEAF

1/2 LB. TROUT FILLETS, SKIN ON

1/2 LB. WALLEYE OR OTHER LEAN FISH FILLETS, SKIN ON

1/2 LB. RAW SHRIMP, PEELED AND DEVEINED

1   CAN (6 1/2 OZ.) MINCED CLAMS, DRAINED

---

6 to 8 servings

In Dutch oven, cook and stir green pepper, onion and garlic in olive oil over medium heat until onion is tender, about 4 minutes. Add fish stock, clam-tomato juice, tomatoes, sugar, salt, thyme, turmeric, pepper and bay leaf. Heat to boiling. Reduce heat. Cover and simmer, stirring occasionally to break up tomatoes, for 15 minutes.

Cut trout and walleye fillets into 1-inch pieces. Add fish, shrimp and clams to stew. Cook over medium heat, stirring gently, until fish flakes easily and shrimp turns opaque, about 5 minutes.

Or substitute 1 can (14 1/2 oz.) chicken broth and 1 1/4 cups water; omit the salt.

Per Serving: Calories: 179 • Protein: 20 g. • Carbohydrate: 9 g. • Fat: 6.5 g. • Cholesterol: 84 mg. • Sodium: 502 mg. — Exchanges: 2 1/4 very lean meat, 2 vegetable, 1 fat

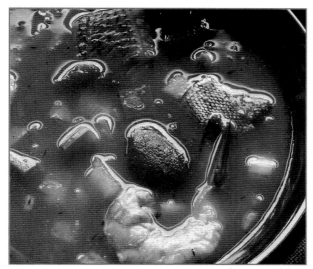

Fisherman's Bouillabaisse

POBLANO CATFISH IN LEEK

2 LEEKS

1 MEDIUM RED OR GREEN PEPPER, THINLY SLICED

1 POBLANO PEPPER (1 OZ.), SEEDED AND THINLY SLICED

3 TABLESPOONS FRESH CILANTRO LEAVES, CHOPPED

2 CLOVES GARLIC, THINLY SLICED

2 SMALL LIMES, THINLY SLICED

2 WHOLE DRAWN CATFISH (ABOUT 1¼ LBS. EACH), HEAD AND SKIN REMOVED

2 TEASPOONS PREPARED CAJUN SEASONING

2 to 3 servings

Per Serving: Calories: 243 • Protein: 30 g. • Carbohydrate: 16 g. • Fat: 7 g. • Cholesterol: 90 mg. • Sodium: 671 mg. — Exchanges: 3 lean meat, 3 vegetable

How to Prepare Poblano Catfish in Leek

1 Prepare grill for medium-high direct heat. Remove 4 large outer leaves from leeks. Set aside. Cut leeks in half lengthwise; rinse. Chop to equal 1 cup. In medium mixing bowl, combine chopped leeks, pepper slices, cilantro and garlic.

2 Spray 20-inch fish-grilling basket with nonstick vegetable cooking spray. On one side of basket, layer half of reserved leek leaves, half of lime slices and half of pepper mixture.

3 Sprinkle both sides of each catfish evenly with Cajun seasoning. Arrange fish in basket. Top with remaining pepper mixture and lime slices. Cover with remaining leek leaves. Secure basket.

4 Place basket on cooking grate. Grill, covered, for 15 minutes. Turn basket over. Grill, covered, for 15 to 20 minutes longer, or until fish begins to flake when fork is inserted at backbone in thickest part of fish.

HERB-STUFFED BARBECUED SALMON

- 1   TABLESPOON OLIVE OIL
- 1   MEDIUM ONION, THINLY SLICED
- 3   LBS. SALMON, OR SUBSTITUTE, FILLETS (8 OZ. EACH), SKIN ON
- 3   CLOVES GARLIC, MINCED
- 1   TEASPOON SNIPPED FRESH CHIVES
- ¼   TEASPOON SALT
- ¼   TEASPOON FRESHLY GROUND PEPPER
- 6   THIN LEMON SLICES
- 1   MEDIUM TOMATO, THINLY SLICED (6 SLICES)
- 3   SPRIGS FRESH DILL WEED
- 3   FRESH BASIL LEAVES
- 3   TABLESPOONS MARGARINE OR BUTTER

6 servings

Prepare grill for medium direct heat. Spray one side of each of three 20 × 18-inch sheets of heavy-duty foil with nonstick vegetable cooking spray. Set aside.

In 8-inch skillet, heat oil over medium heat. Add onion. Cook for 4 to 5 minutes, or until tender, stirring frequently. Set aside.

Place 1 fillet skin side down in center of each sheet of prepared foil. Sprinkle evenly with garlic, chives, salt and pepper. Arrange 2 slices each of lemon and tomato on each fillet. Top evenly with onion, dill and basil. Dot evenly with margarine. Top with remaining fillets, skin-side-up.

Fold long sides of foil together in locked folds. Fold and crimp short ends; seal tightly. Arrange packets on cooking grate. Grill, covered, for 12 minutes. Turn packets over. Grill, covered, for 12 to 15 minutes longer, or until fish is firm and opaque and just begins to flake. Garnish with additional lemon and tomato slices, if desired.

Per Serving: Calories: 415 • Protein: 46 g. • Carbohydrate: 5 g. • Fat: 23 g. • Cholesterol: 125 mg. • Sodium: 263 mg. — Exchanges: 6 lean meat, 1 vegetable, 1 fat

GRILLED MARINATED FROG LEGS

- 6   PAIRS FROG LEGS (ABOUT 2 LBS.), SKIN REMOVED

MARINADE
- ½   CUP VEGETABLE OIL
- 3   TABLESPOONS FINELY CHOPPED RED ONION
- 2   TABLESPOONS SNIPPED FRESH PARSLEY
- 1   TABLESPOON GRATED LEMON PEEL
- 1   TABLESPOON PLUS 1½ TEASPOONS LEMON JUICE
- 1   TEASPOON SALT
- 1   TEASPOON DRY MUSTARD
- 1   TEASPOON DRIED BASIL LEAVES

- ¼   CUP MARGARINE OR BUTTER
- 1   CLOVE GARLIC, MINCED

3 to 6 servings

Arrange frog legs in single layer in 11 × 7-inch baking dish. In small mixing bowl, combine marinade ingredients. Reserve ⅓ cup marinade. Cover with plastic wrap. Chill. Pour remaining marinade over frog legs, turning to coat. Cover with plastic wrap. Chill 3 hours, turning legs over occasionally.

Spray cooking grate with nonstick vegetable cooking spray. Prepare grill for medium direct heat. Drain and discard marinade from frog legs. Arrange legs on prepared cooking grate. Grill, covered, for 3 minutes. Turn legs over. Grill, covered, for 3 to 5 minutes longer, or until meat is no longer pink and begins to pull away from the bone.

In 1-quart saucepan, combine reserved marinade with margarine and garlic. Cook over medium heat for 1 to 2 minutes, or until mixture is hot and margarine is melted, stirring frequently. Before serving, pour margarine mixture over frog legs.

Per Serving: Calories: 206 • Protein: 16 g. • Carbohydrate: 1 g. • Fat: 15 g. • Cholesterol: 49 mg. • Sodium: 422 mg. — Exchanges: 2¼ lean meat, ¼ vegetable, 1½ fat

NORTHERN BEER BITES

Serve as an appetizer or a main dish.

6   WOODEN SKEWERS (10-INCH)

MARINADE
1/4 CUP MARGARINE OR BUTTER
1   TABLESPOON OLIVE OIL
4   TO 5 CLOVES GARLIC, CRUSHED
1/4 TEASPOON INSTANT MINCED ONION
1/4 TEASPOON SNIPPED FRESH DILL WEED
1/4 TEASPOON SALT
1/8 TEASPOON FRESHLY GROUND PEPPER

1/2 CUP BEER
2   NORTHERN PIKE OR OTHER LEAN FISH FILLETS
    (12 OZ. EACH), SKIN REMOVED

4 to 6 servings

Soak wooden skewers in water for 1/2 hour. In 1-quart saucepan, combine marinade ingredients. Cook over medium-low heat for 3 to 5 minutes, or until margarine is melted and mixture is hot, stirring occasionally. Remove from heat. Blend in beer. Set aside.

Cut each fillet lengthwise into three 10 × 1-inch strips. Thread 1 strip on each skewer, accordion-style. Arrange skewers in a single layer in 11 × 7-inch baking dish. Pour marinade mixture over fish, turning skewers to coat. Cover with plastic wrap. Refrigerate 8 hours or overnight, turning over occasionally.

Spray cooking grate with nonstick vegetable cooking spray. Prepare grill for medium direct heat. Drain and discard marinade from fish. Arrange skewers on prepared cooking grate. Grill, covered, for 3 minutes. Turn skewers over. Grill, covered, for 2 to 3 minutes longer, or until fish is firm and opaque and just begins to flake. Serve with drawn butter and lemon wedges, if desired.

Per Serving: Calories: 151 • Protein: 22 g.
• Carbohydrate: 1 g. • Fat: 6 g. • Cholesterol: 44 mg.
• Sodium: 137 mg. — Exchanges: 3 lean meat

Northern Beer Bites

GRILLED LEMON TROUT WITH ROSEMARY

MARINADE
1/2 CUP OLIVE OIL
1/4 CUP LEMON JUICE
1/4 CUP SNIPPED FRESH ROSEMARY LEAVES
3   CLOVES GARLIC, MINCED
1/4 TEASPOON SALT
1/4 TEASPOON PEPPER

4   WHOLE DRAWN STREAM TROUT (8 OZ. EACH)
6   TO 10 BRANCHES WET ROSEMARY
    LEMON WEDGES

4 servings

In 11 × 7-inch baking dish, combine marinade ingredients. Place trout in baking dish, turning to coat. Cover with plastic wrap. Refrigerate 8 hours or overnight, turning trout over once.

Spray cooking grate with nonstick vegetable cooking spray. Prepare grill for medium direct heat. Drain and discard marinade from fish. Drop a few wet rosemary branches over coals. Arrange trout on prepared cooking grate. Grill, covered, for 8 to 12 minutes, or until fish begins to flake when fork is inserted at backbone in thickest part of fish, turning over once. Continue dropping wet rosemary branches over hot coals to keep smoking constant. Serve with lemon wedges.

Per Serving: Calories: 295 • Protein: 29 g.
• Carbohydrate: 2 g. • Fat: 19 g. • Cholesterol: 80 mg.
• Sodium: 110 mg. — Exchanges: 4 lean meat, 1 1/3 fat

SPICY MARINATED SALMON WITH AVOCADO SALSA

(Recipe is pictured on cover inset)

MARINADE
- 1 CUP VERMOUTH
- 3/4 CUP OLIVE OIL
- 1 TABLESPOON MINCED FRESH GARLIC
- 1 JALAPEÑO PEPPER, SEEDED AND FINELY CHOPPED (1 TABLESPOON)
- 1 TABLESPOON FRESH LEMON OR LIME JUICE
- 1 1/2 TEASPOONS FRESHLY GROUND PEPPER
- 2 TEASPOONS RED PEPPER SAUCE
- 1 1/4 TEASPOONS SALT

- 6 SALMON OR OTHER OILY FISH STEAKS (8 OZ. EACH), 1 INCH THICK

SALSA
- 2 RIPE AVOCADOS, PEELED, SEEDED AND FINELY CHOPPED
- 1/4 CUP FINELY CHOPPED RED ONION
- 2 TABLESPOONS OLIVE OIL
- 2 TABLESPOONS RICE WINE VINEGAR
- 1 TABLESPOON SNIPPED FRESH CILANTRO LEAVES
- 1/4 TEASPOON SALT

6 servings

In 11 × 7-inch baking dish, combine marinade ingredients. Arrange steaks in a single layer in baking dish, turning to coat. Cover with plastic wrap. Chill 2 hours, turning steaks over occasionally.

In medium mixing bowl, combine salsa ingredients. Cover with plastic wrap. Chill 2 hours.

Spray cooking grate with nonstick vegetable cooking spray. Prepare grill for medium direct heat. Drain and discard marinade from steaks. Arrange steaks on prepared cooking grate. Grill, covered, for 8 to 10 minutes, or until fish is firm and opaque and just begins to flake, turning over once.

Per Serving: Calories: 400 • Protein: 26 g. • Carbohydrate: 6 g. • Fat: 30 g. • Cholesterol: 67 mg. • Sodium: 282 mg. — Exchanges: 3 lean meat, 1 1/4 vegetable, 4 fat

---

KEONI'S ISLAND BROIL

MARINADE
- 1/2 CUP SOY SAUCE
- 1/4 CUP PORT WINE
- 1/4 CUP WATER
- 1/4 CUP PACKED BROWN SUGAR
- 1/4 CUP SLICED GREEN ONIONS
- 4 TO 6 CLOVES GARLIC, MINCED
- 1 TABLESPOON PLUS 1 1/2 TEASPOONS SESAME OIL
- 1 TABLESPOON TOASTED SESAME SEEDS
- 2 LBS. SALMON OR OTHER OILY FISH FILLETS (8 OZ. EACH), SKIN ON

4 servings

In small mixing bowl, combine marinade ingredients. Reserve 1/4 cup marinade. Cover with plastic wrap and chill. Arrange fillets in a single layer in 11 × 7-inch baking dish. Pour remaining marinade over fillets, turning to coat. Cover with plastic wrap. Chill 3 hours, turning fillets over occasionally.

Spray cooking grate with nonstick vegetable cooking spray. Prepare grill for medium direct heat. Drain and discard marinade from fish. Arrange fillets on prepared cooking grate. Grill, covered, for 5 minutes. Turn fillets over. Grill for 3 to 5 minutes longer, or until fish is firm and opaque and just begins to flake, basting occasionally with reserved marinade. Serve with hot cooked rice, if desired.

Per Serving: Calories: 373 • Protein: 41 g. • Carbohydrate: 12 g. • Fat: 16 g. • Cholesterol: 110 mg. • Sodium: 1573 mg. — Exchanges: 6 lean meat, 2/3 fruit

Keoni's Island Broil

FISH MELT

1 1/2 CUPS FLAKED COOKED NORTHERN PIKE OR OTHER LEAN FISH

1/4 CUP FINELY CHOPPED CUCUMBER

2 TABLESPOONS CHOPPED RADISH

1 TABLESPOON MAYONNAISE OR SALAD DRESSING

1 TABLESPOON SOUR CREAM

1/2 TEASPOON SALT

1/8 TEASPOON PEPPER

4 LARGE THIN TOMATO SLICES

4 TO 8 SLICES WHOLE WHEAT BREAD, TOASTED

4 SLICES AMERICAN CHEESE

2 to 4 servings

Set oven to broil and/or 550°F. In small bowl, mix fish, cucumber, radish, mayonnaise, sour cream, salt and pepper. Place one tomato slice on each of four toasted bread slices. Spread fish mixture over tomatoes; spread to edges of bread. Top each piece with one piece of cheese. Place sandwiches on baking sheet. Broil 2 to 3 inches from heat until cheese melts, about 2 minutes. Top each sandwich with another piece of toast, if desired.

Per Serving:
Calories: 319
• Protein: 24 g.
• Carbohydrate: 28 g.
• Fat: 13 g.
• Cholesterol: 41 mg.
• Sodium: 50 mg.
— Exchanges: 1 3/4 starch, 2 1/2 very lean meat, 1/2 vegetable, 2 fat

SALMON LOUIS

DRESSING

1/2 CUP MAYONNAISE OR SALAD DRESSING

3 TABLESPOONS KETCHUP

2 TABLESPOONS DAIRY SOUR CREAM

2 TABLESPOONS HALF-AND-HALF

1 TABLESPOON CHOPPED GREEN ONION

2 TEASPOONS CHOPPED SWEET PICKLE

1 TEASPOON FRESH LEMON JUICE

1/2 TEASPOON WORCESTERSHIRE SAUCE

SALAD

4 CUPS TORN ICEBERG LETTUCE

2 CUPS FLAKED COOKED SALMON

1 TOMATO, CUT INTO WEDGES

1 HARD-COOKED EGG, SLICED, OPTIONAL

1/4 CUP SLICED BLACK OLIVES, OPTIONAL

4 to 6 servings

In small bowl, blend dressing ingredients. Refrigerate at least 30 minutes. Arrange lettuce in medium bowl or on serving plate. Mound fish in center. Arrange tomato wedges, egg slices and olives around fish. Pour half of dressing over salad. Reserve remaining dressing for serving.

Per Serving:
Calories: 258
• Protein: 14 g.
• Carbohydrate: 6 g.
• Fat: 20 g.
• Cholesterol: 38 mg.
• Sodium: 248 mg.
— Exchanges: 1 2/3 very lean meat, 1 vegetable, 4 fat

Salmon Louis

SALMON PÂTÉ

1 SALMON OR OTHER OILY FISH STEAK (8 OZ.),
   1 INCH THICK
1 RECIPE COURT BOUILLON, PAGE 18
1/3 CUP SNIPPED FRESH PARSLEY
1/4 CUP SLICED GREEN ONIONS
1 CLOVE GARLIC, MINCED
4 OZ. CREAM CHEESE, SOFTENED
2 TABLESPOONS MARGARINE OR BUTTER, SOFTENED
1/2 TEASPOON DRIED THYME LEAVES
1/4 TEASPOON SALT
1/8 TEASPOON PEPPER

1 1/2 cups, 12 servings

Poach salmon in Court Bouillon as directed.
Drain and discard poaching liquid. Cool
salmon slightly. Remove skin and bones; flake
meat. Set aside.

In food processor, combine parsley, onions and
garlic. Process until finely chopped. Add cream
cheese, margarine, thyme, salt and pepper. Process
until smooth. Stir in salmon.

Spoon into small soufflé dish or 2-cup serving
dish. Cover with plastic
wrap. Refrigerate several
hours or overnight.
Serve as a spread with
crackers or celery and
carrot sticks, if desired.

Per Serving: Calories: 75
• Protein: 4 g.
• Carbohydrate: 1 g.
• Fat: 6 g. • Cholesterol:
20 mg. • Sodium: 104 mg.
— Exchanges: 1/2 lean
meat, 1 fat

PARTY TROUT DIP

2 WHOLE DRAWN STREAM TROUT (8 OZ. EACH)
1 RECIPE COURT BOUILLON, PAGE 18
12 OZ. CREAM CHEESE, SOFTENED
1 CUP SOUR CREAM
1/2 CUP SLICED GREEN ONIONS
1/3 CUP SALAD DRESSING OR MAYONNAISE
3 TABLESPOONS DRIED PARSLEY FLAKES
1 JAR (2 OZ.) DICED PIMIENTO, DRAINED
1/4 TEASPOON SALT
1/8 TEASPOON PEPPER

4 cups, 32 servings

Poach trout in Court Bouillon as directed.
Drain and discard poaching liquid. Cool trout
slightly. Remove heads, skin and bones; flake
meat. Set aside.

In medium mixing bowl, combine cream cheese,
sour cream, onions, salad dressing, parsley flakes,
pimiento, salt and pepper. Stir in trout. Cover
with plastic wrap. Refrigerate several hours or
overnight. Serve as a spread with crackers or celery and carrot sticks, if desired.

Per Serving: Calories: 73
• Protein: 3 g.
• Carbohydrate: 1 g.
• Fat: 6 g. • Cholesterol: 20
mg. • Sodium: 72 mg. —
Exchanges: 1/3 lean meat,
1/4 vegetable, 1 fat

Salmon Pâté

TROPICAL SMOKED SALMON

BRINE

2	CUPS ORANGE JUICE
1 1/2	CUPS PINEAPPLE JUICE
1/2	CUP WATER
1/2	CUP PACKED BROWN SUGAR
1/4	CUP CANNING OR PICKLING SALT
1/4	CUP HONEY
3	TABLESPOONS LEMON JUICE
1	TABLESPOON LEMON PEPPER
1	CLOVE GARLIC, MINCED
1	LB. SALMON OR OTHER OILY FISH FILLETS (8 OZ. EACH), 1 INCH THICK, SKIN ON

4 servings

In 5-quart glass or plastic container, combine brine ingredients. Stir until sugar and salt are dissolved. Add fillets to brine. Cover and refrigerate 12 hours or overnight.

Drain and discard brine from fillets. Rinse with water. Pat dry with paper towels. Arrange fillets on cooling racks. Air dry for 1 hour, or until fillets are shiny and dry.

Place oven thermometer in smoker. Heat dry smoker for 20 minutes, or until temperature registers 100°F. Spray smoker racks with nonstick vegetable cooking spray. Arrange fillets on prepared racks, spacing at least 1/2 inch apart. Smoke fillets according to smoker manufacturer's directions (approximately 4 to 6 hours), or until fish is firm and opaque and internal temperature registers 180°F in thickest part of fillet, adding wood chips as necessary to impart desired flavor and to maintain desired level of smoke. Store smoked fish, loosely wrapped, in refrigerator no longer than 2 weeks. Serve with crackers.

Per Serving: Calories: 379 • Protein: 45 g.
• Carbohydrate: 14 g. • Fat: 14 g. • Cholesterol: 125 mg.
• Sodium: 1704 mg. — Exchanges: 7 lean meat, 1 fruit

GUIDE'S SECRET SMOKED FISH

BRINE

4 CUPS WATER

2 CUPS SOY SAUCE

2 CUPS APPLE JUICE

1 CUP PACKED BROWN SUGAR

1/2 CUP CANNING OR PICKLING SALT

2 TABLESPOONS WHOLE BLACK PEPPERCORNS

1 TEASPOON GARLIC POWDER

1 TEASPOON ONION POWDER

1 TEASPOON FRESHLY GROUND PEPPER

3 LBS. LAKE TROUT OR OTHER OILY FISH FILLETS (8 OZ. EACH), 1 INCH THICK, SKIN ON

12 servings

In 5-quart glass or plastic container, combine brine ingredients. Stir until sugar and salt are dissolved. Add fillets to brine. Cover and refrigerate 12 hours or overnight.

Drain and discard brine from fillets. Rinse with water. Pat dry with paper towels. Arrange fillets on cooling racks. Air dry for 1 hour, or until fillets are shiny and dry. Place oven thermometer in smoker. Heat dry smoker for 20 minutes, or until temperature registers 100°F. Spray smoker racks with nonstick vegetable cooking spray. Arrange fillets on prepared racks, spacing at least 1/2 inch apart. Smoke fillets according to smoker manufacturer's directions (approximately 6 to 8 hours), or until fish is firm and opaque and internal temperature registers 180°F in thickest part of fillet, adding wood chips as necessary to impart desired flavor and to maintain desired level of smoke. Store smoked fish, loosely wrapped, in refrigerator no longer than 2 weeks. Serve with crackers.

Per Serving: Calories: 185 • Protein: 24 g. • Carbohydrate: 4 g. • Fat: 8 g. • Cholesterol: 66 mg. • Sodium: 870 mg. — Exchanges: 3 lean meat, 1/4 fruit

WATER-SMOKED PERCH & BACON BUNDLES

BRINE

4 CUPS WATER

2 TABLESPOONS PACKED BROWN SUGAR

2 TABLESPOONS CANNING OR PICKLING SALT

1 SMALL BAY LEAF

3/4 TEASPOON GROUND CINNAMON

1/4 TEASPOON PEPPER

1/4 TEASPOON GARLIC SALT

1/4 TEASPOON ONION SALT

1/4 TEASPOON RED PEPPER SAUCE

1 LB. YELLOW PERCH OR OTHER LEAN FISH FILLETS, SKIN REMOVED, CUT INTO 4 X 3/4 X 1/4-INCH STRIPS (APX. 36 STRIPS)

4 TO 6 CUPS HICKORY WOOD CHIPS

18 STRIPS BACON, CUT IN HALF CROSSWISE

PAPRIKA

4 CUPS WATER

2 CUPS WHITE WINE

12 servings

In 2-quart saucepan, combine brine ingredients. Bring to a rolling boil over high heat. Reduce heat to low, and simmer brine, partially covered, for 30 minutes. Remove from heat. Cool completely. Place perch strips in 2-quart glass or plastic container. Pour brine over strips. Cover and refrigerate 12 hours or overnight.

Place wood chips in mixing bowl. Cover with water. Soak for 1 hour. Drain and discard brine from fish strips. Rinse with water. Pat dry with paper towels. Arrange strips on cooling racks. Air dry for 1 hour, or until strips are shiny and dry. In 10-inch skillet, fry bacon pieces over low heat until lightly browned but not crisp. Drain on paper towel–lined plate. Place 1 strip of fish on each bacon piece. Roll up and secure with wooden picks. Sprinkle bundles with paprika.

Place oven thermometer in smoker. Add 4 cups water and the wine to water pan in smoker. Heat wet smoker with filled water pan for 20 minutes, or until temperature registers 100°F. Spray smoker racks with nonstick vegetable cooking spray. Arrange bundles on prepared racks, spacing at least 1/2 inch apart. Drain and discard water from wood chips. Smoke bundles with wet chips according to smoker manufacturer's directions (approximately 2 to 3 hours), or until fish is firm and opaque, turning bundles over once.

Per Serving: Calories: 92 • Protein: 10 g. • Carbohydrate: 1 g. • Fat: 5 g. • Cholesterol: 42 mg. • Sodium: 390 mg. — Exchanges: 1 1/2 lean meat

CAPTAIN ANDY'S SUGAR-SMOKED WALLEYE

<u>BRINE</u>
- 8 CUPS APPLE JUICE
- 3/4 CUP CANNING OR PICKLING SALT
- 1/4 CUP PACKED BROWN SUGAR

- 3 LBS. WALLEYE, SALMON OR OTHER FRESHWATER FISH FILLETS (8 OZ. EACH), 1/2 TO 1 INCH THICK, SKIN ON
- 4 TO 6 CUPS CHERRY WOOD CHIPS
- 8 CUPS APPLE JUICE
- 1/4 CUP PACKED BROWN SUGAR

<u>GLAZE</u>
- 1/2 CUP APPLE JUICE
- 1 TABLESPOON PACKED BROWN SUGAR
- 1 TEASPOON HONEY

12 servings

In 5-quart glass or plastic container, combine brine ingredients. Stir until salt and sugar are dissolved. Add fillets to brine. Cover and refrigerate 12 hours or overnight.

Place wood chips in large mixing bowl. Cover with water. Soak chips for 1 hour. Drain and discard brine from fillets. Rinse with water. Pat dry with paper towels. Arrange fillets on cooling racks. Air dry for 1 hour, or until fillets are shiny and dry.

Place oven thermometer in smoker. Add 8 cups apple juice and 1/4 cup brown sugar to water pan in smoker. Heat wet smoker with filled water pan for 20 minutes, or until temperature registers 100°F. Spray smoker racks with nonstick vegetable cooking spray. Arrange fillets on prepared racks, spacing at least 1/2 inch apart. Drain and discard water from wood chips.

Smoke fillets with wet chips according to smoker manufacturer's directions (approximately 2 to 3 hours), or until fish flakes easily with fork and internal temperature registers 180°F in thickest part of fillet.

In 1-quart saucepan, combine glaze ingredients. Cook over medium heat for 2 to 3 minutes, or until mixture is hot and sugar is dissolved, stirring frequently. Brush glaze over fillets. Continue smoking for 30 minutes to 1 hour, or until glaze is set. Store smoked fish, loosely wrapped, in refrigerator no longer than 2 weeks. Serve cold as an appetizer, or hot as a main dish.

Per Serving: Calories: 134 • Protein: 22 g. • Carbohydrate: 8 g. • Fat: 2 g. • Cholesterol: 98 mg. • Sodium: 943 mg. — Exchanges: 3 lean meat, 1/2 fruit

Five Recipe Ideas for Using Smoked Fish

Smoked Salmon Triangles—Spread a mixture of 1/2 cup softened butter, 2 tablespoons snipped fresh chives, 1 tablespoon prepared horseradish and garlic salt to taste on thinly sliced rye or wheat bread. Top with flaked smoked salmon or other fish; garnish with sliced tomato and fresh dill.

Spinach Pasta with Creamy Smoked Fish Sauce—Reduce 2 cups heavy cream by one-third over low heat, then add 3 tablespoons Parmesan cheese, salt and pepper to taste, and a few tablespoons chopped fresh dill. Stir in 1 cup flaked smoked fish. Toss with cooked spinach pasta.

Smoked Fish Quiche—Follow your favorite quiche recipe, adding 1 cup flaked smoked fish before baking.

Smoked Fish Omelet—Blend 3 eggs with 2 tablespoons milk and salt and pepper to taste. Cook in skillet with 1 tablespoon butter or margarine until eggs are just set, then sprinkle half of the omelet with 1/2 cup flaked smoked fish and 1/4 cup shredded cheddar or Swiss cheese. Fold other half over filling and cook until cheese melts. For variety, add some sautéed mushrooms and onions with the fish.

Smoked Fish Spread—Combine 8 ounces softened cream cheese, 1 cup flaked smoked fish, 1/4 cup sour cream, a pinch of cayenne and salt and pepper to taste; for variety, add a clove minced garlic and 1/4 cup sliced pimiento-stuffed olives. Chill at least 1 hour before serving with bread sticks or crackers.

HONEY-GLAZED SMOKED SALMON

8	CUPS WATER
3/4	CUP CANNING OR PICKLING SALT
1/3	CUP PACKED BROWN SUGAR
1/2	TEASPOON PEPPER
1/2	TEASPOON ONION POWDER
3	LBS. SALMON OR OTHER OILY FISH FILLETS (8 OZ. EACH), 1 INCH THICK, SKIN REMOVED, CUT INTO 3 × 4-INCH PIECES
1/2	CUP MARGARINE OR BUTTER, MELTED
1	CUP HONEY

12 servings

In 5-quart glass or plastic container, combine water, salt, sugar, pepper and onion powder. Stir until salt and sugar are dissolved. Add salmon pieces to brine. Cover and refrigerate 8 hours or overnight.

Drain and discard brine from salmon. Rinse with water. Pat dry with paper towels. Arrange salmon pieces on cooling racks. Air dry for 1 hour, or until pieces are shiny and dry. Heat oven to 350°F. Spray two 13 × 9-inch baking dishes with nonstick vegetable cooking spray. Arrange salmon pieces in a single layer in each dish. In small mixing bowl, combine melted margarine and honey. Spoon honey mixture evenly over salmon in each dish. Bake for 20 to 30 minutes, or until fish is firm, basting once or twice. Cool slightly. Cover dishes with plastic wrap. Chill 3 hours.

Place oven thermometer in smoker. Heat dry smoker for 20 minutes, or until temperature registers 100°F. Spray smoker racks with nonstick vegetable cooking spray. Arrange salmon pieces on prepared racks, spacing at least 1/2 inch apart. Smoke fillets according to smoker manufacturer's directions (approximately 1 1/2 to 3 hours), or until fish is firm and opaque and internal temperature registers 180°F in thickest part of fillet, adding wood chips as necessary to impart desired flavor and to maintain desired level of smoke. Store smoked fish, loosely wrapped, in refrigerator no longer than 2 weeks. Serve with crackers.

Per Serving: Calories: 243 • Protein: 23 g. • Carbohydrate: 13 g. • Fat: 11 g. • Cholesterol: 62 mg. • Sodium: 894 mg. — Exchanges: 3 lean meat, 3/4 fruit, 1/2 fat

PICKLING FISH

Pickled fish is usually the first item to disappear from the appetizer tray. Most people like to eat it with crackers.

Practically any kind of fish can be pickled, but small fish with delicate flesh generally work better than large fish with coarse meat. Bony fish, such as northern pike, are often pickled because the acid in the pickling liquid helps dissolve the small bones.

There are dozens of different pickling techniques. Generally, the fish is soaked in a vinegar-salt brine and then in a pickling liquid consisting of vinegar, sugar and seasonings. Use soft or distilled water with canning or pickling salt for brining. The minerals in hard water and ordinary table salt result in off flavors and colors. Total brining and pickling time varies from 4 to 20 days, depending on the recipe.

Normally, the fish are packed in canning jars (with two-part sealing lids) along with spices and onions.

Seviche is another popular appetizer made by marinating uncooked fish in citrus juice and adding onions, tomatoes, peppers and spices.

Fresh, uncooked fish should be frozen for at least 48 hours before pickling, in case the meat contains tapeworms. This is seldom a problem, but the broad-fish tapeworm, found mainly in Canada, can be transmitted to humans and produce symptoms much like intestinal flu. If a recipe recommends cooking the fish in the brine, there is no need to freeze the meat first.

CREAMED SALMON

3½ LBS. SALMON OR OTHER OILY FISH FILLETS (8 OZ. EACH), SKIN REMOVED
3 TO 4 MEDIUM ONIONS, SLICED
4 CUPS DISTILLED WHITE VINEGAR
2 CUPS PLUS 2 TABLESPOONS SUGAR, DIVIDED
¼ CUP MIXED PICKLING SPICES
½ CUP CANNING OR PICKLING SALT
1 CARTON (16 OZ.) SOUR CREAM

3 quarts

Freeze fish 48 hours at 0°F. Defrost. Cut into 1- to 2-inch pieces. Set aside. In large glass mixing bowl, combine onions, vinegar, 2 cups sugar, the spices and salt. Stir until sugar and salt are almost dissolved.

Add fish. Cover with plastic wrap. Refrigerate 7 days, stirring mixture once every day. Drain and discard brine, reserving fish, onions and spices.

In large mixing bowl, combine sour cream and remaining 2 tablespoons sugar. Add fish mixture. Stir gently to coat. Loosely pack mixture into three 1-quart jars. Seal jars, using two-part sealing lids. Store in refrigerator no longer than 4 weeks.

Nutritional information not available.

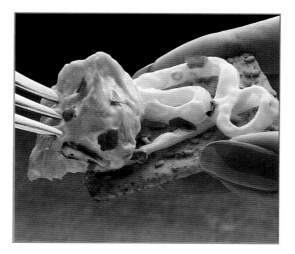

SWEET PEPPER PICKLED FISH

2 TO 3 LBS. ANY FRESHWATER FISH FILLETS (4 TO 6 OZ. EACH), SKIN REMOVED
8 CUPS APPLE CIDER VINEGAR
¼ CUP CANNING OR PICKLING SALT
1½ CUPS SUGAR
3 TABLESPOONS MIXED PICKLING SPICES
½ CUP CHOPPED RED PEPPER
1 LARGE WHITE ONION, SLICED

2 quarts

Freeze fish 48 hours at 0°F. Defrost. Cut into 1- to 2-inch pieces. Set aside. In large glass mixing bowl, combine vinegar and salt. Stir until salt is almost dissolved. Add fish. Cover with plastic wrap. Refrigerate 2 days.

With slotted spoon, remove fish from brine. Rinse fish with cold water until rinse water is clear. Reserve 3 cups brine. Cover and chill fish. Pour reserved brine into 4-quart saucepan. Add sugar, spices and red pepper. Bring mixture to a boil over medium-high heat, stirring constantly until sugar is dissolved. Remove from heat. Cool completely.

In two 1-quart jars, loosely layer fish and onion. Pour pickling liquid over fish to cover. Seal jars, using two-part sealing lids. Refrigerate 1 week before serving. Store in refrigerator no longer than 4 weeks.

Nutritional information not available.

Sweet Pepper Pickled Fish

HOT PEPPER PICKLED FISH

3½ LBS. ANY FRESHWATER FISH FILLETS (4 TO 6 OZ. EACH), SKIN REMOVED
1 MEDIUM ONION, THINLY SLICED
5 SMALL WHOLE DRIED HOT CHILIES
2 CUPS DISTILLED WHITE VINEGAR
1 CUP SUGAR
¾ CUP ROSÉ WINE
¼ CUP CANNING OR PICKLING SALT
1 TABLESPOON MIXED PICKLING SPICES

2 quarts, 1 pint

Freeze fish 48 hours at 0°F. Defrost. Cut into 1- to 2-inch pieces. In two 1-quart jars and one 1-pint jar, loosely layer fish, onion and chilies. Cover and chill. In 2-quart saucepan, combine remaining ingredients. Bring mixture to a boil over medium-high heat, stirring constantly until sugar is dissolved. Remove from heat. Cool completely. Pour pickling liquid over fish to cover. Seal jars, using two-part sealing lids. Refrigerate 10 days before serving. Store in refrigerator no longer than 4 weeks.

Nutritional information not available.

Pickled Jacks

PICKLED JACKS

   3 LBS. NORTHERN PIKE OR OTHER LEAN FISH FILLETS
      (4 TO 6 OZ. EACH), SKIN REMOVED
   4 CUPS WATER
   1 CUP CANNING OR PICKLING SALT
   8 CUPS DISTILLED WHITE VINEGAR, DIVIDED
   1 LARGE RED OR WHITE ONION, THINLY SLICED
2½ CUPS SUGAR
   1 TABLESPOON PLUS 1 TEASPOON MUSTARD SEED
   6 BAY LEAVES
  10 WHOLE CLOVES

3 quarts

Freeze fish 48 hours at 0°F. Defrost. Cut into
½-inch strips. In large glass mixing bowl, combine water and salt. Stir until salt is almost dissolved. Add fish. Cover with plastic wrap.
Refrigerate 2 days. Drain and discard brine. Rinse
fish in cold water until rinse water is clear. Drain.

In same bowl, place fish and 4 cups vinegar.
Cover with plastic wrap. Refrigerate 1 day. Drain
and discard vinegar. Do not rinse fish. In three
1-quart jars, loosely layer fish and onion. Cover
and chill.

In 2-quart saucepan, combine remaining 4 cups
vinegar, the sugar and remaining ingredients.
Bring mixture to a boil over medium-high heat,
stirring constantly until sugar is dissolved.
Reduce heat to medium-low and simmer for 15
minutes. Remove from heat. Cool completely
Pour pickling liquid over fish to cover. Seal jars,
using two-part sealing lids. Refrigerate 1 week
before serving. Store in refrigerator no longer
than 4 weeks.

Nutritional information not available.

TROUT SEVICHE

   1 LB. STREAM TROUT OR OTHER SMALL OILY FISH FILLETS
      (2 OZ. EACH), SKIN REMOVED
   1 CUP FRESH KEY LIME JUICE
  ¼ CUP MINCED JALAPEÑO PEPPERS
   4 MEDIUM TOMATOES, SEEDED AND CHOPPED (4 CUPS)
   1 CUP FINELY CHOPPED RED ONION
   1 CUP THINLY SLICED CELERY
  ¼ CUP HALVED PIMIENTO-STUFFED GREEN OLIVES
   1 TEASPOON FRESHLY GROUND BLACK PEPPER
   1 TEASPOON SALT

16 servings

Freeze fish 48 hours at 0°F. Defrost. Cut into
½-inch pieces. Place fish in large glass or plastic
bowl. Add lime juice and jalapeño peppers. Mix
well. Add remaining ingredients, except salt, stirring gently to combine. With back of spoon, gently press mixture down into juices. Sprinkle salt
evenly over top. Cover with plastic wrap. Chill 1
hour. Serve on toasted tortilla bits or crackers.
Store in refrigerator no longer than 1 to 2 days.

Per Serving: Calories: 56 • Protein: 7 g. • Carbohydrate:
5 g. • Fat: 1 g. • Cholesterol: 16 mg. • Sodium: 208 mg.
— Exchanges: ¾ lean meat, 1 vegetable

PEPPERCORN FISH PICKLES

6	LBS. NORTHERN PIKE OR OTHER LEAN FISH FILLETS (4 TO 6 OZ. EACH), SKIN REMOVED
2	GALLONS WATER, DIVIDED
3½	CUPS CANNING OR PICKLING SALT, DIVIDED
11	CUPS DISTILLED WHITE VINEGAR, DIVIDED
1	LARGE ONION, THINLY SLICED
4½	CUPS SUGAR
2	TABLESPOONS MUSTARD SEED
6	BAY LEAVES
3	TEASPOONS WHOLE CLOVES
1	TO 2 TABLESPOONS WHOLE BLACK, RED OR GREEN PEPPERCORNS

4 quarts, 1 pint

Freeze fish 48 hours at 0°F. Defrost. Cut into 1- to 2-inch pieces. Set aside. In large glass mixing bowl, combine 1 gallon water and 1 cup salt. Stir until salt is almost dissolved. Add fish. Soak for 1 hour. Drain and discard brine.

In another large glass bowl, combine remaining 1 gallon water and 2½ cups salt. Stir until salt is almost dissolved. Add fish. Cover with plastic wrap. Refrigerate 12 hours. Drain and discard brine. Rinse fish with cold water until rinse water is clear. In same bowl, pour 5 cups vinegar over fish. Cover with plastic wrap. Refrigerate 2 days. Drain and discard vinegar.

In four 1-quart jars and one 1-pint jar, loosely layer fish and onion. Cover and chill. In 4-quart saucepan, combine remaining 6 cups vinegar and remaining ingredients. Bring mixture to a boil over medium-high heat. Boil for 5 minutes. Cool completely. Pour pickling liquid over fish to cover. Seal jars, using two-part sealing lids. Refrigerate 2 to 3 days before serving. Store in refrigerator no longer than 4 weeks.

Nutritional information not available.

GRAVLAX INGREDIENTS

2	SALMON OR OTHER OILY FISH FILLETS, 2 TO 2½ POUNDS EACH, SKIN ON
⅓	CUP SALT
¼	CUP SUGAR
1	TABLESPOON DRIED DILL WEED
2	TABLESPOONS COARSELY GROUND BLACK PEPPER

Mix salt, sugar, dill weed and pepper before placing on fillets. Follow directions below.

SALT-CURING FISH: GRAVLAX

Gravlax originated in Scandinavia as a method of salt-curing fish. The salt draws moisture from the fish, delaying spoiling. The salt-curing process requires 4 days, but it is very easy and the finished dish is delicious.

Gravlax is usually made from salmon, though other large oily fish can be used. To make gravlax, scale and fillet a 4- to 6-pound fish. Leave the skin attached. Cut the tail sections off at the vent and save them for another recipe. Use only the large fillets. Freeze fish for at least 48 hours before preparing.

For extra flavor, substitute fresh, chopped dill for the dry dill weed. If a sweet-tasting gravlax is desired, add extra sugar to the ingredients.

Gravlax is most commonly offered as an appetizer, though it is served for breakfast in Norway. Serve gravlax plain or with lime juice. A sauce detracts from its unique flavor and texture.

How to Prepare Gravlax

1 Arrange one fillet, skin side down, in a glass dish. Sprinkle with ingredients. Place second fillet on top, thick side over thin side. Cover the dish with aluminum foil or plastic wrap. Lay a pan or book over the entire length of the fillets. Add about 5 pounds of weight. Refrigerate fish. Rearrange the weight if it shifts to one side. After 24 hours, remove from refrigerator. Take off weight and foil.

2 Drain the liquid and turn fillets over; replace foil and weight and refrigerate. Repeat draining and turning steps two more times, 24 hours apart. Scrape the salt mixture from the flesh on the fourth day. Wrap each fillet in aluminum foil. Refrigerate no longer than 2 weeks.

3 Place the gravlax, skin side down, on a cutting board. Using a fillet knife, slice thin strips at a slight angle. Turn the knife to free flesh from skin. Sprinkle lime juice on gravlax. Serve as an appetizer with crackers. If desired, spread mayonnaise on the cracker.

FISH SAUCES

MUSTARD SAUCE DIJON

Excellent with perch and walleye, as an alternative to tartar sauce.

1/3   CUP DIJON MUSTARD
1/4   CUP VEGETABLE OIL
2   TABLESPOONS SUGAR
1   TEASPOON SNIPPED FRESH PARSLEY
1   TEASPOON SNIPPED FRESH CHIVES
1   TEASPOON WHITE WINE VINEGAR
1   CLOVE GARLIC, MINCED

4 servings

In medium mixing bowl, combine all ingredients. Mix well with whisk. Serve with poached, fried or baked fish. Store, covered, in refrigerator no longer than 1 week.

Per Serving: Calories: 170 • Protein: 0 g. • Carbohydrate: 9 g. • Fat: 15 g. • Cholesterol: 0 mg. • Sodium: 594 mg. — Exchanges: 2/3 fruit, 3 fat

SUMMER-SPICED TOMATO PEPPER SAUCE

This sauce is excellent served over mild fish.

1   MEDIUM TOMATO, PEELED, SEEDED AND CHOPPED (1 CUP)
1/2   CUP FINELY CHOPPED YELLOW PEPPER
1/2   CUP FINELY CHOPPED GREEN PEPPER
1/2   CUP FINELY CHOPPED RED ONION
1   TABLESPOON FINELY CHOPPED PICKLED HOT CHILI PEPPERS
1   TEASPOON FRESH LEMON JUICE
1   TEASPOON RED WINE VINEGAR
1   CLOVE GARLIC, MINCED
1/4   TEASPOON SALT

8 servings

In medium mixing bowl, combine all ingredients. Cover with plastic wrap. Chill at least 2 hours. Serve with poached, fried or baked fish. Store, covered, in refrigerator no longer than 1 week.

Per Serving: Calories: 12 • Protein: 1 g. • Carbohydrate: 3 g. • Fat: 0 g. • Cholesterol: 0 mg. • Sodium: 86 mg. — Exchanges: 1/2 vegetable

MOREL MUSHROOM SAUCE

1/2   OZ. DRIED MOREL MUSHROOMS
1   CUP BOILING WATER
2   TABLESPOONS MARGARINE OR BUTTER
1/4   CUP SLICED GREEN ONIONS
2   TABLESPOONS ALL-PURPOSE FLOUR
1/4   TEASPOON SALT
1/4   TEASPOON GROUND GINGER
1/8   TEASPOON PEPPER
3/4   CUP HALF-AND-HALF
1   TABLESPOON DRY SHERRY

4 servings

In medium mixing bowl, combine mushrooms and boiling water. Let stand for 30 minutes to rehydrate. Drain, reserving 1/2 cup of soaking liquid. Coarsely chop morels. Set aside.

In 2-quart saucepan, melt margarine over medium heat. Add onions and mushrooms. Cook for 2 minutes, or until vegetables are tender, stirring constantly. Stir in flour, salt, ginger and pepper. Blend in reserved morel liquid and the half-and-half. Cook over medium heat, stirring constantly, until mixture thickens and bubbles. Stir in sherry. Serve with poached or baked fish.

Per Serving: Calories: 142 • Protein: 2 g. • Carbohydrate: 8 g. • Fat: 11 g. • Cholesterol: 17 mg. • Sodium: 222 mg. — Exchanges: 1/3 starch, 1/2 vegetable, 1/4 skim milk, 2 fat

RECIPES FOR
Big Game

Big-game meat, if cooked properly, is even tastier than choice beef. And because it's leaner than beef, it also has fewer calories. But the lean meat can become tough and dry if cooked incorrectly.

To make sure big-game meat doesn't dry out, cook it with moist heat or keep it on the rare side. The only exceptions are the meat of bears and wild pigs. Always cook these meats thoroughly, like pork, because they may carry the parasite that causes trichinosis.

The external fat of big game is strong tasting and tallowy, so remove it before cooking. To tenderize tough cuts, marinate them in a mixture of oil and wine or in a packaged beef marinade.

Most recipes for deer work equally well for antelope, elk and moose. Generally, antelope and elk meat is finer-grained than deer and moose meat. Of the antlered animals, elk probably tastes most like beef; antelope, least like it. Bear meat is stronger, darker and coarser than other big game and is usually prepared with more seasoning.

How good the meat tastes, however, depends less on the species of animal than on its sex and age, the time of year it was killed and the care you take with it after the kill. A buck taken during the rut, for instance, is usually stronger tasting and tougher than one taken earlier in the season.

The animal's diet also affects the flavor. A corn-fed deer is much tastier than one forced to eat low-nutrition foods like red cedar. If you store meat from several animals in your freezer and notice that meat from one tastes particularly strong, mark all the other packages from that animal. Then you can prepare this meat in a way that minimizes the flavor.

Tips for Preparing Big-game Meat

REMOVE silverskin with a fillet knife. Cut into one end of the meat to the silverskin. Turn blade parallel to silverskin. Hold silverskin firmly with fingertips and push knife away from them as though skinning a fish fillet. Very little meat is removed with the silverskin this way.

LARD venison roasts before oven roasting to keep them moist. Line the channel of a larding needle with a ¼"-strip of pork fat, available from your butcher. Pierce the roast completely with the needle, then pull the needle out while holding the fat in. Repeat as many times as desired, spacing fat strips evenly. For additional flavor, the fat can be seasoned or marinated prior to larding.

BUTTERFLY small-diameter backstraps or tenderloins to make larger steaks. Cut a steak twice as thick as you want. Then slice it into two "wings" of equal thickness; leave the two wings joined by an edge of meat. Open steak up and flatten slightly.

CUT *across* the grain of the meat when steaking it or making slices for sautéing. Cut *with* the grain, however, when making slices for jerky. Partially frozen meat is easiest to slice.

CHOP or grind trimmed big-game scrap with 15 to 20 percent beef fat to make burger. Use a food processor or meat grinder; the blades must be sharp. Fat is easiest to chop if kept very cold.

How to Chop Venison Coarsely by Hand

1 Cut meat across the grain into thin strips. Cut strips lengthwise into smaller strips.

2 Chop strips crosswise into small pieces.

BIG-GAME SUBSTITUTION GUIDE

Although there are differences in flavor, texture and fat content among the meats from the various hoofed big-game species, you can successfully substitute them for deer in a recipe, keeping in mind the tenderness of the specified cut and that of the substitute.

The substitution chart below shows the various big-game cuts you can substitute for the most common deer cuts. In addition, suggested cooking methods help you make the most of specific cuts.

Big-game Substitution Chart

DEER CUT	TENDERNESS	SUBSTITUTE	COOKING METHOD
TENDERLOIN (WHOLE)	VERY TENDER	•TENDERLOIN PORTION FROM MOOSE, ELK OR CARIBOU •LOIN PORTION FROM CARIBOU, DEER OR ANTELOPE	OVEN ROAST, GRILL
LOIN (PORTION)	TENDER	•LOIN PORTION FROM MOOSE, ELK OR CARIBOU •TENDERLOIN (WHOLE) FROM MOOSE, ELK OR CARIBOU	OVEN ROAST, BROIL, GRILL, PAN-BROIL, PANFRY
LOIN STEAK	TENDER	•LOIN STEAK FROM MOOSE, ELK OR CARIBOU •TENDERLOIN FROM MOOSE, ELK, CARIBOU, DEER OR ANTELOPE	BROIL, GRILL, PAN-BROIL, PANFRY
LOIN CHOP	TENDER	•LOIN CHOP FROM ANY BIG-GAME ANIMAL	BROIL, GRILL, PAN-BROIL, PANFRY
RUMP ROAST	INTERMEDIATE TENDER	•RUMP ROAST FROM ANY BIG-GAME ANIMAL •DEER SIRLOIN TIP •ROLLED, TIED BOTTOM ROUND FROM DEER OR ANTELOPE •EYE OF ROUND FROM MOOSE, ELK OR CARIBOU	OVEN ROAST, GRILL, BRAISE
ROUND STEAK	INTERMEDIATE TENDER	•ROUND STEAK FROM ANY BIG-GAME ANIMAL •SIRLOIN STEAK FROM ANY BIG-GAME ANIMAL •LOIN CHOP FROM MOOSE, ELK, CARIBOU, DEER OR ANTELOPE	BROIL, GRILL, PAN-BROIL, PANFRY, STIR-FRY (STRIPS)
BONELESS ROLLED SHOULDER ROAST	LESS TENDER	•BONELESS ROLLED SHOULDER ROAST FROM ANY BIG-GAME ANIMAL •ROLLED RIB ROAST FROM MOOSE, ELK OR CARIBOU •BONELESS CHUCK ROAST FROM MOOSE, ELK OR CARIBOU	BRAISE
BONE-IN CHUCK ROAST	LESS TENDER	•BONE-IN CHUCK ROAST FROM ANY BIG-GAME ANIMAL •BLADE POT ROAST FROM MOOSE, ELK OR CARIBOU	BRAISE

Peppered Venison Roast

ROAST BONELESS SIRLOIN TIP

(High-temperature Roasting)

1   TO 2 TABLESPOONS OLIVE OIL OR VEGETABLE OIL
1   BONELESS VENISON SIRLOIN TIP, ROLLED TOP ROUND OR RUMP ROAST, 2 TO 5 INCHES THICK

2 to 4 servings per lb.

Heat oven to 450°F. In medium skillet or Dutch oven, heat oil over medium-high heat. Add roast and sear it on all sides. Place roast on rack in roasting pan. Roast to desired doneness (see chart, p. 117), 20 to 30 minutes per pound. Remove roast from oven when internal temperature is 5°F less than desired. Let meat rest for 10 minutes before carving.

Per Serving: Calories: 146 • Protein: 26 g. • Carbohydrate: 0 g. • Fat: 4 g. • Cholesterol: 95 mg. • Sodium: 46 mg. — Exchanges: 3 very lean meat, 3/4 fat

PEPPERED VENISON ROAST

(Low-temperature Roasting)

2   MEDIUM CLOVES GARLIC
1   VENISON SIRLOIN TIP, ROLLED TOP ROUND, BOTTOM ROUND OR RUMP ROAST, 3 TO 5 LBS.
    VEGETABLE OIL
    CRACKED BLACK PEPPER
8   TO 10 SLICES BACON

2 to 4 servings per lb.

Heat oven to 325°F. Cut each garlic clove into 4 or 5 slivers. Make 8 or 10 shallow slits in roast. Insert a garlic sliver into each slit. Place roast on rack in roasting pan; brush with oil. Sprinkle pepper liberally over roast . Cover roast with bacon slices. Roast to desired doneness (see chart, p.117), 22 to 32 minutes per pound; remove roast when temperature is 5°F less than desired. Allow meat to rest for 10 to 15 minutes before carving. Serve with pan juices.

Per Serving: Calories: 213 • Protein: 27 g. • Carbohydrate: 0 g. • Fat: 11 g. • Cholesterol: 104 mg. • Sodium: 133 mg. — Exchanges: 3 1/4 very lean meat, 2 fat

BIG GAME BELGIUM

Slow braising tenderizes the shoulder roast in this recipe. You may substitute any big-game roast for the elk shoulder.

1/2	CUP ALL-PURPOSE FLOUR
2	TEASPOONS DRIED THYME LEAVES
1/4	TEASPOON SALT
1/2	TEASPOON PEPPER
3-	LB. ELK SHOULDER ROAST OR SUBSTITUTE, ABOUT 2 INCHES THICK
3	TABLESPOONS OLIVE OIL OR VEGETABLE OIL
1/2	LB. SALT PORK, DICED
3	TABLESPOONS BUTTER OR MARGARINE
3	MEDIUM ONIONS, THINLY SLICED
1	TABLESPOON GRANULATED SUGAR
1	BOTTLE (12 OZ.) DARK BEER
2	TABLESPOONS PACKED BROWN SUGAR
1	TABLESPOON SNIPPED FRESH PARSLEY

4 to 6 servings

Heat oven to 325°F. In large plastic food-storage bag, combine flour, thyme, salt and pepper; shake to mix. Add meat; shake to coat. In Dutch oven, brown meat in oil over medium heat. Remove meat; set aside. Add salt pork to Dutch oven. Cook over medium heat, stirring frequently, until salt pork is crisp and golden brown.

With slotted spoon, transfer salt pork to small mixing bowl; set aside. Melt butter in Dutch oven. Add onions. Cook and stir over medium heat until tender. Add granulated sugar. Cook and stir until onions are brown, about 10 minutes. Add beer and brown sugar. Stir, scraping bottom of pan to loosen browned bits. Return meat to Dutch oven. Add reserved salt pork. Cover; bake until meat is tender, about 2 hours. Transfer meat to platter. Garnish with parsley. Serve with pan juices if desired.

Per serving: Calories: 753 • Protein: 56 g. • Carbohydrate: 24 g. • Fat: 46 g. • Cholestrol: 175 mg. •Sodium: 830 mg. — Exchanges: 1/2 starch, 7 1/2 very lean meat, 1 1/2 vegetable, 8 1/2 fat

PEPPERY SOUTHWESTERN VENISON ROAST

3-	TO 4-LB. BONELESS VENISON RUMP ROAST OR SUBSTITUTE
1/2	CUP KETCHUP
1/4	CUP PACKED BROWN SUGAR
1	TABLESPOON PREPARED MUSTARD
1	TABLESPOON LIQUID SMOKE FLAVORING (OPTIONAL)
1	TABLESPOON FRESH LEMON JUICE
1	TABLESPOON SOY SAUCE
2	TEASPOONS WORCESTERSHIRE SAUCE
2	TEASPOONS CELERY SALT
2	TEASPOONS COARSELY GROUND PEPPER
1	TEASPOON GARLIC POWDER
1	TEASPOON ONION POWDER
1/4	TEASPOON CRUSHED RED PEPPER FLAKES
	DASH GROUND NUTMEG

14 servings

Heat oven to 350°F. Place roast in bottom of 3-quart roasting pan with cover. Set aside. In medium mixing bowl, combine remaining ingredients. Pour mixture over roast. Cover tightly. Bake for 2 to 2 1/2 hours, or until meat is tender. Remove cover. Bake for 30 minutes longer. Let roast stand for 10 minutes. Carve roast across grain into thin slices.

Per Serving: Calories: 164 • Protein: 26 g. • Carbohydrate: 7 g. • Fat: 3 g. • Cholesterol: 96 mg. • Sodium: 348 mg. — Exchanges: 3 lean meat, 1 vegetable

Internal Temperature of Meat at Various Degrees of Doneness

DEGREE OF DONENESS	INTERNAL TEMPERATURE
RARE	130° TO 135°
MEDIUM-RARE	135° TO 140°
MEDIUM	140° TO 145°
MEDIUM-WELL	145° TO 155°
WELL-DONE	155° TO 160°

VENISON SAUERBRATEN

<u>MARINADE</u>

6	CUPS WATER
1	LARGE ONION, SLICED
2	TEASPOONS SALT
10	WHOLE BLACK PEPPERCORNS
10	WHOLE JUNIPER BERRIES, OPTIONAL
6	WHOLE CLOVES
1	BAY LEAF
½	CUP VINEGAR

3½- TO 4-POUND DEER, ELK OR MOOSE ROAST
2 TABLESPOONS VEGETABLE OIL
1 MEDIUM RED OR GREEN CABBAGE (ABOUT 2½ POUNDS), CUT INTO 8 WEDGES
15 GINGERSNAPS, FINELY CRUSHED
2 TEASPOONS SUGAR

6 to 8 servings

In large saucepan, combine all marinade ingredients except vinegar. Heat to boiling. Add vinegar. Cool slightly. Place roast in large glass or ceramic mixing bowl. Pour cooled marinade over roast. Cover tightly with plastic wrap. Refrigerate 2 to 3 days, turning meat once or twice.

Remove roast from marinade, reserving marinade. In Dutch oven, brown roast on all sides in oil over medium heat. Add marinade. Reduce heat; cover. Cook over low heat until tender, 2 to 3 hours. Heat oven to 175°F just before meat is tender. With slotted spoon, transfer roast to ovenproof serving platter. Keep warm in oven.

Strain cooking liquid into 2-quart measure. Add water if necessary to equal 5 cups. Return liquid to Dutch oven. Heat to boiling. Add cabbage wedges. Return to boiling. Reduce heat; cover. Simmer until cabbage is tender, 15 to 20 minutes. With slotted spoon, transfer cabbage to platter with meat. In small bowl, combine crushed gingersnaps and sugar. Stir into liquid in Dutch oven. Cook over low heat, stirring occasionally, until bubbly and slightly thickened. Serve gingersnap sauce with roast and cabbage wedges.

Per serving: Calories: 366 • Protein: 52 g. • Carbohydrate: 23 g. • Fat: 7 g. • Cholesterol: 180 mg. • Sodium: 790 mg. — Exchanges: 1 starch, 6 very lean meat, 2 vegetable, ½ fat

APRICOT-WALNUT STUFFED ROLLED ROAST

STUFFING

4 SLICES WHOLE-GRAIN BREAD, CUT INTO 1/2-INCH CUBES (2 CUPS)

1/2 CUP CHOPPED WALNUTS

1 TABLESPOON BUTTER OR MARGARINE

1 MEDIUM ONION, CHOPPED (1 CUP)

1 STALK CELERY, CHOPPED (1/2 CUP)

1/2 CUP CHOPPED DRIED APRICOTS

1 TABLESPOON DRIED PARSLEY FLAKES

1 TEASPOON DRIED THYME LEAVES

1/2 TEASPOON SALT

1/4 TEASPOON PEPPER

1/2 TO 3/4 CUP BEEF OR VENISON STOCK

2- TO 3-LB. BONELESS VENISON HINDQUARTER ROAST, BUTTERFLIED TO 1-INCH THICKNESS

4 SLICES BACON, HALVED

8 to 12 servings

Heat oven to 350°F. Spread bread cubes and walnuts in a single layer on large baking sheet. Bake for 8 to 10 minutes, or until cubes are toasted and walnuts are lightly browned, stirring once or twice. Set aside. Reduce oven temperature to 325°F.

In 12-inch nonstick skillet, melt butter over medium heat. Add onion and celery. Cook for 3 to 5 minutes, or until vegetables are tender, stirring occasionally. Remove from heat. Stir in bread cubes, walnuts and remaining stuffing ingredients, except stock. Stir in stock just until stuffing is moistened. See directions at right for rolling the roast.

Roast to desired doneness (see chart on page 117), 20 to 25 minutes per pound. Remove and discard bacon slices.

Per Serving: Calories: 210 • Protein: 23 g. • Carbohydrate: 10 g. • Fat: 8 g. • Cholesterol: 83 mg. • Sodium: 241 mg. — Exchanges: 1/2 starch, 2 1/2 very lean meat, 1/2 vegetable, 1 3/4 fat

How to Roll & Tie a Stuffed Roast

1 Spread and pack stuffing evenly on roast. Roll up roast jelly roll-style, rolling with the grain of the meat.

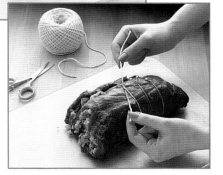

2 Tie roast at 1-inch intervals, using kitchen string. Place roast on rack in roasting pan. Top evenly with bacon slices. Continue with directions in recipe.

SWEET & SOUR VENISON POT ROAST

1 TABLESPOON VEGETABLE OIL

4- LB. VENISON CHUCK ROAST OR SUBSTITUTE,
   TIED IF NECESSARY

2 LARGE ONIONS, SLICED

¼ CUP SUGAR

¼ CUP HONEY

¼ CUP LEMON JUICE

½ TEASPOON GRATED LEMON PEEL

¼ TEASPOON GROUND CLOVES

1 TEASPOON SALT

½ TEASPOON FRESHLY GROUND PEPPER

3 MEDIUM CARROTS, CUT INTO 2-INCH PIECES

1 LB. RED POTATOES, CUT INTO 2-INCH PIECES

8 servings

Heat oven to 325°F. In 6-quart Dutch oven, heat oil over medium-high heat. Add roast. Cook roast for 7 to 10 minutes, or until browned on all sides, turning frequently. Remove from heat. Drain. Add onions.

In 2-cup measure, combine sugar, honey, lemon juice and peel, and cloves. Pour mixture over roast and onions. Sprinkle roast evenly with salt and pepper. Cover tightly. Roast for 1 hour, basting occasionally with pan juices. Add carrots and potatoes, pushing them into the pan juices. Continue roasting for 1½ to 2 hours, or until meat and vegetables are tender. Serve roast with pan juices.

Tips: For a reduced sauce, remove roast and vegetables from Dutch oven. Boil pan juices over medium-high heat until desired consistency.

To make gravy from pan juice, strain 2 cups liquid from pan juices; discard remainder. Return 2 cups liquid to Dutch oven. In 1-cup measure, combine ¹/₄ cup all-purpose flour and ¹/₃ cup water. Gradually whisk flour mixture into pan juices. Bring to a boil over medium-high heat. Cook for 1 to 1¹/₂ minutes, or until thickened, stirring constantly. Add salt and pepper to taste.

Per Serving: Calories: 426 • Protein: 54 g. • Carbohydrate: 34 g. • Fat: 7 g. • Cholesterol: 193 mg. • Sodium: 409 mg. — Exchanges: ¹/₂ starch, 6 very lean meat, 1¹/₂ vegetable, 1¹/₂ fat

SPICED BEAR ROAST

3 1/2- TO 4-LB. BONELESS BEAR RUMP ROAST
     OR SUBSTITUTE, WELL TRIMMED

12 WHOLE CLOVES

1 1/2 CUPS THINLY SLICED CARROTS

1 1/2 CUPS THINLY SLICED CELERY

1 CUP CHOPPED ONIONS

1 CUP DRY RED WINE

3/4 CUP WATER

1/4 CUP MARGARINE OR BUTTER, MELTED

2 TEASPOONS CAYENNE

1 TEASPOON GROUND ALLSPICE

1/2 TEASPOON PEPPER

2 SLICES BACON, CUT IN HALF CROSSWISE

14 to 16 servings

Heat oven to 400°F. Place roast in bottom of 3-quart roasting pan with cover. With sharp knife, cut 12 slits, 1/2 inch deep, in top of roast. Place 1 clove in each slit. In medium mixing bowl, combine remaining ingredients, except bacon. Pour mixture over roast. Arrange bacon slices across roast. Insert meat thermometer in roast. Cover tightly. Bake for 20 minutes.

Reduce heat to 325°F. Bake for 2 to 2 1/2 hours, or until meat is tender and internal temperature registers 165°F. Remove cover. Bake for 15 minutes longer. Let roast stand for 10 minutes. Carve roast across grain into thin slices.

Per Serving: Calories: 225 • Protein: 22 g. • Carbohydrate: 3 g. • Fat: 13 g. • Cholesterol: N/A • Sodium: N/A — Exchanges: 3 lean meat, 2/3 vegetable, 1 fat

GRILLED GARLIC-ROSEMARY ROAST

MARINADE

1 1/2 CUPS DRY RED WINE

1/2 CUP PACKED BROWN SUGAR

1/2 OZ. FRESH ROSEMARY SPRIGS, CUT INTO
     1-INCH PIECES (1/2 CUP)

4 TO 5 CLOVES GARLIC, CRUSHED

1/2 TEASPOON FRESHLY GROUND PEPPER

2- LB. VENISON TOP ROUND ROAST OR
     SUBSTITUTE, 1 1/2 TO 2 INCHES THICK

6 to 8 servings

In 4-cup measure, combine all marinade ingredients. Stir to dissolve sugar. Place roast in large sealable plastic bag. Add marinade, seal bag and turn to coat roast. Refrigerate roast several hours or overnight, turning bag occasionally.

Prepare grill for medium direct heat. Drain and reserve marinade from roast. Strain marinade through fine-mesh sieve, if desired. Grill roast, covered, 30 to 40 minutes for medium-rare, or until desired doneness (see chart, p. 117), turning roast and basting with reserved marinade every 10 minutes. Remove from grill; tent. Let roast stand for 10 minutes.

Per Serving: Calories: 224 • Protein: 26 g. • Carbohydrate: 15 g. • Fat: 3 g. • Cholesterol: 95 mg. • Sodium: 54 mg. — Exchanges: 3 very lean meat, 1/2 fat

Uses for Leftover Cooked Venison

Big Game Sandwich Filling—In food processor, combine 2 cups leftover diced cooked big game, a 4¹/2-ounce can deviled ham, 1/4 cup coarsely chopped onion and salt and pepper to taste. Chop to desired consistency, adding up to 1/2 cup beef broth.

Skillet Game Hash—Sauté 2 cups diced cooked potatoes and 1/2 cup chopped onion in vegetable oil, then add 2 cups diced cooked big game, 1 cup gravy and seasoning to taste. Cook over low heat 5 minutes.

Venison Sandwich Rolls—Spread flour tortillas or other soft wraps with chive-flavored cream cheese. Top with very thinly sliced cooked venison roast, then top venison with fresh spinach leaves and roasted bell pepper strips. Roll up jelly-roll style.

BARBECUED VENISON ROAST

2   CANS (12 OZ. EACH) CARBONATED COLA BEVERAGE
2/3   CUP WORCESTERSHIRE SAUCE
3-   TO 4-LB. VENISON TOP OR BOTTOM ROUND ROAST
1   MEDIUM ONION, SLICED
1/2   CUP WATER
1/4   TO 1/2 TEASPOON PEPPER
1/2   TO 1 CUP BARBECUE SAUCE

12 to 16 servings

In large sealable plastic bag, combine cola and Worcestershire sauce. Add roast, seal bag and turn to coat roast. Refrigerate at least 4 hours, turning roast occasionally.

Heat oven to 325°F. Spray roasting pan with non-stick vegetable cooking spray. Drain and discard marinade from roast. Place roast in pan. Add onion and water to pan. Sprinkle roast evenly with pepper. Cover with lid or foil. Bake for 2¹/2 to 3¹/2 hours, or until meat is tender, basting two or three times with pan juices. Let roast stand, covered, for 10 minutes. Drain and discard liquid from pan.

Cut roast into thin slices. Return to pan. Pour barbecue sauce over meat. Bake, covered, for 20 to 30 minutes, or until hot. Serve meat over mashed potatoes, on hamburger buns or on toast.

Per Serving: Calories: 151 • Protein: 26 g.
• Carbohydrate: 3 g. • Fat: 3 g. • Cholesterol: 95 mg.
• Sodium: 157 mg. — Exchanges: 3 very lean meat, 1/2 fat

SLOW-LANE VENISON

This recipe can also be prepared in a crockpot or in a covered roaster in campfire coals. The secret is long, slow roasting at low temperatures.

3-   TO 4-LB. BONELESS VENISON RUMP ROAST OR SUBSTITUTE
3   SLICES BACON, CUT IN HALF CROSSWISE
1   CAN (8 OZ.) TOMATO SAUCE
1/2   CUP KETCHUP
1/2   CUP CHOPPED ONION
2   TABLESPOONS PACKED BROWN SUGAR
2   TABLESPOONS WORCESTERSHIRE SAUCE
2   TABLESPOONS CIDER VINEGAR
1/2   TEASPOON GARLIC POWDER
1/2   TEASPOON COARSELY GROUND PEPPER

14 servings

Heat oven to 325°F. Place roast in bottom of 3-quart roasting pan with cover. Arrange bacon slices across roast. In medium mixing bowl, combine remaining ingredients. Pour mixture over roast. Cover tightly.

Bake for 2 to 3 hours, or until meat is tender. Let roast stand for 10 minutes. Carve roast across grain into thin slices, or shred. Serve in buttered hamburger buns with coleslaw and chilled cranberry sauce, if desired.

Per Serving: Calories: 190 • Protein: 27 g.
• Carbohydrate: 7 g. • Fat: 6 g. • Cholesterol: 100 mg.
• Sodium: 315 mg. — Exchanges: 3 medium-fat meat, 1¹/4 vegetable

BARBECUED VENISON SANDWICHES

3- LB. VENISON TOP OR BOTTOM ROUND ROAST
1 CAN (11½ OZ.) TOMATO JUICE
1 LARGE ONION, SLICED
½ TEASPOON PEPPER

BARBECUE SAUCE
1 SMALL ONION, CHOPPED (½ CUP)
½ CUP WATER
3 CUPS KETCHUP
⅔ CUP PACKED BROWN SUGAR
½ CUP WORCESTERSHIRE SAUCE
½ CUP WHITE VINEGAR
2 TABLESPOONS LEMON JUICE
2 TEASPOONS CELERY SEED
1 TEASPOON SALT
¼ TO ½ TEASPOON CAYENNE
½ TEASPOON LIQUID SMOKE (OPTIONAL)

24 HAMBURGER BUNS

24 servings

Place roast in 6-quart Dutch oven. Add tomato juice, onion and pepper. Bring to a boil over high heat. Reduce heat to low. Cover. Simmer for 1 to 1½ hours, or until meat is tender, turning meat occasionally. Remove roast from pan and let stand until meat is cool enough to handle. (If desired, refrigerate roast overnight.) Using fork, shred meat along grain. Set aside.

To make sauce, combine onion and water in 4-quart saucepan. Cook over medium heat for 4 to 6 minutes, or until onion is tender and water is boiled off, stirring frequently. Stir in remaining sauce ingredients. Bring to a boil. Reduce heat to low. Simmer for 10 to 15 minutes, or until flavors are blended.

In 6-quart Dutch oven, combine shredded venison and barbecue sauce. Cook over medium heat for 10 to 15 minutes, or until heated through, stirring occasionally. Spoon mixture into hamburger buns to serve.

Per Serving: Calories: 261 • Protein: 18 g. • Carbohydrate: 39 g. • Fat: 4 g. • Cholesterol: 48 mg. • Sodium: 828 mg. — Exchanges: 1½ starch, 1½ very lean meat, 2 vegetable, ½ fat

VENISON BOMBERS

3- LB. BONELESS VENISON RUMP ROAST OR SUBSTITUTE
6 CUPS BEEF OR VENISON STOCK
2 MEDIUM RED OR GREEN PEPPERS, CUT INTO 2 X ½-INCH STRIPS
2 MEDIUM ONIONS, CUT INTO ¾-INCH WEDGES
1 BULB GARLIC, SEPARATED INTO CLOVES, PEELED AND SLICED
2 DRIED HOT PEPPERS, CRUMBLED, SEEDS REMOVED (OPTIONAL)
2 TEASPOONS DRIED OREGANO LEAVES
1½ TEASPOONS DRIED ROSEMARY LEAVES
1½ TEASPOONS DRIED THYME LEAVES
1½ TEASPOONS PEPPER
12 HARD ROLLS, SPLIT
1½ CUPS SHREDDED LETTUCE
12 SLICES (1.2 OZ. EACH) PROVOLONE CHEESE
24 PEPPERONCINI PEPPERS, STEMS REMOVED, CUT INTO STRIPS (OPTIONAL)
4 MEDIUM TOMATOES, THINLY SLICED

12 servings

In 6-quart ovenproof Dutch oven or stockpot, combine roast, stock, red or green pepper strips, onions, garlic, dried peppers, oregano, rosemary, thyme and pepper. Bring to a boil over medium-high heat. Reduce heat to low. Cover. Cook for 2½ to 3½ hours, or until meat is tender. Remove meat from stock. Cool slightly. Carve roast across grain into thin slices. Return slices to broth. Cook over medium-low heat for 10 to 15 minutes, or until hot.

Heat oven to 350°F. Scoop out about half of inside portion of each roll to make a well. (Reserve scooped-out bread for future use.) Place tops and bottoms of rolls together and arrange on baking sheet. Bake for 5 to 8 minutes, or until hot. Spoon about ½ cup sliced meat mixture into bottom half of each roll. Spoon some of broth over meat. Top with lettuce, cheese, pepperoncini peppers and tomatoes. Place tops of rolls over cheese. Serve with additional broth for dipping, if desired.

Per Serving: Calories: 469 • Protein: 43 g. • Carbohydrate: 39 g. • Fat: 15 g. • Cholesterol: 120 mg. • Sodium: 1085 mg. — Exchanges: 2 starch, 4¾ lean meat, 2 vegetable

Venison with Blue Cheese-Port Sauce

GRILLED LOIN WITH BROWN SUGAR BASTE

2 TO 4 LBS. DEER, ANTELOPE, ELK OR MOOSE LOIN PORTION OR WHOLE BACKSTRAP

3 TABLESPOONS BUTTER OR MARGARINE

3 TABLESPOONS SOY SAUCE

3 TABLESPOONS PACKED BROWN SUGAR

2 or 3 servings per lb.

Start charcoal briquets in grill. Remove all fat and silverskin from meat. Cut into lengths about 4 inches long, or about 6 to 8 ounces each. In small saucepan, melt butter over medium heat. Add soy sauce and brown sugar. Cook, stirring constantly, until brown sugar dissolves and sauce bubbles.

When charcoal briquets are covered with ash, spread them evenly in grill. Place grate above hot coals. Place meat on grate. Grill on one side until seared. Turn meat over; brush with brown sugar mixture. Continue grilling, brushing frequently with brown sugar mixture and turning occasionally to grill all sides, until desired doneness.

Per serving: Calories: 233 • Protein: 34 g. • Carbohydrate: 5 g. • Fat: 7 g. • Cholesterol: 135 mg. • Sodium: 440 mg. — Exchanges: 5 very lean meat, 1 fat

VENISON WITH BLUE CHEESE-PORT SAUCE

MARINADE

1 CUP TAWNY PORT

1 CAN (5.5 OZ.) SPICY VEGETABLE JUICE

1/3 CUP THINLY SLICED GREEN ONIONS

2 CLOVES GARLIC, MINCED

1/2 TEASPOON COARSELY GROUND PEPPER

1/4 TEASPOON GROUND ALLSPICE

1- LB. VENISON TOP ROUND STEAK OR SUBSTITUTE, 1/2 TO 3/4 INCH THICK

1/2 CUP BEEF OR VENISON STOCK

2 TO 4 OZ. BLUE CHEESE, CRUMBLED

4 servings

In large sealable plastic bag, combine marinade ingredients. Using sharp knife, score steak at 1-inch intervals in a crisscross pattern to 1/8-inch depth. Place steak in bag, seal bag and turn to coat steak. Refrigerate 4 hours, turning bag occasionally.

Prepare grill for medium-direct heat. Drain and reserve marinade from steak. Set steak aside. Place marinade in 2-quart saucepan. Bring to a boil over medium-high heat. Boil for 6 to 8 minutes, or until sauce is reduced to 1 cup. Add stock. Return to a boil. Boil for 4 to 6 minutes, or until sauce is reduced to 1 cup again. Stir in cheese. Set sauce aside and keep warm.

Grill steak, covered, for 8 to 10 minutes, or until meat is desired doneness, turning steak over once. Cut steak into slices or serving-size pieces and serve with sauce.

Per Serving: Calories: 257 • Protein: 31 g. • Carbohydrate: 11 g. • Fat: 9 g. • Cholesterol: 111 mg. • Sodium: 479 mg. —Exchanges: 3 3/4 very lean meat, 3/4 vegetable, 1 3/4 fat

RUM-SPICED VENISON CHOPS

1   TABLESPOON OLIVE OIL

1   MEDIUM ONION, FINELY CHOPPED (1 CUP)

2   JALAPEÑO PEPPERS OR OTHER HOT CHILI PEPPERS, SEEDED AND FINELY CHOPPED

4   CLOVES GARLIC, MINCED

½   TEASPOON DRIED THYME LEAVES

½   TEASPOON GROUND CINNAMON

⅛   TEASPOON GROUND NUTMEG

⅛   TEASPOON GROUND CLOVES

1   BAY LEAF

¼   CUP DARK RUM

2   TABLESPOONS FRESH LIME JUICE

¼   TEASPOON SALT

4   BONE-IN VENISON LOIN CHOPS (6 OZ. EACH), ½ TO ¾ INCH THICK

4 servings

In 10-inch nonstick skillet, heat oil over medium heat. Add onion, jalapeños, garlic, thyme, cinnamon, nutmeg, cloves and bay leaf. Cook for 8 to 10 minutes, or until mixture is deep golden brown, stirring frequently.

Increase heat to medium-high. Stir in rum, lime juice and salt. Cook for 1½ to 2½ minutes, or until most liquid has boiled away. Remove from heat. Remove and discard bay leaf. Cool marinade completely.

Place chops in shallow dish. Spread half of marinade over chops. Turn chops over and spread with remaining marinade. Cover with plastic wrap. Chill 4 hours.

Prepare grill for medium-direct heat. Spray cooking grid with non-stick vegetable cooking spray. Do not remove marinade from meat. Grill chops, covered, for 10 to 12 minutes, or until desired doneness, turning chops over once.

Per Serving: Calories: 192 • Protein: 27 g. • Carbohydrate: 6 g. • Fat: 6 g. • Cholesterol: 95 mg. • Sodium: 184 mg. —Exchanges: 3 very lean meat, 1¼ vegetable, 1¼ fat

OLD-FASHIONED STEAKS WITH PAN GRAVY

1/4 CUP PLUS 3 TABLESPOONS ALL-PURPOSE FLOUR, DIVIDED
3/4 TEASPOON FRESHLY GROUND PEPPER
1/2 TEASPOON SALT
1/4 TEASPOON PAPRIKA
3 TABLESPOONS BUTTER OR MARGARINE
4 BONELESS VENISON LOIN STEAKS OR SUBSTITUTE (4 OZ. EACH), 3/4 TO 1 INCH THICK
1¾ CUPS 1% MILK

---

4 servings

In shallow dish, combine 1/4 cup flour, the pepper, salt and paprika. Dredge steaks in flour mixture to coat.

In 12-inch nonstick skillet, melt butter over medium heat. Add steaks. Cook for 6 to 8 minutes, or until browned and desired doneness, turning steaks over once. Remove steaks from skillet and keep warm.

In small mixing bowl, combine milk and remaining 3 tablespoons flour. Stir until smooth. Whisk mixture into drippings in skillet. Cook over medium heat for 2 to 3 minutes, or until gravy bubbles, stirring constantly. Cook for 1 minute longer, stirring constantly. Season to taste with salt and pepper. Serve gravy over steaks.

Tip: If you prefer thinner gravy, add a small amount of milk or water.

Per Serving: Calories: 308 • Protein: 31 g. • Carbohydrate: 16 g. • Fat: 13 g. • Cholesterol: 124 mg. • Sodium: 473 mg. — Exchanges: 3/4 starch, 3 very lean meat, 1/4 low-fat milk, 2¼ fat

GRILLED SZECHUAN STEAKS

MARINADE
1/4 CUP SLICED GREEN ONIONS
1½ TABLESPOONS SOY SAUCE
1 TABLESPOON LEMON JUICE
1 TABLESPOON TOASTED SESAME SEEDS
2 TEASPOONS HOT CHILI SAUCE WITH GARLIC
1 TEASPOON SUGAR
1 TEASPOON GRATED FRESH GINGERROOT

4 BONELESS VENISON ROUND STEAKS OR SUBSTITUTE (4 OZ. EACH), 3/4 TO 1 INCH THICK
1/4 TEASPOON CORNSTARCH

---

4 servings

In shallow dish, combine all marinade ingredients. Add steaks, turning to coat. Cover with plastic wrap. Chill 30 minutes, turning steaks over once.

Prepare grill for medium-direct heat. Spray cooking grid with nonstick vegetable cooking spray. Drain and reserve marinade from meat. Grill steaks, covered, for 10 to 12 minutes, or until desired doneness, turning steaks over once.

Meanwhile, in 1-quart saucepan, combine reserved marinade and the cornstarch. Bring to a boil over medium-low heat, stirring constantly. Serve as sauce over steaks.

Tip: For more intense flavor, marinate steaks for several hours or overnight.

Per Serving: Calories: 160 • Protein: 26 g. • Carbohydrate: 4 g. • Fat: 4 g. • Cholesterol: 95 mg. • Sodium: 454 mg. — Exchanges: 3 very lean meat, 3/4 fat

VENISON STEAKS WITH RED PEPPER SAUCE

1 TABLESPOON BUTTER OR MARGARINE

3 LARGE TOMATOES, PEELED, SEEDED AND
  CHOPPED (2 CUPS)

2 ROASTED RED PEPPERS*, CHOPPED

¾ TEASPOON DRIED OREGANO LEAVES

½ TEASPOON GARLIC POWDER

½ TEASPOON PAPRIKA

¼ TEASPOON CAYENNE

4 BONELESS VENISON LOIN STEAKS OR SUBSTITUTE
  (4 OZ. EACH), ¾ TO 1 INCH THICK

4 servings

In 1-quart saucepan, melt butter over medium heat. Add tomatoes and peppers. Cook for 3 to 4 minutes, or until tomatoes are soft, stirring frequently. Stir in oregano, garlic powder, paprika and cayenne. Cook for 3 to 5 minutes, or until sauce is thickened, stirring frequently. Set aside and keep warm.

Spray rack in broiler pan with nonstick vegetable cooking spray. Arrange steaks on rack. Broil with surface of steaks 4 to 5 inches from heat for 6 to 8 minutes, or until desired doneness, turning steaks over once. Serve steaks with sauce.

*See Classic Mushroom-Wild Rice Casserole (page 144) for technique for roasting peppers.

Per Serving: Calories: 195 • Protein: 27 g. • Carbohydrate: 7 g. • Fat: 6 g. • Cholesterol: 103 mg. • Sodium: 162 mg. — Exchanges: 3 very lean meat, 1½ vegetable, 1 fat

Java-Schnitz

JAVA-SCHNITZ

1/3 CUP ALL-PURPOSE FLOUR

1/2 TEASPOON SALT

1/4 TEASPOON PEPPER

8 JAVELINA LOIN STEAKS (2 TO 3 OZ. EACH), POUNDED TO 1/4 -INCH THICKNESS

2 EGGS, BEATEN

1/2 CUP UNSEASONED DRY BREAD CRUMBS

3 TABLESPOONS VEGETABLE OIL

1/2 CUP BUTTER

1/4 CUP SNIPPED FRESH PARSLEY

4 TO 8 LEMON WEDGES

---

4 servings

In shallow dish, combine flour, salt and pepper. Dredge steaks in flour mixture to coat. Dip floured steaks first in eggs and then dredge in bread crumbs to coat.

In 12-inch nonstick skillet, heat oil over medium heat. Add steaks. Cook for 5 to 7 minutes, or until meat is well done, turning steaks over once. Transfer steaks to warm platter. Cover to keep warm. Set aside. Wipe out skillet with paper towels.

In same skillet, melt butter over medium-low heat. Cook for 1 to 2 minutes longer, or until lightly browned. Sprinkle parsley over steaks. Pour browned butter over steaks. Serve with lemon wedges.

Nutritional information not available.

STEAKS WITH MUSTARD SAUCE

4 BONELESS VENISON LOIN STEAKS (4 OZ. EACH), POUNDED TO 1/4-INCH THICKNESS

SALT AND PEPPER TO TASTE

1 TABLESPOON BUTTER

1/4 CUP FINELY CHOPPED ONION

2 CUPS BEEF OR VENISON STOCK

2 TABLESPOONS CORNSTARCH

1/4 CUP SNIPPED FRESH MARJORAM, PARSLEY OR THYME*

1/4 CUP DIJON MUSTARD

2 TABLESPOONS LEMON JUICE

1 TEASPOON WORCESTERSHIRE SAUCE

3 TABLESPOONS MADEIRA WINE

FRESH HERB SPRIGS FOR GARNISH

---

4 servings

Heat 12-inch nonstick skillet over medium heat. Spray with nonstick vegetable cooking spray. Add steaks. Cook for 3 to 4 minutes, or until meat is desired doneness, turning steaks over once. Remove steaks to serving platter. Sprinkle with salt and pepper. Set aside and keep warm.

In same skillet, melt butter over medium heat. Add onion. Cook for 2 to 3 minutes, or until onion is tender, stirring occasionally. In medium mixing bowl, combine stock and cornstarch. Stir stock mixture, fresh herbs, mustard, lemon juice and Worcestershire sauce into skillet. Cook for 2 to 3 minutes, or until sauce thickens and bubbles, stirring constantly. Stir in Madeira. Cook for 1 minute. Spoon sauce over steaks and garnish with fresh herb sprigs.

*A combination of fresh herbs equaling 1/4 cup may also be used.

Per Serving: Calories: 227 • Protein: 27 g.
• Carbohydrate: 7 g. • Fat: 6 g. • Cholesterol: 104 mg.
• Sodium: 824 mg. — Exchanges: 3 very lean meat, 1 1/4 fat

VENISON SATAY WITH SPICY PEANUT SAUCE

Satay is an Indonesian favorite consisting of marinated meat threaded on skewers, grilled or broiled and served with a spicy peanut sauce for dipping.

1   LB. VENISON LOIN STEAKS OR SUBSTITUTE, WELL TRIMMED, CUT INTO 4 X 1/2 X 1/4-INCH STRIPS

1/4   CUP RICE VINEGAR

1/4   CUP SOY SAUCE

12   WOODEN SKEWERS (6-INCH)

PEANUT SAUCE

1/3   CUP CHUNKY PEANUT BUTTER

2   TABLESPOONS WATER

2   TABLESPOONS SOY SAUCE

2   TABLESPOONS RICE VINEGAR

2   CLOVES GARLIC, MINCED

2   TEASPOONS GRATED FRESH GINGERROOT

1   TEASPOON SUGAR

1/4   TEASPOON CRUSHED RED PEPPER FLAKES

1/4   TEASPOON HOT PEPPER SAUCE (OPTIONAL)

6 servings

In shallow dish, combine venison strips, vinegar and soy sauce. Cover with plastic wrap. Refrigerate 30 minutes. Soak skewers in warm water for 30 minutes. Drain. In small mixing bowl, combine sauce ingredients. Set aside.

Drain and discard marinade from meat strips. Evenly thread strips, accordion-style, on skewers. Spray rack in broiler pan with nonstick vegetable cooking spray. Arrange skewers on prepared rack. Place skewers under broiler with surface of meat 4 to 5 inches from heat. Broil for 4 to 5 minutes, or until meat is no longer pink, turning skewers over once. Serve skewers hot with peanut sauce.

Per Serving: Calories: 183 • Protein: 21 g. • Carbohydrate: 5 g. • Fat: 9 g. • Cholesterol: 63 mg. • Sodium: 614 mg. — Exchanges: 2 3/4 very lean meat, 1 3/4 fat

CURRIED WILD PIG

2   LBS. BOAR ROUND STEAK, WELL TRIMMED, CUT INTO 1-INCH PIECES

1/2   TEASPOON MEAT TENDERIZER

1/4   CUP CORNSTARCH

3   TO 4 TABLESPOONS CURRY POWDER

1   TEASPOON SALT

1/2   TEASPOON GARLIC POWDER

1/4   TO 1/2 TEASPOON CRUSHED RED PEPPER FLAKES

1   CAN (14 1/2 OZ.) CHICKEN BROTH

3   TABLESPOONS VEGETABLE OIL

2   CUPS FRESH BROCCOLI FLOWERETS

2   CUPS SLICED CARROTS (1/2-INCH SLICES)

2   CUPS SLICED CELERY (1-INCH LENGTHS)

6 to 8 servings

In medium mixing bowl, combine boar pieces and tenderizer. Stir to coat. Cover with plastic wrap. Chill 1 hour. In small mixing bowl, combine cornstarch, curry powder, salt, garlic powder and pepper flakes. Blend in broth. Set aside.

In 12-inch nonstick skillet or wok, heat oil over medium-high heat. Add broccoli, carrots and celery. Cook for 5 to 7 minutes, or until vegetables are tender-crisp, stirring frequently. With slotted spoon, remove vegetables from skillet. Set aside.

In same skillet, cook meat over medium-high heat for 3 to 5 minutes, or until browned, stirring frequently. Return vegetables to skillet. Stir to combine. Add broth mixture to skillet. Cook for 2 to 3 minutes, or until sauce is thickened and translucent, stirring constantly. Serve over hot cooked rice, if desired.

Per Serving: Calories: 257 • Protein: 27 g. • Carbohydrate: 15 g. • Fat: 10 g. • Cholesterol: N/A • Sodium: N/A — Exchanges: 1/2 starch, 3 1/4 lean meat, 1 1/2 vegetable

GARLIC VENISON STIR-FRY

SAUCE

 1 CUP CHICKEN BROTH
 2 TABLESPOONS HOISIN SAUCE
 1 TABLESPOON SZECHUAN SAUCE
 1 TABLESPOON CORNSTARCH
 1 TABLESPOON SESAME SEEDS
 1½ TEASPOONS HOT CHILI SAUCE
 1 TEASPOON SUGAR
 ½ TEASPOON GROUND GINGER

 1 TABLESPOON GARLIC-FLAVORED OIL OR SESAME OIL
 1 LB. BONELESS VENISON TOP ROUND OR SUBSTITUTE, CUT INTO 1-INCH CUBES
 2 CUPS FRESH BROCCOLI FLOWERETS
 1 MEDIUM RED PEPPER, SEEDED AND CUT INTO ½-INCH CHUNKS (1½ CUPS)
 4 OZ. FRESH SNOW PEA PODS, TRIMMED (1½ CUPS)
 1 MEDIUM RED ONION, SLICED
 1 CUP SLICED FRESH MUSHROOMS
 1 CUP BABY CARROTS
 ½ CUP BEAN SPROUTS
 4 TO 6 CLOVES GARLIC, MINCED

6 servings

In 1-cup measure, combine sauce ingredients. Set aside. Heat wok or 12-inch nonstick skillet over medium-high heat. Add oil and swirl for 30 seconds. Add venison. Cook for 3 to 5 minutes, or until meat is no longer pink, stirring constantly. Stir in remaining ingredients. Stir sauce mixture and add to wok.

Bring to a boil, stirring occasionally. Reduce heat to medium-low. Simmer for 6 to 8 minutes, or until vegetables are tender-crisp, stirring occasionally. Serve over hot cooked rice, if desired.

Per Serving: Calories: 209 • Protein: 22 g. • Carbohydrate: 18 g. • Fat: 6 g. • Cholesterol: 64 mg. • Sodium: 411 mg. — Exchanges: 2 very lean meat, 3½ vegetable, 1 fat

Tip: Stir-fry recipes cook up very quickly, so it is best to prepare all the ingredients and have them in bowls next to the stove when you are ready to begin cooking. The rice should be prepared ahead of everything, so it is ready when the stir-fry is.

CRANBERRY VENISON & RICE

2   TABLESPOONS VEGETABLE OIL, DIVIDED

2   LBS. VENISON TOP ROUND OR SUBSTITUTE, CUT INTO
    1-INCH CUBES, DIVIDED

3   MEDIUM ONIONS, EACH CUT INTO 8 WEDGES

2   CUPS BEEF OR VENISON STOCK

1   CUP DRY RED WINE

2   TABLESPOONS BALSAMIC VINEGAR

3   CLOVES GARLIC, MINCED

1   TEASPOON DRIED THYME LEAVES

1   TEASPOON SALT

1/2 TEASPOON PEPPER

1   PACKAGE (12 OZ.) FRESH CRANBERRIES

1/2 CUP PACKED BROWN SUGAR

1/2 CUP ALL-PURPOSE FLOUR

1/2 CUP WATER

8   CUPS HOT COOKED WHITE RICE
    SNIPPED FRESH PARSLEY (OPTIONAL)

8 servings

In 6-quart Dutch oven, heat 1 tablespoon oil over medium-high heat. Add half of venison cubes. Cook for 4 to 6 minutes, or until meat is no longer pink, stirring frequently. Using slotted spoon, remove meat from pot. Set aside. Drain pot. Repeat with remaining oil and venison.

Return meat to pot. Stir in onions, stock, wine, vinegar, garlic, thyme, salt and pepper. Bring to a boil over high heat. Reduce heat to low. Cover. Simmer for 1 to 1 1/2 hours, or until meat is tender, stirring occasionally.

In medium mixing bowl, combine cranberries, brown sugar, flour and water. Stir into meat mixture. Cook for 5 to 8 minutes, or until sauce is thickened, stirring frequently. Serve mixture over rice. Garnish with parsley.

Per Serving: Calories: 564 • Protein: 34 g.
• Carbohydrate: 88 g. • Fat: 7 g. • Cholesterol: 96 mg.
• Sodium: 526 mg. — Exchanges: 3 3/4 starch, 3 very lean meat, 1 vegetable, 1/4 fruit, 1 1/2 fat

Leftover Stew?

Leftover thick stew makes a great filling for split pita breads. It can also be used to make a game pie. Follow standard pie-making procedures, filling pie pastry-lined pie plate with leftover stew. Top with second pastry. Brush with beaten egg and bake at 375°F until crust is golden brown.

SLOW-COOKING OVEN VENISON STEW

This hearty stew is very easy to throw together, then put in the oven and forget about until dinnertime. It's perfect when you are entertaining a large crowd.

4	CUPS BEEF OR VENISON STOCK
1½	LBS. VENISON CHUCK ROAST OR SUBSTITUTE, CUT INTO 1-INCH CUBES
1	CAN (28 OZ.) DICED TOMATOES, UNDRAINED
1	LB. RED POTATOES, QUARTERED
1	LB. BABY CARROTS
1	PKG. (16 OZ.) FROZEN SMALL WHITE ONIONS
1	PKG. (10 OZ.) FROZEN CUT GREEN BEANS
4	STALKS CELERY, CUT INTO 1-INCH PIECES (2 CUPS)
2	TABLESPOONS QUICK-COOKING TAPIOCA
1	CLOVE GARLIC, MINCED
1	TEASPOON DRIED THYME LEAVES
½	TEASPOON PEPPER
½	TEASPOON SALT
1	BAY LEAF

8 to 10 servings

Heat oven to 325°F. In 6-quart Dutch oven or roasting pan, combine all ingredients. Cover. Bake for 4 to 4½ hours, or until vegetables are tender, stirring occasionally. Remove and discard bay leaf.

Per Serving: Calories: 196 • Protein: 19 g. • Carbohydrate: 25 g. • Fat: 2 g. • Cholesterol: 58 mg. • Sodium: 614 mg. — Exchanges: ½ starch, 1½ very lean meat, 3½ vegetable, ½ fat

VENISON RAGOUT

2	TABLESPOONS VEGETABLE OIL
2	MEDIUM ONIONS, COARSELY CHOPPED (2 CUPS)
2	LBS. VENISON CHUCK ROAST OR SUBSTITUTE, CUT INTO ½-INCH CUBES
3	CANS (12 OZ. EACH) LAGER-STYLE BEER, ROOM TEMPERATURE
4	CUPS WATER, BEEF STOCK OR VENISON STOCK
2	TABLESPOONS SWEET HUNGARIAN PAPRIKA
1	CLOVE GARLIC, MINCED
1	TEASPOON CARAWAY SEED
1	TEASPOON SALT
½	TEASPOON PEPPER
3	MEDIUM TOMATOES, PEELED, SEEDED AND COARSELY CHOPPED (3 CUPS)
1	LB. RUSSET POTATOES, PEELED AND CUT INTO ¼-INCH CUBES (2½ CUPS)
2	TEASPOONS HOT PEPPER SAUCE
⅓	CUP SNIPPED FRESH PARSLEY

8 servings

In 8-quart stockpot, heat oil over medium-high heat. Add onions. Cook for 4 to 6 minutes, or until tender, stirring occasionally. Add venison. Cook for 3 to 5 minutes, or until meat is no longer pink, stirring occasionally.

Stir in beer, water, paprika, garlic, caraway seed, salt and pepper. Bring to a boil over medium-high heat, stirring occasionally. Reduce heat to medium. Simmer for 1 hour. Stir in tomatoes, potatoes and pepper sauce. Simmer for 20 to 25 minutes, or until potatoes are tender, stirring occasionally. Stir in parsley just before serving.

Per Serving: Calories: 266 • Protein: 29 g. • Carbohydrate: 22 g. • Fat: 7 g. • Cholesterol: 96 mg. • Sodium: 385 mg. — Exchanges: ½ starch, 3 very lean meat, 1½ vegetable, 1¼ fat

BLACK BEAN & RICE CASSEROLE

1 PKG. (6 OZ.) SPANISH RICE MIX

2 TEASPOONS OLIVE OIL

1 LB. BONELESS VENISON TOP ROUND OR
   SUBSTITUTE, CHOPPED (PAGE 114)

1 CAN (15 OZ.) BLACK BEANS, RINSED AND DRAINED

1 CAN (14½ OZ.) DICED TOMATOES WITH CHILIES,
   UNDRAINED

½ CUP SLICED GREEN ONIONS

2 TEASPOONS CHILI POWDER

1 TEASPOON GROUND CUMIN

⅛ TEASPOON CAYENNE (OPTIONAL)

½ CUP (2 OZ.) SHREDDED COLBY-JACK CHEESE (OPTIONAL)

   SOUR CREAM FOR GARNISH (OPTIONAL)

6 servings

Heat oven to 375°F. Prepare rice as directed on package. Meanwhile, in 12-inch nonstick skillet, heat oil over medium heat. Add venison. Cook for 3 to 5 minutes, or until meat is no longer pink, stirring occasionally. Remove from heat. Drain.

Stir in remaining ingredients, except cheese and sour cream. Mix well. Spoon mixture into 2-quart casserole. Sprinkle evenly with cheese. Bake, uncovered, for 25 to 30 minutes, or until casserole is hot and bubbly around edges. Garnish with sour cream.

Tip: Casserole can also be served as a filling for flour tortillas.

Per Serving: Calories: 260 • Protein: 23 g.
• Carbohydrate: 32 g. • Fat: 4 g. • Cholesterol: 64 mg.
• Sodium: 812 mg. — Exchanges: 1½ starch, 2 very lean meat, 2 vegetable, ¾ fat

MEXICAN BURGERS

1	LB. LEAN GROUND VENISON, CRUMBLED	4	HAMBURGER BUNS, SPLIT
1	PKG. (1 1/4 OZ.) TACO SEASONING MIX	4	SLICES TOMATO
2	TABLESPOONS COLD WATER	4	LETTUCE LEAVES
8	SLICES (1 OZ. EACH) CHEDDAR OR AMERICAN CHEESE	1/4	CUP SALSA
		1/4	CUP SOUR CREAM

4 servings

In medium mixing bowl, combine venison, seasoning mix and water. Shape mixture into four 1/2-inch-thick patties.

Heat 12-inch nonstick skillet over medium heat. Spray skillet with nonstick vegetable cooking spray. Add patties. Cook for 6 to 8 minutes, or until desired doneness, turning patties over once. Remove from heat. Top each patty with 2 slices cheese.

Place patties in buns with tomato slices, lettuce leaves, salsa and sour cream.

Per Serving: Calories: 659 • Protein: 40 g. • Carbohydrate: 30 g. • Fat: 40 g. • Cholesterol: 160 mg. • Sodium: 1550 mg. — Exchanges: 1 1/2 starch, 3 3/4 high-fat meat, 1 1/2 vegetable, 3/4 fat

RANCH BURGERS

1/3	CUP SOUR CREAM
1	TABLESPOON PLUS 1 TEASPOON RANCH DRESSING MIX, DIVIDED
1	LB. LEAN GROUND VENISON, CRUMBLED
1/4	CUP SLICED GREEN ONIONS
2	TABLESPOONS COLD WATER
1/8	TEASPOON PEPPER
4	HAMBURGER BUNS, SPLIT

4 servings

In small mixing bowl, combine sour cream and 1 teaspoon dressing mix. Cover with plastic wrap. Chill.

In medium mixing bowl, combine venison, green onions, water, pepper and remaining 1 tablespoon dressing mix. Mix well. Shape mixture into four 1/2-inch-thick patties.

Heat 12-inch nonstick skillet over medium heat. Spray skillet with nonstick vegetable cooking spray. Add patties. Cook for 6 to 8 minutes, or until meat is desired doneness, turning patties over once. Place patties in buns and top evenly with sour cream mixture.

Per Serving: Calories: 412 • Protein: 26 g. • Carbohydrate: 25 g. • Fat: 22 g. • Cholesterol: 102 mg. • Sodium: 560 mg. — Exchanges: 1 1/2 starch, 3 medium-fat meat, 1 1/2 fat

To broil patties, spray rack in broiler pan with non-stick vegetable cooking spray. Place patties on rack. Broil patties 4 to 5 inches from heat for 8 to 10 minutes, or until meat is desired doneness, turning patties over once.

To grill patties, place them on cooking grid over medium-direct heat. Grill for 8 to 10 minutes, or until meat is desired doneness, turning patties over once.

ITALIAN MEATBALL SOUP

<u>MEATBALLS</u>

1 1/2   LBS. LEAN GROUND VENISON, CRUMBLED
2/3   CUP SEASONED DRY BREAD CRUMBS
1/3   CUP FINELY CHOPPED ONION
1/4   CUP GRATED PARMESAN CHEESE
1   EGG, SLIGHTLY BEATEN
1/4   TEASPOON SALT
1/4   TEASPOON PEPPER

1   JAR (28 OZ.) PREPARED MARINARA SAUCE
3   CUPS WATER
1   CAN (14 1/2 OZ.) DICED TOMATOES, UNDRAINED
8   OZ. FRESH MUSHROOMS, QUARTERED
1   CUP FROZEN CUT GREEN BEANS
3   CLOVES GARLIC, MINCED
1   TEASPOON DRIED ITALIAN SEASONING
8   OZ. UNCOOKED BOWTIE PASTA

8 to 10 servings

In large mixing bowl, combine all meatball ingredients. Form meatballs into 1-inch balls (about 45 meatballs). Heat 6-quart Dutch oven or stockpot over medium heat. Add meatballs. Cook for 5 to 7 minutes, or until browned, turning meatballs occasionally. (Brown meatballs in batches, if necessary.) Drain.

Stir in remaining ingredients, except pasta. Bring to a boil over high heat. Cover. Reduce heat to medium-low. Simmer for 10 minutes. Stir in pasta. Re-cover. Simmer for 15 to 20 minutes, or until pasta is tender. Garnish individual servings with shredded fresh Parmesan cheese, if desired.

Per Serving: Calories: 364 • Protein: 21 g. • Carbohydrate: 35 g. • Fat: 16 g. • Cholesterol: 81 mg. • Sodium: 908 mg. — Exchanges: 1 1/2 starch, 1 3/4 medium-fat meat, 2 1/2 vegetable, 1 1/2 fat

Herbed Meatloaf

HERBED MEATLOAF

MEATLOAF

 1 LB. LEAN GROUND VENISON, CRUMBLED
1/2 LB. GROUND PORK
3/4 CUP DRY SEASONED STUFFING MIX
 1 SMALL ONION, FINELY CHOPPED (1/2 CUP)
1/3 CUP CHOPPED CELERY
 1 EGG, BEATEN
 2 CLOVES GARLIC, MINCED
3/4 TEASPOON SALT
1/2 TEASPOON RUBBED SAGE
1/2 TEASPOON DRIED THYME LEAVES
1/4 TEASPOON PEPPER

SAUCE

 3 TABLESPOONS FINELY CHOPPED SHALLOTS
 1 TABLESPOON BUTTER OR MARGARINE
 1 TABLESPOON ALL-PURPOSE FLOUR
 1 CUP BEEF BROTH
1/4 TEASPOON DRIED THYME LEAVES
1/8 TEASPOON PEPPER

6 to 8 servings

Heat oven to 375°F. Spray 9 × 5-inch loaf pan
with nonstick vegetable cooking spray. In large
mixing bowl, combine meatloaf ingredients. Press
mixture into prepared pan.

Bake for 50 to 60 minutes, or until meat is firm
and internal temperature reads 150°F. Let stand
for 5 minutes before slicing.

Meanwhile, combine shallots and butter in 1-quart
saucepan. Cook over medium heat for 2 to 3 minutes, or until shallots are tender, stirring frequently.
Stir in flour. Gradually blend in broth, thyme and
pepper. Cook for 2 to 3 minutes, or until gravy
thickens and bubbles, stirring constantly. Serve
meatloaf with gravy.

Per Serving: Calories: 286 • Protein: 18 g.
• Carbohydrate: 8 g. • Fat: 20 g. • Cholesterol: 102 mg.
• Sodium: 471 mg. — Exchanges: 1/2 starch, 2 1/4
medium-fat meat, 1 3/4 fat

ITALIAN MEATLOAF

1 1/2 LBS. LEAN GROUND VENISON, CRUMBLED
1 1/2 CUPS ONION AND GARLIC-FLAVORED CROUTONS
 1 CAN (14 1/2 OZ.) DICED TOMATOES WITH ITALIAN
    SEASONINGS, DRAINED
 1 EGG, BEATEN
 1 TABLESPOON DRIED PARSLEY FLAKES
 2 TEASPOONS ITALIAN SEASONING
1/4 TEASPOON CRUSHED RED PEPPER FLAKES (OPTIONAL)
1/4 TEASPOON FRESHLY GROUND PEPPER

6 to 8 servings

Heat oven to 375°F. In large mixing bowl, combine all ingredients. Shape mixture into an oval.
Place in 9 × 5-inch loaf pan.

Bake for 1 hour to 1 hour 15 minutes, or until
meat is firm and internal temperature reads
150°F. Let stand for 5 minutes before slicing.

Per Serving: Calories: 279 • Protein: 18 g.
• Carbohydrate: 7 g. • Fat: 19 g. • Cholesterol: 103 mg.
• Sodium: 234 mg. — Exchanges: 1/4 starch, 2 1/4
medium-fat meat, 1/2 vegetable, 1 3/4 fat

VENISON BURRITOS

2	LBS. LEAN GROUND VENISON OR SUBSTITUTE, CRUMBLED
1	CAN (16 OZ.) REFRIED BEANS
1	CAN (15 OZ.) TOMATO SAUCE
1	CUP CHOPPED ONIONS
1	CUP SHREDDED CHEDDAR CHEESE
1	CAN (4 OZ.) CHOPPED GREEN CHILIES, DRAINED
1 1/2	TEASPOONS CHILI POWDER
1/2	TEASPOON GROUND CUMIN
1/2	TEASPOON PEPPER
1/4	TEASPOON GROUND CLOVES
16	FLOUR TORTILLAS (10-INCH)

TOPPINGS

SHREDDED LETTUCE

SHREDDED CHEDDAR CHEESE

SALSA

SOUR CREAM

16 servings

Heat oven to 350°F. In 12-inch nonstick skillet, cook ground venison over medium heat for 10 to 12 minutes, or until meat is no longer pink, stirring frequently. Drain. Stir in remaining ingredients, except tortillas and toppings. Reduce heat to medium-low. Cook for 30 to 40 minutes, or until flavors are blended, stirring occasionally.

Warm tortillas as directed on package. Place about 1/2 cup meat mixture in the center of each tortilla. Fold bottom half of tortilla over filling. Fold sides over folded half of tortilla. Fold top half of tortilla over filling. Place burritos seam-side-down on baking sheet. Bake for 8 to 10 minutes, or until hot. Serve with desired toppings.

Per Serving: Calories: 400 • Protein: 20 g. • Carbohydrate: 39 g. • Fat: 18 g. • Cholesterol: 58 mg. • Sodium: 658 mg. — Exchanges: 2 1/2 starch, 1 1/2 lean meat, 1/4 vegetable, 2 1/2 fat

BARBECUED MEATBALLS

MEATBALLS

1	LB. LEAN GROUND VENISON, CRUMBLED
1/2	CUP INSTANT WHITE RICE
1/4	CUP FINELY CHOPPED ONION
1/2	TEASPOON SALT
1/4	TEASPOON FRESHLY GROUND PEPPER
1/8	TEASPOON CAYENNE

SAUCE

1	BOTTLE (12 OZ.) CHILI SAUCE
2/3	CUP GRAPE JELLY
1/4	TEASPOON GARLIC POWDER
1/4	TEASPOON CAYENNE

4 servings

Heat oven to 400°F. In large mixing bowl, combine all meatball ingredients. Shape mixture into 16 meatballs, about 1 1/2 inches in diameter. Arrange meatballs in 8-inch square baking dish. Bake for 15 minutes. Drain. Meanwhile, combine all sauce ingredients in 1-quart saucepan. Bring to a boil over medium-high heat. Cook for 3 to 4 minutes, or until jelly is melted, stirring constantly.

Pour heated sauce over drained meatballs. Bake for 10 to 12 minutes, or until sauce is hot and bubbly. Serve meatballs over mashed potatoes or hot cooked noodles, if desired. This recipe can also be made into an appetizer using smaller meatballs.

Per Serving: Calories: 542 • Protein: 25 g. • Carbohydrate: 68 g. • Fat: 20 g. • Cholesterol: 98 mg. • Sodium: 1478 mg. — Exchanges: 3/4 starch, 3 medium-fat meat, 2 vegetable, 3/4 fat

Barbecued Meatballs

Microwave Venison Chip Dip

MICROWAVE VENISON CHIP DIP

1/2 LB. LEAN GROUND VENISON, CRUMBLED

1- LB. PASTEURIZED PROCESS CHEESE LOAF WITH JALAPEÑO PEPPERS, CUT INTO 1-INCH CUBES

1 CUP CHOPPED SEEDED TOMATO, DIVIDED

1 CAN (4 OZ.) CHOPPED GREEN CHILIES, DRAINED

1/4 CUP SLICED BLACK OLIVES

1/4 TEASPOON GROUND CUMIN

1/4 TEASPOON GARLIC POWDER

1/4 CUP SLICED GREEN ONIONS

3 cups, 12 servings

In 2-quart casserole, microwave ground venison on high for 2 to 4 minutes, or until meat is no longer pink, stirring once to break apart. Drain. Add cheese, 3/4 cup tomato and the remaining ingredients, except green onions. Mix well.

Microwave on high for 4 to 6 minutes, or until mixture is hot and cheese is melted, stirring once. Garnish dip with remaining 1/4 cup chopped tomato and the sliced green onions. Serve with tortilla chips or use as a potato topper, if desired.

Per Serving: Calories: 166 • Protein: 10 g. • Carbohydrate: 6 g. • Fat: 12 g. • Cholesterol: 44 mg. • Sodium: 679 mg. — Exchanges: 1¼ medium-fat meat, 1 vegetable, 1¼ fat

WILD RICE & FRUIT-STUFFED SQUASH

2 MEDIUM ACORN SQUASH (1½ LBS. EACH)

3 TABLESPOONS BUTTER OR MARGARINE, MELTED
  SALT AND PEPPER TO TASTE
  HOT WATER

3/4 LB. UNCOOKED FRESH VENISON SAUSAGE, CRUMBLED

1 CUP COOKED WILD RICE

1/2 CUP DRIED CRANBERRIES

1/4 CUP SLICED GREEN ONIONS

1/4 CUP GOLDEN RAISINS

1/2 TEASPOON DRIED ROSEMARY LEAVES

1/2 TEASPOON SALT

1/8 TEASPOON WHITE PEPPER

4 servings

Heat oven to 350°F. Cut squash in half lengthwise. Scoop out and discard seeds. Place squash halves cut side up in 13 × 9-inch baking dish. Brush evenly with melted butter. Sprinkle with salt and pepper to taste. Pour hot water in bottom of baking dish to 1/4-inch depth. Cover tightly with foil. Bake for 45 to 50 minutes, or until squash is tender.

Meanwhile, in 12-inch nonstick skillet, cook sausage over medium heat for 4 to 6 minutes, or until meat is no longer pink, stirring occasionally. Drain. Stir in remaining ingredients. Cook for 3 to 4 minutes, or until filling is heated through, stirring frequently. Spoon filling evenly into squash halves. Serve immediately.

Per Serving: Calories: 474 • Protein: 20 g. • Carbohydrate: 55 g. • Fat: 21 g. • Cholesterol: 94 mg. • Sodium: 408 mg. — Exchanges: 2¼ starch, 2¼ medium-fat meat, 1¼ fruit, 2 fat

MOOSE MEATBALLS WITH CRANBERRY BARBECUE SAUCE

MEATBALLS
2   LBS. LEAN GROUND MOOSE OR VENISON, CRUMBLED
1   CUP CORNFLAKE CRUMBS
2   EGGS
1/4 CUP SNIPPED FRESH PARSLEY
2   TABLESPOONS SOY SAUCE
1/2 TEASPOON GARLIC POWDER
1/2 TEASPOON PEPPER

SAUCE
1   CAN (16 OZ.) WHOLE-BERRY CRANBERRY SAUCE
1   BOTTLE (12 OZ.) CHILI SAUCE
1/3 CUP KETCHUP
2   TABLESPOONS PACKED BROWN SUGAR
1   TABLESPOON LEMON JUICE
2   TEASPOONS INSTANT MINCED ONION

6 to 8 servings

Heat oven to 350°F. In large mixing bowl, combine meatball ingredients. Shape mixture into 42 meatballs, about $1^{1}/2$ inches in diameter. Arrange meatballs in a single layer in 13×9-inch baking dish. Bake for 30 to 35 minutes, or until meatballs are firm and no longer pink, turning meatballs over once. Drain.

In medium mixing bowl, combine sauce ingredients. Pour over meatballs. Bake for 30 to 35 minutes, or until sauce is hot and bubbly and flavors are blended. Serve with hot cooked rice, if desired.

Per Serving: Calories: 526 • Protein: 25 g. • Carbohydrate: 52 g. • Fat: 24 g. • Cholesterol: 131 mg. • Sodium: 1213 mg. — Exchanges: $3/4$ starch, $2^{3}/4$ lean meat, $1^{1}/2$ vegetable, $2^{1}/4$ fruit, 3 fat

Substituting Venison for Ground Beef

＊☞ ☜＊

Ground venison can be easily substituted for ground beef in your favorite recipes; the flavor will be fuller, but the basic recipe will work fine. Most butchers grind venison with beef fat so the mixture approximates regular hamburger; however, if your ground venison is very lean, you may need to add additional oil, butter or other fat.

CHEDDAR-FILLED VENISON ROLL

$1^{1}/2$ LBS. LEAN GROUND VENISON, CRUMBLED
1/2 CUP UNSEASONED DRY BREAD CRUMBS
1   EGG, BEATEN
1/4 CUP BARBECUE SAUCE, DIVIDED
1/2 TEASPOON SALT
1/4 TEASPOON PEPPER
1   CUP SHREDDED CHEDDAR CHEESE
1/4 CUP SLICED GREEN ONIONS

8 servings

Heat oven to 350°F. Lightly grease 12×8-inch baking dish. Set aside. In medium mixing bowl, combine ground venison, bread crumbs, egg, 2 tablespoons barbecue sauce, the salt and pepper. On sheet of wax paper, shape meat mixture into 14×8-inch rectangle. Sprinkle cheese and onions evenly over meat mixture to within 1 inch of edges. Starting with the short side, roll up tightly, peeling back wax paper while rolling. Discard wax paper. Pinch ends and seam of venison roll to seal.

Place venison roll seam side down in prepared baking dish. Bake for 1 to $1^{1}/2$ hours, or until meat is firm and no longer pink. Spoon remaining barbecue sauce evenly over meatloaf. Bake for 10 minutes. Let stand for 10 minutes before slicing. Serve slices in lettuce-lined hamburger buns, if desired.

Per Serving: Calories: 322 • Protein: 21 g. • Carbohydrate: 6 g. • Fat: 23 g. • Cholesterol: 117 mg. • Sodium: 390 mg. — Exchanges: $1/3$ starch, 3 medium-fat meat, $1^{1}/2$ fat

VENISON & BEANS

6	SLICES BACON, CHOPPED
1½	POUNDS LEAN GROUND VENISON
1	MEDIUM ONION, CHOPPED
1	CAN (16 OZ.) PORK AND BEANS
1	CAN (16 OZ.) KIDNEY BEANS, DRAINED
1	CAN (16 OZ.) BUTTER BEANS OR GREAT NORTHERN BEANS, DRAINED
⅓	CUP PACKED BROWN SUGAR
1	CUP KETCHUP
2	TABLESPOONS VINEGAR
1	TABLESPOON WORCESTERSHIRE SAUCE
½	TEASPOON SALT
¼	TEASPOON PREPARED MUSTARD

8 to 10 servings

Heat oven to 350°F. In Dutch oven, cook bacon over medium-low heat, stirring occasionally, until crisp. Remove with slotted spoon; set aside. Drain all but 1 tablespoon bacon fat from Dutch oven. Add meat and onion. Cook over medium heat, stirring occasionally, until meat is no longer pink and onion is tender. Add reserved bacon and remaining ingredients to Dutch oven; mix well. Cover and bake until bubbly around edges, about 45 minutes.

Per serving: Calories: 376 • Protein: 21 g. • Carbohydrate: 36 g. • Fat: 18 g. • Cholesterol: 70 mg. • Sodium: 880 mg. — Exchanges: 2 starch, 2½ very lean meat, 3 fat

CABBAGE ROLLS WITH RAISIN SAUCE

12	CUPS WATER
6	LARGE WHITE CABBAGE LEAVES, THICKEST PART OF STEM REMOVED
1	LB. LEAN GROUND VENISON, CRUMBLED
1	SMALL ONION, CHOPPED (½ CUP)
1	CUP COOKED WILD OR BROWN RICE
1	CUP FRESH WHITE BREAD CRUMBS*
½	CUP CHOPPED FRESH MUSHROOMS
2	EGGS, BEATEN
¼	CUP CHOPPED TART APPLE
1	TEASPOON SALT
½	TEASPOON PEPPER

SAUCE

1	CAN (10½ OZ.) BEEF CONSOMMÉ
1	CAN (8 OZ.) TOMATO SAUCE
¾	CUP GOLDEN RAISINS
1	TABLESPOON LEMON JUICE
2	TEASPOONS PAPRIKA
1	TEASPOON SUGAR
½	TEASPOON WHITE PEPPER

6 servings

Heat oven to 375°F. In 4-quart saucepan, bring water to a boil over high heat. Immerse cabbage leaves in water for 1 minute, or until color brightens. Remove leaves from water; drain on paper towels.

In 10-inch skillet, combine venison and onion. Cook over medium heat for 6 to 8 minutes, or until meat is no longer pink, stirring occasionally. Drain. Stir in rice, bread crumbs, mushrooms, eggs, apple, salt and pepper. Mix well.

Spoon approximately ⅔ cup venison mixture onto center of each cabbage leaf. Roll leaves up tightly, folding in sides. Place rolls seam side down in 8-inch square baking dish. Set aside.

In 4-cup measure, combine sauce ingredients. Pour sauce over rolls. Cover with foil. Bake for 30 to 40 minutes, or until sauce is bubbly and centers of rolls are hot.

To make fresh bread crumbs, remove crust from white bread. Process in blender or food processor until finely ground (1 slice = ½ cup crumbs).

Per Serving: Calories: 332 • Protein: 22 g. • Carbohydrate: 34 g. • Fat: 13 g. • Cholesterol: 134 mg. • Sodium: 1034 mg. — Exchanges: ¾ starch, 2 medium-fat meat, 1½ vegetable, 1 fruit, ½ fat

STUFFED JUMBO SHELLS

6   OZ. UNCOOKED JUMBO PASTA SHELLS (18 SHELLS)
1   LB. LEAN GROUND VENISON, CRUMBLED
1   CUP CHOPPED FRESH MUSHROOMS
1   SMALL ONION, CHOPPED (1/2 CUP)
2   CLOVES GARLIC, MINCED
1   CUP SHREDDED PART-SKIM MOZZARELLA CHEESE
1/2 CUP DRY SEASONED BREAD CRUMBS
1   EGG, SLIGHTLY BEATEN
1   TEASPOON ITALIAN SEASONING
1/4 TEASPOON GROUND NUTMEG
1   JAR (30 OZ.) PREPARED PASTA SAUCE (3 CUPS)
1/2 CUP SHREDDED FRESH PARMESAN CHEESE

4 to 6 servings

Heat oven to 350°F. Prepare shells as directed. Drain. Set aside.

Meanwhile, in 12-inch nonstick skillet, cook venison, mushrooms, onion and garlic over medium heat for 6 to 8 minutes, or until meat is no longer pink, stirring occasionally. Remove from heat. Drain. Stir in mozzarella, bread crumbs, egg, Italian seasoning and nutmeg.

Spoon half of pasta sauce into bottom of 12 × 8-inch baking dish. Stuff each shell with 2 tablespoons meat mixture. Arrange shells in dish. Pour remaining sauce over shells. Sprinkle shells evenly with Parmesan cheese. Cover with foil. Bake for 30 to 35 minutes, or until hot and bubbly.

Per Serving: Calories: 561 • Protein: 31 g. • Carbohydrate: 54 g. • Fat: 24 g. • Cholesterol: 115 mg. • Sodium: 1256 mg. — Exchanges: 1 1/2 starch, 2 medium-fat meat, 6 vegetable, 3 fat

Stuffed Jumbo Shells

TAMALE PIE

1   LB. LEAN GROUND VENISON, CRUMBLED
1   MEDIUM ONION, CHOPPED (1 CUP)
1   MEDIUM GREEN PEPPER, SEEDED AND CHOPPED (1 CUP)
1   CLOVE GARLIC, MINCED
1 1/2 CUPS FROZEN CORN KERNELS, DEFROSTED
1   CAN (15 OZ.) DICED TOMATOES WITH CHILIES, DRAINED
2   TABLESPOONS CHILI POWDER
1/2 TEASPOON SALT
1/4 TEASPOON PEPPER
1   CUP SHREDDED CHEDDAR CHEESE

BATTER
2   CUPS WATER
3/4 CUP YELLOW CORNMEAL
3   TABLESPOONS MARGARINE OR BUTTER, MELTED

8 servings

Heat oven to 350°F. In 12-inch skillet, cook venison, onion, green pepper and garlic over medium heat for 6 to 8 minutes, or until meat is no longer pink, stirring occasionally. Drain.

Stir in corn, tomatoes, chili powder, salt and pepper. Spoon mixture into 13 × 9-inch baking dish that has been sprayed with nonstick vegetable cooking spray. Top evenly with cheese. Set aside.

In medium mixing bowl, combine batter ingredients. Pour batter evenly over meat mixture. Bake for 40 to 50 minutes, or until crust is golden brown.

Per Serving: Calories: 313 • Protein: 17 g. • Carbohydrate: 22 g. • Fat: 18 g. • Cholesterol: 62 mg. • Sodium: 533 mg. — Exchanges: 1 starch, 2 medium-fat meat, 1 1/2 vegetable, 1 1/2 fat

Got Chili?

Leftover chili (or the meat mixture in Warm Venison-Black Bean Salad, below) makes an excellent and quick filling for soft-shelled burritos. You can also use it to make quick nachos, "taco salad" or any other recipe that calls for Mexican-style seasoned meat.

WARM VENISON-BLACK BEAN SALAD

1	LB. LEAN GROUND VENISON, CRUMBLED
1/2	CUP COARSELY CHOPPED RED ONION
2	JALAPEÑO PEPPERS, SLICED AND SEEDED
2	CLOVES GARLIC, MINCED
2	CANS (15 OZ. EACH) BLACK BEANS, RINSED AND DRAINED
2	MEDIUM TOMATOES, SEEDED AND CHOPPED
2	TABLESPOONS FRESH LIME JUICE
1	TEASPOON GROUND CUMIN
1/2	TEASPOON DRIED OREGANO LEAVES
1/2	TEASPOON SALT
1/4	TEASPOON PEPPER
1/8	TO 1/4 TEASPOON CAYENNE
1/3	CUP SNIPPED FRESH CILANTRO
6	CORN TORTILLAS (6-INCH)
1	AVOCADO, PEELED AND SLICED

6 servings

In 12-inch nonstick skillet, cook venison, onion, jalapeños and garlic over medium heat for 6 to 8 minutes, or until meat is no longer pink, stirring occasionally. Drain. Stir in beans, tomatoes, lime juice, cumin, oregano, salt, pepper and cayenne. Cook for 2 to 3 minutes, or until heated through, stirring occasionally. Stir in cilantro. Warm tortillas as directed on package. Spoon salad over tortillas in individual servings. Garnish salad with avocado slices.

Per Serving: Calories: 365 • Protein: 22 g. • Carbohydrate: 32 g. • Fat: 17 g. • Cholesterol: 63 mg. • Sodium: 493 mg. — Exchanges: 1 3/4 starch, 2 medium-fat meat, 1 vegetable, 1 1/2 fat

CHUNKY-STYLE VENISON CHILI

1	TABLESPOON VEGETABLE OIL
1/2	LB. LEAN GROUND VENISON, CRUMBLED
1	LB. VENISON STEW MEAT, WELL TRIMMED, CUT INTO 3/4-INCH CUBES
2	CANS (16 OZ. EACH) DARK RED KIDNEY BEANS, UNDRAINED
1	CAN (28 OZ.) WHOLE TOMATOES, UNDRAINED AND CUT UP
1 1/2	CUPS CHOPPED GREEN PEPPER
1	CUP CHOPPED ONION
1	CAN (6 OZ.) TOMATO PASTE
5	CLOVES GARLIC, MINCED
1	TABLESPOON CHILI POWDER
1	TEASPOON SUGAR
1/2	TEASPOON PEPPER
1/2	TEASPOON SALT

6 to 8 servings

In 6-quart Dutch oven or stockpot, heat oil over medium-high heat. Add ground venison and venison cubes. Cook for 8 to 10 minutes, or until meat is no longer pink, stirring occasionally. Drain.

Stir in remaining ingredients. Bring to a boil. Reduce heat to low. Simmer, partially covered, for 4 to 5 hours, or until meat is very tender, stirring occasionally. Garnish each serving with sour cream, shredded cheese and sliced green onions, if desired.

Per Serving: Calories: 307 • Protein: 27 g. • Carbohydrate: 30 g. • Fat: 10 g. • Cholesterol: 74 mg. • Sodium: 911 mg. — Exchanges: 1 1/4 starch, 2 1/2 lean meat, 2 vegetable, 1/2 fat

HERBED VENISON EMPANADAS

FILLING

½ LB. LEAN GROUND VENISON, CRUMBLED
1 MEDIUM ONION, CHOPPED (1 CUP)
1 TABLESPOON PAPRIKA
2 TEASPOONS DRIED OREGANO LEAVES
1 TEASPOON SUGAR
½ TEASPOON SALT
½ TEASPOON BLACK PEPPER
½ CUP CRUMBLED FETA CHEESE

1 PACKAGE (11 OZ.) PIE CRUST MIX
1 EGG, LIGHTLY BEATEN

20 empanadas

In 12-inch nonstick skillet, cook venison and onion over medium-high heat for 10 to 12 minutes, or until venison is no longer pink and onion is tender, stirring occasionally. Drain. Stir in remaining filling ingredients, except feta. Transfer filling to large mixing bowl. Cover and chill. Stir in feta when filling is cool.

Heat oven to 375°F. Prepare pie crust as directed on package. Pinch off enough dough to form 1- to 1½-inch ball. On lightly floured surface, roll ball into 4-inch circle. Place heaping tablespoon filling in center of circle. Brush edges of circle lightly with water. Fold circle in half over filling, pressing edges with tines of fork to seal. Place empanada on parchment-lined baking sheet. Repeat with remaining dough and filling.

Brush empanadas with beaten egg. Bake for 30 to 35 minutes, or until empanadas are golden brown. Serve hot.

Tip: You may substitute your favorite two-crust pie crust recipe for the packaged mix.

Per Piece: Calories: 130 • Protein: 4 g. • Carbohydrate: 9 g. • Fat: 9 g. • Cholesterol: 23 mg. • Sodium: 221 mg. — Exchanges: ½ starch, ½ medium-fat meat, 1 ¼ fat

CLASSIC MUSHROOM-WILD RICE CASSEROLE

2 TABLESPOONS VEGETABLE OIL

16 OZ. FRESH MUSHROOMS, SLICED (6 CUPS)

1 MEDIUM ONION, CHOPPED (1 CUP)

½ CUP SLICED CELERY

4 CLOVES GARLIC, MINCED

1 LB. LEAN GROUND VENISON, CRUMBLED

4 CUPS COOKED WILD RICE

1 CARTON (16 OZ.) LOW-FAT SOUR CREAM

3 TABLESPOONS ALL-PURPOSE FLOUR

1 TEASPOON DRIED THYME LEAVES

1 TEASPOON SALT

½ TEASPOON PEPPER

¼ TEASPOON CAYENNE

½ CUP SLICED ROASTED RED PEPPER*

⅓ CUP SLIVERED ALMONDS

6 servings

Heat oven to 400°F. Spray 3-quart casserole with nonstick vegetable cooking spray. Set aside. In 12-inch nonstick skillet, heat oil over medium-high heat. Add mushrooms, onion, celery and garlic. Cook for 6 to 8 minutes, or until vegetables are tender, stirring frequently. Spoon vegetables into casserole. Set aside.

In same skillet, cook venison over medium-high heat for 5 to 7 minutes, or until meat is no longer pink, stirring frequently. Drain. Add meat and rice to casserole. In small bowl, combine sour cream, flour, thyme, salt, pepper and cayenne. Add sour cream mixture and red pepper to casserole. Stir to combine.

Sprinkle almonds evenly over top of meat mixture. Bake for 40 to 45 minutes, or until casserole is hot and bubbly.

Use roasted red peppers from a jar, or see sidebar above.

Per Serving: Calories: 490 • Protein: 25 g.
• Carbohydrate: 45 g. • Fat: 25 g. • Cholesterol: 87 mg.
• Sodium: 513 mg. — Exchanges: 2 starch, 2 medium-fat meat, 1½ vegetable, 3 fat

Roasting Peppers

To roast a pepper, place it under broiler with surface of pepper 3 to 4 inches from heat. Turn pepper frequently until skin is blackened and blistered. Seal pepper in plastic or paper bag and let steam for 10 minutes to loosen skin. Peel pepper; proceed as directed.

SNAPPY SLOPPY JOES

2 LBS. LEAN GROUND VENISON, CRUMBLED

8 OZ. FRESH MUSHROOMS, SLICED (3 CUPS)

1 MEDIUM ONION, CHOPPED (1 CUP)

1 JAR (12 OZ.) CHILI SAUCE

1 CUP KETCHUP

½ CUP WATER

1 TO 2 TABLESPOONS WORCESTERSHIRE SAUCE

1 TABLESPOON FRESH HORSERADISH

1 TEASPOON RED PEPPER SAUCE

½ TEASPOON GARLIC POWDER

½ TEASPOON CELERY SEED

½ TEASPOON SALT

8 TO 10 HAMBURGER BUNS, SPLIT

8 to 10 servings

In 6-quart Dutch oven or stockpot, combine venison, mushrooms and onion. Cook over medium heat for 12 to 15 minutes, or until meat is no longer pink, stirring occasionally. Drain.

Stir in remaining ingredients, except buns. Bring to a simmer. Simmer for 20 to 25 minutes, or until flavors are blended and mixture is desired thickness, stirring occasionally. Serve mixture on buns. Serve with dill pickle and tomato slices, if desired.

Per Serving: Calories: 436 • Protein: 23 g.
• Carbohydrate: 40 g. • Fat: 21 g. • Cholesterol: 81 mg.
• Sodium: 1169 mg. — Exchanges: 2 starch, 2 medium-fat meat, 2 vegetable, 2 fat

VENISON SAUSAGE JAMBALAYA

1 1/2 LBS. SPICY BRATWURST-STYLE VENISON SAUSAGES, SLICED
3 STALKS CELERY, CUT INTO 1/2-INCH SLICES (1 1/2 CUPS)
1 MEDIUM ONION, CHOPPED (1 CUP)
1 MEDIUM GREEN PEPPER, SEEDED AND CHOPPED (1 CUP)
2 CLOVES GARLIC, MINCED
1 TABLESPOON CAJUN SEASONING
1 BAY LEAF
1 CAN (28 OZ.) DICED TOMATOES, UNDRAINED
2 CUPS WATER
1 CAN (15 OZ.) TOMATO SAUCE
2 CUPS UNCOOKED CONVERTED WHITE RICE
1/2 CUP SLICED GREEN ONIONS

8 servings

In 6-quart Dutch oven or stockpot, cook sausages, celery, chopped onion, green pepper and garlic over medium heat for 10 to 12 minutes, or until meat is browned and vegetables are tender, stirring occasionally. Drain. Return to heat.

Stir in Cajun seasoning and bay leaf. Cook for 2 minutes, stirring constantly. Blend in tomatoes, water and tomato sauce. Bring to a boil over medium-high heat. Stir in rice and green onions. Return to a boil. Cover. Reduce heat to low. Simmer for 15 to 20 minutes, or until rice is nearly tender. Remove from heat. Let stand, covered, for 5 minutes. Remove and discard bay leaf.

Per Serving: Calories: 454 • Protein: 21 g. • Carbohydrate: 51 g. • Fat: 18 g. • Cholesterol: 69 mg. • Sodium: 1141 mg. — Exchanges: 2 3/4 starch, 2 medium-fat meat, 2 vegetable, 1 1/4 fat

Mock Chicken Fried Steak

MOCK CHICKEN FRIED STEAK

1 1/2 LBS. LEAN GROUND VENISON, CRUMBLED
1/3 CUP FINELY CHOPPED ONION
3/4 TEASPOON SEASONED SALT
1 1/2 CUPS BUTTER-FLAVORED CRACKER CRUMBS (APPROXIMATELY 36 CRACKERS)
1 EGG, BEATEN
1/4 CUP SKIM MILK
3 TABLESPOONS VEGETABLE OIL, DIVIDED

6 servings

In large mixing bowl, combine venison, onion and salt. Shape mixture into six 1/2-inch-thick patties. Place crumbs in shallow dish. In second shallow dish, combine egg and milk.

Dip patties first in egg mixture, then dredge in crumbs to coat. Heat 1 1/2 tablespoons oil in 12-inch nonstick skillet over medium heat. Cook 3 patties for 4 to 6 minutes, or until browned and meat is no longer pink inside, turning patties over once. Remove patties from skillet. Set aside and keep warm. Repeat with remaining oil and patties.

Per Serving: Calories: 451 • Protein: 24 g. • Carbohydrate: 13 g. • Fat: 33 g. • Cholesterol: 137 mg. • Sodium: 383 mg. — Exchanges: 3/4 starch, 3 medium-fat meat, 3 1/2 fat

145

SALISBURY VENISON STEAKS

1 CAN (10¾ OZ.) CONDENSED CREAM OF MUSHROOM SOUP
1 TABLESPOON PREPARED MUSTARD
2 TEASPOONS WORCESTERSHIRE SAUCE
1 TEASPOON PREPARED HORSERADISH
1½ LBS. LEAN GROUND VENISON, CRUMBLED
½ CUP UNSEASONED DRY BREAD CRUMBS
½ CUP CHOPPED ONION
1 EGG, BEATEN
½ TEASPOON SALT
¼ TEASPOON PEPPER
1 TABLESPOON VEGETABLE OIL
½ CUP WATER
1 TO 2 TABLESPOONS SNIPPED FRESH PARSLEY

6 servings

In medium mixing bowl, combine soup, mustard, Worcestershire sauce and horseradish. Set aside. In large mixing bowl, combine ground venison, bread crumbs, onion, egg, salt, pepper and ¼ cup soup mixture. Shape mixture into six ½-inch-thick patties.

In 12-inch nonstick skillet, heat oil over medium heat. Add patties. Cook for 5 to 7 minutes, or until meat is browned, turning patties over once. Add remaining soup mixture and the water. Cover. Cook for 15 to 18 minutes, or until meat is desired doneness, stirring sauce occasionally. Garnish with parsley. Serve with mixed vegetables and hot cooked noodles or rice, if desired.

Per Serving: Calories: 426 • Protein: 25 g. • Carbohydrate: 12 g. • Fat: 30 g. • Cholesterol: 137 mg. • Sodium: 782 mg. — Exchanges: ¾ starch, 3 medium-fat meat, ¼ vegetable, 3 fat

BACKWOODS LASAGNA

2½ LBS. LEAN GROUND VENISON, CRUMBLED
½ CUP CHOPPED ONION
2 CLOVES GARLIC, MINCED
2 CANS (14½ OZ. EACH) DICED TOMATOES, DRAINED
1 CUP CHOPPED GREEN PEPPER
1 CAN (8 OZ.) TOMATO SAUCE
1 CAN (6 OZ.) TOMATO PASTE
1 TABLESPOON SNIPPED FRESH PARSLEY
1 TEASPOON SALT
1 TEASPOON DRIED OREGANO LEAVES
½ TEASPOON DRIED BASIL LEAVES
½ TEASPOON FRESHLY GROUND PEPPER
1 CUP RICOTTA CHEESE, DRAINED
1 CUP COTTAGE CHEESE, DRAINED
1½ CUPS SHREDDED MOZZARELLA CHEESE
1½ CUPS SHREDDED SWISS CHEESE
12 LASAGNA NOODLES (8 OZ.), COOKED
½ CUP SHREDDED FRESH PARMESAN CHEESE

8 servings

Lightly grease 13 × 9-inch baking dish. Set aside. In 12-inch nonstick skillet, cook ground venison, onion and garlic over medium heat for 8 to 10 minutes, or until meat is no longer pink, stirring frequently. Drain. Add tomatoes, green pepper, tomato sauce and paste, parsley, salt, oregano, basil and pepper. Bring mixture to a boil. Reduce heat to low. Cover. Simmer for 30 minutes. Remove from heat.

Heat oven to 350°F. In small mixing bowl, combine ricotta and cottage cheeses. In medium mixing bowl, combine mozzarella and Swiss cheeses. Arrange 4 lasagna noodles in a single layer in bottom of prepared baking dish. Top with one-third of meat mixture. Drop half of ricotta cheese mixture by spoonfuls over meat mixture. Sprinkle evenly with one-third of mozzarella cheese mixture. Repeat layer once. Top with remaining noodles and meat mixture. Sprinkle evenly with remaining mozzarella cheese mixture and the Parmesan cheese. Bake for 40 to 45 minutes, or until lasagna is hot and bubbly and golden brown. Let stand for 10 minutes before serving.

Per Serving: Calories: 703 • Protein: 52 g. • Carbohydrate: 37 g. • Fat: 38 g. • Cholesterol: 178 mg. • Sodium: 1225 mg. — Exchanges: 1½ starch, 6¼ lean meat, 2 vegetable, ¼ milk, 3¾ fat

Oven-barbecued Venison Ribs

OVEN-BARBECUED VENISON RIBS

SAUCE

½ CUP KETCHUP

½ CUP WATER

¼ CUP CIDER VINEGAR

¼ CUP FINELY CHOPPED ONION

3 TABLESPOONS PACKED BROWN SUGAR

2 TABLESPOONS WORCESTERSHIRE SAUCE

1 TABLESPOON LEMON JUICE

1 TABLESPOON PAPRIKA

1 TEASPOON DRY MUSTARD

1 TEASPOON SALT

1 TEASPOON LIQUID SMOKE FLAVORING

½ TEASPOON PEPPER

¼ TEASPOON CHILI POWDER

2 TO 3 LBS. DEER, ANTELOPE, ELK OR MOOSE RIBS

2 CUPS WATER

4 servings

In small bowl, combine all sauce ingredients. Mix well. In Dutch oven, combine ribs, 2 cups water and ³/4 cup sauce, reserving remaining sauce. Heat rib mixture to boiling. Reduce heat; cover. Simmer until ribs are tender, about 1 hour, rearranging ribs once or twice.

Heat oven to 350°F. Arrange ribs on roasting pan. Brush with reserved sauce. Bake for 10 minutes. Turn ribs over. Brush with sauce. Bake for 10 minutes longer. Serve with remaining sauce.

Per serving: Calories: 268 • Protein: 35 g. • Carbohydrate: 23 g. • Fat: 4 g. • Cholesterol: 125 mg. • Sodium: 1090 mg. — Exchanges: 5 very lean meat, ¹/2 fat

ORIENTAL-STYLE GRILLED VENISON RIBS

MARINADE

1½ CUPS DRY SHERRY

¼ CUP PEANUT OIL OR VEGETABLE OIL

¼ CUP RICE WINE VINEGAR

6 TABLESPOONS SOY SAUCE

6 TABLESPOONS PLUM SAUCE OR 3 TABLESPOONS PLUM JELLY

2 TABLESPOONS HOISIN SAUCE

1 TABLESPOON MINCED FRESH GINGERROOT

4 CLOVES GARLIC, MINCED

2 TO 3 LBS. DEER, ANTELOPE, ELK OR MOOSE RIBS

4 servings

In medium saucepan, combine all marinade ingredients. Heat over medium heat, stirring constantly, until hot. Cool to room temperature. Place ribs in 13 × 9-inch baking pan or in an oven cooking bag. Pour cooled marinade over ribs. Cover pan with plastic wrap or seal bag. Refrigerate ribs for 1 to 2 hours, turning ribs several times.

Start charcoal briquets in grill. When briquets are covered with ash, spread them evenly in grill. Place grate above hot coals. Arrange ribs on grate. Grill until cooked through, 10 to 15 minutes, turning once.

Per serving: Calories: 233 • Protein: 34 g. • Carbohydrate: 7 g. • Fat: 7 g. • Cholesterol: 125 mg. • Sodium: 520 mg. — Exchanges: 5 very lean meat, 1 fat

ORANGE ONION LIVER

¼ CUP ALL-PURPOSE FLOUR

⅛ TEASPOON SALT

⅛ TEASPOON PEPPER

1 LB. DEER, ANTELOPE, ELK OR
   MOOSE LIVER, TRIMMED AND SLICED ½-
   INCH THICK

¼ CUP BUTTER OR MARGARINE

1 MEDIUM YELLOW ONION, THINLY SLICED

1 MEDIUM RED ONION, THINLY SLICED

1 TABLESPOON SUGAR

1 MEDIUM ORANGE, SLICED

¼ CUP BUTTER OR MARGARINE

⅓ CUP BEEF OR VENISON STOCK

¼ CUP BRANDY

¼ TEASPOON DRIED THYME LEAVES

3 or 4 servings

Heat oven to 175°F. On a sheet of waxed paper, mix flour, salt and pepper. Dip liver slices in flour mixture, turning to coat. In large skillet, melt ¼ cup butter over medium heat. Add liver slices; brown on both sides. With slotted spoon, transfer to heated serving platter. Keep warm in oven. Add onions to butter in skillet. Cook and stir over medium heat until tender. Set aside and keep warm.

While onions are cooking, place sugar on a sheet of waxed paper. Coat orange slices on both sides. In medium skillet, melt ¼ cup butter over medium heat. Add orange slices. Fry until golden brown, turning once. Remove orange slices; set aside. Add stock, brandy and thyme to butter in skillet. Cook over low heat for 5 minutes, stirring constantly. Remove from heat. To serve, arrange onions over liver slices. Pour broth mixture over onions and liver. Top with orange slices.

Nutritional information not available.

SAUCES FOR BIG GAME

BIG-GAME BROWN SAUCE

In classic French cooking, many sauces are based on brown sauce, made by reducing rich stock. The following recipes are variations on that idea, simplified for the home cook.

1/3 CUP FINELY CHOPPED ONION
1 SMALL CARROT, FINELY CHOPPED
3 TABLESPOONS BUTTER OR MARGARINE
1/4 CUP DRY WHITE WINE
2 TABLESPOONS ALL-PURPOSE FLOUR
1 CUP VENISON STOCK OR BEEF BROTH
1 TEASPOON LEMON JUICE OR VINEGAR
SALT AND FRESHLY GROUND BLACK PEPPER

About 1 cup

In medium skillet, cook and stir onion and carrot in butter over medium heat until tender. Stir in wine. Cook, stirring occasionally, until reduced by half. Stir in flour. Blend in stock and lemon juice. Cook over medium-high heat, stirring constantly, until thickened and bubbly, 5 to 7 minutes. Strain sauce if desired. Add salt and pepper to taste. Serve warm.

Per serving (1 tablespoon): Calories: 29 • Protein: 0.3 g. • Carbohydrate: 1 g. • Fat: 2 g. • Cholesterol: 5 mg. • Sodium: 75 mg. — Exchanges: 1/2 vegetable, 1/2 fat

Brown Sauce Variations

⟢━◦━⟤

Richer Brown Sauce—Substitute 3/4 cup reduced venison stock (*demi-glace*, page 22) for the regular venison stock.

Pepper-Flavored Brown Sauce—Simmer 1 cup venison stock with 8 whole peppercorns, 1/2 teaspoon dry mustard and a dash of cayenne for 10 minutes. Strain and discard peppercorns. Use as substitute for the regular venison stock in Big-Game Brown Sauce; for additional flavor, substitute vermouth for the white wine.

Orange-Flavored Brown Sauce—Steep 3 tablespoons grated orange rind in 2 cups boiling water for 5 minutes. Strain and reserve orange peel. Omit carrot in Big-Game Brown Sauce; substitute 1/4 cup dry red wine and 1/4 cup orange juice for the white wine. When sauce is thickened and bubbly, stir in reserved orange peel, 1 tablespoon currant jelly and an optional tablespoon cognac. Cook until jelly melts.

Quick and Easy Big-Game Brown Sauce—Omit flour and venison stock. In small bowl, blend 1 package (.78 oz.) brown gravy mix with 1 cup cold water and the lemon juice. Blend gravy mixture into onion mixture; cook as directed.

MADEIRA GAME SAUCE

Excellent with any big-game roast or steaks.

3 TABLESPOONS BUTTER OR MARGARINE
3 TABLESPOONS ALL-PURPOSE FLOUR
1 CUP VENISON STOCK OR BEEF BROTH
2 TABLESPOONS CURRANT JELLY
2 TABLESPOONS MADEIRA WINE

About 1 cup

In small saucepan, melt butter over medium-low heat. Stir in flour. Blend in stock. Cook over medium heat until thickened and bubbly, 5 to 7 minutes. Add jelly; stir until melted. Add Madeira; heat just to boiling. Serve sauce warm.

Per serving (1 tablespoon): Calories: 35 • Protein: 0.3 g. • Carbohydrate: 3 g. • Fat: 2 g. • Cholesterol: 5 mg. • Sodium: 75 mg. — Exchanges: 1/2 starch, 1/2 fat

BIG-GAME SAUSAGES

Fresh big-game sausages are probably the easiest sausages to make, since they require few special ingredients and no smoking. Fresh sausage mixtures can be stuffed into casings or formed into patties or logs. They should be kept in the refrigerator and used within 2 or 3 days or frozen for future use. Cased fresh sausages are also excellent if lightly smoked prior to cooking. Summer sausages and salamis are more complicated and require special ingredients.

Follow the basic sausage-making procedures on pages 61–64 for the recipes in this section. Smoking basics can be found on pages 53–58.

Spicy Bratwurst-style Sausage

Fresh Breakfast Links

SPICY BRATWURST-STYLE SAUSAGE

3   LBS. LEAN GROUND VENISON, CRUMBLED

3   LBS. GROUND PORK, CRUMBLED

2   TABLESPOONS CANNING/PICKLING SALT

2   TABLESPOONS DRIED PARSLEY FLAKES

1   TABLESPOON CRUSHED RED PEPPER FLAKES

1   TABLESPOON DRIED ONION FLAKES

2   TEASPOONS GARLIC POWDER

1   TEASPOON FRESHLY GROUND PEPPER

COLLAGEN CASINGS (32 MM) FOR FRESH SAUSAGE, OR NATURAL HOG CASINGS (29 TO 32 MM)

24 sausages (about 4 oz. each)

In large mixing bowl, combine ground venison and ground pork. In small mixing bowl, combine remaining ingredients, except casings. Sprinkle seasoning mixture evenly over meat. Mix by hand until ingredients are evenly distributed. Cover with plastic wrap. Refrigerate until ready to stuff.

Prepare and stuff casings as directed for natural casings (page 64), using a $3/4$-inch horn and twisting off in 6-inch links. (It may be necessary to hand tie ends of each link with kitchen string if collagen casings are used.) If any air pockets remain on surface of sausages, pierce the casing with a sterilized sausage pricker or needle.

To prepare, place desired number of sausages in saucepan with 1 inch of water or beer. Bring to a boil over high heat. Reduce heat to medium. Cover. Simmer for 4 to 6 minutes, or until sausages are firm. Sausages may be grilled, or cooled, sliced and used in recipes as desired.

Per Sausage: Calories: 299 • Protein: 20 g. • Carbohydrate: <1 g. • Fat: 23 g. • Cholesterol: 92 mg. • Sodium: 424 mg. —Exchanges: 3 medium-fat meat, $1^1/2$ fat

FRESH BREAKFAST LINKS

2   LBS. LEAN GROUND VENISON, CRUMBLED

2   LBS. GROUND PORK, CRUMBLED

$1/3$ CUP PLUS 2 TABLESPOONS ICE WATER

$1^1/2$ TABLESPOONS SALT

1   TEASPOON WHITE PEPPER

1   TEASPOON RUBBED SAGE

1   TEASPOON GROUND THYME

$1/4$ TEASPOON GROUND NUTMEG

$1/4$ TEASPOON GROUND GINGER

COLLAGEN CASINGS (22 MM) FOR FRESH SAUSAGE, OR NATURAL SHEEP CASINGS (22 TO 24 MM)

44 sausages (about $1^1/2$ oz. each)

In large mixing bowl, combine ground venison and ground pork. In small mixing bowl, combine remaining ingredients, except casings. Add to meat mixture. Mix by hand until ingredients are evenly distributed. Cover with plastic wrap. Refrigerate until ready to stuff.

Prepare and stuff casings as directed for natural casings (page 64), using a $1/2$-inch horn and twisting off in 4-inch links. (It may be necessary to hand tie ends of each link with kitchen string if collagen casings are used.) If any air pockets remain on surface of sausages, pierce the casing with a sterilized sausage pricker or needle. Sausages may be panfried or grilled. Wrap tightly and freeze any remaining sausages for future use.

Variation: For sausage patties, prepare recipe as directed above, except omit casings. Shape meat mixture evenly into patties. Freeze patties in sealable plastic bags between layers of wax paper.

Per Sausage: Calories: 108 • Protein: 7 g. • Carbohydrate: 0 g. • Fat: 8 g. • Cholesterol: 33 mg. • Sodium: 245 mg. — Exchanges: 1 medium-fat meat, $3/4$ fat

LEAN FRESH GROUND SAUSAGE

This easy sausage can be formed into patties or used in any recipe that calls for fresh ground sausage.

1	LB. LEAN GROUND VENISON, CRUMBLED
1	TEASPOON FENNEL SEED
1	TEASPOON SALT
1/2	TEASPOON GARLIC POWDER
1/4	TO 1/2 TEASPOON CRUSHED RED PEPPER FLAKES

4 servings

In medium mixing bowl, combine all ingredients. Mix well. Shape mixture into eight 3-inch patties. In 12-inch nonstick skillet, cook patties over medium heat for 5 to 6 minutes, or until meat is no longer pink in center, turning patties over once or twice.

Tip: Patties can be frozen in sealable plastic bags between layers of wax paper. To prepare frozen patties, cook them in a nonstick skillet over medium-low heat for 18 to 20 minutes, or until meat is no longer pink in center, turning patties once or twice.

Per Serving: Calories: 299 • Protein: 22 g. • Carbohydrate: 1 g. • Fat: 23 g. • Cholesterol: 101 mg. • Sodium: 598 mg. — Exchanges: 3 medium-fat meat, 1 1/2 fat

MEXICAN CHORIZO SAUSAGE

Boldly flavored, this sausage can be used for tacos, chili or tiny appetizer meatballs.

2	LBS. TRIMMED DEER OR OTHER BIG-GAME MEAT
2	LBS. BONELESS FATTY PORK SHOULDER OR PORK BUTT
2	TABLESPOONS PAPRIKA
1	TABLESPOON SALT
1	TABLESPOON BLACK PEPPER
2	TEASPOONS CRUSHED RED PEPPER FLAKES
1	TEASPOON SUGAR
1	TEASPOON GARLIC POWDER
1/2	TEASPOON DRIED OREGANO LEAVES
1/4	TEASPOON CUMIN SEED
1/4	CUP WHITE VINEGAR

About 4 pounds

Cut deer and pork into 3/4-inch cubes. Place in large mixing bowl. In small bowl, mix remaining ingredients, except vinegar. Sprinkle over meat; mix well. Chop or grind to medium consistency. Return meat mixture to large mixing bowl. Add vinegar; mix well. Cover bowl tightly with plastic wrap. Refrigerate for at least 1 hour to blend flavors. Cook over medium heat, stirring occasionally, until brown; use for tacos or chili. For cased sausages, prepare and stuff casings as directed for natural casings (page 64), using a 3/4-inch horn and twisting off in 6-inch links. Sausage can also be frozen uncooked.

Per 4-oz. serving: Calories: 209 • Protein: 23 g. • Carbohydrate: 1 g. • Fat: 12 g. • Cholesterol: 90 mg. • Sodium: 500 mg. — Exchanges: 3 1/2 very lean meat, 2 fat

Mexican Chorizo Sausage

SMOKED CAJUN SAUSAGE

3 LBS. LEAN GROUND VENISON, CRUMBLED

3 LBS. GROUND PORK, CRUMBLED

2/3 CUP SOY PROTEIN CONCENTRATE

2 TABLESPOONS MORTON® TENDERQUICK® MIX

1 TABLESPOON PAPRIKA

1 TABLESPOON MINCED DEHYDRATED ONIONS

1 TABLESPOON CAYENNE

1 TABLESPOON SALT

2 TEASPOONS BLACK PEPPER

2 TEASPOONS WHITE PEPPER

2 TEASPOONS GARLIC POWDER

1 TEASPOON GROUND CUMIN

1 TEASPOON THYME LEAVES

1½ TO 3 CUPS HICKORY WOOD CHIPS

COLLAGEN CASINGS (32 MM) FOR SMOKED SAUSAGES, OR NATURAL HOG CASINGS (29 TO 32 MM)

24 sausages

Nutritional information not available.

In large nonmetallic mixing bowl, combine ground venison and ground pork. In small mixing bowl, combine remaining ingredients, except wood chips and casings. Add to meat mixture. Mix by hand until ingredients are evenly distributed. Cover with plastic wrap. Refrigerate until ready to stuff.

Place wood chips in large mixing bowl. Cover with water. Soak chips for 1 hour. Place oven thermometer in smoker. Heat smoker until temperature registers 130°F. Prepare and stuff casings as directed for natural casings (page 64), using a 3/4-inch horn and twisting off in 6-inch links. (It may be necessary to hand tie ends of each link with kitchen string if collagen casings are used.) If any air pockets remain on surface of sausages, pierce the casing with a sterilized sausage pricker or needle.

Drain wood chips. Hang sausages on smokehouse sticks, spacing at least 1 inch apart. Place in smoker. Open damper. Maintain temperature at 130°F for 30 minutes, or until surface of sausages is dry. Partially close damper to raise temperature to 165°F. Place wood chips in smoker. Smoke at 165°F for 2 1/2 to 4 hours, or until internal temperature of largest sausage registers 152°F. (Times are approximate and will vary, depending on size and diameter of sausages, weather conditions and type of smoker used.) Remove sausages from smoker and flush them with cold water until the internal temperature registers 120°F. Store sausages, tightly wrapped, in refrigerator for no longer than 1 week, or wrap tightly and freeze up to 2 months for best quality.

Buffalo Beer Sticks (left), Venison Summer Sausage (center), Elk Salami

BUFFALO BEER STICKS

2	LBS. LEAN GROUND BUFFALO OR VENISON, CRUMBLED
2	TABLESPOONS MORTON® TENDERQUICK® MIX
1½	TEASPOONS GARLIC POWDER
1½	TEASPOONS ONION POWDER
1	TEASPOON FRESHLY GROUND PEPPER
½	TEASPOON GROUND CORIANDER
½	TEASPOON DRY MUSTARD
½	TEASPOON CAYENNE
1½	CUPS HICKORY WOOD CHIPS (OPTIONAL)
19	MM COLLAGEN CASING (OPTIONAL)

32 sticks (about 1 oz. each)

In large nonmetallic mixing bowl, combine all ingredients except wood chips and casing. Mix by hand until ingredients are evenly distributed. Cover with plastic wrap. Refrigerate 8 hours or overnight.

Place wood chips in large mixing bowl. Cover with water. Soak chips for 1 hour. Place oven thermometer in smoker. Heat smoker until temperature registers 150°F. Drain wood chips.

Stuff casings as directed for natural casings (page 64), using a ½-inch horn and cutting off in 4-inch lengths with sharp knife. (If casings are not used, roll meat mixture by hand into ropes 4 inches long and ½ inch in diameter.)

Arrange beer sticks at least 1 inch apart on smoker racks. Place racks in smoker. Open damper. Place wood chips in smoker. When wood chips begin to smoke, close damper, cracking slightly. Smoke beer sticks at 150°F for 1½ to 2¼ hours, or until firm. Cool completely. Store beer sticks, loosely wrapped, in refrigerator for no longer than 1 week, or wrap tightly and freeze up to 2 months.

Variation: To dry beer sticks in conventional oven, add 1 teaspoon liquid smoke flavoring to meat mixture. Continue with recipe as directed, except place oven thermometer in oven. Heat oven to lowest possible temperature setting, propping oven door slightly ajar with wooden spoon to maintain 150°F. Arrange beer sticks on oven racks, spacing as directed. Dry for 1½ to 2¼ hours, or until firm.

Nutritional information not available.

VENISON SUMMER SAUSAGE

8 LBS. LEAN GROUND VENISON OR SUBSTITUTE, CRUMBLED
2 LBS. PORK BACK FAT, CUT INTO 1-INCH PIECES
6 OZ. FERMENTO
1/4 CUP PLUS 2 TABLESPOONS CANNING/ PICKLING SALT
1/4 CUP POWDERED DEXTROSE
1 TABLESPOON FRESHLY GROUND PEPPER
1 TABLESPOON GROUND CORIANDER
2 LEVEL TEASPOONS INSTACURE NO. 1
1 TEASPOON GROUND GINGER
1 TEASPOON DRY MUSTARD
1 TEASPOON GARLIC POWDER (OPTIONAL)
1 1/2 TO 3 CUPS HICKORY WOOD CHIPS
6 TO 8 SYNTHETIC-FIBROUS CASINGS, 3 1/2 X 12 INCHES

About 10 lbs. (2 oz. per serving)

In large nonmetallic mixing bowl, combine ground meat and back fat. In medium mixing bowl, combine remaining ingredients, except wood chips and casings. Add to meat mixture. Mix by hand until ingredients are evenly distributed. Cover with plastic wrap. Refrigerate 24 hours.

Place wood chips in large mixing bowl. Cover with water. Soak chips for 1 hour. Soak casings as directed for synthetic casings (page 63). Grind meat mixture through a 3/16-inch plate. Re-cover meat. Refrigerate until ready to stuff.

Place oven thermometer in smoker. Heat smoker until temperature registers 130°F. Prepare and stuff casings as directed for synthetic casings (page 63), to within 2 inches of top. Secure with butterfly knot. If any air pockets remain on surface of sausages, pierce the casing with a sterilized sausage pricker or needle.

Drain wood chips. Hang sausages on smokehouse sticks, spacing at least 1 inch apart. Place in smoker. Open damper. Maintain temperature at 130°F for 30 minutes, or until surface of sausages is dry. Partially close damper to raise temperature to 150°F. Place wood chips in smoker. Smoke at 150°F for 1 hour. Increase temperature to 165°F. Smoke for 5 to 6 hours longer, or until internal temperature of largest sausage registers 152°F. (Times are approximate and will vary, depending on size and diameter of sausages, weather conditions and type of smoker used.) Remove sausages from smoker and flush them with cold water until internal temperature registers 120°F. Store sausages, tightly wrapped, in refrigerator for no longer than 1 week, or wrap tightly and freeze up to 2 months.

Nutritional information not available.

ELK SALAMI

8 LBS. LEAN GROUND ELK OR SUBSTITUTE, CRUMBLED
2 LBS. PORK BACK FAT, CUT INTO 1-INCH PIECES
2 CUPS COLD WATER
2 CUPS SOY PROTEIN CONCENTRATE
1/4 CUP PLUS 2 TABLESPOONS CANNING/PICKLING SALT
2 TABLESPOONS POWDERED DEXTROSE
2 TABLESPOONS GROUND NUTMEG
1 TABLESPOON WHITE PEPPER
2 LARGE CLOVES GARLIC, MINCED
2 LEVEL TEASPOONS INSTACURE NO. 1
1 1/2 TO 3 CUPS HICKORY WOOD CHIPS
6 TO 8 SYNTHETIC-FIBROUS CASINGS, 3 1/2 X 12 INCHES

About 10 lbs. (2 oz. per serving)

Follow directions for Venison Summer Sausage.

Nutritional information not available.

POTATO SAUSAGE

Fry this sausage in patties for breakfast, brunch or dinner, or use it to make an interesting meatloaf.

1	QUART WATER
2	LBS. PEELED RED POTATOES
1	LB. TRIMMED DEER, ANTELOPE, ELK OR MOOSE
1	LB. BONELESS FATTY PORK SHOULDER OR PORK BUTT
1	MEDIUM ONION, COARSELY CHOPPED
1	EGG, BEATEN
1	TABLESPOON SALT
1/2	TEASPOON GROUND ALLSPICE
1/4	TEASPOON DRIED GROUND SAGE LEAVES
1/4	TEASPOON DRIED BASIL LEAVES
1/4	TEASPOON SUGAR

4 pounds

In 2-quart saucepan, heat water to boiling. Add potatoes. Return to boiling. Reduce heat; cover. Simmer until potatoes are fork-tender, 25 to 35 minutes. Drain. Cool potatoes; cut into 3/4-inch cubes.

Cut deer and pork into 3/4-inch cubes. In large mixing bowl, combine deer, pork, potato cubes, onion and egg. In small bowl, mix remaining ingredients. Sprinkle over meat and potato mixture; mix well. Cover bowl tightly with plastic wrap. Refrigerate at least 1 hour to blend flavors.

Chop or grind meat and potato mixture to medium consistency. Shape into thin patties. Fry in nonstick skillet over medium-low heat in a small amount of vegetable oil until browned and cooked through, turning once.

Per 4 oz. serving: Calories: 156 • Protein: 13 g. • Carbohydrate: 11 g. • Fat: 6 g. • Cholesterol: 60 mg. • Sodium: 480 mg. — Exchanges: 1 starch, 1 1/2 very lean meat, 1 fat

ITALIAN-STYLE SAUSAGE

5	LBS. LEAN GROUND VENISON OR SUBSTITUTE, CRUMBLED
5	LBS. GROUND PORK, CRUMBLED
5	TEASPOONS FENNEL SEED
5	TEASPOONS CRUSHED RED PEPPER FLAKES
5	TEASPOONS CHILI POWDER
5	TEASPOONS DRIED OREGANO LEAVES
2 1/2	TEASPOONS CANNING/PICKLING SALT
1 1/2	TEASPOONS GARLIC POWDER
1 1/4	TEASPOONS FRESHLY GROUND PEPPER
	NATURAL HOG CASINGS (29 TO 32 MM)

32 sausages (about 5 oz. each)

In large mixing bowl, combine ground venison and ground pork. In small mixing bowl, combine remaining ingredients, except casings. Sprinkle seasoning mixture evenly over meat. Mix by hand until ingredients are evenly distributed. Cover with plastic wrap. Refrigerate until ready to stuff.

Prepare and stuff casings as directed (page 64), using a 3/4-inch horn and twisting off in 6-inch links. Sausages may be panfried with sliced onion and green pepper, if desired, or grilled. Wrap tightly and freeze any remaining sausages for future use.

Variation: Italian-style Sausage Patties: Prepare recipe as directed above, except omit casings. Shape meat mixture evenly into patties. Layer patties with wax paper. Stack patties, wrap in foil and freeze no longer than 2 months.

Per Serving: Calories: 376 • Protein: 25 g. • Carbohydrate: 1 g. • Fat: 29 g. • Cholesterol: 114 mg. • Sodium: 189 mg. — Exchanges: 3 3/4 high-fat meat

Potato Sausage

SMOKING RECIPES

SMOKED BUFFALO WITH RED CHILI HONEY CHUTNEY

CHUTNEY

1½ CUPS MAJOR GRAY'S CHUTNEY®
  1 CUP LINGONBERRY PRESERVES
⅓ CUP HONEY
  2 TABLESPOONS CHILI POWDER
  1 TEASPOON SALT
  1 TEASPOON PEPPER

1½ CUPS HICKORY WOOD CHIPS
  1 TABLESPOON PAPRIKA
  2 TO 3 CLOVES GARLIC, MINCED
  2 TEASPOONS COARSELY GROUND PEPPER
  1 TEASPOON DRIED MARJORAM LEAVES
  1 TEASPOON DRIED THYME LEAVES
  1 TEASPOON DRIED ROSEMARY LEAVES
  1 TEASPOON ONION SALT
  5 LBS. BONELESS BUFFALO RIB EYE
    ROAST, ELK LOIN OR SUBSTITUTE,
    WELL TRIMMED

18 servings

In food processor or blender, combine all chutney ingredients. Process until smooth. Cover. Set aside. Place wood chips in large mixing bowl. Cover with water. Soak chips for 1 hour.

In small mixing bowl, combine remaining ingredients, except buffalo. Rub seasoning mixture evenly over roast. Place oven thermometer in smoker. Heat smoker until temperature registers 200°F. Spray smoker rack with nonstick vegetable cooking spray. Place roast on rack. Place in center of smoker. Open damper and maintain 200°F for 1 hour to dry surface of roast. (If juices are released from roast during this time, the temperature is too high.) Drain wood chips. Place wood chips in smoker. When wood chips begin to smoke, close damper, cracking slightly. Smoke roast for 1 hour at 200°F. Remove roast from smoker. On charcoal grill or in preheated 325°F oven, finish cooking roast to desired doneness. Remove from grill. Let roast stand, tented with foil, for 10 minutes before carving. Carve roast across grain into thin slices. Serve with chutney.

Per Serving: Calories: 312 • Protein: 29 g. • Carbohydrate: 34 g. • Fat: 6 g. • Cholesterol: 55 mg. • Sodium: 518 mg. Exchanges: 4 lean meat, 2 fruit

SMOKED CANNED BIG-GAME CHUNKS

Use this meat to make quick stews, or shred and add to barbecue sauce for unusual sloppy joes.

  3 OR MORE LBS. BONELESS BIG-GAME
    STEAKS OR OTHER LARGE CHUNKS,
    ¾ TO 1 INCH THICK

MARINADE (FOR EACH 3 LBS. MEAT)

½ CUP SOY SAUCE
¼ CUP VEGETABLE OIL
  1 TEASPOON SUGAR
  1 TEASPOON BLACK PEPPER
  3 CLOVES GARLIC, CHOPPED
½ TEASPOON WORCESTERSHIRE SAUCE

CANNING BROTH (FOR EACH 3 LBS. MEAT)

  1 CUP VENISON STOCK OR BEEF BROTH
¼ CUP VINEGAR
  1 TEASPOON SUGAR

1½ lbs. meat per pint

Place meat in a single layer in large glass baking dish. In food processor or blender, combine all marinade ingredients; process until smooth. Pour half the marinade over meat. Turn meat over. Cover with remaining marinade. Place plastic wrap directly on surface of meat. Refrigerate at least 3 hours.

Prepare hot smoker. Use 8 to 10 wet chunks of hickory, mesquite, cherry or alder wood. Fill water pan about ⅔ full with water. Drain meat; place on top and bottom racks of hot smoker. Top meat with thinly sliced onion if desired. Smoke until meat is medium doneness, usually 2 to 3 hours, basting meat once with marinade and reversing position of racks. Remove meat from smoker; cool slightly. In medium saucepan, combine all canning-broth ingredients. Heat to boiling. Remove from heat; set aside. Cut meat into 1- to 1½-inch chunks. Follow photo directions on page 66 for canning.

Nutritional information not available.

JERKY-CURED SMOKED ROAST

MARINADE

2	CUPS COLD WATER
1	CAN (12 OZ.) LAGER-STYLE BEER
3	TABLESPOONS MORTON® TENDERQUICK® MIX
2	TABLESPOONS RED WINE VINEGAR
2	TABLESPOONS WORCESTERSHIRE SAUCE
1	TABLESPOON DRIED ONION FLAKES
1	TEASPOON GARLIC POWDER
½	TEASPOON WHITE PEPPER
1½-	TO 2-LB. VENISON ROUND ROAST OR SUBSTITUTE
1½	TO 3 CUPS HICKORY OR MESQUITE WOOD CHIPS

8 to 12 servings

In large nonmetallic mixing bowl, combine marinade ingredients. Stir to dissolve salt cure. Add roast. Cover with plastic wrap. Refrigerate 24 hours, turning roast and stirring marinade occasionally. In large mixing bowl, cover wood chips with water. Soak for 1 hour. Place oven thermometer in smoker. Heat smoker to 130°F.

Spray smoker rack with nonstick vegetable cooking spray. Drain wood chips. Drain and discard marinade from roast. Pat roast dry with paper towels. Place roast on prepared rack. Place rack in smoker. Open damper. Maintain temperature at 130°F for 30 minutes, or until surface of roast is dry. Partially close damper to raise temperature to 150°F. Place wood chips in smoker. Smoke at 150°F for 5 to 6 hours, or until internal temperature of roast registers at least 140°F. (Times are approximate and will vary, depending on size and diameter of roast, weather conditions and type of smoker used.)

Cool roast. Store roast, tightly wrapped, in refrigerator for no longer than 1 week, or wrap tightly and freeze up to 2 months for best quality.

Nutritional information not available.

JERKY RECIPES

CAJUN JERKY

MARINADE

  4 CUPS COLD WATER

  2 TO 3 TABLESPOONS CAJUN SEASONING

  2 TABLESPOONS MORTON® TENDERQUICK® MIX

  1 TABLESPOON SOY SAUCE

  1 TO 2 TEASPOONS PAPRIKA

  2 LBS. BONELESS VENISON ROUND STEAK OR ROAST, CUT INTO 4 × 1 × ¼-INCH STRIPS

1½ TO 3 CUPS HICKORY WOOD CHIPS

11 servings (40 to 50 slices)

Follow directions on page 59.

Nutritional information not available.

To preserve meat, Native Americans and early settlers would hang the meat over a smoky fire until it was dry. Then it could be stored or carried long distances without spoiling.

Any lean game meat without tendons or sinews can be used to make jerky. Cut meat with the grain for a chewy texture or across the grain for a more tender jerky.

Traditionally, jerky is smoked, but it can also be flavored with liquid smoke and dried in a cool oven (directions on page 59) or dehydrator.

Use a curing salt like Morton® TenderQuick® mix when preparing jerky, to help prevent bacterial growth.

GROUND MEAT JERKY

2	LBS. LEAN GROUND VENISON, CRUMBLED
2	TEASPOONS CANNING/PICKLING SALT
2	TEASPOONS FRESHLY GROUND PEPPER
1½	TEASPOONS GARLIC POWDER
1½	TEASPOONS ONION POWDER
½	TEASPOON DRY MUSTARD
1½	TO 3 CUPS HICKORY WOOD CHIPS

18 servings (72 strips)

In large mixing bowl, combine all ingredients except wood chips. Mix well. Using rolling pin, roll mixture in batches between layers of wax paper to ¼-inch thickness. Remove top layer of wax paper. Cut meat into 3 × 1-inch strips. Using spatula, transfer strips to cooling racks that have been sprayed with nonstick vegetable cooking spray, spacing at least ½ inch apart. Smoke jerky as directed on page 59.

<u>Variation</u>: To prepare jerky in oven, add 1 to 2 teaspoons liquid smoke to meat mixture. Follow directions on page 59.

Per Serving: Calories: 134
• Protein: 10 g.
• Carbohydrate: <1 g.
• Fat: 10 g. • Cholesterol: 45 mg. • Sodium: 185 mg.
— Exchanges: 1½ medium-fat meat, ½ fat

PEMMICAN

Pemmican gave Native Americans and pioneers a more nutritious diet than straight jerky did. Then, it was made from powdered jerky, crushed berries and melted animal fat. Wrap individual pieces of our updated version in plastic wrap for a high-energy snack when you are on the trail.

8	OZ. VENISON JERKY
1	CUP RAISINS
1	CUP SNIPPED DRIED APRICOTS
½	CUP GROUND WALNUTS
1	TABLESPOON GRATED FRESH ORANGE PEEL
¼	TEASPOON GROUND ALLSPICE
⅓	CUP VEGETABLE SHORTENING OR LARD, MELTED

40 balls

Process jerky in food processor until very finely chopped. Set aside. In same food processor, combine raisins, apricots, walnuts, orange peel and allspice. Process until finely ground. Return jerky to food processor. Process until mixture forms into ball and no longer sticks to side of bowl.

Roll mixture into 40 1-inch balls. Store pemmican balls between layers of wax paper in airtight container. Store in refrigerator.

Nutritional information not available.

Ground Meat Jerky (bottom), Pemmican (top)

Traditional Venison Jerky

TRADITIONAL VENISON JERKY

SEASONING MIXTURE

2¼ TEASPOONS MORTON® TENDERQUICK® MIX

2¼ TEASPOONS PICKLING SALT

1½ TEASPOONS GARLIC POWDER

1½ TEASPOONS PEPPER

1½ LBS. BONELESS VENISON RUMP OR SUBSTITUTE

About 3/4 pound jerky

In small bowl or empty spice bottle with shaker top, combine all seasoning mixture ingredients. Mix well; set aside. Slice venison with the grain into strips about 1/8 inch thick. Arrange in single layer on cutting board. Sprinkle evenly with seasoning mixture, as though salting heavily. Pound meat lightly with meat mallet. Turn strips over; sprinkle and pound second side.

Smoke jerky as directed on page 59.

Per 1-oz. serving: Calories: 70 • Protein: 13 g. • Carbohydrate: 0.4 g. • Fat: 1.5 g. • Cholesterol: 50 mg. • Sodium: 670 mg. — Exchanges: 2 very lean meat

WILD BILL'S VENISON JERKY

MARINADE

4 CUPS COLD WATER

3 TABLESPOONS MORTON® TENDERQUICK® MIX

2 TABLESPOONS WORCESTERSHIRE SAUCE

1 TABLESPOON SOY SAUCE

1 TABLESPOON FRESHLY GROUND PEPPER

1 TEASPOON GARLIC POWDER

½ TEASPOON RED PEPPER SAUCE

2 LBS. BONELESS VENISON ROUND STEAK OR SUBSTITUTE, CUT INTO 4 X 1 X ¼-INCH STRIPS

1½ TO 3 CUPS HICKORY WOOD CHIPS

11 servings (40 to 50 slices)

Follow directions on page 59.

Per Serving: Calories: 101 • Protein: 19 g. • Carbohydrate: 1 g. • Fat: 2 g. • Cholesterol: 70 mg. • Sodium: 376 mg. — Exchanges: 2 lean meat

BIG-GAME MINCEMEAT

Once you make your own big-game mincemeat, you may never use canned mincemeat again. Try it as a filling for cookies or tarts, as a warm topping for ice cream and, of course, as the main ingredient in the traditional holiday pie.

VENISON MINCEMEAT

2	LBS. LEAN GROUND VENISON, CRUMBLED
1/4	LBS. BEEF SUET, GROUND MEDIUM-FINE
5	CUPS SEEDLESS DARK OR GOLDEN RAISINS
4	CUPS CHOPPED TART APPLE
3	CUPS APPLE CIDER
2	CUPS CURRANTS
2	CUPS PACKED BROWN SUGAR
1 1/2	CUPS GRANULATED SUGAR
1	PACKAGE (8 OZ.) CHOPPED CITRON
3/4	CUP CIDER VINEGAR
1/2	TO 1 CUP COARSELY CHOPPED SLIVERED ALMONDS
	GRATED PEEL FROM 3 OR 4 ORANGES
2	TEASPOONS SALT
2	TEASPOONS GROUND CINNAMON
1 1/2	TEASPOONS GROUND NUTMEG
1	TEASPOON GROUND CLOVES
1	TEASPOON GROUND MACE
1	TEASPOON GROUND ALLSPICE
1/4	CUP BRANDY OR RUM, OPTIONAL

About 4 quarts

In large Dutch oven or stockpot, combine all ingredients except brandy. Mix well. Heat to boiling, stirring frequently. Reduce heat; cover. Simmer 2 hours, stirring occasionally. Cool. Stir brandy into mincemeat. Place mincemeat into pint- or quart-sized containers for storage. Mincemeat can be stored in the refrigerator for 3 or 4 days or frozen for up to a year. Mincemeat may also be canned in a pressure cooker (page 66); process pint jars for 60 minutes at 10 pounds pressure.

Per 1/4-cup serving: Calories: 175 • Protein: 4 g. • Carbohydrate: 30 g. • Fat: 6 g. • Cholesterol:15 mg. • Sodium: 95 mg. — Exchanges: 1/2 very lean meat, 1 1/2 fruit, 1 fat

Big-Game Mincemeat Pie

BIG-GAME MINCEMEAT PIE

4	TO 5 CUPS VENISON MINCEMEAT
	PASTRY DOUGH FOR 2-CRUST PIE*
1	EGG
1	TABLESPOON WATER

9-inch pie

Prepare mincemeat and pie crust as directed. Heat oven to 425°F. On lightly floured board, roll one-half of pastry into thin circle at least 2 inches larger than inverted 9-inch pie plate. Fit crust into pie plate, pressing gently against bottom and side. Trim overhang 1/2 inch from rim. Fill with mincemeat. Roll out remaining pastry. Place on filling. Seal and flute edges. If desired, roll out pastry scraps; cut into decorations and place on pastry top. Cut several slits in pastry top. Blend egg and water. Brush over top. Bake at 425°F for 10 minutes. Reduce heat to 350°F and continue baking until crust is golden brown, 35 to 45 minutes.

*Use your favorite crust recipe or one package (15 oz.) refrigerated pie crust dough.

Per serving: Calories: 707 • Protein: 12 g. • Carbohydrate: 90 g. • Fat: 35 g. • Cholesterol: 70 mg. • Sodium: 560 mg. — Exchanges: 1 1/2 starch, 1 very lean meat, 3 1/2 fruit, 6 1/2 fat

CORNING BIG GAME

Corning is a method of meat preservation developed in the days before refrigeration. After butchering a steer, a farmer would cure the brisket or some other tough cut in a salt-sugar brine for several weeks. The salt acted as a preservative, and the sugar developed flavor and tenderness. Meat cured this way was called "corned" because the salt pellets were about the size of corn kernels.

On a moose or elk, the brisket, or thin meat that covers the bottom of the rib cage, is thick enough for corning. But on smaller animals like antelope and deer, it may be too thin. Flank meat, which lies between the last rib and the hindquarter, is a good choice, as is the shoulder roast.

The corning recipe below requires two types of salt. Canning and pickling salt is pure salt, without any iodine or free-flowing agents that might adversely affect the texture of the meat. Tenderizing salt is a mixture of salt, sugar and preservatives. It adds flavor and tenderness, and the preservatives give the meat its characteristic pink color.

CORNED VENISON

2-	TO 3-LB. BRISKET, FLANK OR SHOULDER ROAST UP TO 1 INCH THICK
2	QUARTS SPRING WATER OR DISTILLED WATER
½	CUP CANNING AND PICKLING SALT
½	CUP TENDERIZING SALT (E.G., MORTON® TENDERQUICK®)
3	TABLESPOONS SUGAR
2	TABLESPOONS MIXED PICKLING SPICE
2	BAY LEAVES
8	WHOLE BLACK PEPPERCORNS
1	OR 2 CLOVES GARLIC, MINCED

4 to 6 servings

Roll brisket or flank loosely and tie (page 119). Place in large glass or pottery mixing bowl, or in large oven cooking bag. In glass or enamel saucepan, combine remaining ingredients. Heat just to boiling. Remove from heat; cool. Pour cooled brine over meat. Cover bowl with plastic wrap; or, if using oven cooking bag, squeeze to remove air, then twist neck of bag and seal. Refrigerate 4 to 5 days, turning meat occasionally. Drain. Rinse meat with cold water.

To prepare corned meat, place in Dutch oven. Cover with cold water. Heat to boiling; drain. Cover with cold water. Heat to boiling. Reduce heat; cover. Simmer until tender, 3½ to 4½ hours.

Per serving: Calories: 233 • Protein: 43 g. • Carbohydrate: 2 g. • Fat: 7 g. • Cholesterol: 160 mg. • Sodium: 1630 mg. — Exchanges: 6 very lean meat, ½ fat

CORNED VENISON WITH VEGETABLES

2-	TO 3-LB. UNCOOKED CORNED VENISON ROAST
5	CARROTS, CUT INTO 2-INCH PIECES
4	MEDIUM RED POTATOES, QUARTERED
2	MEDIUM ONIONS, QUARTERED
1	SMALL HEAD CABBAGE (ABOUT 1¼ LBS.), CORED AND QUARTERED

6 to 8 servings

Drain and rinse corned meat in cold water as directed. Place in Dutch oven. Cover with cold water. Heat to boiling; drain. Cover with cold water. Heat to boiling. Reduce heat; cover. Simmer until almost tender, 2¾ to 3¾ hours. Add carrots; re-cover. Simmer for 20 minutes longer. Add potatoes, onions and cabbage; re-cover. Simmer until meat and vegetables are tender, about 30 minutes longer.

Per serving: Calories: 286 • Protein: 35 g. • Carbohydrate: 27 g. • Fat: 4 g. • Cholesterol: 120 mg. • Sodium: 1260 mg. — Exchanges: 1 starch, 4 very lean meat, 2½ vegetable, ½ fat

Venison Recipes from "KATE'S CORNER"

Kate Fiduccia is a seasoned big-game hunter and chef. She is executive producer of Woods 'n' Water *on the Outdoor Channel and hosts a cooking segment on the show, "Going Wild in Kate's Kitchen."*

FAR EAST VENISON FONDUE

An enameled cast-iron or metal fondue pot works best for this recipe.

2	LBS. VENISON LOIN
2	TEASPOONS BROWN SUGAR
6	TABLESPOONS LOW-SODIUM SOY SAUCE
6	TABLESPOONS DRY SHERRY
3	GARLIC CLOVES, CRUSHED
1	TEASPOON GROUND GINGER
	VEGETABLE OIL (TO FILL 1/3 OF FONDUE POT)

4 servings

Cut the venison into 3/4-inch cubes. In a larger bowl, mix brown sugar, soy sauce, sherry, garlic and ginger. Add the meat, toss to coat, and marinate in the refrigerator about 1 hour.

Heat the oil in a pan on the stove until it reaches about 375°F, then transfer to the fondue pot on the table and keep hot. Skewer venison chunks and dunk in oil until done to taste. Serve with dipping sauces and an Oriental salad. *(A fondue-veteran tip: use color-coded long forks. This way, everyone can easily keep track of their own food).*

DIPPING SAUCES

MUSTARD SAUCE

Combine 1 tablespoon Dijon mustard, 2/3 cup sour cream, 3 tablespoons mayonnaise, salt and pepper to taste. Stir well and serve.

HORSERADISH CREAM SAUCE

Whip 2/3 cup whipping cream until soft peaks form and stir in 1 tablespoon fresh horseradish and 2 chopped scallions.

GARLIC SAUCE

Dampen 2 cups of fresh white bread crumbs with water. Put them in a food processor with 3 garlic cloves and 1/2 teaspoon salt and purée. Add 1 cup of olive oil a little at a time until well blended. Add 4 teaspoons lemon juice and 1 tablespoon white wine vinegar and blend until smooth and creamy.

Nutritional information not available.

VENISON CHILI TOSTADAS

1	TABLESPOON OLIVE OIL, DIVIDED
1	SMALL ONION, CHOPPED
3/4	LB. GROUND VENISON
1 1/2	TEASPOONS CHILI POWDER
1/2	TEASPOON GROUND CUMIN
1/4	TEASPOON SALT
1/8	TEASPOON FRESHLY GROUND BLACK PEPPER
1/4	CUP WATER
1/4	CUP REFRIED BEANS
4	6-INCH FLOUR TORTILLAS
1/4	CUP SHREDDED MONTEREY JACK OR CHEDDAR CHEESE
1	CUP SHREDDED FRESH SPINACH OR LETTUCE
1	CUP CHOPPED FRESH TOMATO
1/4	CUP SOUR CREAM
8	THIN SLICES RED ONION, SEPARATED INTO RINGS

4 servings

Preheat the oven to 375°F.

Heat about 1/2 tablespoon olive oil in a large nonstick skillet over medium heat. Add the onion and cook until soft and translucent, about 3 minutes. Add the ground venison and cook until lightly browned, stirring to break up meat. Stir in chili powder, cumin, salt and pepper and cook for about 1 minute. Add 1/4 cup water and cook, stirring occasionally, until the liquid has evaporated into a thick sauce. Stir in the refried beans and set aside.

Brush the tortillas lightly with the remaining 1/2 tablespoon oil. Place on a baking sheet and bake until crisp and golden, 6 to 8 minutes. Spread the warm venison filling over the tortillas, dividing evenly. Sprinkle 1 tablespoon of the cheese over each. Return the tostadas to the oven and bake 3 to 4 minutes, or until the cheese is melted. Spread a small circle of sour cream in the middle of the tostada. Sprinkle with shredded spinach and chopped tomatoes and top with red onion. Serve at once.

Nutritional information not available.

VENISON FILLET WELLINGTON

Here's an elegant dish that will knock the socks off your deer-camp buddies. It may look complex, but it really is quite simple. From start to finish, Venison Fillet Wellington will take 45 to 60 minutes. Read the directions at least once before preparing this dish, and you will see how quickly it all comes together. You'll find commercial puff pastry in the frozen dessert section of your supermarket.

1 VENISON LOIN
2 TABLESPOONS BUTTER
1 PACKAGE FROZEN PUFF PASTRY, THAWED PER PACKAGE
    DIRECTIONS
1 EGG, SEPARATED
2 TABLESPOONS WATER

FILLING

2 TABLESPOONS CHOPPED SHALLOTS
2 TABLESPOONS BUTTER
3 TABLESPOONS OLIVE OIL
½ LB. FRESH MUSHROOMS, CHOPPED VERY FINE
1 CUP SHREDDED FRESH SPINACH LEAVES
½ CUP GRATED SWISS CHEESE
3 TO 4 STRIPS OF BACON, LIGHTLY COOKED

HUNTER'S SAUCE

2 TABLESPOONS MINCED SHALLOTS
4 TABLESPOONS CLARIFIED BUTTER OR OLIVE OIL
1 CUP SLICED ONIONS
½ CUP DRY WHITE WINE
½ CUP TOMATO SAUCE
1 CUP BROWN SAUCE OR CANNED BROWN GRAVY
    SALT AND PEPPER TO TASTE

Preheat the oven to 400°F. Rub the venison loin with butter and place it in a preheated large sauté pan. Sear the loin over medium-high heat, turning until it turns deep brown on all sides. Then transfer the loin to a roasting pan and bake for about 10 minutes, or until the internal temperature reaches 120°F. Remove it from the oven and let it cool to room temperature.

While the loin is cooling, prepare the savory filling. Sauté the chopped shallots in the butter and oil until they are golden. Like garlic, don't let shallots turn brown, or they will taste bitter. Add the mushrooms and let them sauté until most of the liquid evaporates. Set the mixture aside to cool.

Roll out the puff pastry to a rectangle about 1 to 2 inches larger than the loin. Spread the cooled mushroom-shallot mixture over the pastry, starting in the middle and stopping an inch from the edges of the pastry. In a thin strip (about as wide as the loin) in the center of the mushroom mixture, layer the spinach, cheese and bacon strips. Place the loin on top of the bacon strips. With a pastry brush, brush the edges of the pastry with egg white. This will help hold the pastry together while it is baking. Wrap the pastry around the loin and crimp all the edges to seal. Turn the loin over so that the seam is on the bottom. To give a nice glaze to the pastry while it is baking, brush the outside with a mixture of 1 egg yolk and 2 tablespoons of water.

Place the loin in a baking dish in a preheated 400°F oven. Reduce the heat to 350° and bake for 10 to 15 minutes, or until the pastry is a nice golden brown.

Remove the loin from the oven and serve immediately with Hunter's Sauce. You can use my recipe or you can purchase a premade hunter's sauce, such as McCormick's.

To prepare Hunter's Sauce, sauté the shallots in the butter until they are tender. Add the onions and sauté for about 3 minutes more. Add the white wine and simmer until the liquid is reduced by half. Add the tomato sauce and the brown sauce. Cook over medium-low heat for 10 minutes, stirring frequently, to let the flavors come together. Season with salt and pepper to taste.

Nutritional information not available.

RECIPES FOR
Small Game

The taste and texture of small-game animals vary greatly. Squirrel meat, for example, is mild with a velvety texture, while raccoon is rich, dark and coarse fibered.

The age of an animal also affects taste and texture, which in turn affect the cooking method. Young squirrels are delicious when fried; old ones would be tough and are better stewed or simmered. Rabbits, because of their short life span, are usually tender. Hares, whether young or old, are tougher and gamier. A young raccoon is tasty and tender when roasted, but an old one dressing out at 10 pounds or more is likely to be strong and tough, regardless of the cooking method.

To ensure tenderness, most of the recipes in this section rely on braising or other moist, slow-cooking methods. Pressure-cooking (page 29) also tenderizes quickly and easily, and is usually the best way to cook mature small-game animals.

To prepare a small-game dinner, you need about 3/4 pound of dressed game per person. Gray squirrels dress out at about 3/4 pound, fox squirrels 1 pound, cottontail rabbits 1 1/2 to 2 pounds, snowshoe hares 2 1/2 to 3 pounds, and young raccoons 3 to 6 pounds.

SMALL GAME SUBSTITUTION

Small game flavors vary greatly; although you can substitute different species, remember that the final dish may taste quite different. Be particularly careful when substituting raccoon for rabbit or squirrel; its strong taste can overwhelm a mildly seasoned dish. Hare is tougher than rabbit or squirrel, and requires longer cooking. Domestic rabbit will probably need less cooking time than wild rabbit.

If your recipe calls for a particular leftover or cooked small game, you can substitute any type of cooked small game, or even cooked pheasant, chicken or turkey. Cuts of fresh upland game birds can be easily substituted for small game cuts of similar size, as well.

Small-game Substitution Chart

SPECIES	APPROXIMATE DRESSED WEIGHT	NUMBER OF SERVINGS	SUBSTITUTE	COOKING METHOD
SQUIRREL	3/4 TO 1 LB. (GRAY) 1 TO 1 1/2 LB. (FOX)	1 1 TO 1 1/2	COTTONTAIL RABBIT (1 RABBIT TO 2 SQUIRRELS) HALF OF YOUNG SNOWSHOE HARE PORTION OF YOUNG RACCOON PORTION OF DOMESTIC RABBIT PHEASANT OR SUBSTITUTE (1 PHEASANT TO 2 SQUIRRELS)	PANFRY, BAKE BRAISE, STEW, PRESSURE-COOK
COTTONTAIL RABBIT	1 1/2 TO 2 LBS.	2	2 SQUIRRELS YOUNG SNOWSHOE HARE PORTION OF YOUNG RACCOON PORTION OF DOMESTIC RABBIT 1 PHEASANT OR SUBSTITUTE	PANFRY, BAKE, BRAISE, STEW, PRESSURE-COOK
SNOWSHOE HARE	2 1/2 TO 3 LBS.	2 TO 3	2 SMALL COTTONTAIL RABBITS 2 TO 3 SQUIRRELS DOMESTIC RABBIT HALF OF YOUNG RACCOON (OR PORTION OF LARGE RACCOON)	BRAISE, STEW, PRESSURE-COOK
RACCOON	3 LBS. OF PIECES	3 TO 4	SNOWSHOE HARE, QUARTERED 2 COTTONTAIL RABBITS, QUARTERED 3 OR 4 SQUIRRELS, QUARTERED DOMESTIC RABBIT, CUT INTO PIECES	BRAISE, STEW, STIR-FRY (STRIPS)

BEER-BRAISED RABBIT

2   DRESSED WILD RABBITS OR SUBSTITUTE (1 1/2 TO 2 LBS. EACH), CUT UP

1 1/2   TEASPOONS SALT, DIVIDED

1/2   TEASPOON FRESHLY GROUND PEPPER, DIVIDED

3   TABLESPOONS VEGETABLE OIL

3   MEDIUM RED POTATOES, CUT INTO QUARTERS

2 1/2   CUPS DIAGONALLY SLICED CARROTS (1/2-INCH SLICES)

1   MEDIUM ONION, SLICED

1   CAN (12 OZ.) BEER, DIVIDED

1/4   CUP CHILI SAUCE

1   TABLESPOON PACKED BROWN SUGAR

1   CLOVE GARLIC, MINCED

3   TABLESPOONS ALL-PURPOSE FLOUR

1/3   CUP WATER

4 to 6 servings

Sprinkle rabbit pieces evenly with 1/2 teaspoon salt and 1/4 teaspoon pepper. In 6-quart Dutch oven or stockpot, heat oil over medium heat. Add rabbit pieces. Cook for 8 to 10 minutes, or until meat is browned, turning occasionally. Drain and discard oil from Dutch oven. In same Dutch oven, add potatoes, carrots and onion.

Combine 1 teaspoon salt, 1/4 teaspoon pepper, 1 cup beer, the chili sauce, brown sugar and garlic. Pour over rabbit mixture. Bring to a boil over medium-high heat. Reduce heat to low. Cover. Simmer for 1 to 1 1/2 hours, or until meat and vegetables are tender. Using slotted spoon, transfer food to warm platter. Cover to keep warm. Set aside.

Add enough of remaining beer to broth in Dutch oven to equal 1 1/2 cups (add water if necessary). In small bowl, combine flour and 1/3 cup water. Stir into broth. Cook over medium heat for 4 to 5 minutes, or until sauce thickens and bubbles, stirring frequently. Spoon sauce over rabbit pieces and vegetables.

Per Serving: Calories: 407 • Protein: 49 g. • Carbohydrate: 28 g. • Fat: 10 g. • Cholesterol: 172 mg. • Sodium: 819 mg. — Exchanges: 1 1/4 starch, 5 lean meat, 1 1/2 vegetable

SPANISH RABBIT

3	TABLESPOONS OLIVE OIL
1	DRESSED WILD RABBIT OR SUBSTITUTE (1½ TO 2 LBS.), CUT UP
2	MEDIUM ONIONS, CHOPPED
1	GREEN PEPPER, CUT INTO ½-INCH PIECES
2	CLOVES GARLIC, MINCED
2	CUPS RABBIT STOCK (PAGE 23) OR CHICKEN BROTH
1	CUP UNCOOKED LONG GRAIN RICE
½	CUP SNIPPED FRESH PARSLEY
¾	TEASPOON SALT
¼	TEASPOON CRUSHED SAFFRON THREADS
¼	TEASPOON PEPPER
2	MEDIUM TOMATOES, SEEDED, CHOPPED AND DRAINED
1	CUP LARGE PITTED BLACK OLIVES
1	JAR (2 OZ.) DICED PIMIENTO, DRAINED

2 or 3 servings

In Dutch oven, heat oil over medium heat. Add rabbit pieces. Fry 10 minutes, turning pieces over once. Remove with slotted spoon; set aside. Add onions, green pepper and garlic to oil. Cook and stir until tender. Add rabbit pieces, stock, rice, parsley, salt, saffron and pepper. Heat to boiling. Reduce heat; cover. Simmer until rice is tender and liquid is absorbed, 45 to 55 minutes. Stir in tomatoes, olives and pimiento. Re-cover. Cook until heated through, about 5 minutes.

Per serving: Calories: 736 • Protein: 55 g. • Carbohydrate: 70 g. • Fat: 26 g. • Cholesterol: 170 mg. • Sodium: 1770 mg. — Exchanges: 3 starch, 5 very lean meat, 6 vegetable, 4½ fat

TOMATO-RABBIT CASSEROLE

1	TABLESPOON BUTTER OR MARGARINE
1	TABLESPOON VEGETABLE OIL
1	DRESSED WILD RABBIT OR SUBSTITUTE (1½ TO 2 LBS.), CUT UP
3	MEDIUM POTATOES, QUARTERED
4	TO 6 SMALL ONIONS, QUARTERED OR HALVED
1	CAN (16 OZ.) WHOLE TOMATOES, UNDRAINED
1	CUP VEGETABLE JUICE COCKTAIL
1	BAY LEAF
½	TEASPOON SALT
½	TEASPOON DRIED BASIL LEAVES
¼	TEASPOON DRIED TARRAGON LEAVES
¼	TEASPOON PEPPER

2 or 3 servings

Heat oven to 350°F. In medium skillet, melt butter in oil over medium-low heat. Add rabbit pieces; brown on all sides over medium-high heat. Transfer rabbit pieces to 3-quart casserole. Add remaining ingredients; mix well. Cover; bake until rabbit pieces are tender, about 1½ hours. Discard bay leaf before serving.

Per serving: Calories: 571 • Protein: 54 g. • Carbohydrate: 57 g. • Fat: 14 g. • Cholesterol: 180 mg. • Sodium: 1050 mg. — Exchanges: 2 starch, 5½ very lean meat, 5½ vegetable, 2 fat

Spanish Rabbit

RABBIT STEW

¼ CUP OLIVE OIL

1 DRESSED WILD RABBIT OR SUBSTITUTE (1½ TO 2 LBS.), CUT UP

1 MEDIUM ONION, CHOPPED

2 SHALLOTS, FINELY CHOPPED

1 CAN (16 OZ.) STEWED TOMATOES, UNDRAINED

½ CUP RED WINE

1½ CUPS SLICED FRESH MUSHROOMS

2 MEDIUM CARROTS, SLICED

2 TABLESPOONS BRANDY

2 TABLESPOONS SNIPPED FRESH PARSLEY

1 TEASPOON DRIED OREGANO LEAVES

1 TEASPOON DRIED ROSEMARY LEAVES

½ TEASPOON SALT

¼ TEASPOON PEPPER

1 CUP PITTED BLACK OLIVES

---

2 or 3 servings

In Dutch oven, heat oil over medium-high heat. Add rabbit pieces; brown on all sides. Remove rabbit pieces with slotted spoon; set aside. Add onion and shallots to oil. Cook and stir over medium heat until tender. Add browned rabbit pieces and remaining ingredients except olives. Mix well; cover. Cook over medium heat until rabbit is tender, 50 minutes to 1 hour, turning rabbit pieces occasionally. Add olives; re-cover. Cook about 10 minutes longer.

Per serving: Calories: 557 • Protein: 50 g. • Carbohydrate: 27 g. • Fat: 28 g. • Cholesterol: 170 mg. • Sodium: 1240 mg. — Exchanges: 5½ very lean meat, 5½ vegetable, 5 fat

FRENCH-STYLE RABBIT

¼ CUP OLIVE OIL

2 DRESSED WILD RABBITS OR SUBSTITUTE (1½ TO 2 LBS. EACH), CUT UP

1 CAN (15 OZ.) TOMATO PURÉE

4 OZ. FRESH MUSHROOMS, THINLY SLICED (1½ CUPS)

1 CUP CHOPPED RED PEPPER

⅓ CUP OIL-CURED BLACK OLIVES, PITTED AND SLICED

4 CLOVES GARLIC, MINCED

1 TEASPOON DRIED THYME LEAVES

½ TEASPOON SALT

¼ TEASPOON PEPPER

1 CUP DRY WHITE WINE

---

4 servings

In 6-quart Dutch oven or stockpot, heat oil over medium heat. Add rabbit pieces. Cook for 8 to 10 minutes, or until meat is browned, turning occasionally.

Add remaining ingredients, except wine. Cook for 30 minutes. Add wine. Bring to a boil. Reduce heat to low. Simmer for 30 to 45 minutes, or until meat is tender.

Per Serving: Calories: 585 • Protein: 72 g. • Carbohydrate: 16 g. • Fat: 25 g. • Cholesterol: 257 mg. • Sodium: 1252 mg. — Exchanges: 9 lean meat, 3 vegetable

Rabbit Stew

SOUR CREAM RABBIT WITH HERBS

1/3 CUP PLUS 1 TABLESPOON ALL-PURPOSE FLOUR, DIVIDED

1/2 TEASPOON SALT

1/2 TEASPOON FRESHLY GROUND PEPPER

2 DRESSED WILD RABBITS OR SUBSTITUTE (1 1/2 TO 2 LBS. EACH), CUT UP

3 TABLESPOONS MARGARINE OR BUTTER

3 TABLESPOONS OLIVE OIL

4 MEDIUM ONIONS, CUT INTO 1/2-INCH SLICES

2 CUPS PLUS 2 TABLESPOONS WATER, DIVIDED

1 TABLESPOON TOMATO PASTE

2 TEASPOONS INSTANT BEEF BOUILLON GRANULES

1/4 CUP SOUR CREAM

1 TABLESPOON SNIPPED FRESH PARSLEY

2 TEASPOONS SNIPPED FRESH DILL WEED

---

4 servings

In large plastic food-storage bag, combine 1/3 cup flour, the salt and pepper. Add rabbit pieces, a few at a time, to bag. Shake to coat. In 12-inch non-stick skillet, heat margarine and oil over medium heat. Add rabbit pieces. Cook for 8 to 10 minutes, or until meat is browned, turning occasionally. Remove rabbit pieces from skillet. Set aside.

In same skillet, cook onion slices for 5 to 7 minutes, or until tender, stirring frequently. Add 2 cups water, the tomato paste and the bouillon. Bring to a boil. Return rabbit pieces to skillet. Reduce heat to low. Cover. Simmer for 1 to 1 1/2 hours, or until meat is tender. Transfer rabbit pieces to warm platter. Cover to keep warm. Set aside.

In small bowl, combine remaining 1 tablespoon flour and 2 tablespoons water. Stir flour mixture into liquid in skillet. Cook over medium heat for 3 to 5 minutes, or until mixture thickens and bubbles, stirring constantly. Remove from heat. Stir in sour cream, parsley and dill weed. Pour over rabbit pieces. Serve with hot cooked noodles or rice, if desired.

Variation— Sour Cream Squirrel: Follow recipe as directed, except substitute 3 to 5 squirrels for rabbits. Omit parsley and dill weed. Increase tomato paste to 2 tablespoons and add 1 teaspoon dried oregano leaves, 1 teaspoon chili powder and 1/8 teaspoon garlic powder.

Per Serving: Calories: 676 • Protein: 74 g. • Carbohydrate: 26 g. • Fat: 30 g. • Cholesterol: 264 mg. • Sodium: 999 mg. — Exchanges: 3/4 starch, 9 lean meat, 3 vegetable, 1/2 fat

RABBIT BRAISED WITH BACON & MUSHROOMS

8 SLICES BACON, CUT UP

1/3 CUP ALL-PURPOSE FLOUR

1/2 TEASPOON SALT

1/8 TEASPOON PEPPER

1 DRESSED WILD RABBIT OR SUBSTITUTE (1 1/2 TO 2 LBS.), CUT UP

2 TABLESPOONS BUTTER OR MARGARINE

1 CUP RED WINE

1 MEDIUM ONION, CHOPPED

1/4 CUP BRANDY

1/4 CUP APPLESAUCE

1 TABLESPOON RED WINE VINEGAR

1 TABLESPOON DIJON MUSTARD

2 CLOVES GARLIC, MINCED

1 1/2 CUPS SLICED FRESH MUSHROOMS

SALT AND FRESHLY GROUND BLACK PEPPER

2 or 3 servings

In large skillet, cook bacon over medium heat until crisp, stirring occasionally. Remove skillet from heat. Remove bacon with slotted spoon; set aside. Reserve 2 tablespoons bacon fat in skillet.

In large plastic food-storage bag, combine flour, salt and pepper; shake to mix. Add rabbit pieces; shake to coat. Melt butter in reserved bacon fat in skillet over medium-low heat. Add coated rabbit pieces; brown well on all sides over medium-high heat. Remove rabbit pieces with slotted spoon. Add wine, onion, brandy, applesauce, vinegar, mustard and garlic. Mix well. Return rabbit pieces to skillet. Heat to boiling. Reduce heat; cover. Simmer 45 minutes, turning rabbit pieces occasionally. Add mushrooms and cooked bacon. Re-cover. Simmer until rabbit pieces are tender, 10 to 20 minutes longer. Add salt and pepper to taste.

Per serving: Calories: 579 • Protein: 54 g. • Carbohydrate: 24 g. • Fat: 28 g. • Cholesterol: 215 mg. • Sodium: 1010 mg. — Exchanges: 1 starch, 7 very lean meat, 1/2 fruit, 1 vegetable, 5 fat

RABBIT WITH MUSTARD SAUCE

1 TABLESPOON MARGARINE OR BUTTER

1 DRESSED WILD RABBIT OR SUBSTITUTE (1 1/2 TO 2 LBS.), CUT UP

6 SLICES BACON, CHOPPED

1 TABLESPOON DIJON MUSTARD

1 TABLESPOON ALL-PURPOSE FLOUR

1 CUP DRY WHITE WINE

1 TABLESPOON WHITE WINE VINEGAR

1/2 TEASPOON DRIED ROSEMARY LEAVES, CRUSHED

1/4 TEASPOON SALT

1/4 TEASPOON PEPPER

1/2 CUP SOUR CREAM

2 to 3 servings

Heat oven to 350°F. In 12-inch nonstick skillet, melt margarine over medium heat. Add rabbit pieces. Cook for 8 to 10 minutes, or until meat is browned, turning occasionally. Transfer rabbit pieces to 2-quart casserole. Set aside.

In same skillet, cook bacon over medium heat until brown and crisp. Drain on paper towel–lined plate. Add bacon to casserole. Set aside. Drain and discard all but 1 tablespoon drippings from skillet. Stir in mustard and flour. Blend in wine and vinegar. Cook over medium-low heat for 3 to 5 minutes, or until sauce is slightly thickened, stirring constantly. Stir in rosemary, salt and pepper.

Pour sauce over rabbit pieces. Cover. Bake for 1 to 1 1/2 hours, or until meat is tender. Transfer rabbit pieces to warm platter. Cover to keep warm. Set aside. Stir sour cream into sauce. Bake for 10 to 15 minutes, or until hot. Spoon sauce over rabbit pieces.

Per Serving: Calories: 481 • Protein: 52 g. • Carbohydrate: 5 g. • Fat: 27 g. • Cholesterol: 202 mg. • Sodium: 729 mg. — Exchanges: 1/2 starch, 7 lean meat, 1 fat

OVEN-BARBECUED RABBIT

BARBECUE SAUCE

2 MEDIUM ONIONS, FINELY CHOPPED
2 GREEN PEPPERS, FINELY CHOPPED
1 CLOVE GARLIC, MINCED
1 CUP WATER
1 CUP CIDER VINEGAR
1/2 CUP KETCHUP
1/2 CUP PACKED BROWN SUGAR
1/4 CUP BUTTER OR MARGARINE, CUT UP
2 TABLESPOONS WORCESTERSHIRE SAUCE
1 TEASPOON SALT
1/2 TEASPOON CAYENNE

2 DRESSED WILD RABBITS OR SUBSTITUTE (1 1/2 TO 2 LBS. EACH), CUT UP

4 to 6 servings

Heat oven to 300°F. In medium saucepan, combine all barbecue sauce ingredients. Cook over medium-high heat until bubbly, stirring occasionally. Reduce heat. Simmer 10 minutes. Arrange rabbit pieces in single layer in 13 × 9-inch baking pan. Pour sauce evenly over rabbit pieces. Bake until tender, 2 1/2 to 3 hours, turning rabbit pieces occasionally.

Per serving:
Calories: 439
• Protein: 48 g.
• Carbohydrate: 33 g.
• Fat: 13 g.
• Cholesterol: 195 mg. • Sodium: 870 mg. — Exchanges: 6 very lean meat, 4 vegetable, 2 fat

RABBIT IN APPLE CIDER

1 TABLESPOON BUTTER OR MARGARINE
1 TABLESPOON VEGETABLE OIL
1 DRESSED WILD RABBIT OR SUBSTITUTE (1 1/2 TO 2 LBS.), CUT UP
1 MEDIUM ONION, CUT INTO EIGHTHS
2 MEDIUM CARROTS, DICED
1 1/2 CUPS APPLE CIDER
1/2 TEASPOON SALT
1/4 TEASPOON DRIED THYME LEAVES
1 BAY LEAF
4 WHOLE BLACK PEPPERCORNS
2 MEDIUM COOKING APPLES

2 or 3 servings

In Dutch oven, melt butter in oil over medium-low heat. Add rabbit pieces; brown well on all sides over medium-high heat. Remove rabbit pieces with slotted spoon; set aside. Add onion and carrots to oil. Cook and stir over medium heat until tender. Stir in cider, salt, thyme, bay leaf and peppercorns. Heat to boiling. Add browned rabbit pieces. Reduce heat; cover. Simmer until rabbit pieces are tender, 50 minutes to 1 hour. Core and quarter apples. Add to rabbit pieces. Re-cover. Simmer until apples are just tender, 10 to 15 minutes. Discard bay leaf before serving. If desired, transfer rabbit pieces, vegetables and apples to serving platter with slotted spoon.

Per serving: Calories: 472 • Protein: 48 g.
• Carbohydrate: 39 g.
• Fat: 14 g.
• Cholesterol: 180 mg.
• Sodium: 550 mg. — Exchanges: 6 1/2 very lean meat, 2 fruit, 2 vegetable, 2 fat

Oven-barbecued Rabbit

Rabbit Hunter-style

RABBIT HUNTER-STYLE

2   TABLESPOONS OLIVE OIL
2   DRESSED WILD RABBITS OR SUBSTITUTE (1 1/2 TO 2 LBS. EACH), CUT UP
1   MEDIUM ONION, CUT INTO 1/2-INCH CHUNKS
1   CUP SLICED CELERY (1/2-INCH SLICES)
1/2 CUP SLICED CARROT (1/2-INCH SLICES)
3   CLOVES GARLIC, MINCED
1   CAN (8 OZ.) TOMATO SAUCE
1/4 CUP DRY WHITE WINE
2   TABLESPOONS QUARTERED SPANISH-STYLE OLIVES
1   TABLESPOON CAPERS

4 servings

In 12-inch nonstick skillet, heat oil over medium heat. Add rabbit pieces. Cook for 8 to 10 minutes, or until meat is browned, turning occasionally. Remove rabbit pieces from skillet. Set aside.

In same skillet, cook onion, celery, carrot and garlic over medium-high heat for 3 to 5 minutes, or until vegetables are tender-crisp, stirring frequently. Add rabbit pieces and tomato sauce. Mix well. Reduce heat to low. Cover. Simmer for 1 to 1 1/2 hours, or until meat is tender. Add wine, olives and capers. Simmer for 5 minutes to blend flavors.

Per Serving: Calories: 484 • Protein: 71 g. • Carbohydrate: 11 g. • Fat: 15 g. • Cholesterol: 257 mg. • Sodium: 692 mg. — Exchanges: 8 lean meat, 2 vegetable

HOMESTEADERS' RABBIT OR SQUIRREL WITH CREAM GRAVY

This is based on an old recipe from a Swiss settlement in Wisconsin. Serve with mashed potatoes, pickled beets, green salad, bread, gooseberry jam and thick-sliced Swiss cheese, with cherry pie for dessert.

3   TABLESPOONS ALL-PURPOSE FLOUR
1/2 TEASPOON SALT
1/8 TEASPOON PEPPER
1/8 TEASPOON GROUND NUTMEG
1   DRESSED WILD RABBIT (1 1/2 TO 2 LBS.) OR 2 SQUIRRELS (3/4 TO 1 LB. EACH), CUT UP
2   TABLESPOONS BUTTER OR MARGARINE
2   TABLESPOONS VEGETABLE OIL
3/4 CUP RABBIT STOCK (PAGE 23) OR CHICKEN BROTH
1/2 CUP CHOPPED ONION
1   SMALL BAY LEAF
1/2 CUP HALF-AND-HALF

2 or 3 servings

In large plastic food-storage bag, combine flour, salt, pepper and nutmeg; shake to mix. Add rabbit pieces; shake to coat. Reserve excess flour mixture. In large skillet, melt butter in oil over medium-low heat. Add coated rabbit pieces and excess flour mixture. Brown rabbit pieces on all sides over medium-high heat. Add stock, onion and bay leaf. Heat to boiling. Reduce heat; cover. Simmer until meat is tender, 45 minutes to 1 hour for rabbit, about 1 1/2 hours for squirrel. Stir in cream. Cook over medium-low heat until cream is heated through; do not boil. Discard bay leaf before serving.

Variation: Follow recipe above, substituting 1/2 cup white wine and 1/2 cup water for the rabbit stock. Substitute 1/3 cup dairy sour cream for the half-and-half. Proceed as directed above.

Per serving: Calories: 489 • Protein: 49 g. • Carbohydrate: 11 g. • Fat: 27 g. • Cholesterol: 205 mg. • Sodium: 840 mg. — Exchanges: 1/2 starch, 6 1/2 very lean meat, 1 1/2 vegetable, 4 1/2 fat

WISCONSIN RABBIT PIE

2 DRESSED WILD RABBITS OR SUBSTITUTE (1 1/2 TO 2 LBS. EACH), CUT UP

4 CUPS WATER

1 MEDIUM ONION, CUT INTO QUARTERS

1 CLOVE GARLIC, MINCED

1/2 TEASPOON SALT

1/2 TEASPOON PEPPER

1/4 TEASPOON CAYENNE

4 CUPS PEELED RED POTATOES (4 MEDIUM), CUT INTO 1/2-INCH CUBES

2 CUPS SLICED CARROTS

1/2 CUP SLICED CELERY

1/2 TEASPOON DRIED SAGE OR ROSEMARY LEAVES

CRUST

5 CUPS BUTTERMILK BAKING MIX

1 2/3 CUPS MILK

1 TABLESPOON MARGARINE OR BUTTER, MELTED

6 servings

In 6-quart Dutch oven or stockpot, combine rabbit pieces, water, onion, garlic, salt, pepper and cayenne. Bring to a boil over medium-high heat. Reduce heat to low. Simmer for 1 to 1 1/2 hours, or until meat is tender. Remove from heat. Remove rabbit pieces from broth. Cool slightly. Remove meat from bones. Discard bones. Return meat to broth. Stir in potatoes, carrots, celery and sage. Cook over low heat for 30 to 35 minutes, or until broth is reduced by half and vegetables are tender, stirring occasionally. Remove from heat. Set filling aside.

Heat oven to 425°F. Spray 13 × 9-inch baking dish with nonstick vegetable cooking spray. Set aside. In medium mixing bowl, combine baking mix and milk. Stir with fork until soft dough forms. Divide dough in half.

On lightly floured surface, roll half of dough into 14 × 10-inch rectangle. Fit rectangle into prepared dish, pressing dough over bottom and up sides of dish. Spoon filling evenly into dough-lined dish.

On lightly floured surface, roll remaining dough into 13 × 9-inch rectangle. Place over filling. Roll edges of bottom and top crusts together. Flute edges or press together with tines of fork to seal. Cut several 1-inch slits in top crust to vent. Bake for 20 to 25 minutes, or until crust is golden brown. Brush crust with margarine. Let pie stand for 5 minutes before serving. Garnish with snipped fresh chives, if desired.

Variation: On lightly floured surface, roll dough for top crust to 1/2-inch thickness. Using floured 2- to 3-inch cookie cutters, cut leaf or rabbit shapes. Arrange shapes on top of filling, spacing at least 1 inch apart. Continue as directed above.

Per Serving: Calories: 793 • Protein: 58 g. • Carbohydrate: 90 g. • Fat: 21 g. • Cholesterol: 181 mg. • Sodium: 1722 mg. — Exchanges: 5 1/2 starch, 5 1/2 lean meat, 1 vegetable, 1/4 milk, 1/2 fat

GRANDPA'S FAVORITE RABBIT STEW

1/3 CUP ALL-PURPOSE FLOUR
2 TEASPOONS SALT, DIVIDED
1 TEASPOON FRESHLY GROUND PEPPER, DIVIDED
2 DRESSED WILD RABBITS OR SUBSTITUTE (1 1/2 TO 2 LBS. EACH), CUT UP
3 SLICES BACON
3 TABLESPOONS VEGETABLE OIL
3 CUPS WATER
4 CUPS RED POTATOES (4 MEDIUM), CUT INTO 1/2-INCH CUBES
1 1/2 CUPS CHOPPED CARROTS
2 MEDIUM ONIONS, SLICED
2 CLOVES GARLIC, MINCED
1 CUP SOUR CREAM
1/4 CUP SNIPPED FRESH PARSLEY
2 TO 3 TEASPOONS PAPRIKA

8 to 10 servings

In large plastic food-storage bag, combine flour, 1 teaspoon salt and 1/2 teaspoon pepper. Add rabbit pieces. Shake to coat. Set aside. In 6-quart Dutch oven or stockpot, cook bacon over medium heat for 5 to 7 minutes, or until brown and crisp, turning occasionally. Drain on paper towel–lined plate. Cool slightly. Crumble bacon. Set aside.

In same Dutch oven, heat bacon drippings and oil over medium heat. Add rabbit pieces. Cook for 8 to 10 minutes, or until meat is browned, turning occasionally. Drain and discard oil from Dutch oven.

In same Dutch oven, add remaining 1 teaspoon salt, 1/2 teaspoon pepper, the bacon, water, potatoes, carrots, onions and garlic. Bring to a boil over medium-high heat. Reduce heat to low. Cover. Simmer for 45 minutes to 1 hour, or until meat is tender. Remove from heat. Stir in sour cream, parsley and paprika. Serve immediately.

Per Serving: Calories: 362 • Protein: 31 g. • Carbohydrate: 22 g. • Fat: 16 g. • Cholesterol: 118 mg. • Sodium: 576 mg. — Exchanges: 3/4 starch, 3 1/2 lean meat, 2 1/4 vegetable, 1 fat

INDIANA RABBIT STEW

1/2 CUP ALL-PURPOSE FLOUR
1/2 TEASPOON SALT
1/4 TEASPOON PEPPER
2 DRESSED WILD RABBITS OR SUBSTITUTE (1 1/2 TO 2 LBS. EACH), CUT UP
3 TABLESPOONS BACON DRIPPINGS OR VEGETABLE OIL
4 CUPS CHICKEN BROTH
1 CUP THINLY SLICED CELERY
1 CUP CHOPPED ONION
5 CUPS RED POTATOES (5 MEDIUM), CUT INTO 3/4-INCH CUBES
2 CANS (15 OZ. EACH) TOMATO SAUCE
8 OZ. FRESH MUSHROOMS, SLICED (3 CUPS)
2 1/2 CUPS THINLY SLICED CARROTS
1 LARGE GREEN PEPPER, CUT INTO 1/2-INCH CHUNKS

10 to 12 servings

In large plastic food-storage bag, combine flour, salt and pepper. Add rabbit pieces. Shake to coat. In 6-quart Dutch oven or stockpot, heat bacon drippings over medium heat. Add rabbit pieces. Cook for 8 to 10 minutes, or until meat is browned, turning occasionally. Add broth, celery and onions. Reduce heat to low. Cover. Simmer for 45 minutes to 1 hour, or until meat is tender, stirring occasionally.

Remove from heat. Remove rabbit pieces from broth. Cool meat slightly. Remove meat from bones. Discard bones. Cut meat into 1/4-inch pieces. Return meat to broth. Add remaining ingredients. Bring to a boil over medium heat. Reduce heat to medium-low. Cover. Simmer for 20 to 25 minutes, or until stew thickens slightly and vegetables are tender, stirring occasionally.

Per Serving: Calories: 267 • Protein: 28 g. • Carbohydrate: 26 g. • Fat: 6 g. • Cholesterol: 88 mg. • Sodium: 941 mg. — Exchanges: 1 starch, 2 3/4 lean meat, 2 vegetable

HASENPFEFFER

Marinating tenderizes hare or mature rabbits in this classic German recipe. Serve with hot buttered egg noodles, braised red cabbage, rye bread and a good beer.

1 DRESSED WILD HARE (2½ TO 3 LBS.) OR 2 WILD RABBITS (1½ TO 2 LBS. EACH), CUT UP

MARINADE

2 CUPS RED WINE
1 CUP WATER
½ CUP CIDER VINEGAR
2 CLOVES GARLIC, MINCED
½ TEASPOON DRIED THYME LEAVES
½ TEASPOON DRIED ROSEMARY LEAVES
½ TEASPOON DRIED MARJORAM LEAVES
10 WHOLE BLACK PEPPERCORNS

½ CUP ALL-PURPOSE FLOUR
6 SLICES BACON, CUT UP
8 OZ. FRESH MUSHROOMS, CUT INTO QUARTERS
1 CUP CHOPPED ONION
1 TO 3 TABLESPOONS BUTTER
1 TEASPOON SALT
½ CUP SOUR CREAM

4 to 6 servings

In large glass or ceramic mixing bowl, combine hare pieces and all marinade ingredients. Cover bowl with plastic wrap. Refrigerate for 2 or 3 days, turning hare pieces daily.

Lift hare pieces out of marinade. Pat dry with paper towels; set aside. Strain and reserve 1½ cups marinade, discarding herbs and excess marinade. Place flour on a sheet of waxed paper. Add hare pieces, turning to coat. In Dutch oven, cook bacon over medium heat until almost crisp. Add mushrooms and onion. Cook until onion is tender, stirring occasionally. Remove vegetable mixture with slotted spoon; set aside. Add 1 tablespoon butter to pan. Add hare pieces. Brown on all sides, adding more butter if necessary. Return vegetable mixture to Dutch oven. Add salt and reserved marinade. Heat to boiling. Reduce heat; cover. Simmer until hare pieces are tender, 1 to 1¼ hours. With slotted spoon, transfer hare pieces to heated serving platter. Set aside and keep warm. Blend sour cream into cooking liquid. Cook over medium heat until heated through, stirring occasionally; do not boil. Serve sauce over hare.

Per serving: Calories: 454: Protein: 41 g. • Carbohydrate: 14 g. • Fat: 25 g. • Cholesterol: 170 mg. • Sodium: 680 mg. — Exchanges: ½ starch, 5½ very lean meat, 1½ vegetable, 4½ fat

SHERRIED SQUIRREL

4   DRESSED SQUIRRELS OR SUBSTITUTE (3/4 TO 1 LB. EACH), CUT UP

2   QUARTS WATER

1   TABLESPOON SALT

2   TEASPOONS VINEGAR

1/3 CUP ALL-PURPOSE FLOUR

1   TEASPOON SALT

1/8 TEASPOON PEPPER

2   TABLESPOONS BUTTER OR MARGARINE

2   TABLESPOONS VEGETABLE OIL

8   OZ. FRESH WHOLE MUSHROOMS

SHERRY SAUCE

1   CUP CHICKEN BROTH

1/4 CUP SHERRY

1   TABLESPOON WORCESTERSHIRE SAUCE

1/4 TEASPOON SEASONED SALT

2   OR 3 DROPS HOT RED PEPPER SAUCE

4 to 6 servings

In large glass or ceramic bowl, combine squirrel pieces, water, 1 tablespoon salt and the vinegar. Cover bowl with plastic wrap. Let stand at room temperature 1 hour. Drain, discarding liquid. Pat squirrel pieces dry; set aside.

Heat oven to 350°F. In large plastic food-storage bag, combine flour, 1 teaspoon salt and the pepper; shake to mix. Add squirrel pieces; shake to coat. In large skillet, melt butter in oil over medium-low heat. Add squirrel pieces; brown on all sides over medium-high heat. Transfer squirrel pieces and drippings to 3-quart casserole. Add mushrooms. In 2-cup measure, combine all sherry sauce ingredients. Pour over squirrel pieces and mushrooms. Cover casserole. Bake until tender, about 1 1/2 hours.

Per serving: Calories: 385 • Protein: 47 g. • Carbohydrate: 9 g. • Fat: 16 g. • Cholesterol: 185 mg. • Sodium: 1280 mg. — Exchanges: 1/2 starch, 6 1/2 very lean meat, 1/2 vegetable, 2 1/2 fat

One-pot Squirrel Dinner

SQUIRREL SUPREME

2 TABLESPOONS OLIVE OIL

2 DRESSED SQUIRRELS OR SUBSTITUTE (3/4 TO 1 LB. EACH), CUT UP

1 LARGE ONION, THINLY SLICED

1 CUP WATER

1 TABLESPOON DRIED SAGE LEAVES

2 CLOVES GARLIC, MINCED

1 TEASPOON DRIED BASIL LEAVES

1 TEASPOON DRIED PARSLEY FLAKES

1 CUP DRY RED WINE

---

2 servings

In 10-inch nonstick skillet, heat oil over medium heat. Add squirrel pieces. Cook for 8 to 10 minutes, or until meat is browned, turning occasionally.

Add remaining ingredients, except wine. Reduce heat to low. Cover. Simmer for 1 to 1 1/2 hours, or until meat is tender. Add wine. Cook, uncovered, over medium heat for 10 minutes. Serve over hot cooked rice, if desired.

Per Serving: Calories: 638 • Protein: 69 g.
• Carbohydrate: 14 g. • Fat: 24 g. • Cholesterol: 264 mg.
• Sodium: 338 mg. — Exchanges: 9 lean meat,
2 vegetable

ONE-POT SQUIRREL DINNER

1 PKG. (8 OZ.) CREAM CHEESE, CUT INTO 1-INCH CUBES, SOFTENED

3/4 CUP MILK

1 PKG. (16 OZ.) FROZEN BROCCOLI, CARROTS AND CAULIFLOWER, DEFROSTED AND DRAINED

3 CUPS COOKED RAINBOW FUSILLI OR ROTINI

2 CUPS CUBED COOKED SQUIRREL OR SUBSTITUTE (8 TO 10 OZ.)

1 CAN (4 OZ.) SLICED MUSHROOMS, DRAINED

2 TABLESPOONS DIJON MUSTARD

1/2 TEASPOON DRIED DILL WEED

1/4 TEASPOON SALT

1/4 TEASPOON PEPPER

1/2 CUP SHREDDED FRESH PARMESAN CHEESE

---

6 to 8 servings

In 3-quart saucepan, combine cream cheese and milk. Cook over medium heat for 4 to 6 minutes, or until mixture is smooth, stirring constantly. Add remaining ingredients, except Parmesan cheese. Cook over medium-low heat for 5 to 7 minutes, or until mixture is hot, stirring occasionally. Sprinkle each serving evenly with Parmesan cheese.

Per Serving: Calories: 175 • Protein: 14 g.
• Carbohydrate: 20 g. • Fat: 4 g. • Cholesterol: 35 mg.
• Sodium: 382 mg. — Exchanges: 1 starch, 1 1/3 lean meat, 1 vegetable

SQUIRREL POT PIE

FILLING

2½ CUPS CUBED COOKED SQUIRREL OR SUBSTITUTE (ABOUT 12 OZ.)

2 CUPS PEELED RED POTATOES (2 MEDIUM), CUT INTO ½-INCH CUBES

1½ CUPS FROZEN PEAS AND CARROTS

1 CAN (10¾ OZ.) CONDENSED CREAM OF MUSHROOM SOUP

½ CUP THINLY SLICED CELERY

½ CUP CHOPPED ONION

½ CUP SQUIRREL BROTH OR CHICKEN BROTH

½ TEASPOON INSTANT CHICKEN BOUILLON GRANULES

¼ TEASPOON FRESHLY GROUND PEPPER

CRUST

¾ CUP ALL-PURPOSE FLOUR

1 TEASPOON BAKING POWDER

¼ TEASPOON SALT

¾ CUP MILK

½ CUP MARGARINE OR BUTTER, MELTED

6 servings

Heat oven to 375°F. Spray 8-inch square baking dish with nonstick vegetable cooking spray. Set aside. In 12-inch nonstick skillet, combine filling ingredients. Bring to a boil over medium-high heat. Remove from heat. Spoon filling evenly into prepared dish. Set aside.

In medium mixing bowl, combine flour, baking powder and salt. Add milk and margarine. Stir with fork just until dry ingredients are moistened. Spoon batter evenly over filling, spreading to edges. Bake for 30 to 35 minutes, or until crust is golden brown.

Per Serving: Calories: 411 • Protein: 20 g. • Carbohydrate: 32 g. • Fat: 23 g. • Cholesterol: 59 mg. • Sodium: 1032 mg. — Exchanges: 2 starch, 2 lean meat, ½ vegetable, 3 fat

SOUTHERN FRIED SQUIRREL OR RABBIT WITH GRAVY

⅓ CUP ALL-PURPOSE FLOUR

½ TEASPOON SALT

⅛ TEASPOON BLACK PEPPER

⅛ TEASPOON CAYENNE, OPTIONAL

2 SQUIRRELS (¾ TO 1 LB. EACH) OR 1 WILD RABBIT (1½ TO 2 LBS.), CUT UP

VEGETABLE OIL

3 TABLESPOONS ALL-PURPOSE FLOUR

1½ CUPS MILK OR CHICKEN BROTH

SALT AND PEPPER

BROWN BOUQUET SAUCE, OPTIONAL

2 or 3 servings

In large plastic food-storage bag, combine ⅓ cup flour, salt, black pepper and cayenne; shake to mix. Add squirrel pieces; shake to coat. In large skillet, heat ⅛ inch oil for squirrel, or ¼ inch oil for rabbit, over medium-high heat until hot. Add coated meat; brown on all sides. Reduce heat; cover tightly. Cook over very low heat until tender, 35 to 45 minutes for squirrel, 20 to 25 minutes for rabbit, turning pieces once. Remove cover; cook 5 minutes longer to crisp. Transfer meat to plate lined with paper towels. Set aside and keep warm.

Discard all but 3 tablespoons oil. Over medium heat, stir flour into reserved oil. Blend in milk. Cook over medium heat, stirring constantly, until thickened and bubbly. Add salt and pepper to taste. Add bouquet sauce if darker color is desired. Serve gravy with meat.

Per serving: Calories: 567 • Protein: 51 g. • Carbohydrate: 22 g. • Fat: 29 g. • Cholesterol: 190 mg. • Sodium: 660 mg. — Exchanges: 1½ starch, 7 very lean meat, 5 fat

BRUNSWICK STEW

1/4 CUP ALL-PURPOSE FLOUR

1   TEASPOON SALT

1/4 TO 1/2 TEASPOON PEPPER

3   DRESSED SQUIRRELS (3/4 TO 1 LB. EACH), CUT UP

2   SLICES BACON, CUT UP

2   TABLESPOONS BUTTER OR MARGARINE

5   CUPS WATER

1   CAN (28 OZ.) WHOLE TOMATOES, DRAINED

1   MEDIUM ONION, CHOPPED

1   TABLESPOON PACKED BROWN SUGAR

2   MEDIUM POTATOES

1   PACKAGE (10 OZ.) FROZEN LIMA BEANS

1   CUP FRESH OR FROZEN WHOLE-KERNEL CORN

3   TABLESPOONS ALL-PURPOSE FLOUR, OPTIONAL

3   TABLESPOONS COLD WATER, OPTIONAL

6 to 8 servings

In large plastic food-storage bag, combine 1/4 cup flour, salt and pepper; shake to mix. Add squirrel pieces; shake to coat. Set aside. In Dutch oven, combine bacon and butter. Heat over medium heat until butter melts. Add squirrel pieces; brown on all sides. Fry in two batches if necessary. Add 5 cups water, the tomatoes, onion and brown sugar. Heat to boiling. Reduce heat; cover. Simmer until squirrel pieces are tender, 1 1/2 to 2 hours, stirring occasionally.

Remove squirrel pieces; set aside to cool slightly. Cut potatoes into 1/2-inch cubes. Remove squirrel meat from bones; discard bones. Add squirrel meat, potatoes, beans and corn to Dutch oven. Heat to boiling. Reduce heat; cover. Simmer until potatoes are tender, 25 to 35 minutes. If stew is thinner than desired, blend 3 tablespoons flour and 3 table-spoons cold water in small bowl. Add to stew, stirring constantly. Heat to boiling. Cook over medium heat, stirring constantly, until thickened and bubbly.

Per serving: Calories: 336 • Protein: 31 g. • Carbohydrate: 29 g. • Fat: 11 g. • Cholesterol: 110 mg. • Sodium: 670 mg. — Exchanges: 1 1/2 starch, 3 1/2 very lean meat, 1 1/2 vegetable, 1 1/2 fat

CROCKPOT COON STEW

3   TO 4 LBS. WELL-TRIMMED RACCOON PIECES

8   CUPS WATER

3   CUPS CHOPPED ONION

2   CUPS SLICED CARROTS

2   CUPS RED POTATOES (4 SMALL), CUT INTO 1-INCH CUBES

2   CUPS BEEF BROTH

1   CAN (15 OZ.) TOMATO SAUCE

4   OZ. FRESH MUSHROOMS, CHOPPED (1 1/2 CUPS)

1   CUP SLICED FRESH OR FROZEN OKRA

1   CUP SLICED YELLOW SUMMER SQUASH OR ZUCCHINI SQUASH

1   CUP SHREDDED GREEN CABBAGE

1   CUP CHOPPED CELERY

1/4 CUP DRY RED WINE

1   TABLESPOON ITALIAN HERB BLEND

4   BAY LEAVES

1/4 TEASPOON PEPPER

6 servings

In 6-quart Dutch oven or stockpot, combine rac-coon pieces and water. Bring to a boil over high heat. Reduce heat to low. Cover. Simmer for 1 1/2 to 2 hours, or until meat is tender. Drain and discard broth. Cool meat slightly. Remove meat from bones. Discard bones. Cut meat into 1/4-inch pieces. In 4-quart crockpot, combine meat and remaining ingredients. Cover. Cook on high for 1 hour. Reduce heat to low. Cook for 8 hours, or until vegetables are tender and flavors are blended. Remove and discard bay leaves before serving.

Per Serving: Calories: 355 • Protein: 28 g. • Carbohydrate: 35 g. • Fat: 12 g. • Cholesterol: N/A • Sodium: N/A — Exchanges: 3/4 starch, 2 1/2 lean meat, 4 3/4 vegetable, 1 fat

RECIPES FOR
Waterfowl

The sport of waterfowl hunting has exploded over the last few years, thanks in large part to the incredible rebound in waterfowl numbers. In fact, many die-hard duck and goose hunters believe that hunting is better today than ever before.

During the 1980s and early 1990s, waterfowl numbers were down as a result of a lengthy drought. But because of a break in the drought and the efforts of conservation organizations such as Ducks Unlimited, waterfowl numbers have climbed higher than even the most optimistic wildlife biologist would have predicted.

With this increase in the duck and goose population has come an increase in the daily bag limits for many waterfowl species. As a result of these rule changes, more waterfowl meat is showing up on the dinner table.

The taste of duck varies greatly, depending on the species and the individual duck. Canvasbacks, ringnecks, mallards and teal are the favorites for eating. Redheads, black ducks, wood ducks and pintails are also excellent.

Smell the meat before cooking it. If it has a muddy or fishy odor, you may wish to marinate it or cook it with a flavorful sauce. Next, consider the fat content. The breast is the best place to check for fat. If you can see a yellow layer through the skin, the duck is fat enough for roasting or smoking. If the duck's breast appears dark, however, it may lack fat. Lean ducks require more basting or moist cooking.

Also consider the bird's age. Old, tough birds can be tenderized by long, moist cooking, by parboiling and then roasting, or by pressure-cooking.

Some people enjoy their waterfowl cooked rare. The meat is juicy and flavorful, slightly reminiscent of rare beef. At the other extreme, some prefer it cooked at low heat until the meat literally falls off the bone.

To determine the degree of doneness, prick the bird with a fork. If the juices are rosy, the bird is rare. The juices will run clear on a well-done bird.

Wild geese and ducks are more robustly flavored than domestic waterfowl. They're delicious if properly prepared, although the dark, rich meat is not to everyone's liking. Geese have a milder flavor than ducks and may be a better choice for those who have never tasted wild waterfowl.

WATERFOWL SUBSTITUTION GUIDE

With over 20 species of ducks and geese on this chart, we've taken a "mix-and-match" approach to substitutions. The chart is broken into four areas: Large Geese, Medium-size Geese, Small Geese/Large Ducks and Small Ducks. If the recipe calls for a mallard, locate it on the chart, then substitute any of the other ducks from that same area of the chart.

Breast meat from any of these birds can be substituted for mallard breast in recipes. Domestic ducks are generally too fatty to substitute for wild ducks. Upland game birds with dark meat also make good substitutes for duck if the cuts are the same size.

If a recipe calls for a whole Canada goose, you can substitute any wild goose of similar size. You can also substitute a domestic goose of the proper size, but the flavor is not as rich as that of wild goose. You will have to prick the skin of a domestic goose frequently during roasting to allow the excess fat to drain off; skim the fat from the pan juices prior to making gravy or sauce.

Waterfowl Substitution Chart

	SPECIES	APPROXIMATE DRESSED WEIGHT	NUMBER OF SERVINGS	COOKING METHOD
LARGE GEESE	GIANT CANADA (YOUNG)	4 TO 6 LBS.	4 TO 6	OVEN ROAST, GRILL, PANFRY
	GIANT CANADA (MATURE)	6½ TO 10 LBS.	6 TO 10	PARBOIL/ROAST, BRAISE, STEW
	INTERIOR CANADA (MATURE)	4¾ TO 6 LBS.	5 TO 10	PARBOIL/ROAST, BRAISE, STEW
MEDIUM-SIZE GEESE	LESSER CANADA	3 TO 4½ LBS.	3 TO 6	OVEN ROAST, GRILL, PANFRY
	SNOW OR BLUE GOOSE	3 TO 4 LBS.	3 TO 5	OVEN ROAST, GRILL, PANFRY
	WHITE-FRONTED GOOSE	3½ TO 3¾ LBS.	3 TO 5	OVEN ROAST, GRILL, PANFRY
	INTERIOR CANADA (YOUNG)	3½ TO 4½ LBS.	4 TO 5	OVEN ROAST, GRILL, PANFRY
SMALL GEESE/ LARGE DUCKS	CACKLING CANADA	2 TO 2½ LBS.	2 TO 3	OVEN ROAST, GRILL, PANFRY
	BRANT	1¾ TO 2½ LBS.	2 TO 3	OVEN ROAST, GRILL, PANFRY
	CANVASBACK	1¾ LBS.	2	OVEN ROAST, GRILL, PANFRY
	MALLARD	1¼ TO 1½ LBS.	2	OVEN ROAST, GRILL, PANFRY
	BLACK DUCK	1¼ TO 1½ LBS.	2	OVEN ROAST, GRILL, PANFRY
	REDHEAD	1¼ LBS.	2	OVEN ROAST, GRILL, PANFRY
	GREATER SCAUP (BLUEBILL)	1¼ LBS.	2	OVEN ROAST, GRILL, PANFRY
SMALL DUCKS	GOLDENEYE (WHISTLER)	1 TO 1¼ LBS.	1 TO 1½	OVEN ROAST, GRILL, PANFRY
	PINTAIL	1 TO 1¼ LBS.	1 TO 1½	OVEN ROAST, GRILL, PANFRY
	GADWALL	¾ TO 1 LB.	1 TO 1½	OVEN ROAST, GRILL, PANFRY
	LESSER SCAUP	¾ TO 1 LB.	1 TO 1½	OVEN ROAST, GRILL, PANFRY
	WIDGEON (BALDPATE)	¾ TO 1 LB.	1 TO 1½	OVEN ROAST, GRILL, PANFRY
	RINGNECK (RINGBILL)	¾ LB.	1 TO 1½	OVEN ROAST, GRILL, PANFRY
	WOOD DUCK	½ TO ¾ LB.	1	OVEN ROAST, GRILL, PANFRY
	BUFFLEHEAD	5 OZ. TO ¾ LB.	1	OVEN ROAST, GRILL, PANFRY
	BLUE-WINGED TEAL	½ LB.	1	OVEN ROAST, GRILL, PANFRY
	CINNAMON TEAL	5 OZ. TO ½ LB.	1	OVEN ROAST, GRILL, PANFRY
	GREEN-WINGED TEAL	5 TO 6 OZ.	1 OR LESS	OVEN ROAST, GRILL, PANFRY

FRUITED ROAST GOOSE

1   WHOLE DRESSED CANADA GOOSE (6 TO 8 LBS.), SKIN ON
1/2 TEASPOON SALT
1/2 TEASPOON PEPPER
1   MEDIUM SEEDLESS ORANGE, CUT INTO 8 WEDGES
1   MEDIUM RED COOKING APPLE, CORED AND CUT INTO 8 WEDGES
1   CAN (16 OZ.) SLICED PEACHES IN SYRUP, DRAINED (RESERVE 1/2 CUP SYRUP)
1   TABLESPOON VEGETABLE OIL
13/4 CUPS BEEF BROTH
2   TABLESPOONS CORNSTARCH MIXED WITH 2 TABLESPOONS WATER
1   TABLESPOON SOY SAUCE

6 servings

Heat oven to 350°F. Sprinkle cavity of goose with salt and pepper. Stuff goose loosely with orange, apple and peach slices. Secure legs with string. Tuck wing tips behind back. Brush goose with oil. Place goose breast side up on rack in roasting pan. Pour broth and reserved peach syrup around goose. Bake for 20 to 25 minutes per pound, or until legs move freely and juices run clear, basting occasionally with pan drippings. Transfer goose to warm platter. Let stand, tented with foil, for 10 to 15 minutes.

Meanwhile, strain drippings from bottom of roasting pan. Skim and discard fat from drippings. In 1-quart saucepan, combine 2 cups drippings, the cornstarch mixture and soy sauce. Cook over medium heat for 5 to 7 minutes, or until sauce thickens and bubbles, stirring constantly. Serve sauce with carved goose.

Per Serving: Calories: 770 • Protein: 55 g. • Carbohydrate: 26 g. • Fat: 50 g. Cholesterol: 194 mg. • Sodium: 749 mg. — Exchanges: 8 medium-fat meat, 1 2/3 fruit, 2 fat

MARYLAND WILD GOOSE

1   CUP MARGARINE OR BUTTER
2   CUPS THINLY SLICED CELERY
1/2 CUP CHOPPED ONION
4   CUPS UNSEASONED DRY BREAD CRUMBS
2   MEDIUM RED COOKING APPLES, CORED AND CUT INTO 1-INCH CHUNKS
3   HARD-COOKED EGGS, CHOPPED
1   CUP SNIPPED FRESH PARSLEY
1/2 TEASPOON SALT
1/4 TEASPOON PEPPER
1/4 TEASPOON DRIED BASIL LEAVES
1/4 TEASPOON POULTRY SEASONING
1/8 TEASPOON DRIED THYME LEAVES
    DASH CAYENNE
1   WHOLE DRESSED WILD GOOSE (4 TO 6 LBS.), SKIN ON
4   SLICES BACON

4 to 6 servings

Heat oven to 325°F. In 10-inch nonstick skillet, melt margarine over medium heat. Add celery and onion. Cook for 3 to 4 minutes or until vegetables are tender, stirring occasionally. Remove from heat. In large mixing bowl, combine celery mixture, bread crumbs, apples, eggs, parsley, salt, pepper, basil, poultry seasoning, thyme and cayenne.

Spoon stuffing into cavity of goose. (Wrap extra stuffing in foil and bake separately.) Secure legs with string. Tuck wing tips behind back. Place goose breast side up on rack in roasting pan. Place bacon slices across breast. Bake for 20 to 25 minutes per pound, or until legs move freely and juices run clear, basting occasionally with pan drippings.

Per Serving: Calories: 1180 • Protein: 58g. • Carbohydrate: 63 g. • Fat: 76 g. • Cholesterol: 268 mg. • Sodium: 1354 mg. — Exchanges: 3 1/2 starch, 6 1/2 medium-fat meat, 1/2 fruit, 8 1/2 fat

Fruited Roast Goose

DUCKS WITH ORANGE SAUCE

1   MEDIUM ORANGE

2   WHOLE DRESSED PUDDLE DUCKS (1 1/4 TO 1 1/2 LBS. EACH), SKIN ON

1   SMALL ONION, QUARTERED

2   WHOLE CLOVES GARLIC

1/4   CUP BUTTER, MELTED

2   TEASPOONS DRIED ROSEMARY LEAVES

1   TEASPOON DRIED THYME LEAVES

1   TEASPOON DRIED PARSLEY FLAKES

2/3   CUP CHICKEN BROTH

1/2   CUP ORANGE-FLAVORED LIQUEUR

1/4   CUP ORANGE JUICE

1   TABLESPOON RED WINE VINEGAR

---

4 servings

Heat oven to 400°F. With vegetable peeler, peel 1 tablespoon orange zest from orange. (Do not include white part of orange.) Set zest aside. Cut orange into quarters.

Stuff ducks evenly with orange quarters, onion and garlic cloves. Secure legs with kitchen string. Tuck wing tips behind back. Place ducks breast side up on rack in roasting pan. Brush evenly with butter. Sprinkle ducks evenly with rosemary, thyme and parsley. Roast for 35 to 45 minutes, or until skin is golden brown and meat is desired doneness. Place ducks on serving platter. Set aside and keep warm.

Pour pan juices into 10-inch skillet. Stir in broth, liqueur, orange juice and zest. Bring to a boil over medium-high heat. Boil for 8 to 10 minutes, or until liquid is reduced to 1/2 cup, stirring occasionally. Stir in vinegar. Simmer for 3 minutes. Serve sauce with ducks.

Per Serving: Calories: 563 • Protein: 34 g. • Carbohydrate: 15 g. • Fat: 40 g. • Cholesterol: 181 mg. • Sodium: 391 mg. — Exchanges: 4 1/2 medium-fat meat, 1/2 vegetable, 3 1/2 fat

Ducks with Orange Sauce

ROAST GOOSE IN OVEN COOKING BAG

1   TABLESPOON ALL-PURPOSE FLOUR

1   WHOLE DRESSED WILD GOOSE (ABOUT 8 LBS.), SKIN ON

1   CUP DRY RED WINE

1   CUP WATER

1   PKG. (1 OZ.) ONION SOUP MIX

---

6 to 8 servings

Heat oven to 350°F. Add flour to turkey-size (23 1/2 × 19-inch) oven cooking bag; shake to distribute. Place cooking bag in large roasting pan.

Rinse goose and pat dry with paper towels. Place goose in oven cooking bag. In small mixing bowl, combine wine, water and soup mix. Pour mixture over goose in bag. Secure bag with provided nylon tie. Insert meat thermometer into thickest part of goose breast through top of bag. Make six 1/2-inch slits in top of bag.

Roast goose for 1 1/2 to 2 hours, or until internal temperature registers 180°F. Remove goose from bag. Let stand, tented with foil, for 10 minutes before carving.

Per Serving: Calories: 662 • Protein: 54 g. • Carbohydrate: 1 g. • Fat: 47 g. • Cholesterol: 196 mg. • Sodium: 231 mg. — Exchanges: 7 3/4 medium-fat meat, 1 1/2 fat

Bahama Roast Mallard

MISSISSIPPI PEPPER DUCKS

2   WHOLE DRESSED WILD DUCKS (1 1/4 TO 1 1/2 LBS. EACH), SKIN ON
1   TANGERINE, PEELED AND CUT IN HALF
1   MEDIUM ONION, CUT INTO QUARTERS
1   CUP CHOPPED CELERY
1/2 CUP DRY WHITE WINE
1   TO 2 TABLESPOONS BACON DRIPPINGS, MELTED
1   TEASPOON GREEK SEASONING
2   SLICES BACON, CUT IN HALF CROSSWISE
1/4 CUP HOT RED PEPPER JELLY, MELTED

4 servings

Heat oven to 325°F. Line 13 × 9-inch baking dish with heavy-duty foil, allowing foil to extend about 10 inches on each side. Set aside. Place half of tangerine, half of onion quarters, half of celery and 1/4 cup wine in each duck cavity. Secure legs with string. Place ducks breast side up in prepared dish. Brush ducks with bacon drippings. Sprinkle ducks with seasoning. Place bacon slices across breasts. Fold long sides of foil together in locked folds. Fold and crimp ends. Bake for 40 to 45 minutes, or until meat is tender. Fold back foil. Brush ducks with jelly. Bake, with foil open, for 30 to 35 minutes, or until skin is lightly browned and juices run clear.

Per Serving: Calories: 580 • Protein: 24 g. • Carbohydrate: 21 g. • Fat: 44 g. • Cholesterol: 111 mg. • Sodium: 208 mg. — Exchanges: 3 1/3 high-fat meat, 1 vegetable, 1 fruit, 3 1/2 fat

Cherry Sauce for Waterfowl

Drain juices from 16-oz. can pitted dark sweet cherries into a 2-cup measure; add brandy to equal 1 2/3 cups. In medium saucepan, blend cherry juice mixture with 2 tablespoons cornstarch, 2 tablespoons lemon juice and a dash of salt. Cook over medium heat, stirring constantly, until translucent and bubbly. Add 2 tablespoons honey and 2 tablespoons butter or margarine. Cook and stir over low heat until butter melts. Add cherries and cook until hot.

BAHAMA ROAST MALLARDS

4   WHOLE DRESSED MALLARDS OR SUBSTITUTE (1 1/4 TO 1 1/2 LBS. EACH), SKIN ON
1/4 CUP LIME JUICE
2   TABLESPOONS ORANGE MARMALADE
4   CLOVES GARLIC, MINCED
1   TABLESPOON WATER
1   TEASPOON RUM
1   TEASPOON SEASONED SALT
1   MEDIUM SEEDLESS ORANGE, PEELED AND QUARTERED
4   CLOVES GARLIC
12 PEPPERCORNS

8 servings

Place ducks breast side up in 15 1/2 × 10 1/2-inch jelly roll pan or large roasting pan. Set aside. In small mixing bowl, combine lime juice, marmalade, minced garlic, water and rum. Brush ducks with mixture. Cover with plastic wrap. Chill 6 to 8 hours.

Heat oven to 300°F. Remove ducks from pan. Drain and reserve marmalade mixture. Sprinkle 1/4 teaspoon salt over each duck. Place 1 orange quarter, 1 garlic clove and 3 peppercorns in cavity of each duck. Arrange ducks breast side up in same jelly roll pan. Bake for 1 1/2 to 2 hours, or until meat is desired doneness, brushing several times with reserved marmalade mixture. Serve with hot cooked rice and fried plantains, if desired.

Per Serving: Calories: 428 • Protein: 23 g. • Carbohydrate: 7 g. • Fat: 34 g. • Cholesterol: 100 mg. • Sodium: 231 mg. — Exchanges: 3 1/4 high-fat meat, 1/2 fruit, 1 1/2 fat

CRISP APPLE-GLAZED DUCK

1 WHOLE DRESSED MALLARD OR
   SUBSTITUTE (1¼ TO 1½ LBS.),
   SKIN ON

1 LARGE RED COOKING APPLE, CORED
   AND CUT INTO 1-INCH CHUNKS

1 CUP BOILING WATER

1 TEASPOON INSTANT CHICKEN BOUILLON
   GRANULES

APPLE GLAZE

½ CUP APPLE JELLY

2 TABLESPOONS APPLE JUICE OR DRY
   WHITE WINE

2 servings

Heat oven to 375°F. Stuff duck loosely with apple. Secure legs with string. Tuck wing tips behind back. Place duck breast side up on rack in roasting pan. In small mixing bowl, combine water and bouillon. Stir until bouillon is dissolved. Pour half of bouillon mixture over duck. Bake for 45 minutes, basting occasionally with remaining bouillon mixture.

Meanwhile, in 1-quart saucepan, combine glaze ingredients. Cook over medium heat until jelly is melted. Brush duck with some of glaze. Bake for 10 to 20 minutes, or until meat is desired doneness, basting frequently with glaze. Garnish with apple slices and fresh parsley, if desired. Serve any remaining warm glaze with duck.

Per Serving: Calories: 687 • Protein: 23 g. • Carbohydrate: 74 g. • Fat: 34 g. • Cholesterol: 100 mg. • Sodium: 579 mg. — Exchanges: 3⅓ high-fat meat, 5 fruit, 1½ fat

CREOLE DUCK

1/2 CUP BUTTER OR MARGARINE, DIVIDED

1 MEDIUM GREEN PEPPER, SEEDED AND CHOPPED (1 1/4 CUPS)

1 MEDIUM ONION, CHOPPED (1 CUP)

8 OZ. FRESH MUSHROOMS, SLICED (3 CUPS)

2 CLOVES GARLIC, MINCED

2 CANS (14 1/2 OZ. EACH) DICED TOMATOES

1 CUP CHICKEN BROTH

2 BAY LEAVES

1 1/2 TEASPOONS CHILI POWDER

1 TEASPOON GROUND CUMIN

1/2 TEASPOON DRIED THYME LEAVES

1/4 TEASPOON GROUND ALLSPICE

1/4 TEASPOON RED PEPPER FLAKES

2 WHOLE DRESSED DIVING DUCKS (1 TO 1 1/4 LBS. EACH), SKIN REMOVED, QUARTERED

4 CUPS HOT COOKED WHITE RICE

4 servings

In 2-quart saucepan, melt 1/4 cup butter over medium heat. Add pepper and onion. Cook for 3 to 4 minutes, or until vegetables are tender-crisp, stirring occasionally. Stir in mushrooms and garlic. Cook for 1 to 2 minutes, or until vegetables are tender, stirring occasionally. Stir in remaining ingredients, except ducks and rice. Bring to a boil over high heat. Reduce heat to low. Simmer for 10 to 15 minutes, or until sauce is thickened. Remove and discard bay leaves.

Meanwhile, in 6-quart Dutch oven, melt remaining 1/4 cup butter over medium heat. Add duck pieces. Cook for 3 to 4 minutes, or until browned, turning pieces occasionally. Pour sauce over duck pieces. Bring to a boil. Cover. Reduce heat to medium-low. Simmer for 30 to 40 minutes, or until meat is tender. Serve mixture over rice.

Per Serving: Calories: 705 • Protein: 33 g. • Carbohydrate: 76 g. • Fat: 30 g. • Cholesterol: 150 mg. • Sodium: 903 mg. — Exchanges: 3 1/2 starch, 3 1/4 lean meat, 4 vegetable, 4 fat

Calvados Duck

CALVADOS DUCK

Calvados is a dry apple brandy made in the Normandy region of France. It is often used for cooking poultry. Applejack is its American cousin.

3/4 CUP CALVADOS OR APPLEJACK

3/4 CUP VEGETABLE OIL

2 WHOLE DRESSED DIVING DUCKS (1 TO 1 1/4 LBS. EACH), SKIN REMOVED, QUARTERED

3 SPRIGS FRESH ROSEMARY

1 TABLESPOON JUNIPER BERRIES, CRUSHED

4 servings

In 2-cup measure, combine Calvados and oil. Whisk to blend. Arrange duck halves in 13 × 9-inch baking dish. Pour Calvados mixture over ducks, turning to coat. Place rosemary and juniper berries in dish around ducks. Cover with plastic wrap. Refrigerate overnight, turning ducks occasionally.

Prepare grill for medium-direct heat. Spray cooking grid with nonstick vegetable cooking spray. Drain and discard marinade from ducks. Grill ducks for 15 to 18 minutes, or until meat is desired doneness, turning duck halves occasionally.

Per Serving: Calories: 249 • Protein: 23 g. • Carbohydrate: 4 g. • Fat: 15 g. • Cholesterol: 88 mg. • Sodium: 66 mg. — Exchanges: 3 1/4 lean meat, 1 fat

Quick Recipes for Leftover Waterfowl

Barbecued Sandwiches—Sauté 1/2 cup chopped onion in 1 tablespoon vegetable oil. Add 3 cups shredded cooked waterfowl meat, 1 cup water, 1/2 cup ketchup, 1/2 cup chili sauce, 1 tablespoon brown sugar, 1 tablespoon Worcestershire sauce, 2 teaspoons dry mustard, 1/2 teaspoon red pepper sauce, 1/4 teaspoon garlic powder and salt to taste. Heat to boiling, then simmer for 20 minutes. Serve in buns.

Chopped Waterfowl Sandwiches—Mix together 1 cup chopped cooked waterfowl, 1/3 cup sliced pimiento-stuffed olives, 1/4 cup mayonnaise, 3 tablespoons sliced green onions and pepper to taste. Cover and refrigerate overnight, then spread on bread.

Mandarin Salad—Toss together 12 oz. fresh spinach, 1 cup shredded cooked waterfowl, 1 cup sliced fresh mushrooms, 1 sliced small red onion and 1 small can drained mandarin orange segments. Serve with Oriental-style dressing; top with toasted sliced almonds.

MARMALADE GOOSE BREAST

2	CUPS MILK
1/2	TEASPOON WHITE VINEGAR
1	BONELESS SKINLESS WHOLE CANADA GOOSE BREAST (ABOUT 1 LB.)
1/2	CUP DRY WHITE WINE
1/2	CUP APPLE CIDER OR APPLE JUICE
1/3	CUP FROZEN ORANGE JUICE CONCENTRATE, DEFROSTED
1 1/2	TEASPOONS GRATED ORANGE PEEL
2	TABLESPOONS ORANGE MARMALADE

4 servings

In medium mixing bowl, combine milk and vinegar. Add goose breast, turning to coat. Cover with plastic wrap. Refrigerate 8 hours or overnight, turning once or twice.

Drain and discard milk mixture. In second medium mixing bowl, combine wine, cider, orange juice concentrate and peel. Add goose breast, turning to coat. Cover with plastic wrap. Chill 4 to 6 hours, turning once or twice.

Heat oven to 425°F. Line 8-inch square baking dish with heavy-duty foil, allowing foil to extend about 10 inches on each side. Drain wine mixture, reserving 1/4 cup. Place goose breast in prepared dish. Pour reserved wine mixture over goose. Fold opposite sides of foil together in locked folds. Fold and crimp ends. Bake for 30 to 35 minutes, or until meat is desired doneness.

Fold back foil. Brush marmalade over goose breast. Bake, with foil open, for 5 to 10 minutes, or until meat is browned. Carve breast across grain into thin slices. Serve with hot cooked parsleyed rice, if desired.

Per Serving: Calories: 212 • Protein: 26 g. • Carbohydrate: 5 g. • Fat: 9 g. • Cholesterol: 97 mg. • Sodium: 108 mg. — Exchanges: 3 1/2 lean meat, 1/3 fruit

Seared Duck Breast with Pan Juices

SEARED DUCK BREAST WITH PAN JUICES

Any type of jelly works well in place of the raspberry jam.

2 BONELESS WHOLE WILD DUCK BREASTS (8 TO 12 OZ. EACH), SPLIT IN HALF, SKIN ON
1/4 TEASPOON SALT
1/4 TEASPOON PEPPER
3/4 CUP DRY SHERRY
2 TABLESPOONS RASPBERRY PRESERVES
2 TABLESPOONS MARGARINE OR BUTTER
1/2 CUP CHOPPED ONION

4 servings

Sprinkle breast halves evenly with salt and pepper. Set aside. In small mixing bowl, combine sherry and preserves. Set aside. In 10-inch nonstick skillet, melt margarine over medium heat. Add breast halves. Cook for 3 minutes. Turn breast halves over. Add onion. Cook for 2 to 3 minutes, or until meat is lightly browned.

Pour sherry mixture over breast halves. Cook for 4 to 8 minutes, or until meat is desired doneness and liquid is slightly reduced. To serve, carve breast halves crosswise into slices. Fan slices out slightly over hot cooked pasta, if desired. Top with onion and pan juices.

Per Serving: Calories: 326 • Protein: 29 g. Carbohydrate: 14 g. • Fat: 12 g. Cholesterol: N/A • Sodium: 291 mg. — Exchanges: 4 lean meat, 1/4 vegetable, 3/4 fruit

SAUTÉED WOOD DUCK WITH BALSAMIC-DATE SAUCE

SAUCE
3/4 CUP WATER
1/3 CUP CHOPPED DATES
2 TABLESPOONS BALSAMIC VINEGAR

4 BONELESS SKINLESS WOOD DUCK BREASTS OR SUBSTITUTE (3 TO 4 OZ. EACH), SPLIT IN HALF
SALT AND PEPPER TO TASTE
1 TABLESPOON BUTTER OR MARGARINE
1 SMALL ONION, SLICED

4 servings

In 1-quart saucepan, combine sauce ingredients. Bring to a boil over high heat, stirring occasionally. Reduce heat to low. Simmer for 12 to 15 minutes, or until sauce is desired thickness, stirring occasionally. Set aside and keep warm.

Sprinkle duck breasts evenly with salt and pepper to taste. In 10-inch skillet, melt butter over medium heat. Add breasts and onion. Cook for 5 to 7 minutes, or until meat is desired doneness, turning breasts over once or twice. Serve breasts and onion with sauce.

Per Serving: Calories: 200 • Protein: 20 g. • Carbohydrate: 13 g. • Fat: 7 g. • Cholesterol: 84 mg. • Sodium: 88 mg. — Exchanges: 2 3/4 very lean meat, 1/2 vegetable, 3/4 fruit, 1 1/2 fat

MALLARD SAUTÉ

1/4   CUP ALL-PURPOSE FLOUR

2   TEASPOONS GARLIC POWDER

2   TEASPOONS DRIED TARRAGON LEAVES

1   BONELESS SKINLESS WHOLE MALLARD BREAST OR SUBSTITUTE (8 TO 12 OZ.), CUT INTO 1-INCH STRIPS

1/4   CUP OLIVE OIL

1   TABLESPOON MARGARINE OR BUTTER

4   OZ. FRESH MUSHROOMS, THINLY SLICED (1 1/2 CUPS)

1   MEDIUM GREEN PEPPER, CUT INTO 1/2-INCH STRIPS

1   SMALL ONION, THINLY SLICED

1/4   CUP DRY SHERRY

2 servings

In large plastic food-storage bag, combine flour, garlic powder and tarragon. Add duck strips. Shake to coat.

In 12-inch nonstick skillet, heat oil and margarine over medium heat. Add duck strips. Cook for 3 to 5 minutes, or until meat is browned, turning frequently. Add remaining ingredients, except sherry. Cook over medium heat for 3 to 5 minutes, or until vegetables are tender-crisp, stirring frequently. Add sherry. Cook for 5 to 8 minutes, or until meat is desired doneness. Serve over hot cooked wild rice, if desired.

Per Serving: Calories: 626 • Protein: 33 g. •Carbohydrate: 28 g. • Fat: 39 g. •Cholesterol: N/A • Sodium: 157 mg. — Exchanges: 3/4 starch, 4 lean meat, 1/2 vegetable, 1 fruit, 5 1/2 fat

ORANGE DUCK SALAD WITH TOASTED ALMONDS

4   CUPS MIXED SALAD GREENS

1   MEDIUM ORANGE, PEELED AND SECTIONED, MEMBRANES REMOVED

1   SMALL RED ONION, SLICED

1/2   CUP SLIVERED ALMONDS, TOASTED

4   WHOLE BONELESS SKINLESS TEAL BREASTS OR SUBSTITUTE (3 TO 4 OZ. EACH)

1/4   CUP VEGETABLE OIL

2   TABLESPOONS ORANGE JUICE

1   TABLESPOON OLIVE OIL

1   TABLESPOON DIJON MUSTARD

    FRESHLY GROUND PEPPER TO TASTE

4 servings

Arrange salad greens evenly on individual serving plates. Arrange orange, onion and almonds evenly over greens. Set aside. Prepare grill for medium, direct heat. Spray cooking grid with nonstick vegetable cooking spray. Grill duck breasts for 12 to 15 minutes, or until meat is desired doneness, turning breasts over once or twice. Cut breasts into strips. Arrange strips evenly on serving plates.

In 1-cup measure, combine remaining ingredients, except pepper. Whisk until blended. Drizzle evenly over salads. Sprinkle salads with pepper.

Per Serving: Calories: 388 • Protein: 24 g. • Carbohydrate: 12 g. • Fat: 28 g. • Cholesterol: 76 mg. • Sodium: 166 mg. — Exchanges: 2 3/4 very lean meat, 2 vegetable, 5 1/2 fat

Mallard Sauté

Hot & Sour Duck Soup

HOT & SOUR DUCK SOUP

4 CUPS CHICKEN BROTH
¼ CUP RICE WINE VINEGAR
2 TABLESPOONS SOY SAUCE
1 TABLESPOON CORNSTARCH
1 CUP (4 OZ.) COOKED PUDDLE DUCK STRIPS (1 × ½ × ¼-INCH STRIPS)
⅓ CUP SLICED FRESH SHIITAKE MUSHROOMS
¼ CUP SHREDDED CARROT
¼ CUP SLICED GREEN ONIONS
½ TEASPOON SESAME OIL
¼ TEASPOON WHITE PEPPER

In 2-quart saucepan, combine broth, vinegar, soy sauce and cornstarch. Bring to a boil over medium-high heat, stirring constantly. Stir in remaining ingredients. Cook for 4 to 5 minutes, or until heated through, stirring occasionally.

Per Serving: Calories: 120 • Protein: 10 g. • Carbohydrate: 5 g. • Fat: 6 g. • Cholesterol: 28 mg. • Sodium: 1539 mg. — Exchanges: 1 lean meat, 1 vegetable, ¾ fat

4 servings

SESAME DUCK CABBAGE SALAD

2 TEASPOONS BUTTER OR MARGARINE
2 TABLESPOONS SLICED ALMONDS
2 TABLESPOONS SESAME SEEDS
3 CUPS SHREDDED RED CABBAGE
3 CUPS SHREDDED GREEN CABBAGE
1 TO 2 CUPS SHREDDED COOKED WILD DUCK
2 GREEN ONIONS, SLICED

1 PACKAGE (3 OZ.) CHICKEN-FLAVOR ORIENTAL DRY NOODLE SOUP MIX

DRESSING

3 TABLESPOONS RED WINE VINEGAR
3 TABLESPOONS VEGETABLE OIL
2 TABLESPOONS SUGAR
1 TEASPOON SESAME OIL
¼ TEASPOON SALT
¼ TEASPOON PEPPER

In small skillet, melt butter over medium-low heat. Add almonds and sesame seeds. Cook until light golden brown, stirring constantly. Remove from heat; cool. In large bowl, combine almond mixture, red and green cabbage, duck and onions. Sprinkle dry soup seasoning over salad. Break dry noodles into small pieces; add to salad. Mix well. In small bowl, blend all dressing ingredients. Pour over salad, tossing gently to coat. Serve immediately.

Per Serving: Calories: 211 • Protein: 9 g. • Carbohydrate: 14 g. • Fat: 14 g. • Cholesterol: 25 mg. • Sodium: 340 mg. — Exchanges: 1 lean meat, 3 vegetable, 2 fat

6 to 8 servings

K.B.'S DUCK & SAUSAGE GUMBO

1/4 CUP PLUS 2 TABLESPOONS
    VEGETABLE OIL*

1/2 CUP ALL-PURPOSE FLOUR

1 CUP CHOPPED ONION

1 CUP CHOPPED GREEN PEPPER

1 CUP CHOPPED RED PEPPER

1 CUP SLICED CELERY

5 CUPS WATER, DIVIDED

1 1/2 CUPS CUT-UP COOKED WILD DUCK
    (ABOUT 8 OZ.)

1 LB. SMOKED SAUSAGE LINKS, SLICED

1/2 CUP SLICED GREEN ONIONS

1 CLOVE GARLIC, MINCED

1 TEASPOON SALT

1 TEASPOON PEPPER

1/2 TEASPOON DRIED THYME LEAVES

2 1/4 CUPS SLICED FRESH OR FROZEN OKRA
    (1/2-INCH SLICES)

1 TEASPOON WORCESTERSHIRE SAUCE

1/2 TO 1 TEASPOON RED PEPPER SAUCE

1 TEASPOON FILÉ POWDER

10 to 12 servings

In 6-quart Dutch oven or stockpot, heat oil over medium-low heat. Gradually add flour, stirring constantly with whisk. Cook over medium heat for 25 to 35 minutes, or until mixture is dark golden brown, stirring occasionally. (Do not burn.)

Add chopped onion, pepper and celery. Cook over medium-high heat for 2 to 3 minutes, or until vegetables are tender-crisp, stirring frequently. Add 3 cups water, the duck pieces, sausage, green onions, garlic, salt, pepper and thyme. Bring to a boil. Reduce heat to low. Simmer, covered, for 1 hour.

Add remaining 2 cups water, the okra, Worcestershire sauce and red pepper sauce. Simmer, uncovered, over low heat for 1 hour. Remove from heat. Stir in filé powder. Serve over hot cooked rice, if desired.

*Two tablespoons bacon drippings may be substituted for 2 tablespoons vegetable oil, if desired. Note: Additional cooking makes filé powder tough and stringy. Add filé powder only to portion of gumbo you plan to consume immediately. Add remaining filé powder to reheated leftover portion.

Per Serving: Calories: 293 • Protein: 15 g. • Carbohydrate: 11 g. • Fat: 21 g. • Cholesterol: 43 mg. • Sodium: 789 mg. — Exchanges: 1/4 starch, 1 1/2 medium-fat meat, 1 1/4 vegetable, 2 3/4 fat

CREAMY WILD RICE-DUCK SOUP

This easy recipe is a great way to use leftover wild rice and duck meat.

3	TABLESPOONS BUTTER OR MARGARINE
1/2	CUP FINELY CHOPPED CARROT
1/2	CUP THINLY SLICED CELERY
1/4	CUP FINELY CHOPPED ONION
1/3	CUP ALL-PURPOSE FLOUR
3	CUPS CHICKEN BROTH
2	CUPS COOKED WILD RICE
2	CUPS HALF-AND-HALF
1/3	CUP DRY WHITE WINE
1/4	TEASPOON SALT
1/4	TEASPOON PEPPER
1/8	TEASPOON GROUND NUTMEG
1	CUP (4 OZ.) CUBED COOKED PUDDLE DUCK (1/4-INCH CUBES)

6 servings

In 3-quart saucepan, melt butter over medium-high heat. Add carrot, celery and onion. Cook for 5 to 7 minutes, or until vegetables are tender, stirring occasionally. Stir in flour. Cook for 1 minute, stirring constantly. Blend in broth, stirring until smooth. Bring to a boil.

Stir in rice, half-and-half, wine, salt, pepper and nutmeg. Cook for 8 to 10 minutes, or until hot, stirring constantly. (Do not boil.) Stir in duck. Cook for 2 to 3 minutes, or until heated through, stirring constantly.

Per Serving: Calories: 310 • Protein: 12 g. • Carbohydrate: 22 g. • Fat: 19 g. • Cholesterol: 64 mg. • Sodium: 710 mg. — Exchanges: 1 1/2 starch, 3/4 lean meat, 1/4 vegetable, 3 fat

SLOW-COOKER DUCK & DRESSING

1/2	CUP MARGARINE OR BUTTER
1	CUP THINLY SLICED CELERY
1	CUP CHOPPED ONION
7 1/2	CUPS CRUMBLED CORN BREAD
5 3/4	CUPS DUCK STOCK OR CHICKEN BROTH
4	CUPS UNSEASONED DRY BREAD CRUMBS
3 1/2	CUPS CUT-UP COOKED WILD DUCK OR GOOSE (ABOUT 1 LB.)
2	CUPS CRUSHED SODA CRACKERS
4	EGGS, BEATEN
1/2	CUP MILK
2	TEASPOONS DRIED THYME OR SAGE LEAVES
1/2	TEASPOON BAKING POWDER
1/2	TEASPOON FRESHLY GROUND PEPPER

10 to 12 servings

In 10-inch nonstick skillet, melt margarine over medium heat. Add celery and onion. Cook for 2 to 3 minutes, or until vegetables are tender-crisp, stirring frequently.

In large mixing bowl, combine celery mixture and remaining ingredients. Spoon into 4-quart crockpot. Cover. Cook on high for 1 hour. Reduce heat to low. Cook for 4 to 6 hours longer, or until liquid is absorbed.

Per Serving: Calories: 585 • Protein: 23 g. • Carbohydrate: 67 g. • Fat: 24 g. • Cholesterol: 144 mg. • Sodium: 1590 mg. Exchanges: 4 1/2 starch, 1 1/2 medium-fat meat, 3 1/4 fat

Creamy Wild Rice-Duck Soup

GRILL-SMOKED DUCK

<u>BRINE</u>

6 CUPS COLD WATER

1/2 CUP PLUS 1 TABLESPOON CANNING/PICKLING SALT

1/4 CUP PLUS 2 TABLESPOONS PACKED BROWN SUGAR

3 TABLESPOONS MAPLE SYRUP

2 TABLESPOONS PLUS 1 TEASPOON WHITE VINEGAR

2 TEASPOONS PICKLING SPICE

1 WHOLE DRESSED PUDDLE DUCK (1 1/4 TO 1 1/2 LBS.), SKIN ON

HICKORY WOOD CHIPS

2 TABLESPOONS HONEY

2 TEASPOONS SOY SAUCE

HOT CHICKEN BROTH, BEER OR WATER

3 to 4 servings

In large nonmetallic bowl or sealable plastic bag, combine brine ingredients. Stir until salt and sugar are dissolved. Add duck. Cover. Refrigerate 4 hours, turning duck once or twice. Drain and discard brine from duck. Pat duck dry with paper towels. Let duck air dry for 30 minutes.

While duck is air drying, start large load of charcoal briquets on one side of charcoal grill. Soak wood chips in warm water for 30 minutes; drain. In small bowl, combine honey and soy sauce. When briquets are covered with light ash, toss a handful of wood chips on them. Place pan 2/3 full of hot broth on cooking grid over charcoal. Brush duck with honey mixture and place it on opposite side of cooking grid. Cover grill.

Smoke duck for 3 to 4 hours, or until internal temperature in thickest part of breast registers at least 160°F. (Do not open grill unless necessary.) Temperature in grill should stay between 150° and 200°F. Regulate temperature using vents on grill. Add more wood chips during last hour of smoking.

<u>Tip:</u> *See thermometer tip with Grill-smoked Pheasant, page 214.*

Per Serving: Calories: 239 • Protein: 16 g. • Carbohydrate: 11 g. • Fat: 14 g. • Cholesterol: 75 mg. • Sodium: 667 mg. — Exchanges: 2 1/4 medium-fat meat, 1/2 fat

FRESH DUCK SAUSAGE

3/4 LB. GROUND PUDDLE DUCK BREAST AND THIGHS, CRUMBLED
3/4 LB. GROUND PORK OR VEAL, CRUMBLED
3 TABLESPOONS COLD WATER
2 TEASPOONS SALT
1/2 TEASPOON RUBBED SAGE
1/2 TEASPOON GROUND THYME
1/4 TO 1/2 TEASPOON WHITE PEPPER
1/8 TEASPOON GROUND GINGER
 DASH GROUND NUTMEG

6 servings

To grind duck, cut breast and thighs into 1-inch
pieces, then grind through 3/16-inch plate on meat
grinder. In medium mixing bowl, combine duck and
pork. Mix well. In small bowl, combine remaining
ingredients. Add spice mixture to meat mixture.
Mix by hand until ingredients are evenly distributed.
Shape meat mixture into twelve 3-inch patties.
Panfry or grill patties. To freeze patties, layer
them between sheets of wax paper. Stack patties,
wrap in foil and freeze no longer than 2 months.

Per Serving: Calories: 203 • Protein: 20 g.
• Carbohydrate: <1 g. • Fat: 13 g. • Cholesterol: 75 mg.
• Sodium: 790 mg. — Exchanges: 3 lean meat, 3/4 fat

GOOSE JERKY

MARINADE
2 CUPS COLD WATER
1 CAN (5.5 OZ.) SPICY VEGETABLE JUICE
1/4 CUP SOY SAUCE
1/4 CUP WORCESTERSHIRE SAUCE
1 TO 2 TABLESPOONS MORTON® TENDERQUICK® MIX
2 TEASPOONS ONION POWDER
1/2 TEASPOON GARLIC POWDER
1/2 TEASPOON GROUND GINGER

2 LBS. BONELESS SKINLESS WILD GOOSE MEAT, CUT INTO
 4 × 1 × 1/4-INCH STRIPS
 HICKORY WOOD CHIPS

11 servings (40 to 50 slices)

Follow instructions on page 59.

Per Serving: Calories: 136 • Protein: 19 g.
• Carbohydrate: 1 g. • Fat: 6 g. • Cholesterol: 69 mg.
• Sodium: N/A — Exchanges: 2 1/2 very lean meat, 1 fat

SMOKED GOOSE

BRINE
6 CUPS WATER
1/2 CUP PLUS 2 TABLESPOONS CANNING/PICKLING SALT
1/2 CUP PLUS 2 TABLESPOONS PACKED BROWN SUGAR
3 TABLESPOONS MAPLE SYRUP
2 TABLESPOONS PLUS 1 TEASPOON WHITE VINEGAR
2 TEASPOONS PICKLING SPICE

1 WHOLE DRESSED WILD GOOSE (ABOUT 8 LBS.), SKIN ON
 HICKORY WOOD CHIPS
1/4 CUP HONEY
1 TABLESPOON SOY SAUCE
1/8 TO 1/4 TEASPOON CAYENNE
 HOT WATER OR CHICKEN BROTH

25 2-oz. servings

In large nonmetallic container, combine brine
ingredients. Stir until salt and sugar are dissolved. Add goose. Cover. Refrigerate overnight,
turning goose once or twice. Drain and discard
brine from goose. Pat goose dry with paper towels.
Let goose air dry for 45 minutes.

While goose is air drying, heat water smoker or
insulated smoker to 200°F. Soak wood chips in
warm water for 30 minutes; drain. In small bowl,
combine honey, soy sauce and cayenne. Brush
goose with honey mixture. Place goose on rack in
middle position of smoker. Place pan 2/3 full of
hot water on rack directly under goose.* Place a
handful of wood chips in smoker.

Smoke goose for 8 to 10 hours, or until internal
temperature in thickest part of breast registers
180°F, adding wood chips once or twice.

**Pan of water is for catching dripping fat from goose,
and the steam from the water keeps the goose from
getting too dry.*

Per Serving: Calories: 225 • Protein: 17 g.
• Carbohydrate: 4 g. • Fat: 15 g. • Cholesterol: 63 mg.
• Sodium: 342 mg. — Exchanges: 2 1/2 medium-fat
meat, 1/2 fat

RECIPES FOR
Upland Game Birds

Each autumn, millions of hunters take to the fields and forests in search of upland game birds. And it's easy to understand why. Upland bird hunting offers the unique challenge of combing the countryside in hopes of flushing hard-to-hit quarry from thick cover.

As any avid hunter knows, it's hard to beat the taste of upland game birds. While some people prefer the light-colored meat of chukar partridge, ruffed grouse and quail, others like the dark-colored meat of Hungarian partridge, sharp-tailed grouse, doves and woodcock. Whatever your preference, this section has several recipes sure to suit your taste.

Wild upland birds differ somewhat from their domestic counterparts, so different cooking techniques are required. Wild birds, for one thing, have much less fat. And wild birds have more flavor; the best recipes are those that do not cover up the natural taste.

Exactly how to cook an upland game bird depends on its size, its age, the color of its meat and whether it was plucked or skinned. If the age is in doubt, it's best to cook with moist heat. On most upland birds, the breast meat is lighter in color than the leg or thigh meat. But on some, the breast is dark as well (see the chart below). Light meat dries out more quickly and usually requires less cooking time than dark meat. Plucked birds can be roasted whole or cut up and fried. The skin helps keep the meat moist during roasting, and when fried, it becomes crisp and tasty. Skinned birds are usually cut up and cooked with moist heat.

Meat Color of Upland Birds

TYPE OF BIRD	BREAST	THIGHS/LEGS
SAGE GROUSE	DARK	VERY DARK
RING-NECKED PHEASANT	WHITE	DARK
SHARP-TAILED GROUSE	DARK	DARK
RUFFED GROUSE	VERY WHITE	MEDIUM
CHUKAR PARTRIDGE	WHITE	DARK
HUNGARIAN PARTRIDGE	MEDIUM	DARK
MOUNTAIN QUAIL	WHITE	DARK
SCALED QUAIL	WHITE	DARK
BOBWHITE QUAIL	MEDIUM	MEDIUM
WOODCOCK	DARK	MEDIUM
CALIFORNIA QUAIL	WHITE	DARK
GAMBEL'S QUAIL	WHITE	DARK
MOURNING DOVE	DARK	DARK

UPLAND GAME BIRDS SUBSTITUTION GUIDE

As with small game, there are noticeable differences in meat color and flavor among upland game birds. The subtle berry flavor of a ruffed grouse, for example, may be overpowered in a recipe with strong flavors, just as strong-flavored sharptail may not work in a lightly seasoned dish.

Game-farm birds, such as pheasants, chukar partridge, quail and turkey, can be easily substituted for wild birds in recipes. A game-farm bird will probably have more fat than a wild one, so remove the excess before cooking.

Upland Game Birds Substitution Chart

SPECIES	APPROX. DRESSED WEIGHT	NUMBER OF SERVINGS	SUBSTITUTE	COOKING METHOD
WILD TURKEY (WHOLE)	8 TO 16 LBS.	5 TO 10	DOMESTIC TURKEY OF SIMILAR WEIGHT (NOT PREBASTED TYPE)	OVEN ROAST
WILD TURKEY (ANY PIECES)	3 TO 4½ LBS.	6 TO 8	2 PHEASANTS, QUARTERED 3 RUFFED OR SHARPTAIL GROUSE, HALVED 3 OR 4 CHUKAR OR HUNGARIAN PARTRIDGE, HALVED 3 LBS. DOMESTIC TURKEY PIECES, EXCESS FAT REMOVED	PANFRY, BRAISE, BAKE
PHEASANT (WHOLE)	1½ TO 2¼ LBS.	3 TO 4	2 RUFFED OR SHARPTAIL GROUSE 2 CHUKAR OR HUNGARIAN PARTRIDGE	OVEN ROAST, PAN-BROIL, PANFRY, BRAISE, BAKE
2 PHEASANTS (CUT UP)	3 TO 4½ LBS.	6 TO 8	THIGHS AND LEGS FROM WILD TURKEY 3 OR 4 RUFFED OR SHARPTAIL GROUSE, QUARTERED 4 CHUKAR OR HUNGARIAN PARTRIDGE, QUARTERED 8 QUAIL, HALVED	PANFRY, BRAISE, BAKE
PHEASANT (2 WHOLE BREASTS, BONELESS)	1 LB.	4	BONED BREAST PORTION OR THIGHS FROM TURKEY BONED BREAST AND THIGHS FROM 2 RUFFED OR SHARP-TAIL GROUSE, 2 CHUKAR OR HUNGARIAN PARTRIDGE BONED BREASTS FROM 4 QUAIL BONED BREASTS FROM 6 OR 7 DOVES	PANFRY, BAKE, DEEP-FRY, GRILL, BRAISE,
RUFFED OR SHARPTAIL GROUSE (WHOLE)	1 TO 1¼ LBS.	2 TO 3	½ PHEASANT 1 CHUKAR OR HUNGARIAN PARTRIDGE	OVEN ROAST, PANFRY, BAKE, BRAISE, GRILL
CHUKAR OR HUNGARIAN PARTRIDGE	¾ TO 1 LB.	2	½ PHEASANT 1 RUFFED OR SHARPTAIL GROUSE	OVEN ROAST, PANFRY, BAKE, BRAISE
QUAIL	4 QUAIL (4 TO 6 OZ. EACH)	4	1 PHEASANT, CUT UP 1½ RUFFED OR SHARPTAIL GROUSE, CUT UP 2 CHUKAR OR HUNGARIAN PARTRIDGE, QUARTERED	OVEN ROAST, PANFRY, BAKE, BRAISE, GRILL
WOODCOCK	5 TO 6 WOODCOCK, (5 OZ. EACH)	4	1 PHEASANT, CUT UP 1½ RUFFED GROUSE, CUT UP 2 CHUKAR OR HUNGARIAN PARTRIDGE, CUT UP 4 QUAIL, HALVED	PANFRY, BRAISE, BAKE
DOVE	6 OR 7 DOVES (2 TO 3 OZ. EACH)	4	1 PHEASANT, CUT UP, BREAST SECTION HALVED 1½ RUFFED OR SHARPTAIL GROUSE, CUT UP, BREAST SECTIONS HALVED 2 CHUKAR OR HUNGARIAN PARTRIDGE, CUT UP, BREAST SECTIONS HALVED 4 QUAIL, HALVED	PANFRY, BRAISE, BAKE

HERB-COATED ROAST PHEASANT

3 CUPS LOOSELY PACKED FRESH MIXED HERBS (CURLY-LEAF PARSLEY, FLAT-LEAF PARSLEY, SORREL, TARRAGON, DILL WEED)
1 WHOLE DRESSED PHEASANT (1½ TO 2¼ LBS.), SKIN ON, TRUSSED (SEE P. 37)
1 EGG YOLK, BEATEN
  SALT AND PEPPER TO TASTE
2 TABLESPOONS BUTTER, SOFTENED
1 CUP WATER, DIVIDED

3 to 4 servings

Heat oven to 375°F. In food processor or with chef's knife, finely chop herbs. Set aside. Place pheasant breast side up in small roasting pan. Brush with yolk. Sprinkle evenly with salt and pepper. Pat herb mixture evenly over pheasant. Dot pheasant evenly with butter. Pour ½ cup water in bottom of roasting pan.

Roast pheasant for 50 minutes to 1 hour, or until pheasant is tender and juices run clear, basting occasionally with pan juices. Remove pheasant from oven, draining any juices in cavity of bird into pan. Place pheasant on serving platter and keep warm. Place roasting pan over medium-high heat. Add remaining ½ cup water to pan, scraping bottom of pan to remove any browned bits. Bring to a boil. Boil for 4 to 5 minutes, or until liquid is reduced to desired thickness. Strain liquid. Pour over pheasant.

Per Serving: Calories: 421
• Protein: 44 g.
• Carbohydrate: 5 g. • Fat: 24 g.
• Cholesterol: 199 mg.
• Sodium: 160 mg. —
Exchanges: 6 lean meat,
1 vegetable, 1¼ fat

UPLAND BIRDS IN OVEN COOKING BAG

1 TABLESPOON ALL-PURPOSE FLOUR
½ CUP APPLE CIDER OR ORANGE JUICE
1 WHOLE DRESSED PHEASANT (1½ TO 2¼ LBS.), OR 2 GROUSE OR PARTRIDGE (¾ TO 1 LB. EACH), SKIN ON*
  SALT
3 TABLESPOONS MELTED BUTTER OR MARGARINE
¼ TO ½ TEASPOON BOUQUET GARNI SEASONING OR OTHER HERB MIXTURE
½ APPLE

2 or 3 servings

Heat oven to 350°F. Add flour to regular (10 × 16-inch) oven cooking bag; shake to distribute. Place bag in 10 × 6-inch baking dish. Pour cider into bag; stir with plastic or wooden spoon to blend into flour. Salt body cavity of pheasant. Brush outside of pheasant with melted butter; sprinkle with bouquet garni. Put ½ apple inside body cavity of pheasant (if cooking grouse or partridge, cut apple half into two pieces; place one piece inside cavity of each bird). Place pheasant in cooking bag. Close bag with provided nylon tie. Make six ½-inch slits in top of bag. Roast until juices run clear when thigh is pricked, 1 to 1¼ hours. Slit bag down center and fold back. Continue cooking until pheasant is brown, about 15 minutes. Remove and discard apple. Stir juices and spoon over pheasant, if desired.

*Variation: If birds are skinned, cover with bacon strips if desired; omit butter. Use three bacon strips for a pheasant; two for each grouse or partridge.

Per serving: Calories: 585
• Protein: 56 g. • Carbohydrate: 10 g. • Fat: 34 g. • Cholesterol: 205 mg. • Sodium: 220 mg. —
Exchanges: ½ fruit, 8 lean meat, 2 fat

Herb-coated Roast Pheasant

Sautéed Ruffed Grouse with Thyme

SAUTÉED RUFFED GROUSE WITH THYME

1   TABLESPOON BUTTER OR MARGARINE
2   WHOLE DRESSED RUFFED GROUSE (3/4 TO 1 LB. EACH), SKIN REMOVED, QUARTERED
1   TABLESPOON SNIPPED FRESH THYME
1/2 TEASPOON SALT
1/2 TEASPOON PEPPER
1/4 TEASPOON GARLIC POWDER

4 servings

In 12-inch nonstick skillet, melt butter over medium heat. Add grouse pieces. Cook for 5 to 7 minutes, or until browned, turning grouse pieces once or twice.

Reduce heat to low. Sprinkle thyme, salt, pepper and garlic powder evenly over grouse. Cover. Cook for 20 to 25 minutes, or until meat is tender, turning grouse over occasionally.

Per Serving: Calories: 230 • Protein: 36 g.
• Carbohydrate: <1 g. • Fat: 8 g. • Cholesterol: 108 mg.
• Sodium: 359 mg. — Exchanges: 5 very lean meat,
1 1/2 fat

GRILL-SMOKED CHUKAR PARTRIDGE

MARINADE
1/4 CUP BALSAMIC VINEGAR
2   TEASPOONS DRIED OREGANO LEAVES
2   TEASPOONS WORCESTERSHIRE SAUCE
1   TEASPOON DRIED RUBBED SAGE
1   CLOVE GARLIC, MINCED
1/2 TEASPOON DRIED THYME LEAVES
1/2 TEASPOON SUGAR
1/2 TEASPOON SALT
    DASH GROUND NUTMEG
1   CUP OLIVE OIL

2   WHOLE DRESSED CHUKAR PARTRIDGES (3/4 TO 1 LB. EACH), SKIN ON, HALVED
    APPLE WOOD CHIPS

4 servings

In food processor or blender, combine all marinade ingredients except oil. Process until blended. With processor running, gradually add oil in a slow drizzle until well blended. In shallow dish or sealable bag, combine partridge halves and marinade. Turn partridges to coat. Cover dish with plastic wrap, or seal bag. Refrigerate several hours or overnight, turning partridges occasionally.

Soak wood chips in warm water for 30 minutes; drain. Prepare grill for medium-direct heat. Spray cooking grid with nonstick vegetable cooking spray. Drain and discard marinade from partridges. Sprinkle a handful of wood chips over charcoal in grill. Cover grill until chips begin to smoke.

Arrange partridge halves on cooking grid. Grill, covered, for 15 to 20 minutes, or until meat is tender, turning partridges occasionally.

Per Serving: Calories: 435 • Protein: 39 g.
• Carbohydrate: 1 g. • Fat: 29 g. • Cholesterol: 122 mg.
• Sodium: 218 mg. — Exchanges: 5 1/2 lean meat, 2 1/2 fat

FRUITY GARLIC-ROASTED PHEASANT

- ½ CUP BRANDY OR COGNAC, DIVIDED
- ⅓ CUP RAISINS
- ⅓ CUP DRIED CRANBERRIES
- 1 WHOLE DRESSED PHEASANT (1½ TO 2¼ LBS.), SKIN ON
- 1 CLOVE GARLIC, CRUSHED
- SALT AND PEPPER TO TASTE
- 2 SPRIGS FRESH SAGE
- 8 WHOLE CLOVES GARLIC, PEELED
- 1¼ CUPS DRY RED WINE, DIVIDED
- 1 TEASPOON HONEY

3 to 4 servings

In small bowl, combine ⅓ cup brandy, the raisins and cranberries. Let soak for several hours or overnight or microwave on high for 1 minute.

Heat oven to 375°F. Rinse pheasant and pat dry with paper towels. Rub surface of pheasant with crushed garlic. Sprinkle surface and cavity with salt and pepper. Place sage sprigs in pheasant cavity, and truss pheasant (see trussing technique on page 37). Place pheasant in small roasting pan. Arrange whole garlic cloves around pheasant. Pour 1 cup wine and raisin mixture into pan around pheasant.

Roast pheasant for 50 minutes to 1 hour, or until meat is tender and juices run clear, basting occasionally with pan juices. Remove pheasant from oven, draining any juices in cavity of bird into pan. Place pheasant on serving platter and keep warm.

Place roasting pan over medium-high heat. Add remaining ¼ cup wine and remaining brandy to pan, scraping bottom of pan to remove any browned bits. Bring to a boil. Boil for 5 to 6 minutes, or until liquid is reduced to desired thickness. Whisk in honey. Spoon sauce around pheasant on platter.

Per Serving: Calories: 455 • Protein: 43 g.
• Carbohydrate: 22 g. • Fat: 17 g. • Cholesterol: 131 mg.
• Sodium: 80 mg. — Exchanges: 6 lean meat, 1 fruit

Three Marinades for Game Birds

Lemon-Garlic Marinade—In small saucepan, combine ½ cup fresh lemon juice, ½ cup olive oil or vegetable oil, 2 teaspoons dried oregano leaves, 1 teaspoon Dijon mustard, 3 cloves minced garlic and ⅛ teaspoon pepper. Heat until bubbly. Cool to room temperature before using.

Greek-Style Marinade—In small saucepan, combine ½ cup olive oil, ½ cup sweet vermouth, 1 tablespoon lemon juice, ¾ teaspoon dried tarragon leaves, 1 thinly sliced small red onion and ⅛ teaspoon cracked black pepper. Heat until bubbly. Cool to room temperature before using.

Asian-Style Marinade—Combine ¼ cup sliced green onions, 3 tablespoons soy sauce, 2 tablespoons honey, 1 tablespoon sesame oil and 1 tablespoon molasses; stir well.

GRILLED MARINATED GAME BIRDS

- 2 WHOLE DRESSED PHEASANTS (1½ TO 2¼ LBS.) OR 4 WHOLE PARTRIDGE (¾ TO 1 LB. EACH), SKIN ON
- 1 RECIPE LEMON-GARLIC MARINADE (ABOVE) OR OTHER MARINADE
- SALT AND FRESHLY GROUND BLACK PEPPER

4 servings

Split birds into halves. Place pheasant halves in large plastic food-storage bag. Pour prepared marinade over birds; seal bag. Refrigerate for at least 3 hours or overnight, turning bag over occasionally.

Start charcoal briquets in grill. When briquets are covered with ash, spread them evenly in grill. Place grate above hot coals. Remove birds from marinade; reserve marinade. Arrange birds on grate, skin side down. Grill until breasts are browned, 10 to 15 minutes, basting after every 5 minutes with reserved marinade. Turn birds over; continue grilling and basting until juices run clear when thigh is pricked. Remove from grill; season with salt and pepper.

Per serving: Calories: 788 • Protein: 83 g.
• Carbohydrate: 2 g. • Fat: 47 g. • Cholesterol: 260 mg.
• Sodium: 160 mg. — Exchanges: 12 lean meat, 2½ fat

QUAIL THAT WON'T FAIL

Doves also work well in this recipe.

4	WHOLE DRESSED QUAIL OR SUBSTITUTE (4 TO 6 OZ. EACH), SKIN ON
1/4	TEASPOON SALT
1/4	TEASPOON PEPPER
2	TABLESPOONS MARGARINE OR BUTTER
2	TABLESPOONS VEGETABLE OIL
1/4	CUP ALL-PURPOSE FLOUR
1	CAN (10 1/2 OZ.) CONDENSED BEEF CONSOMMÉ
1	CUP DRY WHITE WINE
1/4	TEASPOON DRIED THYME LEAVES
2	BAY LEAVES

4 servings

Split each quail down the back and flatten. Sprinkle salt and pepper evenly over quail. In 12-inch nonstick skillet, heat margarine and oil over medium-high heat. Add quail. Cook for 6 to 8 minutes, or until meat is browned, turning occasionally.

Remove quail from skillet. Reduce heat to medium. Stir flour into drippings in skillet. Blend in consommé, wine, thyme and bay leaves. Bring to a boil. Return quail to skillet. Reduce heat to low. Cover. Simmer for 30 to 40 minutes, or until meat is tender and juices run clear. Transfer quail to warm platter. Cover to keep warm. Set aside.

Cook sauce, uncovered, for 3 to 5 minutes longer, or until thickened, stirring constantly. Remove and discard bay leaves. Spoon sauce over quail. Serve quail with hot cooked white and wild rice, if desired.

Per Serving: Calories: 404 • Protein: 29 g. • Carbohydrate: 8 g. • Fat: 28 g. • Cholesterol: N/A • Sodium: 659 mg. — Exchanges: 1/2 starch, 4 medium-fat meat, 1 1/2 fat

HUNGARIAN PARTRIDGE WITH JUNIPER

2	WHOLE DRESSED HUNGARIAN PARTRIDGES (3/4 TO 1 LB. EACH), SKIN REMOVED, HALVED
	SALT AND PEPPER TO TASTE
2	TABLESPOONS BUTTER OR MARGARINE
2	MEDIUM CARROTS, SLICED (1 CUP)
2	STALKS CELERY, SLICED (1 CUP)
1	MEDIUM ONION, CHOPPED (1 CUP)
2	CUPS WATER OR CHICKEN BROTH
1/4	CUP BRANDY
10	DRIED JUNIPER BERRIES, CRUSHED
1	BAY LEAF
1/4	TEASPOON DRIED THYME LEAVES
1	SPRIG FRESH PARSLEY
8	OZ. FRESH MUSHROOMS, QUARTERED

4 servings

Heat oven to 400°F. Sprinkle partridge halves with salt and pepper to taste. In 12-inch nonstick skillet, melt butter over medium heat. Add partridges and cook for 4 to 6 minutes, or until browned, turning occasionally. Set aside.

In 13 × 9-inch baking dish, evenly spread carrots, celery and onion. Add water, brandy, juniper berries, bay leaf, thyme and parsley. Arrange partridge halves over vegetables. Arrange mushrooms around partridges. Cover with foil. Bake for 45 to 55 minutes, or until vegetables and meat are tender. Remove and discard bay leaf.

Per Serving: Calories: 300 • Protein: 38 g. • Carbohydrate: 10 g. • Fat: 12 g. • Cholesterol: 116 mg. • Sodium: 154 mg. — Exchanges: 5 very lean meat, 2 vegetable, 2 1/4 fat

APPLE-GINGER RUFFED GROUSE

1	TABLESPOON BUTTER OR MARGARINE
2	WHOLE DRESSED RUFFED GROUSE (3/4 TO 1 LB. EACH), SKIN REMOVED, QUARTERED
1	CAN (14½ OZ.) CHICKEN BROTH
1	MEDIUM ONION, SLICED
2	TEASPOONS GRATED FRESH GINGERROOT
1	STICK CINNAMON (3 INCHES LONG)
½	TEASPOON SALT
¼	TEASPOON PEPPER
2	RED COOKING APPLES, CORED AND SLICED
1	TABLESPOON CORNSTARCH MIXED WITH 2 TABLESPOONS WATER

4 servings

In 12-inch nonstick skillet, melt butter over medium heat. Add grouse pieces. Cook for 5 to 7 minutes, or until browned, turning occasionally. Add broth, onion, gingerroot, cinnamon, salt and pepper. Bring to a simmer. Cover. Reduce heat to low. Simmer for 20 minutes.

Add apple slices to skillet. Re-cover. Simmer for 10 to 15 minutes, or until meat is tender. Remove grouse, apples and onion from skillet and arrange on warm serving platter. Set aside and keep warm.

Whisk cornstarch mixture into pan juices. Bring to a boil over medium-high heat. Boil for 1 minute, stirring constantly. Spoon sauce over grouse.

Per Serving: Calories: 299 • Protein: 37 g. • Carbohydrate: 14 g. • Fat: 10 g. • Cholesterol: 108 mg. • Sodium: 798 mg. — Exchanges: 5 very lean meat, 1 vegetable, ½ fruit, 2 fat

DOVES IN CORN BREAD STUFFING

Moist corn bread stuffing prevents the doves from becoming dry in this classic Southern recipe.

STUFFING

1/2	CUP CHOPPED CELERY
1/4	CUP SLICED GREEN ONION
2	TABLESPOONS SNIPPED FRESH PARSLEY
1/4	CUP BUTTER OR MARGARINE
3	CUPS CORN BREAD STUFFING MIX
1	CUP UPLAND GAME BIRD STOCK (PAGE 23) OR CHICKEN BROTH
1/2	TEASPOON DRIED MARJORAM LEAVES
1/2	TEASPOON SALT
1/8	TEASPOON PEPPER
8	WHOLE BONELESS SKINLESS DOVE BREASTS (ABOUT 1 OZ. EACH)

4 servings

Heat oven to 350°F. Lightly grease 2-quart casserole; set aside. In medium skillet, cook and stir celery, onion and parsley in butter over medium heat until tender. Add remaining stuffing ingredients. Mix until moistened. Place half of stuffing mixture in prepared casserole. Arrange dove breasts over stuffing. Cover completely with remaining stuffing mixture. Bake, uncovered, until dove is cooked through and tender, about 1 hour.

Per serving: Calories: 621 • Protein: 24 g. • Carbohydrate: 53 g. • Fat: 35 g. • Cholesterol: 110 mg. • Sodium: 1460 mg. — Exchanges: 3 1/2 starch, 2 lean meat, 5 1/2 fat

WOODCOCK SUPREME

2	TABLESPOONS MARGARINE OR BUTTER
4	BONELESS SKINLESS WHOLE WOODCOCK BREASTS (2 TO 3 OZ. EACH), SPLIT IN HALF
1	SMALL GREEN PEPPER, THINLY SLICED
1	CUP FINELY CHOPPED ONION
1/2	CUP SLICED FRESH MOREL MUSHROOMS
1/2	CUP CHICKEN BROTH
1/4	CUP DRY WHITE WINE
3	TABLESPOONS RED CURRANT JELLY
1	TABLESPOON CORNSTARCH MIXED WITH 1 TABLESPOON WATER
1/4	TEASPOON SALT

2 servings

In 10-inch nonstick skillet, melt margarine over medium heat. Add breast halves. Cook for 4 to 6 minutes, or just until meat is browned, turning over once. Add pepper, onions and mushrooms. Cook for 4 to 5 minutes, or until vegetables are tender-crisp, stirring occasionally. Add remaining ingredients. Cook over medium heat for 3 to 4 minutes, or until jelly melts and mixture is thickened and translucent, stirring frequently. Serve over hot cooked white or wild rice, if desired.

Nutritional information not available.

Woodcock Supreme

HUNGARIAN HUNS

Buttered spaetzle or kluski noodles, rye bread and green beans complete this meal.

8   SLICES BACON, CUT UP
3/4 CUP ALL-PURPOSE FLOUR
1   TABLESPOON PAPRIKA
3   OR 4 WHOLE DRESSED HUNGARIAN PARTRIDGE (3/4 TO 1 LB. EACH)
1/4 CUP CHICKEN BROTH
3   TABLESPOONS CIDER VINEGAR
1   SMALL HEAD GREEN CABBAGE (ABOUT 1 1/2 LBS), VERY COARSELY CHOPPED
1   MEDIUM ONION, COARSELY CHOPPED
1   APPLE, CORED AND CUT INTO 1/2-INCH CUBES
1/2 TEASPOON CARAWAY SEED
1/2 TEASPOON SALT
1/8 TEASPOON PEPPER

4 to 6 servings

In Dutch oven, cook bacon over medium heat until crisp, stirring frequently. Remove from heat. Remove bacon with slotted spoon; set aside. Reserve 3 tablespoons bacon fat in Dutch oven.

In large plastic food-storage bag, combine flour and paprika; shake to mix. Add one partridge; shake to coat. Repeat with remaining partridge. Add partridge to bacon fat in Dutch oven; brown on all sides over medium-high heat. Add reserved bacon and remaining ingredients to Dutch oven. Reduce heat; cover. Simmer until juices run clear when thigh is pricked, about 1 hour, rearranging birds and stirring vegetables once or twice.

Per serving: Calories: 574 • Protein: 52 g. • Carbohydrate: 25 g. • Fat: 29 g. • Cholesterol: 155 mg. • Sodium: 500 mg. — Exchanges: 1 starch, 1/2 fruit, 6 1/2 lean meat • 2 vegetable • 2 fat

CHUTNEY-GINGER SHARPTAIL

1   WHOLE ACORN SQUASH (ABOUT 1 1/2 LBS.), SLICED INTO 1-INCH RINGS, SEEDS REMOVED
1 1/2 CUPS APPLE JUICE
1   MEDIUM RED COOKING APPLE, CORED AND CHOPPED (1 CUP)
1/2 CUP FRESH CRANBERRIES
1   SMALL ONION, CHOPPED (1/2 CUP)
1   TABLESPOON FRESH THYME LEAVES
2   STICKS CINNAMON (2-INCH LENGTHS)
2   TABLESPOONS OLIVE OIL
1   CLOVE GARLIC, MINCED
1   TEASPOON GROUND GINGER
1/2 TEASPOON GROUND CARDAMOM
1/2 TEASPOON SALT
1/4 TEASPOON WHITE PEPPER
1   WHOLE DRESSED SHARPTAIL GROUSE (3/4 TO 1 LB.), SKIN REMOVED, QUARTERED
1/4 CUP PREPARED MANGO CHUTNEY
4   SPRIGS FRESH THYME FOR GARNISH

2 servings

Heat oven to 350°F. Arrange squash rings in 13 × 9-inch baking dish. Set aside. In medium mixing bowl, combine apple juice, apple, cranberries, onion, thyme leaves and cinnamon. Spoon mixture evenly over squash. Set aside.

In 12-inch nonstick skillet, heat oil over medium heat. Add garlic, ginger, cardamom, salt and pepper. Cook for 30 seconds, stirring constantly. Add sharptail pieces. Cook for 6 to 8 minutes, or until meat is browned, turning pieces occasionally.

Arrange sharptail over squash and apple mixture. Brush pieces evenly with chutney. Cook for 1 to 1 1/4 hours, or until squash is tender. To serve, arrange squash rings on serving plates. Top with fruit mixture, then sharptail pieces. Garnish with sprigs of fresh thyme. Serve with additional chutney, if desired.

Per Serving: Calories: 706 • Protein: 39 g. • Carbohydrate: 95 g. • Fat: 20 g. • Cholesterol: 100 mg. • Sodium: 959 mg. — Exchanges: 1 3/4 starch, 4 3/4 very lean meat, 1 vegetable, 2 1/4 fruit, 4 fat

Deviled Birds

❧══☙

Follow recipe below, adding 3/4 teaspoon dry mustard, 3/4 teaspoon paprika and 1/8 teaspoon cayenne to 3/4 cup stock. Continue as directed.

SMOTHERED BIRDS

The natural flavor of the bird comes through with this simple method. You may substitute 8 to 10 whole doves, 3 split partridge, 2 cut-up grouse or 1 cut-up pheasant for the quail; adjust cooking times as indicated.

6   WHOLE DRESSED QUAIL (4 TO 6 OZ. EACH) OR
    SUBSTITUTE, SPLIT INTO HALVES
1/2 CUP ALL-PURPOSE FLOUR
1/2 TEASPOON SALT
1/8 TEASPOON PEPPER
1/4 CUP BUTTER OR MARGARINE
1 1/4 CUPS UPLAND GAME BIRD STOCK (PAGE 23) OR
    CHICKEN BROTH, DIVIDED

2 or 3 servings

Pat quail halves dry. In large plastic food-storage bag, combine flour, salt and pepper; shake to mix. Add quail halves; shake to coat. Remove quail pieces; set aside. Reserve 2 tablespoons flour mixture; discard remaining flour mixture.

In medium skillet, melt butter over medium heat. Add quail; brown on both sides. Add 3/4 cup stock to skillet. Reduce heat; cover. Simmer until birds are tender, 35 to 45 minutes for quail or doves. Partridge or grouse will take 40 to 50 minutes; pheasant will take 50 to 60 minutes. Transfer quail halves to heated platter. Set aside and keep warm. In measuring cup or small bowl, blend reserved 2 tablespoons flour into remaining 1/2 cup stock. Blend into drippings in skillet. Cook over medium heat, stirring constantly, until thickened and bubbly. Serve gravy over birds.

Per serving: Calories: 709 • Protein: 53 g. • Carbohydrate: 16 g. • Fat: 47 g. • Cholesterol: 235 mg. • Sodium: 1090 mg. — Exchanges: 1 starch, 7 lean meat, 5 fat

HUNGARIAN PARTRIDGE SCALOPPINE

2   WHOLE BONELESS SKINLESS HUNGARIAN PARTRIDGE
    BREASTS (6 OZ. EACH), SPLIT IN HALF, POUNDED
    TO 1/4-INCH THICKNESS
    SALT AND PEPPER TO TASTE
2   TABLESPOONS OLIVE OIL
2   TABLESPOONS BUTTER OR MARGARINE, DIVIDED
2   TABLESPOONS FRESH LEMON JUICE
2   TEASPOONS CAPERS, DRAINED
2   TABLESPOONS SNIPPED FRESH PARSLEY
    LEMON SLICES FOR GARNISH

4 servings

Sprinkle partridge breasts with salt and pepper to taste. In 12-inch nonstick skillet, heat oil and 1 tablespoon butter over medium-high heat. Add breasts. Cook for 5 to 7 minutes, or until meat is browned, turning breasts over once. Set breasts aside and keep warm.

Reduce heat to medium-low. Add lemon juice and capers to skillet. Stir in remaining 1 tablespoon butter until melted. Stir in parsley. Spoon sauce over partridge breasts. Garnish with lemon slices.

Per Serving: Calories: 227 • Protein: 20 g. • Carbohydrate: 1 g. • Fat: 16 g. • Cholesterol: 72 mg. • Sodium: 154 mg. — Exchanges: 3 very lean meat, 3 fat

Hungarian Partridge Scaloppine

RUFFED GROUSE SALAD

4	CUPS MIXED SALAD GREENS
1	CAN (11 OZ.) MANDARIN ORANGES, DRAINED
1	SMALL RED ONION, THINLY SLICED
2	KIWIFRUIT, PEELED AND SLICED
3/4	CUP FRESH RASPBERRIES OR POMEGRANATE SEEDS
1/3	CUP PECAN HALVES, TOASTED
1/3	CUP VEGETABLE OIL
3	TABLESPOONS RASPBERRY VINEGAR
1 1/2	TABLESPOONS SUGAR
1/4	TEASPOON SALT
	DASH RED PEPPER SAUCE
4	WHOLE BONELESS SKINLESS RUFFED GROUSE BREASTS (4 TO 6 OZ. EACH), SPLIT IN HALF

4 servings

Prepare grill for medium, direct heat. On individual serving plates, evenly arrange greens, oranges, onion, kiwifruit, raspberries and pecans. Set aside. In 1-quart saucepan, combine oil, vinegar, sugar, salt and red pepper sauce. Bring to a boil over medium-high heat, stirring frequently. Set dressing aside and keep warm.

Spray cooking grid with nonstick vegetable cooking spray. Arrange grouse breasts on cooking grid. Grill for 8 to 10 minutes, or until meat is no longer pink and juices run clear. Place 2 breast halves on each prepared plate. Drizzle warm dressing evenly over salads. Serve immediately.

Per Serving: Calories: 536 • Protein: 38 g. • Carbohydrate: 33 g. • Fat: 29 g. • Cholesterol: 82 mg. • Sodium: 209 mg. — Exchanges: 5 very lean meat, 2 vegetable, 1 1/2 fruit, 5 1/2 fat

CAJUN PHEASANT FINGERS

SPICE MIX

2½	TEASPOONS GARLIC POWDER
2	TEASPOONS DRIED THYME LEAVES
1½	TEASPOONS BLACK PEPPER
1	TO 2 TEASPOONS CAYENNE
1	TEASPOON WHITE PEPPER
½	TEASPOON SALT
1	CUP APRICOT PRESERVES
¼	CUP DIJON MUSTARD
2	WHOLE BONELESS SKINLESS PHEASANT BREASTS (5 TO 6 OZ. EACH), CUT LENGTHWISE INTO 1-INCH-WIDE STRIPS
2	TABLESPOONS VEGETABLE OIL
1	TABLESPOON BUTTER OR MARGARINE

3 to 4 servings

In shallow dish, combine spice mix ingredients. Set aside. In 1-quart saucepan, combine preserves and mustard. Cook over medium heat for 4 to 5 minutes, or until mixture bubbles and becomes smooth, stirring frequently. Set sauce aside and keep warm.

Dredge pheasant strips in spice mix to coat. In 12-inch skillet, heat oil and butter over medium heat. Add pheasant strips. Cook for 4 to 5 minutes, or until browned, turning strips over once. Remove strips from skillet and drain on paper towel–lined plate. Serve strips with apricot sauce for dipping.

Per Serving: Calories: 412 • Protein: 20 g. • Carbohydrate: 55 g. • Fat: 13 g. • Cholesterol: 53 mg. • Sodium: 722 mg. — Exchanges: 2³/4 very lean meat, 2½ fat

SAGE GROUSE WITH ARTICHOKES & MUSHROOMS

2	WHOLE BONELESS SKINLESS SAGE GROUSE BREASTS (8 TO 10 OZ. EACH), SPLIT IN HALF
¼	TEASPOON SALT
6	TABLESPOONS BUTTER OR MARGARINE, DIVIDED
8	OZ. FRESH MUSHROOMS, SLICED (3 CUPS)
1	JAR (7 OZ.) ARTICHOKE HEARTS IN MARINADE, DRAINED AND HALVED
½	TEASPOON DRIED TARRAGON LEAVES
2	TABLESPOONS ALL-PURPOSE FLOUR
¾	CUP CHICKEN BROTH
¼	CUP DRY SHERRY
1	TABLESPOON SNIPPED FRESH PARSLEY

4 servings

Heat oven to 375°F. Sprinkle grouse breasts evenly with salt. In 12-inch skillet, melt 2 tablespoons butter over medium-high heat. Add grouse breasts. Cook for 4 to 6 minutes, or until meat is browned, turning breasts over once. Arrange breasts in 12 × 8-inch baking dish. Set aside.

Add 2 tablespoons butter to drippings in skillet. Melt over medium heat. Add mushrooms. Cook for 3 to 4 minutes, or until mushrooms are tender, stirring occasionally. Using slotted spoon, spoon mushrooms over grouse breasts. Top with artichoke hearts and tarragon. Set aside.

Add remaining 2 tablespoons butter to drippings in skillet. Melt over medium heat. Whisk flour into drippings. Cook for 1 minute, stirring constantly. Gradually blend in broth. Cook for 3 to 4 minutes, or until sauce is thickened and bubbly, stirring constantly. Remove from heat. Stir in sherry. Pour sauce over grouse. Bake for 30 to 45 minutes, or until meat is no longer pink. Sprinkle with parsley. Serve over rice pilaf, if desired.

Per Serving: Calories: 423 • Protein: 34 g. • Carbohydrate: 10 g. • Fat: 26 g. • Cholesterol: 121 mg. • Sodium: 800 mg. — Exchanges: 4½ very lean meat, 1¼ vegetable, 5 fat

PARMESAN PHEASANT

¹/₂ CUP SEASONED DRY BREAD CRUMBS

¹/₄ CUP SHREDDED FRESH PARMESAN CHEESE

2 TABLESPOONS SNIPPED FRESH PARSLEY

1 TEASPOON GARLIC POWDER

1 EGG, SLIGHTLY BEATEN

4 WHOLE BONELESS SKINLESS PHEASANT BREASTS (5 TO 6 OZ. EACH), SPLIT IN HALF

3 TABLESPOONS MARGARINE OR BUTTER

2 CUPS PREPARED CHUNKY MARINARA SAUCE

4 SLICES (¹/₂ OZ. EACH) PROVOLONE CHEESE, HALVED

3 to 4 servings

In shallow baking dish, combine bread crumbs, Parmesan cheese, parsley and garlic powder. Place egg in second shallow dish. Dip pheasant breast halves in egg, then dredge in crumb mixture to coat.

In 10-inch nonstick skillet, melt margarine over medium-high heat. Add breast halves. Cook for 6 to 8 minutes, or until pheasant is golden brown, turning once.

Pour marinara sauce around breast halves in skillet. Top each breast half with 1 slice Provolone. Cover. Cook for 4 to 5 minutes, or until sauce is heated through and cheese is melted.

Per Serving: Calories: 523 • Protein: 50 g. • Carbohydrate: 25 g. • Fat: 25 g. • Cholesterol: 158 mg. • Sodium: 1590 mg. — Exchanges: ³/₄ starch, 6 lean meat, 2³/₄ vegetable, 1¹/₂ fat

SAVORY CHUKAR

2 TABLESPOONS VEGETABLE OIL

2 TABLESPOONS MARGARINE OR BUTTER

2 TO 3 LBS. BONELESS SKINLESS CHUKAR BREASTS OR SUBSTITUTE, CUT INTO 1-INCH PIECES

¹/₂ TEASPOON SALT

¹/₄ TEASPOON PEPPER

¹/₈ TEASPOON DRIED SUMMER SAVORY

³/₄ CUP WHIPPING CREAM

3 TABLESPOONS MADEIRA WINE

¹/₄ TEASPOON CRUSHED RED PEPPER FLAKES

10 servings

In 10-inch nonstick skillet, heat oil and margarine over medium heat. Add chukar pieces, salt, pepper and summer savory. Cook for 8 to 10 minutes, or just until meat is browned, stirring frequently. Stir in cream, wine and pepper flakes. Reduce heat to low. Cook for 8 to 10 minutes, or until hot, stirring occasionally. Serve over hot buttered rice and garnish with snipped fresh parsley, if desired.

Per Serving: Calories: 265 • Protein: 28 g. • Carbohydrate: 1 g. • Fat: 15 g. • Cholesterol: N/A • Sodium: 181 mg. — Exchanges: 4 lean meat, ³/₄ fat

Parmesan Pheasant

MARINATED PHEASANT SALAD

2½ CUPS (10 OZ.) SHREDDED COOKED
    PHEASANT

  1 CAN (14 OZ.) QUARTERED ARTICHOKE
    HEARTS, DRAINED

 ½ MEDIUM RED ONION, CUT INTO THIN
    WEDGES AND SEPARATED (½ CUP)

 ½ CUP ITALIAN DRESSING

  8 CUPS TORN MIXED BABY SALAD GREENS

  2 ROMA TOMATOES, SLICED

 ½ CUP PITTED HALVED KALAMATA OLIVES

 ½ CUP (2 OZ.) CRUMBLED BLUE CHEESE

4 to 6 servings

In medium mixing bowl, combine pheasant, artichoke hearts, onion and dressing. Toss to coat. Cover with plastic wrap. Chill at least 2 hours, stirring occasionally.

In large salad bowl or mixing bowl, combine greens, tomatoes and olives. Add pheasant mixture. Toss to combine. Sprinkle cheese over top of salad.

Per Serving: Calories: 279 • Protein: 20 g. • Carbohydrate: 11 g.
• Fat: 18 g. • Cholesterol: 49 mg. • Sodium: 534 mg. — Exchanges: 2¼ very lean meat, 2 vegetable, 3½ fat

EASY PHEASANT PIE

1 PACKAGE (16 OZ.) FROZEN STEW VEGETABLES
  (POTATOES, CARROTS, ONION AND CELERY)
1 PACKAGE (.87 OZ.) CHICKEN-FLAVORED GRAVY MIX
1¾ CUPS (7 OZ.) CHOPPED COOKED PHEASANT
1 CUP FROZEN PEAS
1 TEASPOON SNIPPED FRESH ROSEMARY
  PASTRY DOUGH FOR 2-CRUST PIE*

6 servings

Heat oven to 425°F. Prepare vegetables as
directed on package, cooking just until tender-
crisp. Drain. Set aside. Prepare gravy mix as
directed on package. Add pheasant, peas and
rosemary to gravy. Set aside.

On lightly floured surface, roll half of pastry
dough into 12-inch circle. Fit circle into 9-inch
pie plate. Spread vegetables in bottom of crust.
Top with pheasant mixture. Roll remaining dough
into 11-inch circle. Cut vents in circle with sharp
knife. Place circle over top of pie. Roll edges of
bottom and top crusts together. Flute edges or
press together with tines of fork to seal.

Bake for 15 minutes. Reduce heat to 400°F.
Bake for 15 to 20 minutes longer, or until filling
is bubbly and crust is browned. Let stand for 10
minutes before serving.

*Use your favorite crust
recipe or 1 package
(15 oz.) refrigerated pie
crust dough.*

Per Serving: Calories: 432
• Protein: 16 g.
• Carbohydrate: 41 g.
• Fat: 22 g. • Cholesterol:
29 mg. • Sodium: 593
mg. — Exchanges: 2¼
starch, 1 very lean meat, 1
vegetable, 4¼ fat

PARTRIDGE & HAZELNUT SALAD

2 CUPS CUT-UP COOKED HUNGARIAN PARTRIDGE OR
  SUBSTITUTE (ABOUT 10 OZ.)
½ CUP COARSELY CHOPPED HAZELNUTS, TOASTED, DIVIDED
1 CUP THINLY SLICED CELERY
½ CUP HALVED SEEDLESS GREEN GRAPES
½ CUP HALVED SEEDLESS RED GRAPES
½ CUP MAYONNAISE OR SALAD DRESSING
¼ CUP PLAIN NONFAT OR LOW-FAT YOGURT
1 TABLESPOON HONEY
1 TABLESPOON LEMON JUICE
½ TEASPOON GROUND GINGER
⅛ TEASPOON SALT

4 servings

In large mixing bowl, combine partridge pieces,
¼ cup hazelnuts, the celery and grapes. Set
aside. In small mixing bowl, combine remaining
ingredients, except remaining hazelnuts. Spoon
mayonnaise mixture over partridge mixture. Toss
to coat. Serve salad on lettuce-lined plates, if
desired. Sprinkle servings evenly with remaining
¼ cup hazelnuts.

Per Serving: Calories: 474 • Protein: 27 g.
• Carbohydrate: 15 g. • Fat: 35 g. • Cholesterol: N/A
• Sodium: 302 mg.— Exchanges: 4 medium-fat meat,
1 fruit, 3 fat

Partridge & Hazelnut Salad

PHEASANT HOT DISH

6 OZ. UNCOOKED MINI LASAGNA NOODLES (4 CUPS)
3½ CUPS CUT-UP COOKED PHEASANT OR SUBSTITUTE (ABOUT 1 LB.)
1¼ CUPS MILK
1 CAN (10¾ OZ.) CONDENSED CREAM OF MUSHROOM SOUP
1 CUP SHREDDED PASTEURIZED PROCESS CHEESE LOAF
1 CAN (4 OZ.) SLICED MUSHROOMS, DRAINED
1 CLOVE GARLIC, MINCED
1 TEASPOON INSTANT CHICKEN BOUILLON GRANULES
½ TEASPOON PEPPER
½ TEASPOON DRIED THYME LEAVES
1 TABLESPOON MARGARINE OR BUTTER
1 CUP THINLY SLICED CELERY
½ CUP CHOPPED GREEN PEPPER
½ CUP CHOPPED RED PEPPER
½ CUP CHOPPED ONION
1 CUP CRUSHED POTATO CHIPS

6 to 8 servings

Heat oven to 350°F. Spray 3-quart casserole with nonstick vegetable cooking spray. Set aside. Prepare noodles as directed on package. Rinse and drain. In large mixing bowl, combine noodles, pheasant pieces, milk, soup, cheese, mushrooms, garlic, bouillon, pepper and thyme. Set aside.

In 10-inch nonstick skillet, melt margarine over medium heat. Add celery, peppers and onion. Cook for 3 to 5 minutes, or until vegetables are tender-crisp, stirring occasionally. Add to pheasant mixture.

Spoon pheasant mixture into prepared casserole. Sprinkle top evenly with potato chips. Bake for 30 to 35 minutes, or until mixture is hot and bubbly and topping is golden brown.

Per Serving: Calories: 345 • Protein: 26 g. • Carbohydrate: 29 g. • Fat: 14 g. • Cholesterol: N/A • Sodium: 792 mg.— Exchanges: 1½ starch, 2¾ lean meat, 1 vegetable, 1¼ fat

GRILL-SMOKED PHEASANT

BRINE
6 CUPS COLD WATER
½ CUP PLUS 1 TABLESPOON CANNING/PICKLING SALT
¼ CUP PLUS 2 TABLESPOONS PACKED BROWN SUGAR
3 TABLESPOONS MAPLE SYRUP
2 TABLESPOONS PLUS 1 TEASPOON WHITE WINE VINEGAR
2 TEASPOONS PICKLING SPICE

1 WHOLE DRESSED PHEASANT (1½ TO 2¼ LBS.), SKIN ON
  APPLE OR CHERRY WOOD CHIPS
2 TABLESPOONS HONEY
2 TEASPOONS SOY SAUCE
  HOT CHICKEN BROTH, BEER OR WATER

3 to 4 servings

In large nonmetallic bowl or sealable plastic bag, combine brine ingredients. Stir until salt and sugar are dissolved. Add pheasant. Cover. Chill 4 hours, turning pheasant once or twice. Drain and discard brine from pheasant. Pat pheasant dry with paper towels. Let pheasant air dry for 30 minutes.

While pheasant is air drying, start large load of charcoal briquets on one side of charcoal grill. Soak wood chips in warm water for 30 minutes; drain. In small bowl, combine honey and soy sauce. When briquets are covered with light ash, toss a handful of wood chips on them. Place pan ⅔ full of hot broth on cooking grid over charcoal. Brush pheasant with honey mixture and place it on opposite side of cooking grid. Cover grill.

Smoke pheasant for 2 to 3 hours, or until pheasant is fully cooked. (Do not open grill unless necessary.) Temperature in grill should stay between 150° and 200°F. Regulate temperature using vents on grill. Add more wood chips during the last hour of smoking.

Per Serving: Calories: 379 • Protein: 42 g. • Carbohydrate: 12 g. • Fat: 17 g.• Cholesterol: 131 mg. • Sodium: 1041 mg. — Exchanges: 6 lean meat

BUTTERY SMOKED PHEASANT WITH ONIONS

¼ CUP BUTTER, MELTED
½ TEASPOON SUGAR
½ TEASPOON DRY MUSTARD
½ TEASPOON SALT
¼ TEASPOON PAPRIKA
⅛ TEASPOON CAYENNE
1 DRESSED PHEASANT OR SUBSTITUTE (1½ TO 2¼ LBS), CUT UP, SKIN REMOVED
1½ CUPS APPLE OR CHERRY WOOD CHIPS
1 MEDIUM ONION, SLICED

3 or 4 servings

In medium mixing bowl, combine all ingredients except pheasant pieces, wood chips and onion. Add pheasant pieces, turning to coat. Cover with plastic wrap. Chill 1 hour. Meanwhile, place wood chips in large mixing bowl. Cover with water. Soak chips for 1 hour. Place oven thermometer in smoker. Heat smoker until temperature registers 250°F. Drain wood chips.

Arrange onion slices in bottom of 9-inch square disposable foil baking pan. Arrange pheasant pieces over onion. Remelt any remaining butter mixture and pour over pheasant pieces. Place pan on top rack of smoker. Open damper. Place wood chips in smoker. When wood chips begin to smoke, close damper, cracking slightly. Smoke pheasant pieces for 1½ to 2 hours at 250°F, or until juices run clear. Serve pheasant with onion and pan drippings.

Per Serving: Calories: 454 • Protein: 42 g. • Carbohydrate: 4 g. • Fat: 29 g. • Cholesterol: 31 mg. • Sodium: 465 mg. — Exchanges: 5¼ medium-fat meat, 1 vegetable, ¾ fat

SMOKY PHEASANT SOUP

2 TABLESPOONS MARGARINE OR BUTTER
¼ CUP FINELY CHOPPED ONION
1 CLOVE GARLIC, MINCED
¼ CUP ALL-PURPOSE FLOUR
½ TEASPOON SALT
½ TEASPOON FRESHLY GROUND PEPPER
4 CUPS CHICKEN BROTH, DIVIDED
2½ CUPS COOKED WILD RICE
2 CUPS CUT-UP SMOKED PHEASANT OR SUBSTITUTE (ABOUT 10 OZ.)
1 CUP THINLY SLICED CARROTS
1 BAY LEAF
1 CUP HALF-AND-HALF
2 TABLESPOONS DRY SHERRY

8 servings

In 6-quart Dutch oven or stockpot, melt margarine over medium heat. Add onion and garlic. Cook for 2 to 3 minutes, or until onion is tender, stirring frequently. In 4-cup measure, combine flour, salt and pepper. Blend in 2 cups broth. Stir into onion mixture. Add remaining 2 cups broth and remaining ingredients, except half-and-half and sherry. Bring to a boil over medium-high heat. Reduce heat to low. Simmer for 30 to 35 minutes, or until carrots are tender. Stir in half-and-half and sherry. Simmer for 10 to 15 minutes longer, or until flavors are blended. Remove and discard bay leaf before serving.

Per Serving: Calories: 222 • Protein: 16 g. • Carbohydrate: 18 g. • Fat: 9 g. • Cholesterol: 54 mg. • Sodium: 700 mg. — Exchanges: 1 starch, 1½ lean meat, ½ vegetable, ¾ fat

Smoky Pheasant Soup

RECIPES FOR
Wild Turkey

Thanks to organizations like the National Wild Turkey Federation, the opportunity to hunt and harvest a wild turkey has never been better. Across the country, today's hunter has an outstanding chance to hear the thunderous gobble of a tom turkey and try to call the wary bird within shooting range.

Why is turkey hunting so popular? Perhaps it's the chance to carry a gun or bow during the warm spring months. Or maybe it's the rush of watching a gobbler fan its tail feathers as he saunters toward your decoys. Whatever the reason, turkey hunting is totally addicting.

Hunters who are lucky enough to harvest a bird are treated to a large amount of tasty meat. In fact, many people—hunters and nonhunters alike—prefer the flavor of wild turkey to that of domestic turkey.

This section contains many mouthwatering recipes to make the most out of your harvested bird. From "Roasted Wild Turkey" to "Wild Turkey Picatta with Morels," the following dishes are sure to please.

As a special bonus, you'll learn how to deep-fry a whole wild turkey. This technique has become extremely popular in the last few years. Not only is this the fastest way to prepare a wild turkey, but the meat stays incredibly moist and absolutely delicious.

Savvy cooks have learned that brining the traditional Thanksgiving bird before roasting produces moist meat. Wild turkeys benefit even more from this treatment, as they have less fat than their domestic counterparts.

For the best results, brine your turkey overnight. You'll need a large, nonaluminum container to hold the turkey and brine; a stockpot or a clean, food-safe bucket such as a pickle pail works well.

Dissolve 2 cups canning/pickling salt or kosher salt in 2 gallons of cold water in the brining container. Add the turkey and place a heavy ceramic plate on top of it to keep it submerged. Cover the container and refrigerate it overnight, turning the bird once if possible. The next day, rinse the bird and pat it dry; it's now ready for your regular roasting preparations.

Some cooks add additional flavor to the brine by mixing in a cup or so of brown sugar, molasses or maple syrup. You can also add about 2 tablespoons mixed pickling spices or a few sprigs of fresh herbs to add a light flavor note to the turkey.

ROASTED
WILD TURKEY

An oven bag is an excellent tool when roasting wild birds such as turkey. It helps keep an otherwise lean and dry bird moist.

1   TABLESPOON ALL-PURPOSE FLOUR
1   WHOLE DRESSED WILD TURKEY, SKIN ON
    SALT AND PEPPER TO TASTE
    PREPARED BREAD DRESSING, OPTIONAL
2   STALKS CELERY, CUT INTO 3-INCH PIECES
1   MEDIUM ONION, QUARTERED
3   TABLESPOONS VEGETABLE OIL

6 to 8 servings

Heat oven to 350°F. Add 1 tablespoon flour to turkey-size ($23^1/2 \times$ 19-inch) oven cooking bag; shake to distribute. Place cooking bag in 13×9-inch roasting pan.

Season cavity of turkey with salt and pepper. Stuff loosely with dressing, as shown at right, or place celery and onion in cavity of turkey. Tuck tips of wings behind turkey's back. Truss legs with kitchen string. Brush entire turkey with oil. Place turkey in cooking bag; secure bag with provided nylon tie. Insert meat thermometer into thickest part of thigh through top of bag. Make six $1/2$-inch slits in top of bag.

Roast turkey according to chart (right), until internal temperature reads 180°F. Remove turkey from bag. Let stand, tented with foil, for 20 minutes before carving.

Per Serving (without stuffing or gravy):
Calories: 608 • Protein: 82 g. • Carbohydrate: 1 g.
• Fat: 28 g. • Cholesterol: 239 mg. • Sodium: 212 mg.
— Exchanges: 11 lean meat

Uses for Leftover Roast Turkey

Substitute an equal amount of leftover roast turkey for the game meat in any of these recipes:

- One-Pot Squirrel Dinner, page 179
- Squirrel Pot Pie, page 180
- Marinated Pheasant Salad, page 212
- Easy Pheasant Pie, page 213
- Partridge & Hazelnut Salad, page 213
- Pheasant Hot Dish, page 214

Stuff turkey loosely with dressing if desired; place celery and onion in oven cooking bag before adding stuffed turkey. Place any extra dressing in buttered casserole and refrigerate until ready to bake. Bake extra dressing for last 35 minutes.

Roasting Timetable for Wild Turkey in Oven Cooking Bag

TURKEY	WEIGHT BEFORE STUFFING	APPROXIMATE COOKING TIME
STUFFED	4 TO 8 LBS.	2 TO 2¾ HOURS
	8 TO 12 LBS.	2½ TO 3 HOURS
	12 TO 15 LBS.	3 TO 3½ HOURS
	15 TO 20 LBS.	3½ TO 4 HOURS
	20 TO 25 LBS.	4½ TO 5 HOURS
UNSTUFFED	4 TO 8 LBS.	1¾ TO 2¼ HOURS
	8 TO 12 LBS.	2 TO 2½ HOURS
	12 TO 15 LBS.	2½ TO 3 HOURS
	15 TO 20 LBS.	3 TO 3½ HOURS
	20 TO 25 LBS.	4 TO 4½ HOURS

PECAN TURKEY WITH MAPLE SAUCE

1/4 CUP PURE MAPLE SYRUP

2 TABLESPOONS DARK CORN SYRUP

3 TABLESPOONS APPLEJACK BRANDY

1 TABLESPOON BUTTER, MELTED

1 WHOLE BONE-IN WILD TURKEY BREAST (3 TO 4 LBS.), SKIN ON

3/4 CUP FINELY CHOPPED PECANS

6 to 8 servings

Heat oven to 350°F. In small bowl, combine syrups, brandy and butter. Reserve 1/4 cup and set remaining mixture aside. Place turkey breast skin side up in roasting pan. Brush evenly with 2 tablespoons reserved syrup mixture. Press pecans evenly over breast to coat. Cover with foil.

Bake for 1 hour 15 minutes. Brush remaining 2 tablespoons reserved mixture over breast. Bake, uncovered, for 15 to 30 minutes, or until internal temperature registers 180°F in thickest part of breast. Serve with remaining syrup mixture.

Per Serving: Calories: 389 • Protein: 40 g. • Carbohydrate: 14 g. • Fat: 18 g. • Cholesterol: 105 mg. • Sodium: 109 mg. — Exchanges: 5 1/2 very lean meat, 3 1/2 fat

BARBECUE-SMOKED TURKEY

RUB MIX

1/2	CUP KETCHUP
2	TABLESPOONS PACKED BROWN SUGAR
1	TABLESPOON PREPARED YELLOW MUSTARD
1	TABLESPOON WORCESTERSHIRE SAUCE
1	TEASPOON CHILI POWDER
1	TEASPOON SALT
1	TEASPOON HOT PEPPER SAUCE
1/2	TEASPOON GARLIC POWDER
1/2	TEASPOON FRESHLY GROUND PEPPER
1	WHOLE DRESSED WILD TURKEY (8 TO 10 LBS.), SKIN ON
	HICKORY WOOD CHIPS
	HOT WATER, CHICKEN BROTH OR BEER

6 to 8 servings

In small mixing bowl, combine rub mix ingredients. Spread mixture evenly in cavity and over surface of turkey. Let turkey air dry for 45 minutes. Soak wood chips in warm water for 30 minutes; drain. Heat smoker to 200°F.

Position smoker rack at lowest setting in smoker. Fill 13 × 9-inch pan half full with hot liquid and place on rack. Spray second smoker rack with nonstick vegetable cooking spray. Place prepared rack at position just above water pan. Place turkey breast side up on rack above pan. Place chips in smoker.

Smoke turkey for 6 to 8 hours, or until internal temperature in thickest part of breast registers 180°F. Keep smoker temperature between 200° and 250°F, and refill water pan if necessary.

Per Serving: Calories: 491 • Protein: 64 g. • Carbohydrate: 8 g. • Fat: 21 g. • Cholesterol: 186 mg. • Sodium: 682 mg. — Exchanges: 9 very lean meat, 4 fat

ROAST TURKEY WITH CORN & SAUSAGE STUFFING

1	LB. UNSEASONED BULK PORK SAUSAGE, CRUMBLED
2	CUPS CHOPPED ONION
16	SLICES DAY-OLD BREAD, CUT INTO 1/2-INCH CUBES (8 CUPS)
1	CAN (15 OZ.) CREAM-STYLE CORN
1	TABLESPOON SNIPPED FRESH PARSLEY
1 1/2	TEASPOONS POULTRY SEASONING
1	TEASPOON SALT
1/4	TEASPOON PEPPER
1	WHOLE DRESSED WILD TURKEY (10 TO 12 LBS.), SKIN ON

8 to 10 servings

Heat oven to 350°F. In 12-inch nonstick skillet, combine sausage and onions. Cook over medium heat for 6 to 8 minutes, or until meat is no longer pink and onions are tender, stirring occasionally. Drain, reserving 1/4 cup drippings.

In large mixing bowl, combine sausage mixture, reserved drippings, the bread cubes, corn, parsley, poultry seasoning, salt and pepper.

Sprinkle cavity of turkey with additional salt and pepper. Spoon stuffing lightly into cavity. Secure legs with string. Tuck wing tips behind back. Place turkey breast side up in roasting pan. Bake for 2 1/2 to 3 hours, or until legs move freely and juices run clear.

Per Serving: Calories: 850 • Protein: 88 g. • Carbohydrate: 31 g. • Fat: 39 g. • Cholesterol: 256 mg. • Sodium: 1039 mg. — Exchanges: 1 1/2 starch, 11 1/2 lean meat, 1 3/4 vegetable, 1 fat

WILD TURKEY PICATTA WITH MORELS

In many states, spring turkey-hunting season coincides with the wild morel mushroom season. Hunters gather morels on their way to their hunting spots. This dish combines both of these special ingredients.

	HALF OF WILD TURKEY BREAST, SKIN AND BONES REMOVED
2	CUPS MILK
1	CUP ALL-PURPOSE FLOUR
1/2	TEASPOON SALT
1/4	TEASPOON PAPRIKA
	DASH PEPPER
4	TO 6 TABLESPOONS BUTTER OR MARGARINE
3/4	CUP COARSELY CHOPPED FRESH MORELS*
3	TABLESPOONS BUTTER OR MARGARINE
2	TABLESPOONS COARSELY CHOPPED FRESH CHIVES
	SALT AND FRESHLY GROUND BLACK PEPPER

4 or 5 servings

Cut turkey breast into 1/2-inch-thick slices across the grain. Place a slice on a cutting board between two sheets of waxed paper. Pound gently to 1/4-inch thickness with saucer or flat side of meat mallet. Repeat with remaining slices. Place turkey slices in 12 × 8-inch baking dish. Add milk. Let stand at room temperature for 30 minutes. Remove turkey slices. Place milk in small bowl; set aside.

Heat oven to 175°F. In large plastic food-storage bag, combine flour, salt, paprika and pepper; shake to combine. Remove 3 tablespoons flour mixture; stir into reserved milk. Set aside. Add 1 turkey

slice to remaining flour mixture in bag. Shake gently to coat. Remove and repeat with remaining slices. In medium skillet, melt 4 tablespoons butter over medium heat. Add half the turkey slices. Cook until golden brown and cooked through, turning once. Transfer turkey slices to heated platter; keep warm in oven. Add additional butter to skillet, if necessary. Repeat with remaining turkey slices.

In same skillet, cook and stir mushrooms in 3 tablespoons butter over medium heat until tender. Stir in reserved milk mixture and chives. Cook over medium heat, stirring constantly, until thickened and bubbly. Salt and pepper to taste. If necessary, blend in additional milk to desired consistency. Serve sauce over turkey slices.

*Variation: Substitute 1/2 ounce dried morels, available at specialty food stores, for fresh morels. Place dried morels in plastic bag. Add 1/4 cup hot water. Squeeze out excess air; seal bag with tie. Set aside to rehydrate for about 15 minutes.

Per Serving: Calories: 635 • Protein: 77 g. • Carbohydrate: 24 g. • Fat: 24 g. •Cholesterol: 240 mg. • Sodium: 610 mg. – Exchanges: 1 1/2 starch, 10 very lean meat, 1/2 whole milk, 3 fat

WILD TURKEY BREAST WITH PECANS

¼   CUP ALL-PURPOSE FLOUR
¾   TEASPOON CURRY POWDER
¼   TEASPOON SEASONED SALT
4   UNCOOKED WILD TURKEY BREAST SLICES (3 OZ. EACH), ½-INCH THICK
2   TABLESPOONS MARGARINE OR BUTTER, DIVIDED
2   TABLESPOONS OLIVE OIL, DIVIDED
¾   CUP THINLY SLICED CARROT
½   CUP THINLY SLICED CELERY
1   CUP PECAN HALVES
¼   CUP GOLDEN RAISINS (OPTIONAL)
½   CUP DRY WHITE WINE

4 servings

In shallow dish, combine flour, curry powder and seasoned salt. Dredge breast slices in flour mixture to coat. In 12-inch nonstick skillet, heat 1 tablespoon margarine and 1 tablespoon oil over medium heat. Add breast slices. Cook for 3 to 5 minutes, or until meat is golden brown, turning over once. Transfer breast slices to warm platter. Set aside.

In same skillet, heat remaining 1 tablespoon margarine and 1 tablespoon oil over medium heat. Add carrot, celery, pecans and raisins. Cook for 5 to 8 minutes, or until vegetables are tender-crisp and pecans are toasted, stirring occasionally.

Arrange breast slices over vegetable mixture. Pour wine around breast slices. Cook for 5 to 8 minutes, or until vegetables are tender and liquid in pan thickens slightly. Serve with hot cooked brown and wild rice, if desired.

Per Serving: Calories: 446 • Protein: 24 g. • Carbohydrate: 14 g. • Fat: 31 g. •Cholesterol: 53 mg. • Sodium: 207 mg. — Exchanges: ½ starch, 3 lean meat, 1 vegetable, 4½ fat

Wild Turkey Breast with Pecans

TURKEY TRACKS

PASTRY

1   PACKAGE (8 OZ.) CREAM CHEESE, SOFTENED
1   CUP MARGARINE OR BUTTER, SOFTENED
2   CUPS ALL-PURPOSE FLOUR

FILLING

3½   CUPS COOKED WILD TURKEY OR SUBSTITUTE (ABOUT 1 LB.), CUT INTO ¼-INCH CUBES
⅓   CUP SHREDDED PASTEURIZED PROCESS CHEESE LOAF
⅓   CUP THINLY SLICED CELERY
⅓   CUP MAYONNAISE OR SALAD DRESSING
2   TABLESPOONS SLICED GREEN ONION
2   TABLESPOONS SOUR CREAM
¼   TEASPOON SALT
¼   TEASPOON PEPPER

16 servings

Heat oven to 400°F. In medium mixing bowl, cut cream cheese and margarine into flour until soft dough forms. Cover with plastic wrap. Chill 1 hour.

Shape dough into 48 balls, about 1 inch in diameter. Press each ball into bottom and up sides of ungreased 1¾-inch muffin cups. Bake for 8 to 10 minutes, or until golden brown.

In large mixing bowl, combine all filling ingredients. Spoon about 1 tablespoon turkey mixture into each pastry shell. Bake for 3 to 5 minutes, or until cheese is melted.

Per Serving: Calories: 310 • Protein: 13 g. • Carbohydrate: 13 g. • Fat: 23 g. • Cholesterol: 46 mg. • Sodium: 333 mg. — Exchanges: ¾ starch, 1½ medium-fat meat, 3 fat

TURKEY CHOWDER

1	CUP WATER
1	LARGE POTATO, PEELED AND CUT INTO ¼-INCH CUBES (1 CUP)
1	MEDIUM ONION, CHOPPED (1 CUP)
2	TEASPOONS CHICKEN BOUILLON GRANULES
1	CLOVE GARLIC, MINCED
¼	TEASPOON PEPPER
2	CUPS 2% MILK
1	CAN (15 OZ.) CREAM-STYLE CORN
1	CAN (4 OZ.) DICED GREEN CHILIES
¾	TO 1 TEASPOON GROUND CUMIN
1½	CUPS (6 OZ.) CHOPPED COOKED WILD TURKEY
1	MEDIUM TOMATO, SEEDED AND CHOPPED (1 CUP)
¾	CUP (3 OZ.) SHREDDED COLBY-JACK CHEESE OR CHEDDAR CHEESE

6 servings

In 3-quart saucepan, combine water, potato, onion, bouillon, garlic and pepper. Bring to a boil over medium-high heat, stirring occasionally. Reduce heat to medium-low. Simmer for 12 to 15 minutes, or until vegetables are tender.

Stir in milk, corn, chilies and cumin. Increase heat to medium. Cook for 10 to 15 minutes, or until mixture is very hot, stirring occasionally. Stir in turkey. Cook for 4 to 6 minutes, or until turkey is heated through, stirring occasionally. To serve, top each serving evenly with tomato and cheese.

Per Serving: Calories: 241 • Protein: 17 g. • Carbohydrate: 27 g. • Fat: 8 g. • Cholesterol: 41 mg. • Sodium: 827 mg. — Exchanges: 1¼ starch, 1½ very lean meat, 1 vegetable, ¼ low-fat milk, 1¼ fat

TURKEY STEW WITH DUMPLINGS

3   TABLESPOONS BUTTER OR MARGARINE

4   MEDIUM CARROTS, SLICED (2 CUPS)

1/4   CUP CHOPPED ONION

1/2   CUP ALL-PURPOSE FLOUR

2   CUPS CHICKEN BROTH

1 2/3   CUPS 2% MILK, DIVIDED

3   CUPS (12 OZ.) CHOPPED COOKED
    WILD TURKEY

1   CUP FROZEN PEAS, DEFROSTED

1/2   CUP FROZEN CORN KERNELS, DEFROSTED

1/2   TEASPOON DRIED THYME LEAVES

1/2   TEASPOON SALT

1/2   TEASPOON PEPPER

2   CUPS BUTTERMILK BAKING MIX

1/2   TEASPOON SNIPPED FRESH ROSEMARY
    LEAVES (OR 1/4 TEASPOON CRUSHED
    DRIED ROSEMARY)

4 to 6 servings

Heat oven to 400°F. Spray 11 × 7-inch baking dish with nonstick vegetable cooking spray. Set aside. In 3-quart saucepan, melt butter over medium heat. Add carrots and onion. Cook for 3 to 5 minutes, or until vegetables are tender-crisp, stirring occasionally. Stir in flour. Cook for 1 minute, stirring constantly. Gradually blend in broth and 1 cup milk. Cook for 5 to 6 minutes, or until mixture is thickened and bubbly, stirring constantly.

Remove from heat. Stir in turkey, peas, corn, thyme, salt and pepper. Spoon mixture into prepared dish. Set aside. In small mixing bowl, combine baking mix, remaining 2/3 cup milk and the rosemary; stir just until moistened. Drop batter onto turkey mixture by spoonfuls to form 6 dumplings. Bake for 30 to 35 minutes, or until stew is hot and bubbly and dumplings are golden brown.

Per Serving: Calories: 430 • Protein: 25 g. • Carbohydrate: 43 g. • Fat: 17 g. • Cholesterol: 65 mg. • Sodium: 1181 mg. — Exchanges: 2 1/4 starch, 2 very lean meat, 1 vegetable, 1/4 low-fat milk, 3 fat

TURKEY LENTIL SOUP

1   TURKEY CARCASS, FAIRLY MEATY

8   CUPS WATER

1   MEDIUM ONION, QUARTERED

1/4   CUP SNIPPED FRESH PARSLEY

1   CLOVE GARLIC, MINCED

2   TEASPOONS SALT

1/4   TEASPOON DRIED MARJORAM LEAVES

1/4   TEASPOON PEPPER

1/8   TEASPOON DRIED THYME LEAVES

1   CUP THINLY SLICED CARROT

3/4   CUP DRIED LENTILS

1/2   CUP THINLY SLICED CELERY

1/2   TEASPOON SALT

    DASH PEPPER

2 quarts

In Dutch oven, combine turkey carcass (cut up if desired), water, onion, parsley, garlic, 2 teaspoons salt, marjoram, 1/4 teaspoon pepper and thyme. Heat to boiling. Reduce heat; cover. Simmer until meat is very tender, 1 1/2 to 2 hours. Strain broth through several layers of cheesecloth; reserve broth. Remove meat from carcass; discard carcass and skin.

Return broth and meat to Dutch oven. Stir in remaining ingredients. Heat to boiling. Reduce heat; cover. Simmer until lentils are tender, about 30 minutes.

Per Serving: Calories: 144 • Protein: 16 g. • Carbohydrate: 14 g. • Fat: 3 g. •Cholesterol: 25 mg. • Sodium: 870 mg. — Exchanges: 1 starch, 2 very lean meat, 1/2 vegetable, 1/2 fat

Turkey Lentil Soup

DEEP-FRYING A WHOLE WILD TURKEY

If you've never had a deep-fried whole turkey, you may be in for a surprise. This southern-inspired method produces a bird with deliciously moist meat and crispy skin; the hot oil seals the outside almost immediately, preventing the meat from absorbing oil and becoming greasy.

Many cooks flavor the meat with a marinade or seasoned brine, which is usually injected into the turkey (often a day or two before cooking); others simply season the outside of the bird and let the seasonings permeate a few hours to overnight before cooking. Injection-seasoning adds flavor to the bird, but also may obscure the delicious natural flavor of the wild bird.

Commercial brines and flavorings are available from turkey-fryer manufacturers, as are the special poultry needles used to inject the birds with the seasoned liquid.

Special turkey fryers are very helpful for this technique. Without such a specialty appliance, you need to rig up a very large pot, powerful heat source and a method of getting the turkey into—and out of—boiling-hot fat. Whether you use a special turkey fryer or a homemade setup, plan on cooking the turkey out-of-doors. Spattering oil and fumes would be a problem in an indoor setting. Follow all safety instructions carefully, to avoid an accident with the hot oil.

DEEP-FRIED WILD TURKEY

1   DRESSED WILD TURKEY, PREFERABLY SKIN-ON

1¼   CUPS MARINADE (PURCHASED, OR FROM THE RECIPE BELOW), OPTIONAL

CREOLE SEASONING BLEND, OR OTHER SEASONING BLEND OF YOUR CHOICE

PEANUT OIL OR VEGETABLE OIL (APPROXIMATELY 5 GALLONS)

Follow the step-by-step instructions on the next page.

EASY CREOLE MARINADE

¼   CUP CRAB BOIL SPICES, SUCH AS ZATARAIN'S

1¼   CUPS WATER

Combine crab boil spices and water in small saucepan. Heat to boiling, stirring to blend. Remove from heat and allow to cool completely. Strain out whole spices and reserve, using liquid to inject turkey. Rub reserved spices in cavity of bird after injecting.

How to Deep-Fry a Whole Turkey

1 Turkey fryers make the task of frying a whole turkey easy. These specialty appliances include a basket or rack that holds the turkey in the hot oil. Most use a propane heat source and are intended for outdoor use. Smaller cookers work well for smaller birds and can also be used to deep-fry fish, onion rings or other foods.

2 Place the turkey in the fryer basket, then place into the empty cooking pot. Add cold water to cover the turkey by 1 to 2 inches. Remove the basket and turkey, and note the water level in the pot; this is the amount of oil you should use. You may also measure the water.

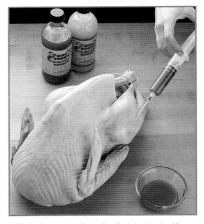

3 Add flavoring to the turkey by injecting it with marinade, using a special meat injector pump. (This step is optional, but it does add flavor and juiciness.) Fill the pump, push the tip into the turkey and gradually depress the plunger while slowly pulling the tip out, until pump is empty. Inject marinade once in each leg, and twice in each thigh and breast, or follow instructions on injector package. You may wrap the injected turkey in plastic and refrigerate it for up to 2 days before cooking, or cook the same day.

4 Rub the outside of the turkey with seasoning mix after patting it dry; sprinkle the inside generously with additional seasoning. If you have injected the bird, rub the seasoning on the bird just before cooking; otherwise, you may want to season the bird and refrigerate it for a few hours (or overnight) to allow the spices to penetrate. Heat the measured amount of oil in the cooker until it reaches 350°F. Place turkey in basket.

6 Cook turkey for 3½ minutes per pound, then carefully remove turkey and check temperature of thigh meat. It will read 180°F when done. If necessary, return turkey to oil until done. Place cooked turkey on newspapers that have been covered with paper towels, cover with a tent of paper and drain for 15 to 30 minutes before carving.

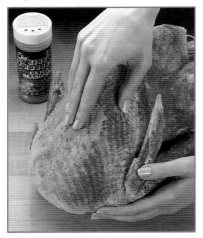

5 Lower the turkey very slowly and carefully into the pot of hot oil. If you add it too quickly, the oil may splash out and burn you. Keep children and pets away from the cooker at all times. Follow all safety precautions indicated in the manual that came with the cooker.

TURKEY JERKY

MARINADE

3 1/2 CUPS COLD WATER

3 TABLESPOONS MORTON® TENDERQUICK® MIX

2 TABLESPOONS WORCESTERSHIRE SAUCE

2 TABLESPOONS SOY SAUCE

1 1/2 TEASPOONS ONION POWDER

1/2 TEASPOON GARLIC POWDER

1/2 TEASPOON PEPPER

2 LBS. BONELESS SKINLESS WILD TURKEY BREAST, CUT INTO 4 X 1 X 1/4-INCH STRIPS

1 1/2 TO 3 CUPS APPLE WOOD CHIPS

11 servings (40 to 50 slices)

Follow directions on page 59.

Per Serving: Calories: 93 • Protein: 20 g.
• Carbohydrate: 0 g. • Fat: 1 g. • Cholesterol: 51 mg.
• Sodium: 396 mg. – Exchanges: 2 lean meat

WILD TURKEY SAUSAGE

1 1/4 LBS. BONELESS FATTY PORK (SUCH AS SHOULDER), CUT INTO 1-INCH PIECES

1/2 LB. BONELESS SKINLESS TURKEY MEAT, CUT INTO 1-INCH PIECES

1 CUP FINELY CHOPPED ONION

1/2 CUP UNSEASONED DRY BREAD CRUMBS

2 EGGS

1/3 CUP MILK

1 TEASPOON CANNING/PICKLING SALT

1 TEASPOON WHITE PEPPER

1 TEASPOON GROUND NUTMEG

1/2 TEASPOON CHILI POWDER

NATURAL SHEEP CASINGS (22 TO 24 MM)

14 sausages (about 2 oz. each)

In large mixing bowl, combine meats. In medium mixing bowl, combine remaining ingredients, except casings. Add to meat mixture. Mix by hand until ingredients are evenly distributed. Grind mixture through a 3/16-inch plate. Cover with plastic wrap. Refrigerate until ready to stuff. Prepare and stuff casings as directed (page 64), using a 1/2-inch horn and twisting off in 4-inch links. Sausages may be panfried or grilled. Wrap tightly and freeze any remaining sausages for future use.

Variation: Wild Turkey Sausage Patties: Prepare recipe as directed above, except omit casings. Shape meat mixture evenly into patties. Layer patties with wax paper. Stack patties, wrap in foil and freeze no longer than 2 months.

Per Serving: Calories: 238 • Protein: 10 g. • Carbohydrate: 4 g. • Fat: 20 g. • Cholesterol: 81 mg. • Sodium: 229 mg. — Exchanges: 1/4 starch, 1 lean meat, 1/4 vegetable, 3 1/4 fat

Camp & Cabin
RECIPES

Fishing and hunting often take us to places where the conveniences of home are far away. Cooking may be done over an open fire, or on a woodstove, with primitive equipment. But the rewards of this style of cooking are great. Fish never tastes as good as it does when it is minutes from the water. And there are choice venison cuts that can be enjoyed right away at camp, as a reward for work well done.

The recipes in this section offer some tips on open-fire cooking, including panfrying and foil cooking over an open fire. While it's true that almost any recipe that calls for panfrying can be cooked over an open fire, the recipes in this section were especially selected because of their suitability for open-fire cooking. Similarly, the panfried dishes in this section can be cooked at home, on a modern stove … but they will be missing that special tang that open-fire cooking imparts to foods. Foil-wrapped dishes from this section will work as well on a modern home grill as they do over an open fire in the woods or on the shore.

The game recipes in this section focus on the cuts that are most likely to be eaten in deer camp, namely the tenderloin, heart and liver.

These recipes also use simple cooking methods suitable for primitive cooking conditions.

The best cut of all, of course, is the tenderloin. This is the one cut that often doesn't make it home, since it is easy to remove from the cavity of a field-dressed deer and seems to taste best when fresh. Often, the best way to prepare it is to simply panfry it in a little butter with nothing more than salt and pepper to season it. We've included some different tenderloin recipes that are easy to prepare and won't overwhelm this excellent cut.

Other cuts that are at their best when fresh are the heart and liver. In the following pages, you will find an easy technique for cutting up the heart, along with two simple but flavorful recipes. We've also included a version of the most popular liver recipe—Liver & Onions. For waterfowl enthusiasts, there's even a delicious foil-wrapped dish that is cooked over an open fire.

These fish and game recipes provide delicious new ways to enjoy fresh fish and game in the outdoors, using simple ingredients that are easy to pack. We've kept preparation simple, so you won't have to wait long to enjoy your dinner.

OPEN-FIRE COOKING

Whether it's a shore lunch after a hard morning of fishing, or an evening meal to prepare the first bounty from a successful hunt, open-fire cooking is unforgettable. The wood smoke adds a unique savor to the food, and the simple cooking methods allow the flavor of the fish or game to shine through.

Build a small fire using dry, nonresinous hardwoods, preferably small logs about 3 to 4 inches in diameter ignited with smaller kindling. If it has been raining, you may have to use newspaper or dry tinder to get the fire started. Stack the wood in log-cabin or tepee style over the tinder.

The most important part of open-fire cooking is heat control. Many outdoor cooks build a larger fire, then scoop hot coals from that into a smaller cooking area. The larger fire is fed with fresh wood, to provide a steady supply of hot coals; this way, you don't have to cook over the open flame of the hot fire. Place a grate over the coals, using rocks around the edge to support the grate.

When you're done with the fire, be sure to extinguish it completely, either by dousing it thoroughly with water or by covering it with dirt or sand. You should not feel any warm areas or wood chunks if you stir the extinguished embers with your hand.

How to Cook Foil-wrapped Foods in Coals

2 Set the foil package in the middle of the coals. Cooking time will vary depending on weather, size of package and intensity of heat.

1 Double-wrap food by first crisscrossing two sheets of heavy-duty aluminum foil. Wrap food in top sheet as shown; repeat with bottom sheet.

3 Cook for half the recommended time. Using long-handled tongs, turn package over and cook for remaining time. Open package to test doneness.

How to Cook in a Frying Pan over an Open Fire

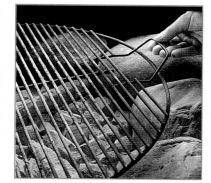

2 Place rocks around the fire to hold the grate about 4 to 8 inches above the coals. Lower the height of the grate for more heat or raise it for less heat.

1 Test the coals by blowing on them; when they glow bright red, the fire is ready. Don't attempt to cook until the flames disappear.

3 Add 2 or 3 tablespoons of cooking oil (or as directed in recipe) to the frying pan and heat for 1 to 2 minutes. Add food with long-handled tongs.

Tips for Open-fire Cooking

A SMALL FIRE is important. If it is too large, fish will burn on the outside, but will be raw on the inside. Gather an ample supply of dry twigs and add them to the fire at regular intervals to provide even heat.

HOLD your hand 6 to 8 inches above grate to judge heat. If you can hold it there 2 to 4 seconds, the heat is high; 5 to 7 seconds, medium, 8 to 10 seconds, low.

ROAST small whole fish over an open fire by impaling it on the sharpened end of a sturdy green hardwood stick. Cook until flesh at backbone flakes easily. Cool slightly and eat in a corn-on-the-cob fashion.

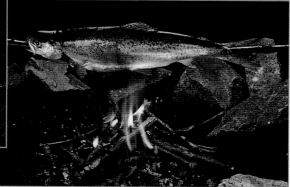

COOK whole skin-on fish directly on the grate; brush grate and fish with oil or butter to prevent sticking. Place skinless fillets on foil cut to size; brush with butter or oil.

Salsa-stuffed Trout

SALSA-STUFFED TROUT

1   WHOLE DRAWN LAKE TROUT OR SUBSTITUTE
    (1½ TO 2 LBS.), HEAD REMOVED
3   ROMA TOMATOES, SEEDED AND CHOPPED (¾ CUP)
⅓   CUP SLICED GREEN ONIONS
½   CUP THINLY SLICED CELERY
⅓   CUP SNIPPED FRESH PARSLEY
3   TABLESPOONS SNIPPED FRESH CILANTRO LEAVES
1   JALAPEÑO PEPPER, SEEDED AND MINCED (2 TABLESPOONS)
1   TABLESPOON SNIPPED FRESH BASIL LEAVES
1   TEASPOON SALT
½   TEASPOON WHITE PEPPER

3 to 4 servings

Build a campfire and allow it to burn down to glowing coals. Cut two 30 × 18-inch sheets of heavy-duty foil. Place trout in center of one sheet. In medium mixing bowl, combine remaining ingredients. Stuff cavity of fish with vegetable mixture, spreading any excess mixture on top of fish.

Fold long sides of foil together in locked folds. Fold and crimp short ends; seal tightly. Place packet seam side down on second sheet of foil. Fold as directed above. Place packet on cooking grate over campfire. Cook for 10 minutes. Turn packet over. Cook for 5 to 10 minutes longer, or until fish begins to flake when fork is inserted at backbone in thickest part of fish.

Per Serving: Calories: 238 • Protein: 32 g. • Carbohydrate: 4 g. • Fat: 10 g. • Cholesterol: 87 mg. • Sodium: 647 mg. — Exchanges: 4 lean meat, ½ vegetable

CAMPFIRE TROUT

2   WHOLE DRAWN STREAM TROUT (8 OZ. EACH)
1   SMALL ONION, CUT INTO 6 WEDGES
2   TABLESPOONS SNIPPED FRESH SORREL OR WILD DOCK
    LEAVES
2   TEASPOONS MARGARINE OR BUTTER
¼   TEASPOON SALT
¼   TEASPOON PEPPER
4   TO 6 LARGE FRESH SORREL, WILD DOCK OR BIBB
    LETTUCE LEAVES

2 servings

Build a campfire and allow it to burn down to glowing coals. Cut two 18 × 14-inch sheets of heavy-duty foil. Place 1 trout in center of each sheet. Stuff each fish evenly with onion, snipped sorrel and margarine. Sprinkle cavity of each fish evenly with salt and pepper. Wrap body of each fish with sorrel leaves, leaving head and tail exposed. Fold long sides of foil together in locked folds. Fold and crimp short ends; seal tightly. Place packets directly on coals. Cook for 4 minutes. Turn packets over. Cook for 4 to 6 minutes longer, or until fish begins to flake when fork is inserted at backbone in thickest part of fish.

Per Serving: Calories: 210 • Protein: 29 g. • Carbohydrate: 4 g. • Fat: 8 g. • Cholesterol: 76 mg. • Sodium: 353 mg. —Exchanges: 4 lean meat, ½ vegetable

LEMONY APPLE-STUFFED SALMON

1   WHOLE DRAWN SALMON OR SUBSTITUTE (2½ TO 3 LBS.), HEAD REMOVED

1   TEASPOON DRIED DILL WEED

1   MEDIUM RED COOKING APPLE, CORED AND CUT INTO THIN WEDGES

½   MEDIUM ONION, THINLY SLICED

4   THIN LEMON SLICES

½   CUP MARGARINE OR BUTTER, MELTED

4 servings

Build a campfire and allow it to burn down to glowing coals. Cut two 36 × 18-inch sheets of heavy-duty foil. Place salmon in center of one sheet. Turn up edges slightly. Sprinkle cavity of fish with dill. Stuff cavity of fish with apple, onion and lemon slices. Brush fish lightly with margarine. Pour remaining margarine over stuffing.

Fold long sides of foil together in locked folds. Fold and crimp short ends; seal tightly. Place packet seam side down on second sheet of foil. Fold as directed above. Place packet on cooking grate over campfire. Cook for 15 minutes. Turn packet over. Cook for 15 to 20 minutes longer, or until fish begins to flake when fork is inserted at backbone in thickest part of fish.

Per Serving: Calories: 492 • Protein: 37 g. • Carbohydrate: 7 g. • Fat: 35 g. • Cholesterol: 102 mg. • Sodium: 350 mg. — Exchanges: 3 lean meat, ⅓ fruit, 2½ fat

RIVERSIDE BULLHEADS

1   TABLESPOON MARGARINE OR BUTTER, SOFTENED

6   WHOLE DRAWN BULLHEADS (4 TO 6 OZ. EACH), SKIN AND HEADS REMOVED

8   OZ. FRESH MUSHROOMS, SLICED (2 CUPS)

⅔   CUP DRY WHITE WINE

¼   CUP CHOPPED ONION

2   TABLESPOONS VEGETABLE OIL

1½   TABLESPOONS DRIED PARSLEY FLAKES

1½   TABLESPOONS FRESH LEMON JUICE

¼   TEASPOON SALT

¼   TEASPOON FRESHLY GROUND PEPPER

¼   TEASPOON DRIED THYME LEAVES

3 servings

Build a campfire and allow it to burn down to glowing coals. Cut six 18 × 14-inch sheets of heavy-duty foil. Spread ½ teaspoon margarine on each sheet of foil. Place 1 bullhead in center of each sheet. Turn up edges slightly. In medium mixing bowl, combine remaining ingredients. Spread heaping ⅓ cup of mixture evenly over each fish.

Fold long sides of foil together in locked folds. Fold and crimp short ends; seal tightly. Place packets on cooking grate over campfire. Cook for 9 minutes. Turn packets over. Cook for 5 to 9 minutes longer, or until fish begins to flake when fork is inserted at backbone in thickest part of fish.

Per Serving: Calories: 288 • Protein: 20 g. • Carbohydrate: 5 g. • Fat: 17 g. • Cholesterol: 57 mg. • Sodium: 293 mg. — Exchanges: 3 lean meat, 1 vegetable, ¼ fruit, 1¾ fat

Lemony Apple-stuffed Salmon

STEAK À LA WOODSMAN

- 2 SALMON, OR SUBSTITUTE, STEAKS (8 OZ. EACH), 1 INCH THICK
- 1½ TEASPOONS SALT
- 3 TABLESPOONS MARGARINE OR BUTTER

2 servings

Build a campfire and allow it to burn down to glowing coals. Remove all moisture from surface of steaks by blotting with paper towels. Set aside.

Sprinkle salt in even layer over bottom of 8-inch cast-iron skillet. Place skillet on cooking grate over campfire. When drop of water flicked onto skillet dances across it, squarely drop steaks into skillet. Sear steaks for 10 seconds on each side. Add margarine to skillet. Cook for 4 minutes. Turn steaks over. Cook for 4 to 6 minutes longer, or until fish is firm and opaque and just begins to flake.

Per Serving: Calories: 436 • Protein: 40 g. • Carbohydrate: 1 g. • Fat: 30 g. • Cholesterol: 110 mg. • Sodium: 1936 mg. — Exchanges: 5 lean meat, 3 fat

LAYERED FISH & VEGETABLE BAKE

- 2 TABLESPOONS MARGARINE OR BUTTER
- 1 MEDIUM ONION, THINLY SLICED
- 1 MEDIUM TOMATO, THINLY SLICED
- 2 MEDIUM RED POTATOES, THINLY SLICED
- 1½ LBS. WALLEYE, SALMON OR SUBSTITUTE FILLETS (6 OZ. EACH), SKIN REMOVED
- 2 CUPS FRESH BROCCOLI FLOWERETS
- 2 TABLESPOONS FRESH LEMON JUICE
- 1 CLOVE GARLIC, MINCED
- ¼ TEASPOON SALT
- ¼ TEASPOON FRESHLY GROUND PEPPER

4 servings

Build a campfire and allow it to burn down to glowing coals. Dot 11 × 9 × 1-inch foil pan with margarine. Layer onion, tomato, potatoes, fillets and broccoli in pan. Sprinkle lemon juice, garlic, salt and pepper evenly over broccoli.

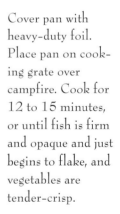

Cover pan with heavy-duty foil. Place pan on cooking grate over campfire. Cook for 12 to 15 minutes, or until fish is firm and opaque and just begins to flake, and vegetables are tender-crisp.

Per Serving: Calories: 308 • Protein: 37 g. • Carbohydrate: 22 g. • Fat: 8 g. • Cholesterol: 146 mg. • Sodium: 313 mg. — Exchanges: 3/4 starch, 4 lean meat, 2 vegetable

Steak à la Woodsman

Hot Waldorf Crayfish

HOT WALDORF CRAYFISH

1 LB. COOKED CRAYFISH TAILS, IN SHELL
2 MEDIUM RED OR GREEN COOKING APPLES, EACH CORED AND CUT INTO 8 WEDGES
1/2 CUP CHOPPED PECANS OR WALNUTS
1/4 CUP MARGARINE OR BUTTER

2 servings

Build a campfire and allow it to burn down to glowing coals. Cut four 18 × 14-inch sheets of heavy-duty foil. Place half of crayfish tails in center of each of 2 sheets of foil. Top each with half of apple wedges and pecans. Dot evenly with margarine.

Fold long sides of foil together in locked folds. Fold and crimp short ends; seal tightly. Place packets seam side down on remaining 2 sheets of foil. Fold as directed above. Place packets directly on coals. Cook for 4 minutes. Turn packets over. Cook for 3 to 5 minutes longer, or until apples are tender-crisp and mixture is hot.

Per Serving: Calories: 639 • Protein: 39 g.
• Carbohydrate: 26 g. • Fat: 44 g. • Cholesterol: 271 mg.
• Sodium: 371 mg. — Exchanges: 5 lean meat, 1 1/2 fruit, 5 3/4 fat

BLACKENED FISH

CAJUN SEASONING
1 TABLESPOON PAPRIKA
2 1/2 TEASPOONS SALT
1 TEASPOON ONION POWDER
1 TEASPOON GARLIC POWDER
1 TEASPOON CAYENNE
3/4 TEASPOON WHITE PEPPER
3/4 TEASPOON BLACK PEPPER
1/2 TEASPOON DRIED THYME LEAVES, CRUSHED
1/2 TEASPOON DRIED OREGANO LEAVES
2 1/4 LBS. CATFISH, LAKE TROUT OR SUBSTITUTE FILLETS (6 OZ. EACH), SKIN REMOVED, CUT IN HALF CROSSWISE

6 servings

Build a campfire and allow it to burn down to glowing coals. In shallow bowl, combine seasoning ingredients. Set aside. Place cast-iron skillet on cooking grate over campfire. When drop of water flicked onto skillet dances across it, skillet is hot. Dredge both sides of each fillet in seasoning mixture.

Squarely drop fillets into skillet. Cook for 2 minutes on each side, or until fish is firm and opaque and just begins to flake.

Per Serving: Calories: 261 • Protein: 36 g.
• Carbohydrate: 2 g. • Fat: 11 g. • Cholesterol: 99 mg.
• Sodium: 1005 mg. — Exchanges: 5 lean meat

TROUT CAKES WITH CELERY SAUCE

2 TABLESPOONS MARGARINE OR BUTTER

1 MEDIUM ONION, FINELY CHOPPED

1 SMALL RED PEPPER, SEEDED AND FINELY CHOPPED

1 CUP WATER

1 TEASPOON INSTANT CHICKEN BOUILLON GRANULES

1/2 TEASPOON WORCESTERSHIRE SAUCE

1/2 TEASPOON RED PEPPER SAUCE

1/2 TEASPOON FRESHLY GROUND PEPPER

1 LB. STREAM TROUT OR SUBSTITUTE FILLETS

1 TEASPOON FRESH LEMON JUICE

1 CAN (10¾ OZ.) CONDENSED CREAM OF CELERY SOUP, DIVIDED

2 CUPS INSTANT POTATO BUDS OR FLAKES

1/2 CUP SEASONED DRY BREAD CRUMBS

6 TABLESPOONS VEGETABLE OIL

12 SLICES (¾ OZ. EACH) PASTEURIZED PROCESS AMERICAN CHEESE (OPTIONAL)

1/4 CUP EVAPORATED MILK

---

6 servings

Per Serving: Calories: 411 • Protein: 20 g. • Carbohydrate: 30 g. • Fat: 24 g. • Cholesterol: 52 mg. • Sodium: 929 mg. — Exchanges: 1¾ starch, 2 lean meat, ½ vegetable, 3½ fat

1 Build campfire; allow to burn down to glowing coals. Place 10-inch cast-iron skillet on grate over coals. Melt margarine in skillet. Add onion and red pepper. Cook for 1 to 2 minutes. Add water, bouillon, Worcestershire sauce, red pepper sauce and pepper. Cook for 1 to 2 minutes. Add trout fillets. Cook for 3 to 5 minutes, or until fish is firm and completely flaked.

2 Remove skillet from cooking grate. Add lemon juice and 1/3 can of soup (about 1/3 cup). Gradually stir in potato flakes until mixture is stiff. Let cool for 5 minutes. Place bread crumbs on plate. Divide fish mixture into 12 portions. Shape each into 3½-inch patty. Dredge both sides of each patty in bread crumbs. Wipe out skillet. Place on cooking grate. Heat 2 tablespoons oil.

3 Add 4 patties. Cook for 4 to 6 minutes, or until golden brown, turning once and topping with cheese during final minutes of cooking time. Place on plate. Cover to keep warm. Repeat with remaining oil, patties and cheese.

4 Wipe out skillet. Add remaining soup and the evaporated milk. Cook mixture for 5 to 6 minutes, or until hot, stirring constantly. Spoon about 1 tablespoon sauce over each cake.

FIVE QUICK & EASY SHORE LUNCHES

One of the best meals going is a mess of fish cooked over an open fire on the bank of a lake or stream. The scenery is terrific, and the fish is guaranteed fresh. But preparing a shore lunch takes up a lot of fishing time, so you'll want something simple and fast. Many of the ingredients can be prepared at home and put in sealable plastic containers or parceled up and wrapped in the foil you'll use for cooking.

Most any kind of fish can be used with these recipes. You can cook on a grate, directly on the coals or on a camp stove.

One of the biggest problems when cooking in foil over an open fire is telling when the food is done, because cooking time varies with the type of wood, wind and outside temperature. With any of these recipes, simply open the foil and test the food with a fork. The fish should flake easily, and the vegetables should be tender. If the food is not done, reseal the package and put it back on the fire.

FILLETS WITH BACON, MAYO AND ONION

Form a shallow tray with an 18 × 18-inch piece of heavy-duty aluminum wrap. Place several pats of butter and thin slices of onion on the foil. Lay a medium-sized fillet on the onions. Spread mayonnaise on the fillet and season with salt and pepper. Top the fish with bacon strips and grated sharp cheddar. Seal the aluminum foil; cook the packet for 15 to 20 minutes. Open the foil to check the bacon. When it's done, so is the fish.

SEASONED FISH AND VEGETABLES

Place a medium-sized fillet on an 18 × 18-inch piece of heavy-duty aluminum foil. Sprinkle the fish with 1/8 teaspoon salt, 1/8 teaspoon pepper and 1/2 teaspoon of dried basil leaves. Top the fish with one thinly sliced (1/4-inch thick) medium-sized potato, two thinly sliced carrots, one onion sliced and separated into rings, and 1 tablespoon of butter. Sprinkle salt and pepper on the vegetables. Wrap and seal the foil. Place the fish on the grate and cook for 15 to 20 minutes.

BACON-BAKED FISH AND PEPPER STRIPS

Lay a medium-sized fillet on an 18 × 18-inch piece of heavy-duty aluminum foil. Top it with a small green pepper cut into strips, a small onion sliced and separated into rings, and two slices of bacon cut into 1-inch pieces. Salt and pepper to taste. Wrap and seal the foil, and cook the fish 15 to 20 minutes. Then open the foil to see if the bacon is done.

TERIYAKI FISH FILLET

Place a medium-sized fillet on an 18 × 18-inch piece of foil. Top the fillet with sliced green pepper and onion. In a small bowl, combine 2 tablespoons lemon juice, 1 tablespoon brown sugar and 1 tablespoon soy sauce (or a single restaurant packet). Pour the mixture over the fish and vegetables. Wrap and seal the foil. Cook for 15 to 20 minutes.

FISH À L'ORANGE

Place a medium-sized fillet on an 18 × 18-inch piece of foil. Top the fillet with 1 tablespoon of butter and orange slices with the skin left on. Salt and pepper to taste. Wrap the aluminum foil and seal it. Cook the fish for 15 to 20 minutes.

OPEN-FIRE COOKING: GREAT LAKES FISH BOIL

Fish boils are popular along the shores of the Great Lakes. Lumbermen originated them over 100 years ago when they wanted easy one-pot meals.

For best results, use large, oily fish such as lake trout, salmon, brown trout and steelhead. Always scale the fish and cut it into steaks. The skin and bones will hold the fish together during cooking. The fish can be fresh or thawed. Use medium-sized potatoes, which are normally done the same time as the fish.

Special fish boil kettles are usually 8-quart or 12-quart pots. However, any large, sturdy pot with vents in the lid and a basket will work. The ingredients (below) are for an 8-quart kettle. In a 12-quart pot, double the ingredient amounts, but increase the water just enough to cover the food.

For good results, the water must actively bubble for the entire 30 minutes of cooking time. Maintaining a hard boil requires a large fire and a good supply of dry wood.

FISH BOIL INGREDIENTS

FOR 8-QUART KETTLE

5   QUARTS WATER
6   MEDIUM POTATOES
6   ONIONS
1   CUP SALT
3   LBS. FISH STEAKS, 1 TO 1½ INCHES THICK, SCALED

6 servings

How to Prepare a Fish Boil

1 Build a large fire. Enclose it on three sides with cement blocks. Place a sturdy grill rack on the blocks. Have extra wood ready to maintain the fire.

2 Place the kettle on the rack. Remove the basket. Add water. Cover, with vents open, and heat the water to boiling.

240

3 Scrub the potatoes, but do not peel. Cut a thin slice from each end. Put the potatoes in the basket. Remove the skin from the onions.

4 Lower the basket into the boiling water; cover. Return to boiling. Add onions and salt; cover. Boil, with vents open, for 18 minutes.

5 Add the steaks to the basket. Cover and return to boiling. Boil 12 minutes. Test potatoes and fish with a fork. The fish should flake easily. Remove the basket; drain thoroughly. Serve immediately with lemon wedges and melted butter. Coleslaw and hard rolls are traditional accompaniments.

SPICED GRILLED TENDERLOIN

Make the spice mix ahead of time and keep it in a small jar with your camping gear.

SPICE MIX

1 ½ TEASPOONS PEPPER

1 ½ TEASPOONS GROUND ALLSPICE

  1 TEASPOON SALT

¾ TEASPOON GROUND CINNAMON

¾ TEASPOON GROUND CLOVES

½ TEASPOON GROUND NUTMEG

  1 TABLESPOON VEGETABLE OIL OR OLIVE OIL

    VENISON TENDERLOIN (ABOUT 1 LB.)

3 to 4 servings

In small bowl, combine spice mix ingredients. Add oil and mix well to make a paste. Rub all sides of tenderloin evenly with spice paste. Set aside.

Prepare grill or campfire for medium, direct heat. Place tenderloin on cooking grid. Grill for 12 to 14 minutes, or until meat is desired doneness, turning tenderloin occasionally. Let stand for 5 minutes before slicing.

Per Serving: Calories: 173 • Protein: 26 g. • Carbohydrate: 2 g. • Fat: 6 g. • Cholesterol: 95 mg. • Sodium: 598 mg. — Exchanges: 3 very lean meat, 1¼ fat

BACON-WRAPPED TENERLOIN *(photo on page 230)*

1/4 TEASPOON SALT
1/4 TEASPOON ONION POWDER
1/4 TEASPOON GARLIC POWDER
1/4 TEASPOON PEPPER
    VENISON TENDERLOIN (ABOUT 1 LB.)
2 STRIPS BACON
1 TABLESPOON BUTTER OR MARGARINE

3 to 4 servings

In small bowl, combine salt, onion powder, garlic powder and pepper. Rub all sides of tenderloin evenly with spice mixture. Wrap bacon strips in a spiral around tenderloin, securing ends with wooden picks.

Heat 10-inch cast-iron skillet over medium heat. Melt butter in skillet. Add tenderloin. Cook for 4 to 6 minutes, or until meat is browned on all sides. Reduce heat to low or set skillet off direct heat. Cover. Cook for 12 to 15 minutes, or until meat is desired doneness, turning tenderloin occasionally. Let stand for 5 minutes before slicing.

Per Serving: Calories: 226 • Protein: 27 g. • Carbohydrate: <1 g. • Fat: 12 g. • Cholesterol: 112 mg. • Sodium: 300 mg. — Exchanges: 3 1/4 very lean meat, 2 1/2 fat

STEVE'S GRILLED DUCK

2 BONELESS SKINLESS WHOLE WILD DUCK BREASTS (8 TO 12 OZ. EACH), SPLIT IN HALF
1 MEDIUM RED COOKING APPLE, CORED AND CUT INTO 1/4-INCH SLICES
1 MEDIUM ONION, SLICED
1 CAN (8 OZ.) SLICED WATER CHESTNUTS, RINSED AND DRAINED
1/2 TEASPOON SEASONED SALT
1/4 TEASPOON FRESHLY GROUND PEPPER

4 servings

Build a campfire and allow it to burn down to glowing coals. Place 1 breast half in center of 12 × 12-inch square of heavy-duty foil. Repeat with remaining breast halves. Arrange apple, onion and water chestnuts evenly over breast halves. Sprinkle evenly with salt and pepper.

Fold opposite sides of foil together in locked folds. Fold and crimp ends. Place packets on cooking grate over coals. Cook for 30 to 45 minutes, or until meat is tender and juices run clear.

Per Serving: Calories: 240 • Protein: 29 g. • Carbohydrate: 16 g. • Fat: 6 g. • Cholesterol: N/A • Sodium: 242 mg. — Exchanges: 3 3/4 lean meat, 2 vegetable, 1/3 fruit

Steve's Grilled Duck

BLACKENED WILD GAME

This Cajun treatment is a natural for outdoor cooking, where the smoke produced by the cooking isn't a problem, as it is in a kitchen. You'll need a cast-iron skillet for this technique.

The tenderloin is the venison cut that is most often cooked in camp. However, this method works equally well for duck or goose breasts.

Here are two spice mixtures you can use for blackening; each is enough for about a pound of meat. Make the mixture up at home, and carry it to camp in a plastic bag or small container.

BLACKENING MIXTURE I

2	TEASPOONS CHILI POWDER
1	TEASPOON GROUND CUMIN
1/2	TEASPOON BLACK PEPPER
1/4	TEASPOON WHITE PEPPER

BLACKENING MIXTURE II

1 1/2	TABLESPOONS MEDIUM-GRIND BLACK PEPPER
1 1/2	TEASPOONS CAYENNE
2	TABLESPOONS PAPRIKA
1	TABLESPOON GARLIC POWDER
1	TABLESPOON ONION POWDER
2	TEASPOONS SALT

BLACKENED VENISON TENDERLOIN

VENISON TENDERLOIN (ABOUT 1 LB.), CUT INTO 1/2-INCH SLICES
2 TABLESPOONS BUTTER OR MARGARINE, MELTED
ONE OF THE BLACKENING MIXTURES (LEFT)

Pound or press tenderloin slices to 1/4-inch thickness. Dip slices first in melted butter, then dredge in blackening mixture to coat. Follow cooking instructions below.

BLACKENED DUCK OR GOOSE BREAST

1 LB. BONELESS, SKINLESS DUCK OR GOOSE BREAST
2 TABLESPOONS BUTTER OR MARGARINE, MELTED
ONE OF THE BLACKENING MIXTURES (LEFT)

Cut the meat into individual portions; if meat is more than 1/2 inch thick, slice horizontally to half-inch thickness. Dip meat first in melted butter, then dredge in blackening mixture to coat. Follow cooking instructions below.

HOW TO COOK BLACKENED WILD GAME

Build a campfire and allow it to burn down to glowing coals. Place cast-iron skillet on cooking grate over campfire. When drop of water flicked onto skillet dances across it, skillet is hot. Squarely drop seasoned meat into skillet. Cook until meat is richly colored on first side, 2 or 3 minutes. Turn and cook on second side until meat is desired doneness. Venison and waterfowl breasts are best when cooked to no more than medium doneness; medium-rare is preferred.

KOREAN VENISON BARBECUE

Mix up the marinade for this flavorful dish at home, then take it to deer camp in a small, tightly sealed jar or container.

MARINADE

1/3 CUP SOY SAUCE

3 TABLESPOONS SUGAR

2 TABLESPOONS SESAME OIL

2 TEASPOONS DEHYDRATED MINCED ONIONS

1/2 TEASPOON GROUND GINGER

1/4 TEASPOON GARLIC POWDER

FRESHLY GROUND PEPPER TO TASTE

VENISON TENDERLOIN (ABOUT 1 LB.), CUT INTO
1/4-INCH SLICES

3 to 4 servings

In shallow dish, combine marinade ingredients. Add tenderloin slices, stirring to coat. Let stand for 15 minutes, stirring occasionally.

Heat 10-inch cast-iron skillet over medium-high heat. Using slotted spoon, transfer tenderloin to skillet. Cook for 3 to 4 minutes, or until meat is no longer pink, stirring frequently. Serve tenderloin slices on bread or buns, or over a baked potato, if desired.

Per Serving: Calories: 191 • Protein: 26 g. • Carbohydrate: 6 g. • Fat: 6 g. • Cholesterol: 95 mg. • Sodium: 746 mg. — Exchanges: 3 very lean meat, 1 1/4 fat

Liver & Onions

LIVER & ONIONS

⅓ CUP ALL-PURPOSE FLOUR

½ TEASPOON SALT

¼ TEASPOON PEPPER

1 LB. VENISON LIVER, CUT INTO ½-INCH SLICES

4 SLICES BACON, CUT INTO 1-INCH PIECES

2 MEDIUM ONIONS, SLICED

4 servings

In shallow dish or on sheet of wax paper, combine flour, salt and pepper. Dredge liver slices in flour mixture to coat. Set aside.

In 10-inch cast-iron skillet, cook bacon over medium heat for 4 to 5 minutes, or until bacon is crisp, turning occasionally. Remove bacon from skillet and drain on paper towels.

Add liver and onions to bacon drippings in skillet. Cook for 6 to 8 minutes, or until meat is well done, stirring occasionally. Top liver and onions with bacon pieces.

Nutritional information not available.

HEART WITH HORSERADISH SAUCE

HORSERADISH SAUCE

⅓ CUP MAYONNAISE

2 TABLESPOONS PREPARED HORSERADISH, WELL DRAINED

1 TEASPOON SUGAR

¼ TEASPOON WORCESTERSHIRE SAUCE

2 TABLESPOONS ALL-PURPOSE FLOUR

½ TEASPOON PAPRIKA

¼ TEASPOON SEASONED SALT

1 VENISON HEART (8 OZ.), CUT CROSSWISE INTO ¼-INCH SLICES

2 TABLESPOONS VEGETABLE OIL

2 servings

In small mixing bowl, combine all sauce ingredients. Set aside. In shallow dish or on sheet of wax paper, combine flour, paprika and salt. Dredge heart slices in flour mixture to coat. In 10-inch cast-iron skillet, heat oil over medium heat. Add heart slices. Cook for 4 to 6 minutes, or until meat is desired doneness. Serve with horseradish sauce.

Nutritional information not available.

STUFFED VENISON HEART ROLLS

Mix up the stuffing ingredients ahead of time and carry them to camp in a small, sealable plastic bag.

1 VENISON HEART (8 OZ.), SLICED AS DIRECTED AT RIGHT

STUFFING

½ CUP UNSEASONED DRY BREAD CRUMBS

1 TEASPOON DRIED PARSLEY FLAKES

¼ TEASPOON DRIED THYME LEAVES

¼ TEASPOON RUBBED SAGE

¼ TEASPOON SEASONED SALT

3 TABLESPOONS WATER

PEPPER TO TASTE

4 STRIPS BACON

2 TABLESPOONS BUTTER OR MARGARINE

2 servings

In small mixing bowl, combine stuffing ingredients and water. Stir until evenly moistened. Spoon and pack stuffing mixture on cut side of heart. Roll up heart, enclosing stuffing. Sprinkle heart with pepper to taste.

Wrap bacon strips around heart, securing with wooden picks. Cut heart between picks into 4 rolls.

Heat 10-inch cast-iron skillet over medium heat.

Melt butter in skillet. Add rolls. Cook for 8 to 10 minutes, or until meat is desired doneness, turning rolls over once or twice.

Nutritional information not available.

How to Slice Heart for Stuffed Venison Heart Rolls

1 Slip knife lengthwise into outer wall of heart, penetrating only half the thickness of the wall.

2 Slice in spiral fashion, from outside to center, "unrolling" heart into one long strip. Remove and discard membranes. Continue with recipe directions.

Cleaning Techniques

Fish & Wild Game

Cleaning fish or dressing wild game are the final steps of the outdoor adventure, but ones that are critical to ensure good eating. Unfortunately, many anglers and hunters overlook this important fact, and the fish or game languishes in the freezer because it has a bad texture or just doesn't taste that good.

This is a terrible waste, and one that can be avoided by taking proper care of fish and game—in the field and later, during cutting up and other processing steps. In this final section of the book, you'll find all the information you need to take the proper care of your hard-won fish and game.

In earlier days, most cooks were familiar with the steps necessary to process an animal for the table. It was common for the cook to catch a chicken in the barnyard, then kill it and dress it for the roaster. In modern times, however, we've become insulated from the steps involved in food production. Meat is something that comes on styrofoam trays; fish is displayed on ice in a case.

Anglers and hunters often have no one to turn to for help in learning the best ways to care for fish and game. Written descriptions in books can be difficult and confusing for the novice to follow, and diagrams never look quite the same as the animal in front of you.

This book takes a different approach, and shows actual photos of cleaning and dressing techniques, accompanied by easy-to-follow text that takes the mystery out of these processes. Sensitive photos show everything from pan-dressing small fish to field-dressing and butchering big game. The final chapter explains the best ways to freeze fish and game, and includes charts for freezer storage times.

By following the instructions in this chapter you'll avoid that "off flavor" so often associated with wild game, and you will be able to serve fish and game dinners that will have family and guests coming back for more.

Cleaning & Storing Fish

For top flavor, clean and cook your gamefish within 2 hours after catching it. However, most anglers have to keep their catch for a longer time.

The colder the storage temperature, the longer the fish can be held. If handled and cleaned properly, fish can be refrigerated for 24 hours with little flavor loss. Fish stored on crushed ice will remain fresh for 2 or 3 days, but they must be drained often. Super-chilled fish can be kept up to 7 days.

Lean fish can be stored longer than oily fish; whole fish longer than fillets or steaks.

To prepare fish for storing, wipe with paper towels. Rinse in cold water if intestines were penetrated during cleaning.

Super-Chilling Fish

It's hard to keep fish fresh on long trips into the backcountry. You'll be lucky to keep them for more than 2 or 3 days on ordinary ice. But you can keep them for a full week by "super-chilling" them with a mixture of ice and salt. Because the ice-salt combination has a lower melting point, about 28°F, the fish stay colder.

You can super-chill fillets, steaks or whole fish that have been gutted and gilled. Wrap the fish in aluminum foil or plastic wrap. Add 1 pound of coarse ice cream salt to 20 pounds of crushed ice and stir thoroughly. If you need less of the salt-ice mixture, reduce the ingredients proportionately.

Place the wrapped fish on a 4-inch bed of the salt-ice. Add alternating layers of fish and salt-ice (photo at left), finishing with a generous topping of the salt-ice mixture. Later, as the ice melts, drain the cooler and add more of the salt-ice.

How to Refrigerate Fish

1 Wipe fillets, steaks or whole fish with paper towels. Or rinse them quickly with cold water and pat dry.

2 Refrigerate fish on paper towels. Cover them tightly with plastic wrap or aluminum foil.

INITIAL CARE

Fish are extremely perishable. Fish that do not have red gills, clear eyes and a fresh odor should be discarded. Proper care insures firm flesh for cooking.

The secret to preserving your catch is to keep it alive or cold. If the surface water is cool, a stringer or wire basket can keep some fish species alive. Bring the fish aboard when moving the boat to a new spot. Return them to the water as soon as possible.

Aerated live wells in many boats keep bass, northern pike and other hardy fish alive. Limit the number of fish; remove dead ones to ice immediately.

Check your catch often, whether the fish are on a stringer or in a wire basket or live well. Transfer dead ones to an ice-filled cooler immediately. Dead fish left in water spoil rapidly.

Burlap bags, newspapers, moss or other materials that "breathe" help preserve fish when ice is not available. Keep the covering moist;

Clip-type stringers (left) are preferable to the rope style because fish are not crowded. However, rope stringers are better for very large fish. Wire baskets or net bags hung over the side of the boat keep small fish alive. The fish should have ample room to move around.

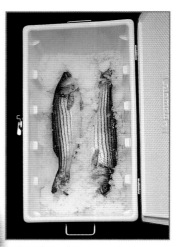

Coolers filled with ice keep fish cold. Crushed ice chills faster than a solid block. Drain the cooler often so the catch does not soak in water.

evaporation helps cool fish. Large gamefish should be killed immediately. Use a stout stick and rap the fish across the back of the head. Their flesh can bruise if they flop around in a boat. Field-dress (opposite page) as soon as possible and place the fish on ice.

Keeping fish in good condition on extended trips is difficult. Fish held longer than 2 days should be super-chilled (page 251), frozen or smoked. You can often take advantage of motel facilities to keep your catch cold or frozen. If shipping fish by plane, place them in a Styrofoam® cooler wrapped with a layer of heavy cardboard.

Wicker creels are used by wading anglers. Place layers of moss, ferns or grass between the fish to provide ventilation. Transfer to ice as soon as possible.

FIELD-DRESSING

For top quality and flavor, fish should be field-dressed as quickly as possible by removing the gills, guts and kidney, all of which spoil fast in a dead fish.

Field-dress fish that are to be cooked whole or steaked. It is not necessary to field-dress fish if they are to be filleted within an hour or two. Scale fish that are to be cooked with their skin on, but only if they have large scales. These fish include bluegills, perch, crappies, black bass, striped bass, walleyes, northern pike and large salmon.

When field-dressing and scaling at home, place your catch on several layers of newspaper to ease cleanup. Before field-dressing, wipe the fish with paper towels to remove slime. This makes it easier to hold the fish firmly. If you puncture the guts, wash the body cavity with cold water. Use water sparingly, because it softens the flesh.

The head can be removed after scaling. Paper towels are excellent for wiping off scales and blood spots, and for drying fish.

Field-dressing is easier if you have the right tools and if you clean the fish in a convenient location. Practice the different cleaning techniques until you can clean fish quickly and with little waste.

Scaling fish is quick and easy with a scaler, though a dull knife or a spoon can be used. Wet the fish and scrape off the scales, working from tail to head. This job should be done outdoors, because scales fly in all directions. Or line the kitchen sink with newspapers and scale as carefully as possible.

How to Field-dress *Small Trout & Salmon*

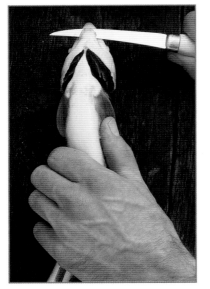

1 Slice the throat connection, the tissue that connects the lower jaw and the gill membrane.

2 Insert the knife in the vent; run the blade tip up the stomach to the gills. Try not to puncture the intestines.

3 Push your thumb into the throat; pull gills and guts toward the tail. Scrape out the bloodline with a spoon.

How to Field-dress *Other Fish*

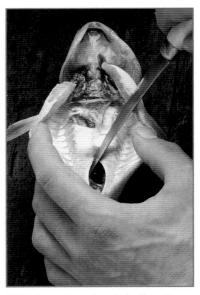

1 Remove gills by cutting the throat connection, then along both sides of the arch so the gills pull out easily.

2 Insert the knife in the vent. Run the blade tip to the gills. Pull the guts and gills out of the cavity.

3 Cut the membrane along the backbone. Scrape out the kidney or bloodline underneath the membrane.

PAN-DRESSING FISH

Panfish, including bluegills, crappies and yellow perch, are often too small for filleting. They are usually pan-dressed instead. Scales, fins, guts and head are always removed. The tail is quite tasty and can be left on. Most of the tiny fin bones in a fish are removed by pan-dressing.

How to Pan-dress Whole Fish

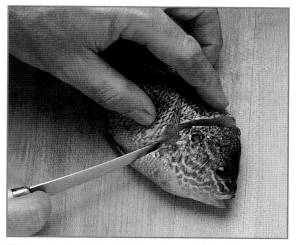

1 Slice along the dorsal fin of the scaled panfish. Make the same cut on the other side, then pull out the fin.

2 Cut along both sides of the anal fin. Remove the fin by pulling it toward the tail.

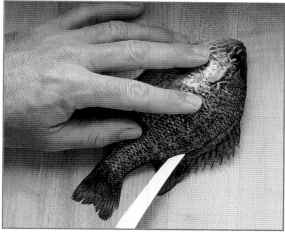

3 Remove the head. Angle the blade over the top of the head to save as much flesh as possible.

4 Slit the belly and pull out the guts. Cut off tail, if desired. Rinse fish quickly; dry with paper towels.

The Art of Filleting

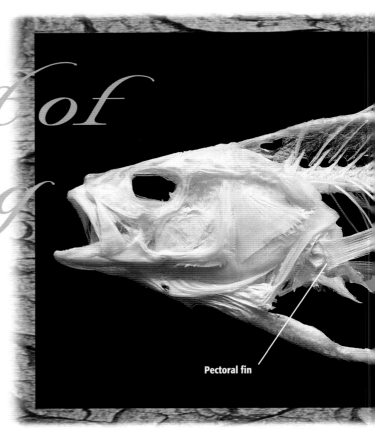

Pectoral fin

Filleting is the most common method of cleaning fish. It is easily mastered with a little practice and some knowledge of the bone structure and location of the various fins (right). The technique is popular because most of the flesh can be quickly removed from the bones without touching the intestines. In addition, the boneless fillets can be cooked in many ways and are easy to eat.

A sharp knife is essential when filleting fish. Use a sharpening stone and steel to touch up knife blades. Fillet knives of hard steel will hold their edge longer than soft steel. However, soft steel requires less effort to sharpen. It is interesting and helpful to watch butchers sharpen and realign knives.

Ideally, the length of the blade should fit the fish. Because good fillet knives last many years, it pays to have two or three sizes. A wooden fillet board with a clip on one end is useful for holding fish. Outdoors, fillet your fish on an oar, a paddle or the lid of a plastic cooler.

How to Select & Sharpen Fillet Knives

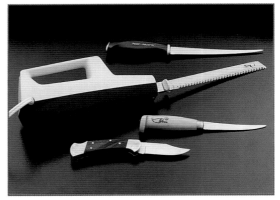

FILLETING is easiest with a thin, flexible knife. Some anglers, however, prefer a short, firm blade. Electric carving knives are also used.

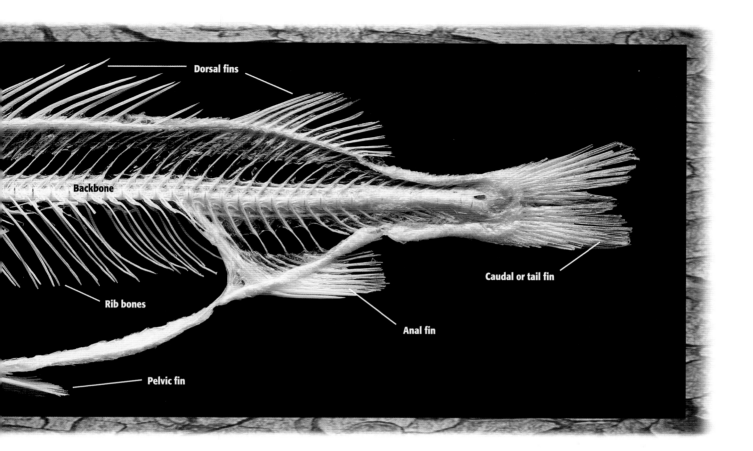

Dorsal fins

Backbone

Rib bones

Pelvic fin

Anal fin

Caudal or tail fin

REALIGN the cutting edge with a sharpening steel. Alternately draw each side of the blade into the steel at a 20- to 30-degree angle, about 10 strokes per side.

SHARPEN a knife by pushing the blade into a honing stone, as if cutting a thin slice of stone. The blade should be at a 15- to 20-degree angle to the stone.

HONING OIL can be added to lubricate a stone, resulting in a finer cutting edge. Most stones have two sides, one a coarse texture and the other fine.

BASIC FILLETING TECHNIQUE

How to Fillet & Skin a Fish

1 Lift the pectoral fin. Angle the knife toward the back of the head and cut to the backbone.

2 Turn the blade parallel to the backbone. Cut toward the tail with a sawing motion. Cut fillet off.

Anglers use a variety of filleting techniques. The method shown on the next two pages is the easiest and quickest for most anglers. Fillets can be stripped from the backbone in 30 seconds with a very sharp knife. Removing the rib bones takes a few additional seconds. Other methods are described on following pages.

If your fillet board does not have a clip, you can use a fork to pin the head of a small fish. A fork or pliers can also be useful during skinning. Salt on the hands helps hold a slippery fish.

The skin can be removed or left on. Fish such as largemouth bass have strong-tasting skin, so many anglers remove it. However, the skin on small trout and panfish is tasty. Panfish have large scales that must be removed if the skin is retained.

Keep the skin on fillets that will be charcoal grilled. This helps prevent the flesh from falling apart, sticking to the grill and overcooking. Cut long fillets into serving-size pieces before they are cooked or stored. Thick fillets can be divided into two thin fillets for easier cooking.

Remove the thin strip of fatty belly flesh on oily fish such as salmon and large trout. Any contaminants will settle into this fatty tissue. To clean fillets, wipe with paper towels or rinse quickly under cold running water. Dry thoroughly with paper towels.

After filleting, rinse hands with clean water before using soap. Rub hands with vinegar and salt, lemon juice or toothpaste to remove the fishy smell.

Save the bones and head after filleting. These pieces can be used for stock, chowder, fish cakes or other dishes.

Freshwater "Scallops"

Many anglers cut fillets off walleyes and discard the rest. They don't realize they're throwing away some of the best meat — the cheeks. They have a taste and texture very much like scallops. But the cheeks of even a good-sized walleye don't give you much to hold onto. Here's a trick that makes the job quicker and easier.

3 Remove the rib bones by sliding the blade along the ribs. Turn fish over and remove second fillet.

1 Cut under the cheek, leaving the cheek connected to the fish by a small flap of skin just behind the eye.

4 Cut off the strip of fatty belly flesh. Discard guts and belly. Save bones and head for stock.

2 Skin the cheek meat by peeling it off with your thumb and forefinger.

5 Skin the fillet, if desired, by cutting into the tail flesh to the skin. Turn the blade parallel to the skin. Pull the skin firmly while moving the knife in a sawing action between the skin and the flesh.

CANADIAN FILLETING TECHNIQUE

Some anglers find this technique easier than the basic method (page 258–59), especially when used on fish with a heavy rib structure, such as crappies. The Canadian technique takes a little longer and leaves more flesh on the bones. But many anglers are comfortable with this method, because it eliminates the extra step of cutting the rib bones from the fillet. As a bonus, your knife stays sharp longer, because the boneless fillet is removed without cutting through the rib bones. Be careful when cutting the belly so the knife does not penetrate the guts.

How to Fillet Using the Canadian Technique

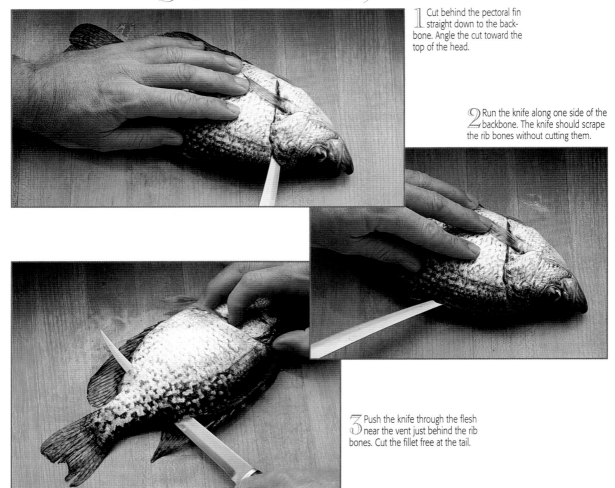

1 Cut behind the pectoral fin straight down to the backbone. Angle the cut toward the top of the head.

2 Run the knife along one side of the backbone. The knife should scrape the rib bones without cutting them.

3 Push the knife through the flesh near the vent just behind the rib bones. Cut the fillet free at the tail.

4 Cut the flesh carefully away from the rib cage. To save flesh, the blade should graze the bones.

5 Remove the first boneless fillet by cutting through the skin of the stomach area.

6 Turn the fish over. Remove the second fillet using the same technique.

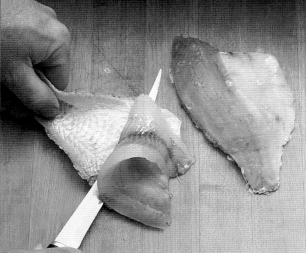

7 Skin fillets, if desired. Hold the tail with your fingertips and cut between flesh and skin with a sawing motion. Rinse fillets quickly with cold water or wipe with paper towels. Save the head and skeleton for stock.

FILLETING WITH AN ELECTRIC KNIFE

An electric knife is particularly useful for fillet-ing panfish, catfish or any large fish that has heavy rib bones. Scale fish before filleting if the skin will be retained for cooking. Skin is usual-ly removed from largemouth bass, striped bass and other fish that have strong-tasting skin.

How to Fillet with an Electric Knife

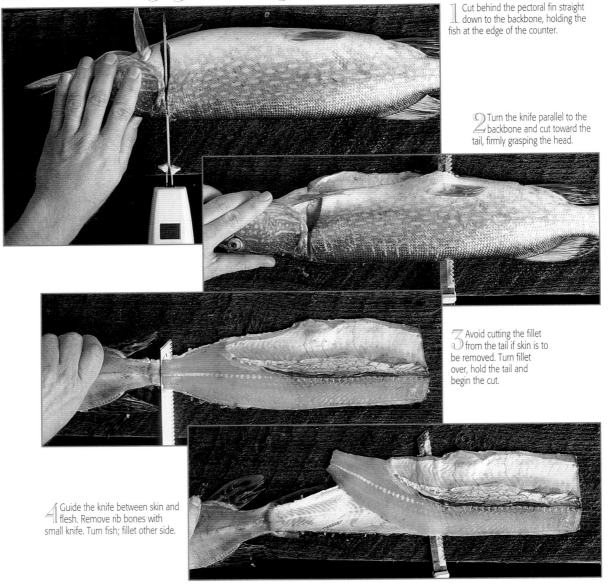

1 Cut behind the pectoral fin straight down to the backbone, holding the fish at the edge of the counter.

2 Turn the knife parallel to the backbone and cut toward the tail, firmly grasping the head.

3 Avoid cutting the fillet from the tail if skin is to be removed. Turn fillet over, hold the tail and begin the cut.

4 Guide the knife between skin and flesh. Remove rib bones with small knife. Turn fish; fillet other side.

THE LATERAL LINE

Some gamefish, such as largemouth bass, striped bass, northern pike and white bass, have a lateral line of strong-tasting flesh.

For cleaning and cooking purposes, the lateral line is defined as the band of dark-colored flesh along the side of a fish. It covers the entire side of some fish. This flesh spoils easily and develops an odor when the fish has been frozen too long.

In some species, such as trout and salmon, the lateral line does not have a strong flavor and may be retained. Many people enjoy the "fishy" taste of the lateral line. It is particularly flavorful when the fish is smoked or cooked and served cold.

Many anglers remove the lateral line if the fish are taken from waters of marginal quality. Contaminants tend to concentrate in the lateral line flesh.

Contaminants

Many waters harbor contaminants that are transferred to fish. In several states, health agencies have issued advisories to limit consumption of fish from monitored waters. Particular groups of people (children and pregnant women, for instance) are cautioned not to eat any fish from these waters. Anglers should check with state health agencies for advisories on the waters they are fishing.

Fortunately, the health risk associated with consumption of fish containing trace amounts of most contaminants can be substantially reduced during cleaning. Skin and fillet all fish. The belly flap and the fatty strip along the backbone (the backstrap) should be discarded, as well as all dark reddish meat along the lateral line (red dashed lines in photo). Broiling, baking or grilling fish provides additional risk reduction.

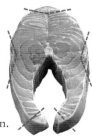

How to Remove the Lateral Line

1 Skin the fillet to expose the lateral line. In most species, it is an oily layer of reddish or brownish flesh.

2 Cut away the shallow band of dark flesh, using an extremely sharp fillet knife. Remove the lateral line; discard.

3 Another method is to tip the blade up while skinning so the lateral line is removed with the skin.

REMOVING Y BONES & EPIPLEURAL RIBS

Members of the pike family have delicious, flaky meat. But the Y bones are bothersome enough that some people refuse to eat these fish.

Although there are a couple of ways to remove these bones, most fishermen don't know how, so they have to pick them out at the table. Here's one way to make boneless

fillets from pike and pickerel. If the fish is already filleted, remove the Y bones as shown on facing page.

The fillets of many kinds of fish contain a row of small bones, called epipleural ribs, that lie right above the rib cage. The facing page shows an easy way to get rid of these bones.

1 Cut down behind the head. Turn the blade toward the tail and run it along the backbone (dashed line). Slice upward just ahead of the dorsal fin, cutting away the back fillet.

2 Loosen the skin along each edge of the back fillet so it will lie flat on the cutting surface. Now you can skin the fillet as you would any other.

3 Remove the side fillets by first cutting down to the backbone, once behind the head, and a second time ahead of the dorsal fin (arrows). Feel along the back to find the Y bones (dotted line). With the fish on its side, insert your knife just above the Y bones and cut away a fillet (shown) so the Y bones remain attached to the fish. Remove the fillet from the other side in the same way. Skin the fillets.

4 Cut off the fillets from each side of the tail section by slicing along the backbone. There are no Y bones in this part of the fish. Skin the tail fillets. You now have five boneless fillets.

How to Remove Y Bones from Pike Fillets

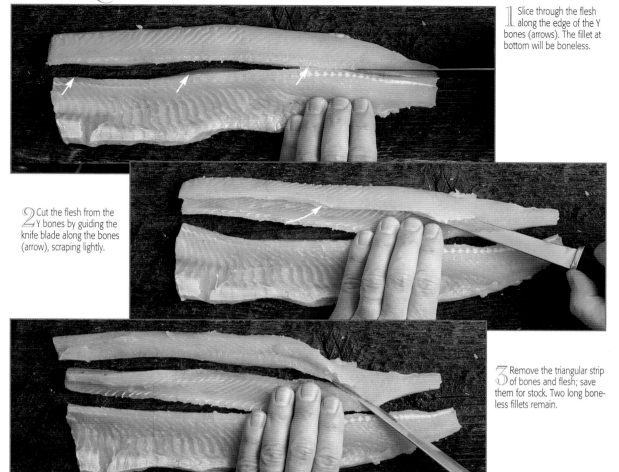

1 Slice through the flesh along the edge of the Y bones (arrows). The fillet at bottom will be boneless.

2 Cut the flesh from the Y bones by guiding the knife blade along the bones (arrow), scraping lightly.

3 Remove the triangular strip of bones and flesh; save them for stock. Two long boneless fillets remain.

How to Remove Epipleural Ribs

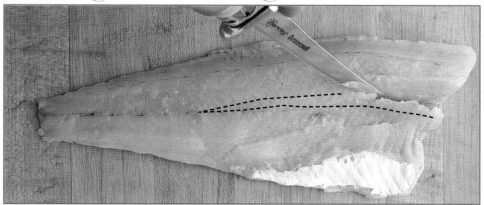

Remove the row of small bones that remains in the fillets of walleyes, largemouth bass and many other kinds of fish by cutting away a narrow strip of meat (dashed lines) just above the rib cage. You can easily locate the bone line by running your finger down the fillet before making your cuts.

CLEANING CATFISH & BULLHEADS

After the fun of fishing for catfish or bullheads has subsided, anglers are faced with the task of cleaning their catch. Some choose to hire someone else to do the job, others suffer through the process and still others, with a little know-how, accomplish the task with relative ease.

Catfish and bullheads should be skinned, regardless of their size. Two basic tools are required: a sharp knife and a set of skinning pliers. A regular set of pliers works, but skinning pliers work better because the jaws are wider, affording a

better grip on the catfish's thin, slippery skin.

Some anglers also use a skinning board clamp or a board with a nail driven through it to hold the head in place. Large fish may have to be hung from a tree limb or other overhead support to facilitate cleaning. Small fish can be handheld. Regardless of how you secure the fish, take care to avoid the sharp pectoral and dorsal spines throughout the cleaning process. Stun the fish with a hammer before you start skinning.

How to Skin & Fillet Catfish & Bullheads

1 Make a cut through the skin behind the head. Start behind the pectoral fin on one side of the fish, and cut up, over and down to the other pectoral fin.

2 Use the point of the knife to split the skin down the middle of the back, from head to tail, running down one side of the dorsal fin.

3 Split the skin on the other side of the dorsal fin, connecting this cut to the one just made. The fish is now ready for skinning.

5 Remove the meat along each side of the fish with a fillet knife. Cut around the rib cage for a totally boneless fillet. Cut away all dark red flesh along the lateral line. This meat often harbors contaminants and can have a strong flavor.

4 Grasp the skin with pliers and pull toward the tail. It should strip off in one or two pieces. Repeat the process on the other side.

How to Clean Catfish & Bullheads for Whole Cooking

1 After skinning, sever the backbone just behind the head, using a heavy serrated knife or cleaver.

2 Pull the head away from the body. The pectoral fins and entrails should come with the head. Slice off the adipose fin and tail.

3 Remove the dorsal and anal fins by gripping each at its rear edge with skinning pliers and lifting toward the head of the fish.

Muddy Flavors?

→❯❮←

Catfish and bullheads may pick up a weedy or muddy taste from the water they live in. But you can get rid of most of this strong flavor by using either of the following methods:

1. Soak the pieces of fish for approximately 30 minutes in a mixture of a quart of water and 1/2 teaspoon of baking soda. After soaking, rinse the fish with water.

2. Soak the fish for an hour in fresh, cold whole milk. Then rinse the fish with water. Many of the molecules that cause the disageeable flavor bind to the proteins in the milk and wash away.

Other Cleaning Tips

SLICE thick fillets from large catfish into thinner fillets or "fingers" for easier cooking.

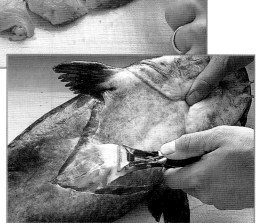

MAKE STEAKS out of large catfish that have been dressed for panfrying. A whole fish of this size would take too long to cook properly.

SAVE the belly flesh of a large catfish by stripping the belly skin toward the head, then cutting away the boneless meat. This meat is fatty but delicious.

STEAKING LARGE FISH

Gamefish of 6 pounds or more *can* be steaked. Fish over 15 pounds *should* be steaked or chunked so they are easier to cook. Before steaking, scale fish that have large scales. Then remove the guts, kidney (blood-line) and dorsal fin. Rinse in cold running water and wipe with paper towels.

Partially frozen fish are easier to cut into steaks. Firm up the flesh by super-chilling (page 251) or by placing the fish in a freezer until they begin to stiffen.

Lay the fish on its side. Use a sharp knife to cut even, 3/4- to 1-inch-thick steaks from the fish. Cut through the backbone with a sturdy knife, electric knife, kitchen saw or frozen-food knife. After steaking, trim fatty belly flesh from oily fish such as salmon, trout or striped bass.

The tail sections of large gamefish can be left whole, filleted or cut into 1 1/2- to 2-inch chunks for baking or smoking. Save the head to make stock (page 23).

Tips for Steaking Fish

TRIM and throw away pieces of fatty belly flesh from the ends of the steaks.

FILLET the tail section by sliding a sharp knife along the backbone in a sawing motion.

268

BUTTERFLYING FISH

Butterflying is an easy way to present fish in a different manner. Fillets from smooth-skinned species such as salmon, trout and catfish can be butterflied to make cutlets if the fish is large enough. The cutlets are easy and quick to make, and because you don't cut through the backbone, your knife stays sharp.

The finished cutlets are easier to eat than steaked fish because there are no rib bones.

Whole fish can also be butterflied for stuffing or grilling. While this technique is most often used with the same species mentioned above, it also works for walleye, especially medium to medium-large fish.

How to Butterfly Fillets to Make Cutlets

Cut a (1) fillet from the fish. Remove the rib bones, but don't skin the fillet. (2) Slice across the fillet, about an inch from the end, cutting through the meat but not the skin. (3) Make a second cut, parallel to the first and about an inch farther from the end; slice completely through both the meat and the skin. (4) Fold the piece of fish backwards along the first cut so the meat is on the outside and the skin is on the inside. Butterfly the rest of the fillet, except the tail section.

How to Butterfly Whole Fish

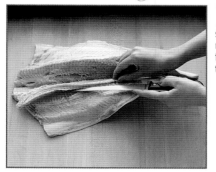

1 Cut from inside cavity along each side of backbone to release bone from flesh; do not cut through skin.

2 Discard bone and spread out two sides of fish so it lies flat. Trim and discard belly meat. Remove rib bones.

Dressing Wild Game

This chapter shows you how to care for any kind of game after it's down. You'll learn how to field-dress and transport big game and how to hang, age and skin it. The section on butchering and boning big game contains complete and concise instructions.

You'll also find step-by-step directions for dressing and portioning small game, upland game birds, wild turkeys and waterfowl. Everything is covered, from wet- and dry-plucking birds to skinning squirrels. There are even tips on removing tough leg tendons from upland birds, finding shot embedded in meat and making a boneless fillet from a bird's thigh.

While many hunters do a good job of field-dressing their game, they make mistakes in caring for the animal after that. You'll be assured of getting fine cuts of meat if you keep in mind the following tips:

• After field-dressing a big-game animal, move it to camp as soon as possible. Leave the hide on to protect the meat from dirt and flies, unless the hide needs to be removed during quartering (page 279). The hide also prevents the surface from drying during aging (page 280-281). In hot weather, however, you may want to remove the hide in the field to help cool the carcass.

• If you plan to skin a big-game animal in the field, bring along a large cloth bag or sheet to keep the meat clean during transport. Never put the carcass or quarters in plastic bags unless the meat is thoroughly chilled. Plastic traps the body heat, and the meat may be ruined. Avoid plastic garbage bags; they may be treated with a toxic disinfectant.

• After dressing small-game animals or game birds, you must cool them properly. Don't put them in a hot car or carry them for hours in the pocket of your hunting coat. Instead, leave them in a shaded spot, out of reach from predators. Some hunters hang their field-dressed animals in a shady tree, so the carcasses can drain as well as cool. Never put a small-game animal or game bird in a plastic bag until it's completely cooled.

• In warm weather, it's best to chill dressed small-game animals and game birds in a cooler. Reusable plastic ice packs are better than plain ice, since they are colder and won't fill the cooler with melted water.

Hunting knives include general-purpose types, such as (1) folding drop-point and (2) folding clip-point. The tip of a clip-point is more acute and curves up higher than that of a drop point; see inset photo below. Special-purpose types include (3) folding bird knife, with a hook for field-dressing birds, as shown on page 297; (4) folding combination knife, with a blunt-tip blade for slitting abdomens without puncturing intestines, a clip-point blade, and a saw for cutting through the breastbones and pelvic bones of big game; and (5) big-game skinner, with a blunt-tip blade to avoid punching holes in the hide.

SELECTING & SHARPENING HUNTING KNIVES

A good hunting knife is one of the best investments a hunter can make. Properly selected, used and cared for, it may well outlive the hunter. A cheap knife, on the other hand, may not last a single hunting season.

When selecting a hunting knife, look closely at the materials, blade length and shape, and workmanship.

The blade steel should be stainless, hard but not brittle. A blade with a Rockwell hardness rating of 57 to 60 is hard enough to hold an edge, but soft enough for easy resharpening at home when it does become dull.

The handle should be made of hardwood, plastic-impregnated wood or a tough synthetic. These materials last longer than brittle plastic or wood you can easily dent with your fingernail.

Choose a knife that feels comfortable in your hand. Remember that your hands may be wet when you're using it, and look for a handle shape that's easy to hold firmly. A blade between 3 1/2 and 4 1/2 inches long is adequate for either big or small game.

Clip-point and drop-point knives (right) are good all-purpose types. The acutely pointed tip of 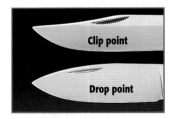 a clip-point is good for delicate cutting and easily penetrates the abdominal skin in field-dressing. The tip of a drop-point is less apt to puncture the intestines when slitting the abdominal skin, or to punch a hole in the hide should you use it for skinning.

For convenience and safety in the field, many hunters prefer folding knives. They are shorter and easier to carry than a straight knife, and the folded blade is safely out of the

The sides of the skinner blade are concave, curving down to a thin edge that's ideal for skinning but prone to chipping when used to cut wood or bone. The other blades shown have sides that slant down straight, with thicker, sturdier edges.

way in the event of a fall.

Choose folding knives carefully, checking for quality construction. When fully opened, the blade should lock in position with no trace of wiggle or sloppiness, and the back of the blade should line up exactly with the back edge of the handle.

Use your knife only for its intended purpose. If you use it to hack wood or pry the lid off a jar, you could destroy the edge. Be sure your knife is clean and dry before you store it at the end of the season. Over time, even modern stainless steel can be corroded by salts or acids.

A sharp blade is safer than a dull one. It gives you more control, and you need less pressure to get the job done. Dress the edge often with a sharpening steel (page 285). A steel does not remove metal from the blade, but simply realigns the edge. When the blade becomes so dull that the steel won't dress it, sharpen it with a whetstone.

How to Sharpen a Knife

1 Select a medium whetstone at least as long as the blade. (If the blade is extremely dull, use a coarse stone first, then the medium stone.) Place the stone on a folded towel for stability, and apply a little honing oil.

2 Hold the base of the blade against the whetstone at the angle at which the blade was originally sharpened (usually between 12 and 17 degrees). Using moderate pressure, push the knife away from you in a smooth arc from base to tip, as if shaving thin pieces off the face of the stone. Keep the edge of the blade at the same angle, in constant contact with the whetstone. Repeat this pushing motion two more times.

3 Draw the knife toward you in an arc three times, maintaining the same angle. Continue sharpening alternate sides, adding oil if necessary, until the blade hangs up when drawn very gently over a fingernail. Repeat the previous steps on a fine whetstone. If the stone clogs, wipe and re-oil it. The knife is sharp when it slices effortlessly through a piece of paper. Clean the whetstone with soapy water for storage.

Handy sharpening devices include (1) pre-angled sharpening kits; (2) ceramic sticks, which have a light sharpening action; and (3) diamond-impregnated sticks, which remove as much metal as a medium stone.

FIELD-DRESSING BIG GAME

A little homework before a big-game hunt can save a lot of time and effort once you've bagged your animal. And it will insure that the meat you bring home will be in prime condition for the table.

Familiarize yourself with state and local regulations. Some states prohibit quartering and skinning in the field; others require that you turn in certain parts for biological study. Be sure to check the regulations booklet available with your license. For more information, contact state or federal wildlife-management agencies.

If you are hunting for a trophy, consult in advance with a reliable taxidermist. He can give you advice on the best ways to handle the head and antlers in the field. There are also several good do-it-yourself kits for antler mounting and hide tanning.

The hides of deer, moose and elk make excellent leather. Many

Hang field-dressed big game in a tree to speed its cooling. Hanging also helps protect it from scavenging animals if you must leave to get help carrying it out. Use a block and tackle for easier lifting.

tanneries will buy rawhides directly from hunters. If you plan to sell the hide, find out how the buyer wants it prepared. Some tanneries will exchange a rawhide for a pair of finished leather gloves. Or you may want to have the hide tanned and returned to you.

Unless you have a reliable cold storage area for holding your animal prior to butchering, make arrangements with a locker plant before you hunt. Ask about the locker's business hours; you don't want to return from hunting on a warm Saturday only to discover that the plant is closed for the weekend.

Before you shoot, consider the location and body position of the animal. Remember that you'll have to get it out of the area after it's down. If you spot an animal across a canyon, consider possible drag routes before shooting. A moose standing in a bog may be a tempting target, but you would probably need several people to move it to dry land for field-dressing and quartering.

Shot placement affects both the quality and quantity of the meat you bring home. A study at Texas A&M University showed that game killed instantly with a clean shot produces meat more tender and flavorful than that of game only wounded with the first shot. Game animals, like humans, produce adrenaline and other chemicals when frightened or stressed. These chemicals make the meat tough and gamey. A poorly placed shot may also damage choice cuts, or rupture the stomach or intestines, tainting the meat.

If possible, shoot an animal that's standing still rather than running. A shot in the heart or lungs will drop it quickly, and you'll lose little meat.

Approach a downed animal with caution, keeping your gun loaded and staying away from the hooves and antlers. Nudge the animal with your foot, or gently touch your gun barrel to its eye. If there's any reaction, shoot it in the head or heart. When you're certain the animal is dead, unload your gun and place it safely out of the way.

Field-dress the animal immediately to drain off the blood and dissipate the body heat. Wear rubber gloves to protect you from any parasites or blood-borne diseases the animal may be carrying, and to make cleanup easier.

The step-by-step instructions on the following pages will guide you through a field-dressing procedure that produces a clean carcass. Splitting the pelvis is optional with this method. In warm weather, you may wish to split the pelvis, because the hams cool faster when separated. However, an animal with a split pelvis

Equipment for Field-Dressing

Some important equipment for field-dressing includes: folding lock-back knife and a spare small whetstone or sharpening stick, several foot-long pieces of kitchen string, two clean sponges, zip-lock plastic bags, rubber gloves, block and tackle and 20 feet of 1/4-inch nylon rope. If hunting moose or elk, also bring cloth bags for carrying out the quarters if skinned and a belt axe or folding game saw for quartering. Hooks can be slipped over the edges of the split rib cage, then tied to trees to hold the body open while gutting. Stow everything but the belt axe in a backpack, along with a first-aid kid and other hunting gear.

is more difficult to drag. The separated hind legs flop around, and the cavity may get dirty.

If you elect to split the pelvis, cut between the hams as described. Then locate the natural seam between the two halves of the pelvic bone, and cut through it with your knife. On a large or old animal, you may need to use a game saw or hatchet. Some hunters stand their knife upright with its tip on the seam, then strike the knife with their palm to split the pelvis. Do not attempt this unless you have a sturdy knife; you could damage the blade.

Be sure to follow state regulations requiring evidence of the sex left on the carcass. Antlers are usually adequate to identify a buck; in some states, antlers must be a certain length for the animal to be legal.

Where the law allows, attach the registration tag after field-dressing, rather than before. The tag may get ripped off during the dressing procedure.

How to Field-dress a Deer (Right-handed Hunter)

1 Run your finger along the breastbone until you can feel the end of it. Pinch the skin away from the body so you don't puncture the intestines, and then make a shallow cut just long enough to insert the first two fingers of your left hand.

2 Form a V with your first two fingers, maintaining upward pressure. Guide the blade between your fingers with the cutting edge up; this way, you won't cut into the intestines. Cut through the abdominal wall back to the pelvic area.

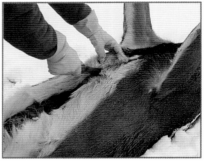
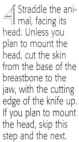

Liver

Lungs

Diaphragm

Jaw

Windpipe

Esophagus

Heart

Stomach

3 Separate the external reproductive organs of a buck from the abdominal wall, but do not cut them off completely. Remove the udder of a doe if she was still nursing. The milk sours rapidly and could give the meat an unpleasant flavor.

4 Straddle the animal, facing its head. Unless you plan to mount the head, cut the skin from the base of the breastbone to the jaw, with the cutting edge of the knife up. If you plan to mount the head, skip this step and the next.

5 Brace your elbows against your legs, with your left hand supporting your right. Cut through the center of the breastbone, using your knees to provide leverage. If the animal is old or very large, you may need to use a game saw or small axe.

6 Slice between the hams to free a buck's urethra, or if you elect to split the pelvic bone on either a buck or doe. Make careful cuts around the urethra until it is freed to a point just above the anus. Be careful not to sever the urethra.

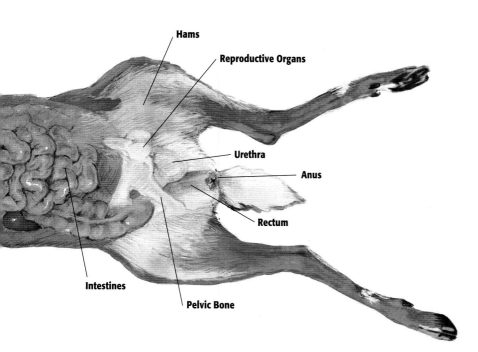

Hams

Reproductive Organs

Urethra

Anus

Rectum

Intestines

Pelvic Bone

7 Cut around the anus; on a doe, the cut should also include the reproductive opening (above the anus). Free the rectum and urethra by loosening the connective tissue with your knife. Tie off the rectum and urethra with kitchen string.

8 Free the windpipe and esophagus by cutting the connective tissue; sever them at the jaw. Grasp them firmly and pull down, continuing to cut where necessary, until they're freed to the point where the windpipe branches out into the lungs.

9 Hold the rib cage open on one side with your left hand. Cut the diaphragm from the rib opening down to the backbone. Stay as close to the rib cage as possible; do not puncture the stomach. Repeat on the other side so the cuts meet over the backbone.

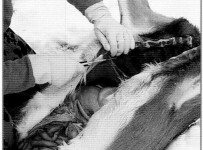

10 Pull the tied-off rectum and urethra underneath the pelvic bone and into the body cavity, unless you have split the pelvic bone. If so, this is unnecessary. Roll the animal on its side so the entrails begin to spill out of the body cavity.

11 Grasp the windpipe and esophagus; pull down and away from the body. If the organs do not pull freely away, the diaphragm may still be attached. Scoop from both ends toward the middle to finish rolling out the entrails. Detach the heart and liver.

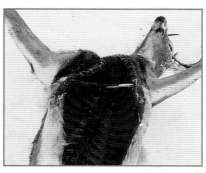

12 Prop the body cavity open with a stick after sponging the cavity clean. If the urinary tract or intestines have been severed, wash the meat with snow or clean water. Hang the carcass from a tree to speed cooling, or drape it over brush or logs with the body cavity down.

TRANSPORTING BIG-GAME ANIMALS

You may have to quarter an elk or moose to transport it from the field (opposite page). Some hunters skin the animal before quartering, so the hide can be tanned in one piece. Others prefer to quarter the animal first. However, a quartered hide is still suitable for tanning; most tanneries split whole elk or moose hides in half to make them easier to handle.

Pile quarters onto a horse, all-terrain vehicle or snowmobile. Skinned quarters should be wrapped in cloth bags. Quarters from smaller animals can be packed out one at a time on a pack frame. If the quarters have not been skinned and the terrain is smooth, they can be dragged out.

Wear blaze-orange clothing and make lots of noise when you move an animal in the field. Hunters have been known to mistakenly shoot at animals being dragged or carried. For this reason, the traditional method of carrying a deer by lashing it to a pole between two hunters is not recommended.

If you must carry an animal this way, drape it completely with blaze-orange cloth.

Once in camp, hang the animal up (pages 280–281). Hanging aids cooling and blood drainage, and the stretching helps tenderize the meat. Clean the clots and excess blood from the heart and liver, then place them in plastic bags on ice.

Ideally, the carcass should be cooled to 40°F within 24 hours. Cool it as rapidly as possible, but don't allow it to freeze. The meat loses moisture if frozen and thawed, and the carcass is difficult to skin when frozen. If the days are warm and the nights cool, keep the carcass covered with a sleeping bag during the day. If the nights are warm as well, store the carcass at a locker plant.

The best way to transport the animal home is in a closed trailer or covered pickup. In cool, dry weather, you can carry an animal on top of your car, with the head forward. Do not carry an animal on the hood, because heat from the engine will spoil the meat. If your trip is long and hot, pack bags of dry ice around the carcass. Or quarter the animal, wrap well in plastic and pack it into coolers with ice. Be sure to check state laws regarding transport of big game.

Drag a deer with each front leg tied to an antler to keep from snagging brush. If the deer is antlerless, tie a rope around the neck. Snow makes dragging easier. If the terrain is dusty, sew the carcass shut with a cord after punching a hole in each side of the rib cage. A bear may be dragged on a heavy tarp, to avoid damaging the fur.

How to Quarter an Elk or Moose (pictured: Elk)

1. Bend a leg sharply, then cut the skin around the joint to remove the lower leg. Repeat on all legs.

2. Saw off the head after skinning the neck area. Sawing it before skinning would force hair into the meat.

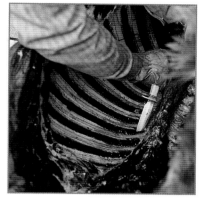

3. Cut between the third and fourth ribs, from the backbone to the tips of the ribs. Cut from inside the body.

4. Separate the front half of the animal from the rear half by sawing through the backbone.

5. Split the hide along the backbone on both halves, then peel it back several inches on each side of the cut.

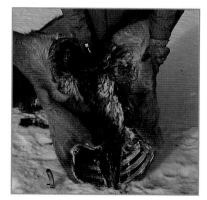

6. Prop one half against your legs, then begin sawing lengthwise through the backbone.

7. Continue cutting while keeping the back off the ground. Gravity will help pull the quarters apart, making the cutting easier. Your saw will not bind, as it would if the half were lying on the ground.

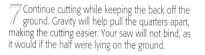

9. Drag out a hindquarter by punching a hole behind the last rib, then threading a rope through and tying as pictured. This way, you drag with the grain of the hair. To drag out a forequarter, tie a rope tightly around the neck.

8. Quartered elk looks like this. Depending on the animal's size, elk quarters weight 60 to 125 pounds each; moose, up to 225 pounds. Where the law allows, some hunters bone the animal in the field to reduce weight.

HANGING & AGING BIG GAME

How should I hang my animal—from the head or by the hind legs? And what about aging—does it improve the meat or spoil it? If I'm going to age the animal, should I leave the hide on during aging or take it off? These questions cause a great deal of debate among hunters.

If you want the head for a trophy, the first question is answered for you: the animal must be hung by the hind legs. Many hunters hang all big game this way, and the U.S. Department of Agriculture recommends this method for butchering beef. Hanging by the hind legs allows the blood to drain from the choice hindquarters. If your animal must be hung outdoors, however, it's better to hang it from the head because of the direction of hair growth. Otherwise, the upturned hair would trap rain and snow.

Many laboratory and taste tests have demonstrated that aging will definitely tenderize the meat. The special tenderness and flavor of beef prime rib result from extended aging. Wild game can benefit in the same way. It's a matter of personal taste: some prefer the aged flavor and tenderness, others don't. Aging is unnecessary if all the meat will be ground into sausage or burger.

To prevent unwanted bacterial growth during the aging process, the carcass temperature must be stabilized between 35° and 40°F. If it fluctuates widely, condensation may form. Temperatures above 40° promote excess bacterial growth and cause the fat to turn rancid. If you age the animal outdoors or in a shed, be prepared to butcher it immediately or take it to a locker should the weather turn warm.

Leave the hide on during aging, if possible. It helps stabilize the temperature of the meat and also reduces dehydration. In a study at the University of Wyoming, an elk carcass was cut in half down the backbone; one half was skinned, the other was not. After two weeks of aging, the skinned side lost over 20 percent more moisture. Animals aged without the hide will have a great deal of dried, dark meat to be trimmed, further reducing your yield.

During aging, enzyme activity breaks down the connective tissue that makes meat tough. Elk has more connective tissue than deer, antelope or bear and can be aged longer. Antelope is probably the most tender of these animals; extended aging may give it a mushy texture. Many people prefer their antelope aged only about 3 days. Bear can age from 3 days to a week. Deer and cow elk reach their prime in a week to 10 days, and bull elk require up to 14 days. These times are for ideal conditions. Do not attempt to age an animal in warm conditions.

Some people prefer to quarter their meat, wrap the quarters in cloth, then age them in a refrigerator or old chest-style pop cooler. The effects are almost the same as hanging a whole carcass. The meat may be slightly less tender, because it doesn't get stretched as much.

If you prefer not to age the animal, delay butchering for at least 24 hours, until the carcass has cooled and the muscles have relaxed. The cuts will be ragged and unappealing if you start before cooling is complete, and the meat will be tough if butchered while the muscles are still contracted.

Hanging an Animal by the Hind Legs

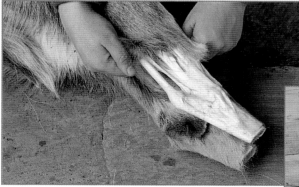

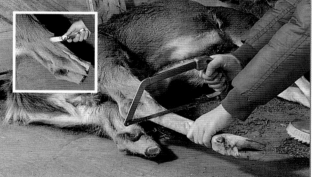

2 Saw off the bottom of each hind leg several inches below the knee. Cutting from inside the skin, slit the skin on each leg to a point about 4 inches above the knee (inset).

1 Make a gambrel out of a 3-foot-long 2 x 2. Cut a shallow notch all around the wood an inch from each end, and another in the middle.

3 Peel the skin over the leg to uncover the large tendon at the back of the leg. Then slit any tissue between the bone and the large tendon. The tendon is needed for hanging the animal, so be careful not to sever it.

4 Insert the gambrel in the slits. Tie each leg to the wood, wrapping the rope in the notch. Tie 6 feet of rope to the center notch, then loop it over a sturdy beam or through a pulley. Hoist the carcass completely off the ground.

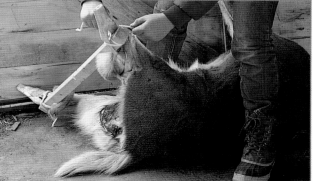

SKINNING BIG GAME

Skinning is easiest while the animal is still warm. If you age the meat, however, it's best to leave the skin on until butchering.

Most hunters skin their animals by hand. The task isn't difficult, requiring only a knife and a saw. For easiest skinning, hang the animal from a pulley. Then you can raise or lower the carcass, so the area you're working on will always be at eye level. Or hoist the animal on a rope running through a heavy-duty screw eye fastened to a solid ceiling beam.

Try to keep hair off the meat during skinning. Keep your knife sharp, touching it up as necessary with a steel or stone. Cut through the skin from the inside out, so your knife slips between the hairs. This way, you avoid cutting hairs in half or driving them into the meat, and your knife won't dull as quickly.

After skinning, lay the hide out on a piece of plywood, skin side up. If you take a few moments to scrape off any bits of meat or fat, you will get a better piece of leather.

Most tanneries prefer to receive a hide salted and rolled. To protect it from rain and animals during the salting process, find a sheltered spot like a shed or garage. Sprinkle the skin side liberally with salt, and rub some into the edges, cuffs and neck area. Tilt the plywood slightly so the hide will drain.

After a day, add more salt and fold the hide in half, skin side in. Roll the folded hide into a bundle and tie it with twine. Don't put the rolled hide in plastic, except for shipping, because it may rot. Keep it cold, and get it to the tannery as soon as possible.

If you have a deer hide, save the tail. It can be used for jig and fly tying, and hide buyers may pay several dollars for it.

If you're not going to butcher the animal yourself, deliver the carcass to the butcher with the hide still on, and let him skin it.

How to Skin an Animal Hanging by the Hind Legs (pictured: Whitetail Deer)

1 Peel the skin over the hind leg to uncover the large tendon at the back of the leg. Carefully slit any tissue between the bone and the large tendon. Place the end of the gambrel into the area between the leg bone and tendon, and hoist the carcass to a comfortable height.

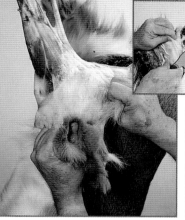

2 Cut the hide along the inner side of each hind leg with the knife blade turned away from the carcass. Rotate the knife blade back toward the meat (inset) and begin skinning the hide around the leg. Pull on the hide with your hands once you reach the outside of each leg.

3 Pull the remaining hide down the outside of each leg until the skinned part reaches the tail. Sever the tail close to the rump, leaving the tailbone inside the hide. Continue skinning down the back by loosening the hide with your knife.

4 Pull the hide down the back with your hands. Use your knife only where necessary, and take care not to cut a hole in the hide. Continue peeling down the back and around the rib cage until you reach the front shoulders.

5 Cut with your knife along the inside of each front leg and peel the hide off the front legs just as you did with the hind legs. Saw off the front legs just above the joint. Peel the hide from the brisket and over the shoulders.

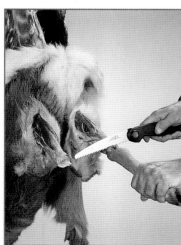

6 Continue peeling the hide down the neck as far as possible. Saw off the head at the base of the skull. After skinning, lay the hide out on a flat surface, scrape off any bits of meat or fat, and salt the hide.

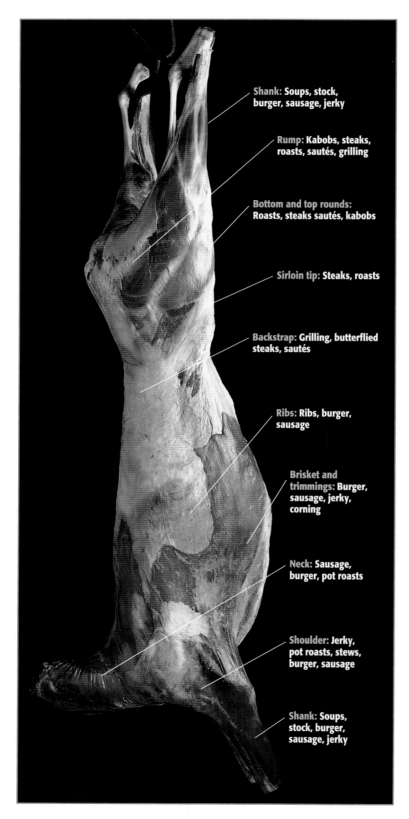

Shank: **Soups, stock, burger, sausage, jerky**

Rump: **Kabobs, steaks, roasts, sautés, grilling**

Bottom and top rounds: **Roasts, steaks sautés, kabobs**

Sirloin tip: **Steaks, roasts**

Backstrap: **Grilling, butterflied steaks, sautés**

Ribs: **Ribs, burger, sausage**

Brisket and trimmings: **Burger, sausage, jerky, corning**

Neck: **Sausage, burger, pot roasts**

Shoulder: **Jerky, pot roasts, stews, burger, sausage**

Shank: **Soups, stock, burger, sausage, jerky**

BUTCHERING BIG GAME

When you do your own butchering, you know that the meat has been handled with care, and you get the cuts you prefer. You will probably be willing to take more time trimming than a butcher would, so your finished cuts may have less gristle, fat and silverskin on them.

In most cases, the animal is butchered while still hanging from the skinning process. Use caution when butchering a hanging animal. When you cut off each portion, you must "catch" it, and this can be tricky with a knife in one hand. A deer leg, for instance, can weigh 20 pounds or more, so you may need a partner to catch it. Be absolutely certain that your partner stays clear of your knife, and never allow him to cut at the same time. For safety, some hunters prefer to butcher on a large table.

The photo sequence on pages 286 and 287 shows how to cut up a deer that is hanging from the head. The procedure is

Dress your knife frequently with a sharpening steel. Hold the base of the blade against the steel at the angle at which it was originally sharpened. Draw the knife toward you in an arc from base to tip. Repeat on the other side. Alternate sides until the blade is sharp.

somewhat different if the animal is hanging by the hind legs. You will not be able to cut off the hind legs because they are supporting the carcass. Instead, remove the front legs, backstrap and ribs as described, then place the hindquarters on a table to finish cutting.

After cutting up the carcass, bone the meat. Boning is easier than bone-in butchering, and usually results in tastier meat. Bone marrow is fatty and can turn rancid, even in the freezer. By boning, you avoid cutting the bones, so there is no bone residue to affect the meat's flavor. In addition, boned meat takes less freezer space and is easier to wrap. There are no sharp edges to puncture the freezer wrap and expose the meat to freezer burn.

On pages 288 and 289, you'll learn an easy method for boning a big-game animal. To roughly estimate the amount of boned meat you will get, divide the field-dressed weight of your animal in half. You will get a smaller yield if the shot damaged much meat, or if you aged the animal.

Work on a large hardwood or plexiglass cutting board. To keep bacterial growth to a minimum, wash the board with a solution of 3 tablespoons of household bleach to 1 gallon of water, and wash it occasionally during the boning process. Keep two large bowls handy for the trimmings. As you bone, place large chunks to be used for stew in one bowl, and small scraps for sausage or burger in the other.

How you make the final boning cuts depends on the animal's size. On a moose, for instance, the rump portion is large enough to yield several roasts. But on an antelope, the same cut is too small for a roast; it is better for steaks, kabobs or stroganoff.

Keep the meat cool throughout the butchering and boning process. Work on the carcass in a cool shed or garage. To reduce bacterial growth, bone and freeze each portion as you remove it, or refrigerate it until you can bone it. You can butcher faster by working in pairs; while one person cuts up the carcass, the other works on boning.

Save the bones if you want to make soup or stock (page 22). The backbone makes particularly good stock. Saw the larger bones into pieces to fit your stockpot.

How to Cut Up a Big-Game Animal

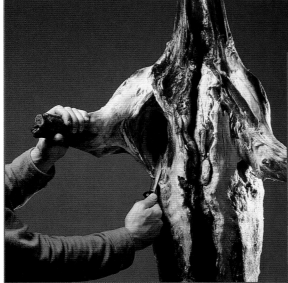

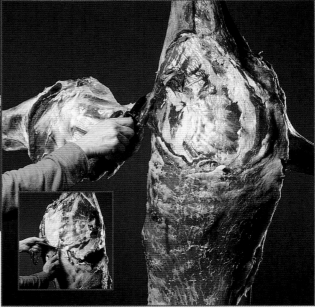

2 Remove the front leg by cutting between the shoulder blade and the back. Repeat with the other leg. Remove the layer of brisket meat over the ribs (inset). Moose or elk brisket is thick enough to be rolled for corning (page 163). Grind thin brisket for burger.

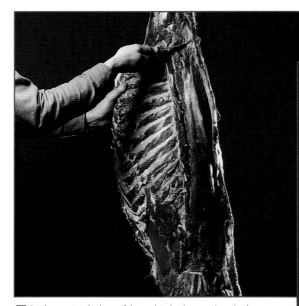

1 Push the front leg away from the body, then begin cutting between the leg and the rib cage. Continue until you reach the shoulder. It helps to have someone steady the carcass, but make sure he or she is safely away from your knife.

4 Make two cuts between the shoulder and rump: one along the spine, the other along the rib tops. Keep your knife close to the bones, removing as much meat as possible. Cut off this first backstrap at the rump, then remove the backstrap on the other side of the spine.

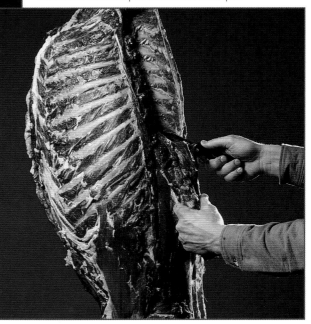

3 Cut the meat at the base of the neck to begin removing a backstrap. There are two backstraps, one on each side of the spine. Backstraps can be butterflied for steaks (page 114), cut into roasts or sliced thinly for sautéing. The lower part, or loin, is most tender.

5 Begin cutting one hind leg away, exposing the ball-and-socket joint (arrow). Push the leg back to pop the joint apart, then cut through the joint. Work your knife around the tailbone and pelvis until the leg is removed. Repeat with the other leg.

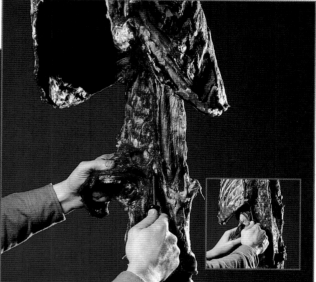

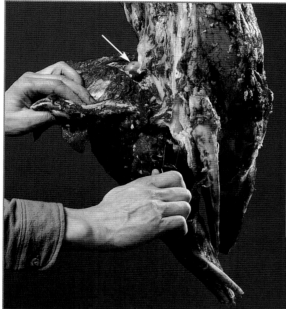

6 Cut the tenderloins from inside the body cavity after trimming the flank meat below the last rib (inset). The flank meat can be ground, or cut into thin strips for jerky. Many hunters remove the tenderloins before aging the animal, to keep them from darkening and dehydrating.

7 Remove the ribs if desired by sawing along the backbone (dashed line). Cut around the base of the neck, then twist the backbone off. Separate the neck and head. Bone the neck to grind for burger, or keep it whole for pot roasting.

8 Trim the ribs by cutting away the ridge of meat and gristle along the bottom. If the ribs are long, saw them in half. Cut ribs into racks of three or four. If you don't want to save the ribs, you can bone the meat between them and grind it for burger or sausage.

How to Bone a Hind Leg (pictured: Antelope)

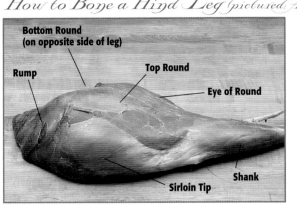

Bottom Round
(on opposite side of leg)

Rump

Top Round

Eye of Round

Sirloin Tip

Shank

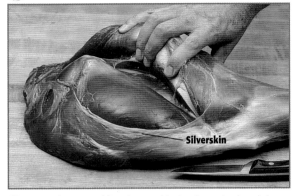

Silverskin

1 A hind leg consists of the sirloin tip, the top and bottom rounds, the eye of round, a portion of the rump, and the shank. The sirloin, rounds and rump are tender cuts for roasting or grilling; the shank is tough and best for ground meat or soups.

2 Separate the top round from the rest of the leg after cutting through the thin layer of silverskin that covers the leg. Work your fingers into the natural seam, then begin pulling the top round away from the leg. Use your knife only where necessary to free the meat.

4 Remove the rump portion. Cut the rump off at the top of the hipbone after removing the silverskin and pulling the muscle groups apart with your fingers. A large rump is excellent for roasting; a small one can be cut for steaks, kabobs or sautés.

3 Cut along the back of the leg to remove the top round completely. The top round is excellent when butterflied, rolled and tied for roasting (see opposite page). Or cut it into two, smaller flat roasts, cube for kabobs or slice for sautés.

5 Cut bottom round away from sirloin tip after turning leg over and separating these two muscle groups with your fingers. Next, carve sirloin tip away from bone. Sirloin tip makes a choice roast or steaks; bottom round is good for roasting, steaks or kabobs.

6 A boned leg will look like this. Cut the shank and upper leg bone apart at the knee joint if you plan on using the shank for soup. Or cut the meat off the shank close to the bone; trim away the tendons and silverskin, and grind the meat for burger or sausage. Use the leftover bones for stock (page 22). On a larger animal, you may wish to separate the eye of round from the top round.

7 Make large-diameter steaks from a whole hind leg by cutting across all the muscle groups rather than boning as described above. First, remove the rump portion as described, then cut the leg into inch-thick steaks. As each steak is cut, work around the bone with a fillet knife, then slide the steak over the end of the bone. Continue steaking until you reach the shank.

Bottom Round

Eye of Round

Top Round

Rump

Sirloin Tip

Shank

How to Bone a Front Leg *(pictured: Deer)*

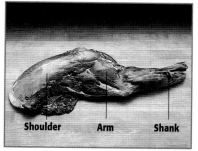

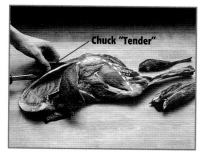

2 Cut along bony ridge in the middle of the shoulder blade. One side yields the small, boneless chuck "tender." Bone the other side along the dashed line to make a shoulder roast.

1 A front leg consists of the shoulder, arm and shank. The meat from the front leg is less tender than that from the hind leg, and is used for pot roasting, stews, jerky or grinding.

3 Trim remaining meat from bones. Use the chuck "tender" for jerky or stews. Pot roast the shoulder roast, cut into stew chunks or use for jerky. Grind the shank meat for burger.

How to Make a Rolled Roast *(pictured: Antelope)*

2 Tie the rolled meat about an inch from the end that is farthest from you; use a 60-inch length of kitchen string. Leave several inches at the short end of the string; you will need to tie the two ends of the string together after making loops around the meat.

1 Butterfly meat that is thicker than 1 inch by cutting into two thinner pieces; leave the meat connected at one edge. Open up the butterflied meat so it lies flat. Roll the meat tightly with the grain, tucking in any irregular edges.

3 Make a loop in the string, then twist the loop once to make a small "braid." Slip the braided loop over the end of the meat closest to you, then slide the loop so it is about 1 inch from the string tied around the far end.

4 Snug up this first loop by pulling on the long end of the string, adjusting its length so the braid lines up with the original knot. The roast will look more attractive when it is served if all the braids are lined up along the top of the roast.

6 Tie the two ends of the string together with a double overhand knot. Trim both ends of the string close to the knot. When you are ready to carve a cooked rolled roast, simply snip the loops along the top of the roast and pull off the string.

5 Continue making loops about an inch apart, snugging them up as you go. Tie on additional string if necessary. When you have made a loop about an inch from the close end, slip the string underneath the roast so it comes out on the far side.

DRESSING SMALL GAME

Proper field care of small game ensures excellent eating. Field-dress rabbits, hares and squirrels as soon as possible, or the delicately flavored meat may pick up an unpleasant taste. Squirrel seems particularly susceptible to off tastes, so knowledgeable hunters take time to field-dress squirrels immediately after shooting. Most raccoon hunters skin and dress their raccoons at home shortly after the hunt. Raccoon meat doesn't suffer from the minor delay, and the pelt is more valuable if it hasn't been cut for field-dressing.

A great deal has been written about small game transmitting diseases to humans. Such diseases are contracted by handling entrails or uncooked meat from infected animals. Bacteria pass through cuts in a person's skin or through the mucous membranes. But infected animals are rarely encountered, because the diseases usually kill them or weaken them so much that predators can easily capture them.

To avoid any danger, never shoot an animal that moves erratically or otherwise appears sick. Wear rubber gloves when dressing or skinning any small game. Never touch your mouth or eyes, and wash your hands thoroughly when finished. Dispose of the entrails and skin in a spot where dogs and cats can't reach them and become infected.

For safer disposal, some hunters carry plastic bags.

When field-dressing small game, you may encounter various internal parasites. Most of these, while visually unappealing, do not harm the meat and are removed during dressing or skinning.

Raccoon populations in some areas of the country carry a roundworm that may be found in the droppings and on the pelt. In very rare circumstances, this parasite can be transmitted to humans. Although the possibility of contamination is slim, raccoon hunters should wear rubber gloves while dressing and skinning.

When handling rabbits, wear gloves not only for dressing and skinning, but also during all stages of kitchen preparation. Rabbits occasionally carry *tularemia,* a bacterial disease that can be transmitted to humans. Thorough cooking destroys the bacteria.

Before skinning, try to determine the animal's age, because this may affect the way you cook it. The tail of a young squirrel tapers to a point, while the tail of an old one is the same width throughout. A young rabbit has soft, flexible ears and a small cleft in the upper lip; an old one has stiffer ears, often with white edges, and a deeply cleft upper lip. In all kinds of small game, the meat of old animals is darker in color. Also, the teeth darken and dull with age, and the claws become blunt.

How to Field-dress Small Game

1 Equipment for field-dressing small game includes: (1) hunting knife, (2) rubber gloves, (3) plastic bags, (4) paper towels, (5) cord for hanging dressed animals in a tree.

2 Make a shallow cut (dashed line) from the vent to the rib cage. Be sure not to puncture the intestines. Some hunters extend the cut through the rib cage to the neck.

3 Pull out all the entrails. Check a rabbit's liver for white spots indicating disease; if it's clean, save it in a plastic bag with the heart. Wipe cavity with paper towels.

How to Skin a Rabbit or Hare

2 Grasp the hide with both hands and pull in opposite directions. Keep pulling until all the legs are skinned up to the feet.

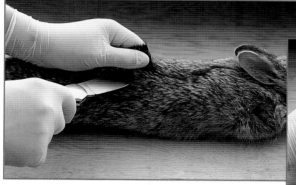

1 Pinch the hide up and away from the middle of the rabbit's spine. Slit the hide from the spine down the sides, being careful not to cut the meat.

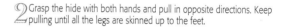

4 Clean body cavity, removing any material left after dressing. Rinse briefly under running water and pat dry. Squirrels can also be skinned this way, but not as easily (see page 292 for an easier squirrel-skinning method).

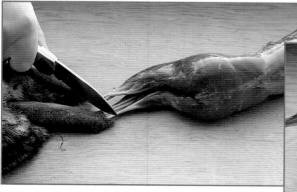

3 Cut off the head, feet and tail. If you did not field-dress the rabbit before skinning, slit the underside from vent to neck, then remove all internal organs. Save liver and heart if desired.

How to Skin a Squirrel

1 Cut through the base of the tailbone, starting on the underside of the tail. Stop when the bone is severed; do not cut the skin on the top side of the tail.

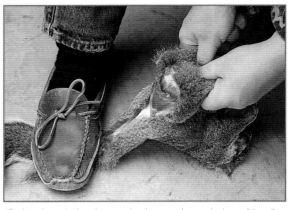

2 Place the squirrel on the ground and set your foot on the base of the tail. Pull up on the rear legs, peeling the skin all the way to the front legs.

3 Peel the "britches" off the rear legs to the ankle joints. Keep your foot firmly on the base of the tail until all skinning is complete.

4 Remove the squirrel's back feet by cutting through the ankle joints with a knife or game shears. If using a knife, cut away from yourself as pictured.

5 Pull each front leg out of the skin, as far as the wrist joint. Use the fingers of your free hand to help loosen the skin at the elbow. Then cut each front foot off at the wrist joint (pictured).

6 Cut the head off. Remove any glands and clean out the body cavity as described in the rabbit-skinning sequence on page 291. Several long hairs usually remain on the wrist; cut these off with your knife or shears.

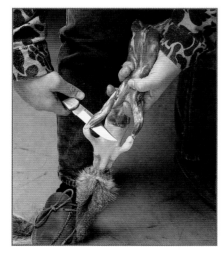

How to Skin a Raccoon (Keeping the Pelt Saleable)

1 Hang the raccoon by the rear legs, and cut the skin around the rear feet. The raccoon in this picture is hanging from a special raccoon-skinning gambrel.

2 Cut along the inside of each rear leg to the base of the tail. Peel the pelt back to the base of the tail. Begin peeling the skin off the abdomen.

3 Use your knife as shown to skin the pelt from the spine above the tail. Cut through the tailbone close to the rump. Leave the tailbone inside the pelt.

4 Continue peeling off the pelt until you reach the shoulders, using your knife only when necessary. Cut the skin around the front feet (pictured).

5 Pull the pelt off the front legs and then off the head, cutting carefully at the eyes and rear base of the ears. Cut the pelt off at the nose. Turn it right side out to dry. Cut and peel the tail skin to remove the bone.

6 Remove the glands that lie under the front legs and above the base of the tail. Cut off the head and feet. Slit the abdomen from vent to neck. Remove the internal organs, rinse the raccoon and pat it dry.

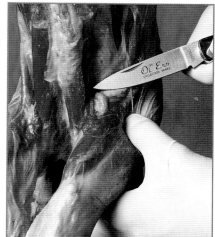

PORTIONING SMALL GAME

Small game is usually cut into serving pieces before it is cooked or frozen. Pieces are more convenient to freeze than a whole carcass, because they can be arranged into a compact bundle with few air spaces.

The portioning method shown below works with squirrels, rabbits, hares and raccoons. The rear legs are the meatiest pieces, followed by the saddle or loin

portion, then the front legs. The ribs contain very little meat, but can be used for making stock.

Game shears are an excellent tool for cutting up squirrels, rabbits and hares. You may need a heavy knife, however, to cut through the thick backbone of a raccoon.

Wear rubber gloves when handling raw rabbit or hare. In some locations, raccoons may carry encephalitis in early fall, so gloves are a good precaution when portioning raccoons taken at that time.

A Simple Method for Cutting Up a Squirrel

1 Cut the squirrel in half behind the ribs (left), or along the backbone(right). If the squirrel is small, no further cutting will be necessary.

2 Quarter a large squirrel by cutting each half apart. Quartered squirrels are easier to fry than halved ones and look more attractive when served.

How to Cut Up Small Game (pictured: Rabbit)

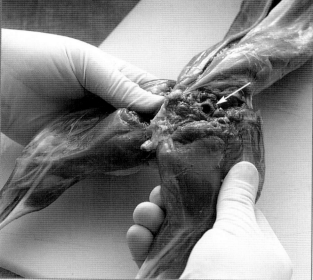

2 Bend the leg back to pop the ball-and-socket joint (arrow). Cut through the joint to remove the leg. Repeat with the other leg. On a large rabbit, hare or raccoon, each rear leg can be split in two at the knee.

1 Place the animal on its back on a cutting board. Cut into the rear leg at a point near the backbone. When you come to the leg bone, stop cutting. If using a game shears, snip the meat around the bone.

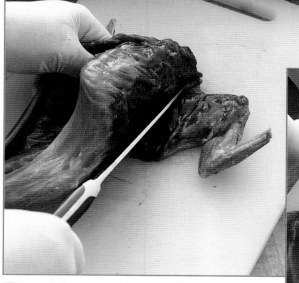

4 Cut the back into two or three pieces, depending on the animal's size. Remove the rib cage, if desired. When portioning a raccoon or large hare, you can also split the back along the spine, making four to six pieces.

3 Remove the front legs by cutting close to the rib cage and behind the shoulder blades. The legs come off easier this way because you don't cut through joints. On a large animal, cut each leg in two at the elbow.

DRESSING UPLAND BIRDS, WILD TURKEYS & WATERFOWL

In warm weather, all birds should be gutted as soon as they're shot. In cool weather, gutting can wait until the end of the day's hunt.

Plucking the birds is seldom practical in the middle of a hunt. But if you do have the opportunity, you'll find the feathers pull out more easily then, while the birds are still warm. When plucking in the field, put the feathers in a bag instead of scattering them around. Be sure to check state laws on the transport of game birds. In many states, at least one wing must remain fully feathered and attached to the carcass.

Before plucking or skinning any water-fowl, try to determine its age. Old birds may be tough unless cooked with moist heat. Young geese and ducks are smaller than old ones, and the plumage may not be fully colored. If you notice a lot of pinfeathers when plucking, the bird is prob-ably young.

Most upland birds have short life spans, but turkeys and pheasants often live several years. Check the spurs on the legs of a tom turkey or rooster pheasant. Long, pointed spurs indicate an old bird; short, rounded spurs, a young one.

Birds, like big game, can be tenderized by aging. Dress the birds but leave the skin and feathers on; then store them, uncovered, in a refrigerator for a few days.

If possible, birds to be served whole should be plucked rather than skinned. The skin helps keep the meat moist. Waterfowl have thick, tough skin that doesn't tear easily, so they're easier to pluck than upland birds. An upland bird that's badly shot up may have to be skinned, because the delicate skin would rip during plucking. Sage grouse, sea ducks and fish-eating ducks like mergansers are usually skinned, because the skin of these birds is strongly flavored.

Skinning a bird saves time, but the meat may dry out in cooking. You can save even more time by using the breasting method shown on page 301, if you like pieces instead of a whole bird.

How to Field-dress Birds (pictured: Pheasant)

1 Equipment for field-dressing upland birds and waterfowl includes: (1) small hunting knife, (2) plastic bags, which can double as gloves, (3) paper towels.

2 Cut the skin from the vent toward the breastbone. Some hunters pluck the feathers between the vent and breastbone before cutting.

3 Make a short slit above the breast toward the chin. Pull out the windpipe. Remove the crop, a flexible sac that lies between the bird's breast and chin, and any undigested food it may contain.

4 Remove the entrails, including the lungs. If desired, save the heart, gizzard and liver, storing them in a plastic bag. Be sure to trim the green gall sac from the liver. Wipe the inside of the bird with paper towels.

How to Wet-pluck a Bird (pictured: Chukar Partridge)

2 Dip the bird several times in simmering (160° to 180°F) water. For waterfowl, add a tablespoon of dish-washing liquid to help saturate the feathers. Rinse any soapy water from the cavity of a field-dressed bird.

1 Wet the bird thoroughly by holding it underneath a running faucet. If wet-plucking waterfowl, rub the breast with your thumb to ensure that the thick down feathers are saturated with water.

4 Cut off the head and tail. Slice off the feet, removing the leg tendons from upland birds (page 302) if desired. Clean the body cavity, and take out the windpipe if still present. Rinse the cavity, and pat the bird dry.

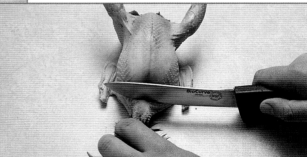

3 Rub the body feathers with your thumb. They should strip off easily. If they don't, dip the bird in hot water again. Pull out the large feathers of the wing and tail, using a pliers if necessary.

How to Dry-pluck a Bird (pictured: Bobwhite Quail)

2 Use a pliers, if necessary, to pull out the wing and tail feathers. Some hunters cut off the outer two joints of the wings; little meat is lost.

1 Grasp only a few feathers at a time, and pull gently in the direction in which they grow. Pluck over a grocery bag to minimize the mess.

3 Singe any downy feathers or "hair" with a gas burner. Finish cleaning as described in the last step of the wet-plucking sequence shown above.

How to Wax Waterfowl (pictured: Mallard)

1 Heat a large pot of water to a gentle boil. Melt several chunks of special duck-picking wax or paraffin in the water. The floating layer of melted wax should be at least ¼ inch thick.

2 Rough-pluck the larger feathers from the body, legs, wings and tail. Pull only a few feathers at a time. Leave the smaller feathers on the bird, since they make the wax adhere better.

3 Dip the bird in the wax and water. Swish it around gently, then slowly remove it from the wax. Hold the bird up until the wax hardens enough that you can set it down on newspapers without sticking. Or hang it by wedging the head between closely spaced nails on a board.

4 Allow the bird to cool until the wax is fairly hard. To speed the process, you can dip the bird in a bucket of cold water. Repeat the dipping and cooling until a layer of wax has built up at least ⅛ inch thick. Allow the wax to cool completely and harden.

5 Peel the hardened wax off the bird. The feathers will come off with the wax, leaving the skin smooth. You can reuse the wax if you melt it again and strain it through cheesecloth to remove the feathers.

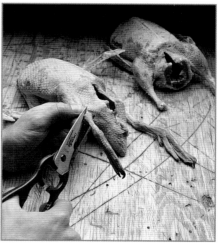

6 Cut off the head, feet and tail. Remove the windpipe and entrails if the bird was not dressed before waxing. Remove wax from the cavity of a dressed bird. Clean the cavity thoroughly, rinse the bird and pat it dry.

How to Skin a Bird (pictured: Pheasant)

2 Place fingers in the slit where the crop was removed during field-dressing; pull to skin breast and legs. If crop is still in, slit skin and remove crop first.

1 Cut off the last two joints of the wing with game shears or a knife. Cut off the feet, removing the leg tendons from an upland bird (page 302) if desired.

4 Remove the head and tail with game shears. If the bird wasn't dressed before skinning, pull out the windpipe and entrails. Clean the cavity thoroughly. Rinse the bird and pat it dry.

3 Pull the skin away from the wing joints, turning the skin inside out over the joints as though peeling off a stocking. Free both wings, then peel the skin off the back of the bird.

How to Breast a Bird to Retain the Legs (pictured: Pheasant)

2 Slice breast halves away from the breastbone, using a fillet knife. Keep the blade as close to the bone as possible. Cut the meat away from the wishbone to free completely.

1 Cut off the feet and pull the skin off the breast and legs as described in the skinning sequence on the opposite page. Do not skin the wings.

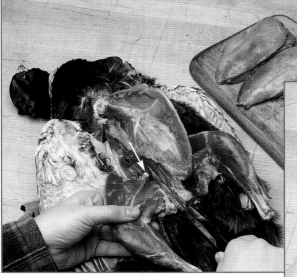

4 Cut apart the thigh and drumstick if desired. Dispose of the carcass. With this method of breasting, the only meat discarded is on the back and wings. The boneless breast halves are easy to cook.

3 Push the leg down, popping the ball-and-socket joint (arrow). Cut through the joint to remove the leg. Remove other leg. If the bird wasn't field-dressed, remove liver, heart and gizzard if you wish to save them.

How to Remove Leg Tendons from Upland Birds

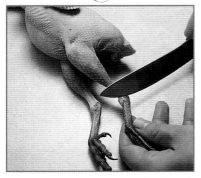

2 Bend the foot back and forth four or five times. This helps loosen the tendons, which connect the foot to the muscles in the leg.

1 Cut the skin around the bottom of the drumstick, either before or after plucking. Do not cut deeply, or you will sever the tendons.

3 Pull the foot off while holding the leg with your other hand. The tendons will come away with the foot.

Tips for Dressing Upland Birds and Waterfowl

REMOVE entrails with a special bird-gutting knife. Insert the hook into the body, then rotate the knife and pull it out. The entrails will twist around the hook. A small forked stick can be used the same way.

MAKE a large cut when field-dressing a turkey (pictured) or large sage grouse so you can get your whole hand inside the body cavity (left). This makes it easier to take out the entrails (right).

PLUCK waterfowl by using a rubber-fingered "power picker." Many shooting pre-serves and some resorts near good waterfowl areas will power-pick your ducks or geese for a small fee.

BONE the thigh of a pheasant (pictured) or other bird to make a boneless fillet. Fold the thigh in half so the bone is on top. Slip your knife or shears under the end of the bone, and cut the meat away.

PORTIONING BIRDS

Whether to portion a bird, and how, depends mainly on its size and the cooking method. Any upland bird or waterfowl can be cooked whole. The larger ones, such as pheasant, turkey, mallard and goose, can be cut into traditional pieces if preferred. Birds up to the size of a pheasant can also be split into halves.

If you portion a bird, skinning is optional. When you cut it up, save the backbone, neck and any bones left from breasting. These parts make excellent stock (page 23). Most cooks do not make stock from small birds like doves, woodcock and quail.

Breasting is quick and easy, and many hunters prefer it when they have a number of birds to process. The breasting method shown on page 301 saves not only the breast but also the thighs and drumsticks, so very little meat is wasted.

How to Split a Bird into Halves

1 Split the back by cutting along one side of the backbone with game shears. If desired, cut along the other side of the backbone and remove it.

2 Cut along one side of the breastbone and through the wishbone. You can remove the breastbone by making a second cut along the other side of it.

How to Cut Up a Bird
(pictured: Pheasant)

1 Remove the wings by cutting through the joint next to the breast. For another way of handling the wings, see the photo sequence of the French portioning technique on page 304.

2 Separate the breast from the back by cutting through the ribs. When you reach the shoulder, grasp the breast in one hand and the back in the other; bend the carcass as if it were hinged. Cut the breast and back apart.

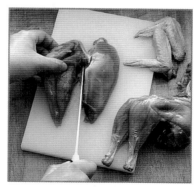

3 Divide the breast into halves by cutting along one side of the breastbone, then cutting away the wishbone. You can also cut along the other side of the breastbone and remove it. Or bone the breast as shown in the breasting sequence on page 301.

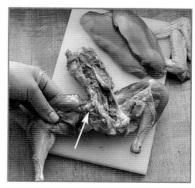

4 Begin cutting the leg away from the backbone, then bend it back to expose the ball-and-socket joint (arrow). Cut through the socket to remove the leg. If desired, separate the thigh from the drumstick by cutting through the knee joint.

How to Cut Up a Bird Using the French Technique (pictured: Pheasant)

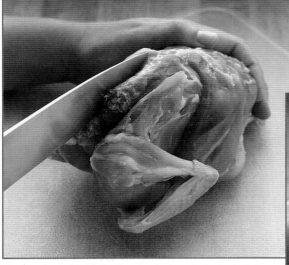

1 Locate the shoulder blade, where the wing is attached to the back of the bird. Slice between the shoulder blade and backbone, sliding the knife next to the ribs. Do not cut the wing completely off.

2 Grasp the breastbone in one hand and the backbone in the other. Then pull as pictured, separating the breast portion from the back portion. The legs will remain attached to the backbone.

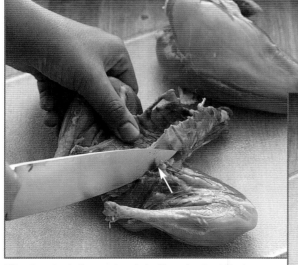

3 Begin cutting the leg away from the backbone, then bend it back to expose the ball-and-socket joint (arrow). Cut through the socket to remove the leg. If desired, separate the thigh from the drumstick by cutting through the knee joint.

4 Split the breast lengthwise, then cut each half as shown. This technique leaves some breast meat attached to the wings, so the serving portions are more nearly even. The added meat from the breast is especially desirable if you haven't saved the last two wing joints.

BIRDS & SMALL GAME: FINAL CLEANING STEPS

A quick rinse before cooking or freezing is often all that is necessary for the final cleaning step. But a little extra effort will often improve the quality of your meat.

Examine birds and small game carefully, looking for shot and for any fur or feathers the shot may have driven in. Pick all these out with fine tweezers, the point of a sharp knife or a fly-tying forceps.

Soak the meat only if it is badly shot up and saturated with blood. Then, immerse it for an hour or two in milk or a solution of 2 quarts water to 1 tablespoon baking soda. If the meat has been cut into portions, soak only the damaged ones. Rinse the meat well after soaking.

Remove all fat from a raccoon before cooking or freezing. The fat is strong-tasting and oily and gives the meat an undesirable flavor. Rabbits, hares and squirrels have little if any fat.

Rinse the hearts and livers to remove any clotted blood. If the top of the heart is ragged, trim it off. The bile sac should have been removed from the liver during field-dressing. Cut away any part of the liver or meat that has a green bile stain.

Many hunters save turkey gizzards, and some save pheasant and waterfowl gizzards. Clean them as shown in the photo sequence below. Gizzards can be fried whole, chopped and mixed into stuffing or added to the stockpot.

How to Clean a Gizzard

1 Split the gizzard between the two lobes, and clean out all food matter and grit. Do not put the contents down a kitchen garbage disposal, since they include small rocks that cannot be ground up.

2 Set the opened gizzard on your cutting board, with the tough inside membrane facing down. Skin the meat from the membrane with a fillet knife. Discard this membrane. The outside membrane can be left on, if desired.

Tips for Final Cleaning

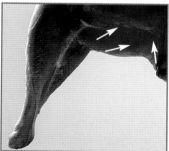

HOLD a piece of upland bird or small game up to a light. The meat is somewhat translucent, so you may be able to see shot (arrows) embedded in it.

USE a game shears to remove fat from a raccoon. Cut down into the fat until some meat is exposed, then snip between the fat and the meat.

Freezing Fish & Game

Many hunters and anglers overlook the importance of proper freezing techniques for their harvest. They wrap fish fillets loosely in plastic wrap or hurriedly throw a gamebird into a used bread bag, then toss the parcel into the freezer. When it comes time to cook, they're surprised that the meat is dried out or freezer burned.

Fish, small game and game birds can be preserved by freezing in water. Any dehydration that occurs will first happen to the ice, not the meat; and if the food is frozen in a milk carton or plastic container, dehydration is greatly reduced.

Even foods frozen in water won't last indefinitely, however, especially if stored in a frost-free freezer. In a freezer of this type, a fan unit pulls moisture out of the air to prevent frost buildup. Unfortunately, it also pulls the moisture out of poorly wrapped fish or game, and it will also eventually cause the ice to be eaten away from foods that have been frozen in water. In addition to these problems, fats in fish and game will slowly begin to oxidize even in the freezer. As a result, fatty fish such as salmon, and many types of game, have a shorter freezer life than other foods.

Big-game steaks, chops and roasts, and any other game or fish that is not frozen in water, should be double-wrapped in plastic wrap and overwrapped in freezer paper before freezing. When cutting up big game for the freezer, remember to keep it in the largest size that is practical, and do any additional cutting to the thawed meat just prior to cooking. Moisture escapes from each cut surface, so smaller pieces of meat lose more moisture than bigger ones. Also, if you freeze a piece of choice venison whole rather than cutting it up, you have the option of cooking it as a roast or cutting it into steaks just prior to cooking.

The same principle applies to freezing stew, burger or sausage meat: freeze larger chunks, then cut to size or grind just before cooking. Game that's been ground with fat for burger meat doesn't keep as long as plain ground meat, because the fat can turn rancid even in the freezer.

Fish fillets and steaks may be treated to extend their freezer life by 3 months. Mix 2 tablespoons of ascorbic acid (available in drugstores) with 1 quart cold water. Place fish in the mixture for 20 seconds, then wrap and freeze immediately.

Never thaw fish or game at room temperature, because bacteria can grow as the food is thawing. Place wrapped packages on a plate in the refrigerator for a day; larger pieces may need even longer to thaw.

Freezer Storage Chart

FISH TYPE	MAXIMUM STORAGE TIME		
	WHOLE	STEAKS	FILLETS
LARGE OILY	2 MONTHS	1 1/2 MONTHS	1 MONTH
SMALL OILY	1 1/2 MONTHS	1 MONTH	1 MONTH
LARGE LEAN	6 MONTHS	4 MONTHS	3 1/2 MONTHS
SMALL LEAN	4 MONTHS	3 MONTHS	2 1/2 MONTHS

TYPE OF MEAT	WRAPPING METHOD*	MAXIMUM STORAGE TIME
BIG-GAME ROASTS	STANDARD BUTCHER WRAP	10 MONTHS
BIG-GAME STEAKS	STANDARD BUTCHER WRAP	8 MONTHS
BIG-GAME RIBS	FOIL WRAP	5 MONTHS
BIG-GAME ORGANS	STANDARD BUTCHER WRAP/WATER PACK	4 MONTHS/6 MONTHS
BIG-GAME CHUNKS	FREEZER BAG AND PAPER	6 MONTHS
BIG-GAME BURGER	FREEZER BAG AND PAPER	4 MONTHS
CUT-UP SMALL GAME	STANDARD BUTCHER WRAP/WATER PACK	8 MONTHS/1 YEAR
SMALL-GAME ORGANS	WATER PACK	10 MONTHS
WHOLE LARGE BIRDS	FOIL PACK	5 MONTHS
WHOLE SMALL BIRDS	STANDARD BUTCHER WRAP/WATER PACK	6 MONTHS/ 1 YEAR
CUT-UP UPLAND BIRDS	STANDARD BUTCHER WRAP/WATER PACK	8 MONTHS/1 YEAR
CUT-UP WATERFOWL	STANDARD BUTCHER WRAP/WATER PACK	8 MONTHS/1 YEAR
BIRD GIBLETS	WATER PACK	4 MONTHS
GAME STOCK	FREEZER CONTAINERS	4 MONTHS

Photo instructions given for wrapping methods on pages 309-312

How to Water-pack Fish or Cut-up Game in Containers

1 Freeze fish, cut-up gamebirds or small game in meal-sized portions, using washed milk cartons or plastic containers. Choose containers based on the size of the game you're freezing; for example, half-gallon cartons work well for ducks, while pint-sized cartons are better for partridge. Tiny game birds, cut-up game, fish fillets, fish cheeks or game-bird giblets can be frozen with a number of pieces in each container. Add cold water to cover the food. Jiggle to eliminate air bubbles, then place on a level spot in the freezer. Freeze until completely solid.

2 Check after the water has frozen to be sure the food is completely covered with a good layer of ice. If not, top off with more cold water and refreeze. If any food sticks out of the ice, it will get freezer burned in a surprisingly short amount of time.

3 Fold the top of a dairy carton closed, if possible. Wrap a band of freezer tape around the carton so it sticks to itself; label the tape. Label the lid of a plastic container.

4 Cut off the top if the carton can't be closed, or if it isn't filled to the fold with ice. Trim at the ice level. Cover the top with heavy-duty aluminum foil. Wrap freezer tape around the edge of the foil and label it.

An Alternate Method: Use a Baking Pan

2 Pop out block of frozen ice and food by running cold water on the bottom; the ice should release easily from the pan.

1 Use small baking pans to freeze meal-sized portions of fish or cut-up game. Cover food with cold water and freeze as described above.

3 Wrap the solid block of ice and food in plastic wrap or aluminum foil. Overwrap with freezer paper, sealing tight.

How to Water-pack Cut-up Game in a Plastic Bag

2 Add water to completely cover the pieces of game. Squeeze out all the air, and seal the top of the bag. Set the pan in the freezer.

1 Place a zip-lock plastic freezer bag in a cake pan, then arrange the pieces in the bag. The bag should lie on its side in the pan.

3 Butcher-wrap the frozen bag with freezer paper. This keeps it from ripping or puncturing, which could open the meat to freezer burn.

Freezing Fish & Game for Individual Use

1 Cover whole fish, fillets or boneless breasts with water as they lie side by side in a resealable bag in a cake pan. Leave a little space between them. Squeeze out the air, and seal the bag. Prepare several bags of food, laying them in the pan in layers. Put the pan in the freezer. When the food is frozen, remove the bags from the pan and stack them in the freezer.

2 Break off as many pieces as you need for a meal by pushing the bag against the edge of a countertop. Don't rip the plastic. Remove the broken-off portion, reseal the bag and return it to the freezer.

Alternate Freezing Techniques

DOUBLE-WRAP whole fish, steaks or fillets that are frozen without a protective block of ice. Separate the fillets or steaks with waxed paper to make thawing easier. This method saves freezer space.

GLAZE whole fish by first freezing without wrapping. Dip frozen fish in very cold water; freeze again. Repeat three to five times, until 1/8 inch of ice builds up. Double-wrap in airtight package, handling fish carefully.

The Standard Butcher Wrap

1 Place the meat on the center of a large piece of plastic wrap. If wrapping a cut-up bird or small-game animal, arrange the pieces to form a compact bundle, with as little space between them as possible.

2 Bring one end of the wrap over the meat, then fold both sides over it. Gently squeeze out as much air as possible. Bring the other end over, or roll the bundle to it, continuing to squeeze out air.

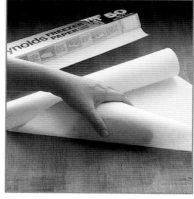

3 Lay the plastic-wrapped bundle on a corner of a large piece of heavy-duty freezer paper (shiny side up).

4 Roll the bundle once, so both the top and bottom are covered with a single layer of freezer paper.

5 Fold one side of the freezer paper over the bundle. Tuck in any loose edges of the paper.

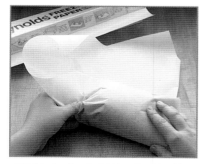

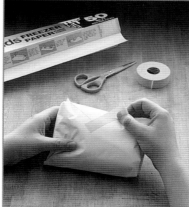

7 Fasten the end with freezer tape when wrapping is complete. Tape the seam also, if desired.

6 Roll the bundle agin. Fold the other side of the freezer paper over the bundle, tucking the corner neatly.

8 Label with a waterproof pen. Note the species, cut, quantity, and date, as well as the maturity of the animal, if known.

The Foil Wrap

1 Use foil instead of plastic wrap for ribs or other odd-shaped cuts. Place the meat on a large piece of heavy-duty aluminum foil.

2 Press the foil around the meat to eliminate air spaces. Be careful not to puncture the foil with the bones. Use two pieces of foil if necessary.

3 Butcher-wrap with freezer paper, eliminating as much air as possible. Seal all seams with freezer tape, and label the package.

How to Wrap a Whole Large Game Bird

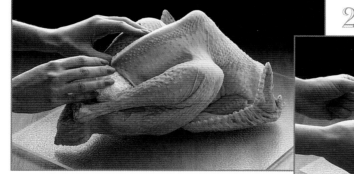

1 Stuff wadded plastic wrap into the body cavity. This reduces the chance of freezer burn.

2 Tie the drumsticks together with kitchen string. They'll stick out less, and wrapping will be easier.

3 Wrap the bird with heavy-duty aluminum foil. You may need several pieces to cover the entire bird. Press the foil snugly around the body.

4 Complete the wrapping with a double layer of heavy-duty freezer paper. Seal all the seams with freezer tape, and label the package.

Tips for Freezing Fish & Game

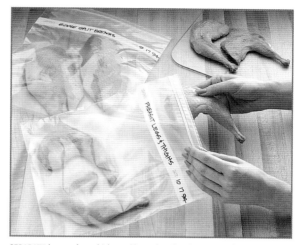

ADD more giblets or fish cheeks to the frozen ones as you get them. Place fresh pieces on top of the frozen ones. Add cold water; refreeze. Keep track of the number of pieces on a piece of tape, until you have enough for a meal.

SEPARATE breasts from thighs and legs when freezing cut-up pheasants, ducks or other birds. Then, if your recipe calls for breast meat only, you won't have to thaw the other parts.

PUT stew chunks or ground meat in a zip-lock plastic freezer bag. To push out air, immerse the bag almost to its top in a sink full of cold water. Seal the bag while it's still in the water. Wrap it in freezer paper.

FREEZE 1-cup batches of cooked fish or game stock in small dairy cartons or plastic freezer containers. When a recipe calls for stock, take a carton from the freezer, hold it under warm water, then slide the frozen stock out.

TUCK the legs of a partridge, quail or other small bird into the body cavity before wrapping. The package will be more compact, with less air inside to dry the meat.

Index